Democracy, Consensus
& Social Contract

SAGE Modern Politics Series

Editorial Board

Democracy, Consensus & Social Contract

Editors
Pierre Birnbaum, Jack Lively, Geraint Parry

SAGE Modern Politics Series   Volume 2
sponsored by the European Consortium for
Political Research / ECPR

 SAGE Publications · London and Beverly Hills

Copyright © 1978 by
SAGE Publications Ltd

For information address

SAGE Publications Ltd
28 Banner Street
London EC1Y 8QE

SAGE Publications Inc
275 South Beverly Drive
Beverly Hills, California 90212

International Standard Book Number
0 8039 9882 1 Cloth
0 8039 9883 X Paper

Library of Congress Catalog Card Number
77-084075

First Printing

Printed in Great Britain by

Contents

Introduction

Wherein lies the value of democracy? Is it to be admired as the system of government which most effectively promotes the interest of the community or, at least, the interests of the vast majority? Or is democracy a condition for and an instrument of personal self-development? Is it, instead, the best guarantee of liberty? Democracy, some sceptics assert, is merely a means towards the more efficient government of states; it presupposes no particular philosophy of life. But can one draw such a contrast? Does commitment to democratic forms require agreement as to the values of liberty or equality? Is it the case that a democratic consensus reflects, or even that it helps conceal, an underlying structure of power, a pattern of cleavage? If such a consensus is necessary, how might it be arrived at, and how might it be justified to the philosophers' rational man or to the more complex, less single-minded citizen for whom politics is but one of his every-day activities?

These questions are, of course, not new. They have formed the core of political reflection ever since democracy began once again to acquire a favourable connotation and are, in any case, distant echoes of questions asked about democracy in classical times. Nevertheless, although traditional, these are issues which have been raised with renewed intensity in the last decade and the ways in which they have been tackled have often involved new techniques of analysis. Politics is an activity requiring co-operation but it is occasioned by conflict. Political thought reflects on this tension between co-operation and conflict and it flourishes to the degree that it detects crisis, actual or latent. The very considerable resurgence in political theory since the mid-1960s is an indication of the widespread sense that something is now amiss with contemporary democracies. If the times are out of joint, there are plenty ready to set them right. The relative calm of the 1950s and 1960s was broken, as previously neglected or under-privileged groups protested that the time had come for democratic governments to live up to the values of liberty and equality on which they claimed to be founded. Demands for implementation of civil rights were supplemented by demands that governments should acknowledge the right to certain substantive conditions of life. Philosphically these developments found expression in an energetic discussion of needs and rights and of the obligation and capacity of government to meet them. The outcome was unexpected and yet logical — a reformulation of the philosophy of rights and contract in an attempt to come to an understanding of the place of the individual in modern states suddenly torn by doubt about the proper role of government. Political debate displayed an ideological division and intensity undreamt of a few years earlier when the end of ideology had been proclaimed.

Increasingly, the demand that government should satisfy civil, social and economic rights was felt to be insufficient. The unequal access of economic and social groups to power was contrasted with the formal equality proclaimed by democrats. The structure of the state and the 'permeability' of institutions was challenged. Citizens began to argue that they should be more than inert recipients of government protection or assistance and that they should act to shape in greater detail the policies and the administrative processes by which they or their community would benefit. Political participation was implied by the value of self-determination. It was also a means of rallying individuals and groups into immediate political action who had previously been quiescent or whose aspirations had lacked direction. In academic terms this was reflected in a growing literature on participation, exploring its implications in the classics of political philosophy and commenting on its apparently subordinate role in more recent democratic thought.

The campaigns for rights and pressures for greater participation had practical implications for the reform of law and institutions. In many countries these activities resulted in disorder. Additionally in the USA a war which failed to carry conviction with large sections of the population led to civil disruption. As a consequence the consensus as to democratic procedures and values was called into question in popular and academic debate. Increasingly commentators demanded that the structure of power which consensus concealed should be displayed in full view. Not only the content but the very need for consensus became an issue.

Finally, the growing assumption that substantive social and economic demands were needs which governments had a duty to meet has presented liberal democracies with a crisis of power and of confidence. The resources required have been such as to present government with a range of unpalatable alternatives — inflation, high levels of taxation and redistributive policies which, whatever their justification, would be likely to arouse severe complaints and even resistance. In response, political scientists and political theorists have felt impelled to re-examine the political consequences of inflation, the problems of so-called 'overload' and the character of 'distributive justice', whether this is seen as the only appropriate conception of justice or is rejected as a 'mirage'.

It is in this intellectual context that the political theory Workshops of the European Consortium for Political Research met from 1975-77. At London in 1975 the theme of the Workshop was 'Ideology and Consensus'; at Louvain-La-Neuve in 1976 it was 'Democracy, Problems of Power and Consciousness', and in 1977 the Workshop at Berlin was devoted to 'Social Contract and Political Community'. Although there was some continuity from one year to the next, the membership of the Workshops underwent considerable change. In making their selection of papers the editors have aimed at representing the range of concerns of the Workshop, since space naturally prevented incorporating anything like all the fifty and more contributions to the discussions. Nearly all the papers have in some way been revised to take account of points raised in the deliberations. In some cases the papers differ substantially from the originals but nevertheless speak to the same basic issues. In the instance of Favre's contribution the editors invited a paper discussing issues central to the discussions from a scholar who had found himself unable to participate as had been hoped in the Workshop itself. In all other cases the editors speak for the authors in thanking those colleagues who, though often individually unacknowledged, made such a vital contribution to the final form of the papers. In all instances the responsibility for the contents of the article remains with each author.

The editors have not sought to emphasise any one approach to political theory or any one issue. They have, however, placed the papers under three broad headings. The first group consists of papers which begin from an examination of a problem in the political theories of the past, but broaden out into reflections on present-day issues seen in the light of traditional concerns. Van Gunsteren outlines the liberal theory of citizenship, with its roots in Enlightenment assumptions about rationality and its hopes that the free choices of rational citizens could ensure a rational ordering of the whole society. He argues that this liberal theory has declined into 'voluntarism' which emphasises not the individual reason but the individual's arbitrary will; and he poses an alternative understanding of citizenship which restricts the wills that can legitimately be asserted by citizens to those individual wills that are in some sense freely formed and are aimed at socially rational objectives. Parry asks whether the traditional concern of the classics of political thought with the question of political knowledge should not be revived in modern discussions of the necessary conditions for genuine citizenship. An 'individualist' and a 'communitarian' conception of man and society are counterposed by Duncan. Modern participatory democrats, in criticising individualism from a communitarian standpoint, have, he argues, left a large number of questions unanswered concerning the relations between face-to-face societies and the larger society and have thus neglected the positive, if impersonal, values of liberty and the rule of law admired in the individualist tradition. The tension within the liberal-democratic tradition between the claims of democracy and the liberal conception of justice as distribution according to desert is the theme of Miller's paper. Contrasting the early liberal attempt to resolve or alleviate the tension by abandoning the principle of political equality with the later liberal attempt to do this by modifying the principle of social justice, he argues that the tension can only be removed by an acceptance of a conception of social justice that incorporates distribution according to need. Rousseau has played a central part in the democratic tradition and Favre re-examines the question posed by Rousseau: what mode of collective decision-making would be required by rational self-interested men to induce them to abandon their independence? Through both the construction of rational choice models and an analysis of the ambiguities in Rousseau's own attitudes towards the .unanimity and majority principles, he concludes that there can be no determinate answer to this question. Finally, Minogue surveys the history of contractarian thought. Discerning a philosophical and a popular version of the theory, he finds both to be a response to fears of a collapse in the most fundamental social relationships. This has occasioned the current recourse to contract notions, even though contemporary contractarianism differs from that of Hobbes or Locke by being concerned not with the distribution of power, but with the distribution of goods — an issue taken up by papers in the third part of the volume.

The articles in the second section examine the consensual values of modern democratic theory. Self-government has long been recognised to be basic to both the aims and the method of democracy yet, as J. S. Mill pointed out, it is an ambiguous notion. Berg subjects the idea of self-determination to detailed analysis, arguing that it has radical implications for political structures when the need for opportunities for choice to be relevant to the individual's life is fully comprehended. American pluralist democratic theory is the subject of papers by both Birnbaum and Lively. Birnbaum's theme is the depoliticisation of democratic theory by the common acceptance of the apolitical, apathetic character of the modern citizen, reinforced by the supposedly consequent necessity for the professionalisation of politics. Democratic consensus is not a product of citizen participation but conceals a structure of domination. Lively also discovers a process of depoliticisation in pluralist thought but understands it differently. Pluralists may regard political activity as neutral umpirage or as one in which politicians constitute one of the competing participants in the process leading to policy decisions. In neither case, however, can the theory encompass politics and the state as representing or embodying a notion of the general interest. Pluralists are forced to place emphasis on an alleged consensus in liberal-democratic societies as a substitute for the formative role of the state in reshaping the political balance. For Windisch consensus is likely to be the product of mobilisation in which ideology plays a crucial role. Citing in support two case studies drawn from Swiss experience of political parochialism and xenophobia, he argues that ideology gains in strength to the extent that it builds upon the day-to-day experience of those whom it seeks to mobilise. This, Windisch suggests, is more readily recognised and exploited by the right, whereas the left undervalue the impact and reality of ideology as a consequence of explaining it in terms of false-consciousness or alienation.

The third part of the volume is devoted to the new contractarian and individualist thought and to the relation between individual choice and collective action. Minogue had earlier suggested that this has emerged as a response to perceptions of social breakdown. This receives some support from Gray's critique of Nozick and, more particularly, of Rawls whose work he sees as an attempt to solve a deep-rooted crisis in liberalism. Rawls, he argues, must fail in his aspiration to universality for his proposed principles of justice. In attempting to elucidate the formal defining features of the moral point of view, Rawls introduces substantive principles of an egalitarian character which point inevitably towards the values of liberal society but which are controversial, and which illegitimately eliminate alternative accounts of morality from consideration. Rawls and Nozick are just two of the authors incorporated in Nurmi's critical review of the literature on individual choice and the 'emergence' of the state. Nurmi focuses on the paradox that the characterisation of rational choice regularly indicates the 'irrationality' of some of the most basic features of political life. He concludes by suggesting the need for a research programme which will further refine the analysis of individual rational choice, balanced by some other non-individualistic approach, so that the two taken together will approximate more to political reality. Lehning's comparison between the views of Rawls and of Buchanan on the foundation and extent of property rights shows him to be somewhat more sympathetic to Rawls than are certain other contributors. Lehning accuses Buchanan of failing fully to realise the moral and political implications of property rights, whereas Rawls offers an approach which might be developed so as to explain such rights as elements in self-development or in what Berg would regard as 'self-relevance' and 'self-choice'. Steiner examines more specifically an issue which Nurmi had surveyed generally — the 'emergence' of the state. He argues that Nozick's attempt to explain it as, like money, the unintended result of separate individual transactions is mistaken — as it is in the case of the money comparison — and that, to the contrary, some collective decision is required to establish the terms of association and protection. Mironesco is critical of the individual choice school and suggests that its plausibility arises largely from its making a number of imperfectly articulated and often unrealistic presumptions concerning the power and interests of the individual actors. The concluding article by Daudt and Rae employs the techniques of rational choice theory to analyse problems raised by several contributors and which were at the basis of the Workshops. The modern democratic welfare state faces a crisis of legitimacy. There is no longer a consensus as to the appropriate role of government, with many groups pressing it to satisfy demands — presented in the vocabulary of needs — and other groups protesting at having to bear the resultant costs of government services. With consensus lacking on the distribution of goods it becomes increasingly difficult to maintain a consensus on such democratic procedures as majority rule. Daudt and Rae examine a range of situations where majoritarian procedures in conditions of dissensus could produce results which might exacerbate rather than resolve tensions between competing interests. Once again a new social contract would appear to be a corrective to the crisis, but on what terms?

Pierre Birnbaum
Jack Lively
Geraint Parry   *Warwick, December 1977*

1 Re-appraisals of Classic Democratic Theories

1 Notes on a Theory of Citizenship

Herman van Gunsteren
University of Leiden, The Netherlands

After a long and distinguished career the concept of citizenship has gone out of fashion among political thinkers. For Marxists, citizenship is part of the bourgeois legal ideology of individualism. Contemporary liberal theorists deny virtually any theoretical status to citizenship. Many of them interpret what used to be called politics – the activities of citizens, in their double capacities as rulers and ruled – in terms of power, elites, ideology, organization and technique. The more democratically minded theorists emphasize either intermediate associations – through which the individual should be able to create his own independent life out of multiple and conflicting dependencies – or direct democracy – assuming that direct participation in the local affairs of daily life can establish an effective mediation between the individual and the wider political system.

This theoretical decline of citizenship is striking in view of the fact that any political theory must contain at least some notion of the place of individuals in the political system. This certainly holds true for liberal and Marxist theories. Liberal theory, given its individualist premises and its acceptance of the legal state as the framework of politics, must logically treat citizenship as one of its principal terms. Marxist theory remains inadequate as long as it does not develop an adequate notion of citizenship under the revolutionary dictatorship of the proletariat, and of the relation between 'spontaneous' citizen action and 'disciplined' class action.

The theoretical decline of citizenship has its roots and effects in practice. Take the example of the ongoing struggle about human rights. The frequent inability of both 'East' and 'West' to listen and adequately

Author's Note: I thank Pat Albin, Etienne Balibar, Hans Daalder, Tim Koopmans, Grahame Lock, David Spitz and Elaine Spitz for their criticisms of earlier versions of this article.

respond to serious criticism from the other side, and the instability and contradictions in the arguments concerning human rights that are presented by one and the same 'party', indicate, among other things, a theoretical uncertainty. Concepts of human rights are part of a family of concepts that have to do with the place of the individual in the political system. They are part of a language of citizenship. Theoretical neglect of language will tend to increase the confusion that surrounds the practice of human rights.

In this article I shall present the theoretical decline of citizenship and the possibilities for its restoration. Section 1 contains some methodological remarks. Section 2 considers the liberal theory of citizenship, emphasizing its roots in Enlightenment thought. Section 3 traces the decline of this theory into voluntarism. Section 4 discusses Marxist critiques of citizenship. Section 5 presents a revised theory of citizenship. Section 6 addresses problems of bureaucracy and professionalism in terms of the revised theory. Section 7 evaluates the revised theory from the perspective of class struggle.

METHODOLOGICAL REMARKS

When studying citizenship one should not assume that one knows — or after some clarification can know — what citizenship *is*, but rather treat it as an essentially contested concept that refers to a conflictual practice. Many studies of citizenship result in vacuous tautologies or restatements of unexamined ideological positions precisely because they assume that we must begin our inquiries by defining what citizenship is. They obscure the fact that notions and practices of citizenship are variable and conflicting.

The ambiguities of citizenship should not be defined away, but rather be conceived as keys, signs to be deciphered, that enable us to get in view real conflicts and problems between a plurality of people whom history has brought together in relations of interdependence and dominance, and who thus have common business to attend to. The ambiguities of citizenship are particularly indicative of conflicts over who will have what kind of say over the definition of common problems and how they will be tackled.

We must then view citizenship as an area of contestation and struggle — including class struggle — in both theory and practice. However, the area of struggle is not given, but historically *produced*. It is produced in part — and in different social formations to different degrees — by citizen struggles in this very area. The liberal fallacy is to accept this area as unproblematically given or alternatively to conceive it as completely productive of itself; the Marxist fallacy is to deny its relatively autonomous existence of this area or alternatively to conceive it to be completely produced by forces that lie outside it.

My general approach in studying citizenship is to inquire how languages, institutions and practices of citizenship are (re)produced and what functions they serve in different social environments. I do not treat citizenship as a reality that is immediately observable in individual people before us, nor as an abstract ideal, but rather as part of a social formation (a structured process) that (re)creates its own realities, facts, aspirations and ideals.

I focus on 'languages,' not on an isolated concept, because in order to understand a particular historical notion of citizenship, one must locate it vis-a-vis related concepts like 'individual,' 'politics,' 'state,' 'public and private.' I focus on the 'functioning' of languages of citizenship because the meaning of a word can only be grasped by observing its use, not when language is idling.

There is a strong temptation to reify notions of citizenship. We see individuals, freely moving bodies with wills or souls of their own. Thus all we need to do, it seems, is to observe individual's attitudes, beliefs and actions in the public sphere. Then we shall know what citizenship is. However, we would thus be committing the same error as those philosophical psychologists who located the 'soul' and the 'will' inside the brain of individuals. They sat at their desks, moving their fingers and trying to catch the fleeting moment, the will that willed the finger to move, without ever catching it. It seems more fruitful to assume that all citizen activities, however concrete they may seem, are loaded with ideology and theory, and that they take place in institutional settings that are also shot through with ideology and theory. Thus one must study citizenship at three related levels: as a theoretically constituted object of political thought, at the level of institutions, and at the level of its practical realization.

The reader will soon discover that this article does not fully live up to the methodological requirements that have been outlined here. It is a first step in a bigger project. This article merely outlines some developments in one language of citizenship (the liberal one) and stays at the level of theory with only occasional excursions to the levels of institutional embodiment and practical realization.

THE LIBERAL NOTION OF CITIZENSHIP

Like so much else in liberal thought, the liberal understanding of citizenship has important roots in Enlightenment conceptions of rationality in man and society. I shall therefore begin by constructing, out of the variety of Enlightenment thought on the subject, an ideal type of rational citizenship.

Earlier schools of political thought had conceived of (the idea of) the just society as *given* — by revelation, grace, tradition or the Legislator (Founder) — in the form of substantive arrangements and substantive rules of law. In contradistinction to this, Enlightenment thinkers saw the just society not as given, but as *produced* by the free activities of rational individuals (e.g. in the form of a social contract). What remained 'given' was only the form of this production process, not the substantive outcomes. Major terms of the language in which it was described were: rationality, freedom, justice, and individuals.

The Enlightenment thinkers held that rationality was both given to, and produced by, man. It was given because it was discovered, and not constructed, by thought. Rationality was produced, because it was realized by men who had freely decided to organize their actions in accordance with rational principles of order. Thus rationality in the tradition of the Enlightenment referred to man who, on the basis of insight, held himself responsible for what happened to him, for his own existence. A correct view of the order of things and of human relationships made adequate orientation possible and this in turn enabled one to act with more freedom. Rational understanding and action served the cause of freedom and emancipation. The more rational connections between human activities on the one hand and what happened in the world on the other were established, the more one could hold human beings responsible for what happened in the world and the more history could be interpreted as the outcome of human choice.

However, people did not live alone. They were dependent on others. As long as webs of dependence and dominance were given, as long as they remained mute and blind, individuals could not lead free lives and be fully rational. The Enlightenment thinkers hoped that dependence and dominance would be transformed into rational order by the rational activities of the state and its free citizens. The state itself could only be rational when human beings could be held responsible for what it did, when its activities could be conceived of as the outcome of human choice. Individuals could only be free when they could conceive of the activities of the state as the outcome of their own rational and therefore free choice. A free state was the product of the rational choice of its free citizens. Thus individual and political rationality were closely related, if not identical. Political rationality could only come about as the product of the rational actions of individual citizens. A rational political order was, in turn, a necessary condition for the exercise of individual self-determination. The citizen, one could say, was the custodian of both political and individual rationality.

As soon as we try to give historical flesh and bones to this Enlightenment conception of citizenship, its ambiguities, dilemmas and contradictions become apparent. Which, and how many, individuals were to act freely and rationally in order to bring about the rationalization of state authority and the just society? The enlightened ruler only? The intellectuals? Enlightened aristocrats? All citizens? In their answers to these questions the 'philosophes' wavered and differed. They did not demonstrate how much individual rational action was minimally required to produce a just society.

Nor were they clear about who had a *right* to act in the public realm, about what it was that made people qualify as citizens. Being an independent property owner? Being educated? Military service? Residence? Being born of citizen parents? Being a partner in a social contract? Or was one to assume that enlightened education would spread out over the earth like air and very soon make all men and women, if not children, qualify as citizens?

The general Enlightenment notion of rational citizenship did not enable one to make distinctions inside the area of citizenship, among its various rights and duties: public education, voting, eligibility for various public offices (juror, judge, delegate, civil servant), military service, welfare rights. Did all citizens necessarily have *all* these rights and duties?

Finally, the Enlightenment theory of citizenship implied a theory of the state that was highly ambiguous. It supposed that exploitation and dominance would come to an end with the rational ordering of the state. Private enlightenment would lead to a rational public order embodied in law. The end of legal inequality and exploitation would be an end to all intolerable inequality and exploitation. The state, it was assumed, would be rational enough to will nothing but legal justice, and powerful enough to transform it into social justice. Enlightenment thought did not deal adequately with the state as a phenomenon of power. While trying to bring about a rational order and use of power, it tended to rationalize power away. It both over- and under-estimated the power of the state. It overestimated it by assuming that the state was the source of *all* oppression, or alternatively, that the state would be powerful enough to combat all oppression by way of law. It underestimated, on the other hand, the degree to which a state needs, in order to be strong or even to continue to exist at all, a power base beyond rational deliberation and choice. The power base of the state lies primarily in its relations to powerful groups and classes, and it is only, or at least mainly, within the limits of these that rational delibera-tion and choice can take place and be effective. Enlightenment thinkers failed to se that the state is but one component in a wider power structure. Thus there was little room in their theory of citizenship for an appreciation of the effects of social and economic inequalities on the actual relations between citizens who supposedly were equals.

What I am doing here is reading back later distinctions and problems into the Enlightenment conception of citizenship, thereby making it appear more ambiguous than it probably was in its own time. The 'philosophes' did not invent citizenship. They analyzed citizenship in terms of contemporary languages and institutions, criticizing some assumptions of these, while implicitly accepting others. In order to better understand the meaning of the Enlightenment conception of citizenship, we must take a brief look at the tradition of discourse within which it developed.

Ancient Greek-Athenian citizenship is one important strand in this tradition. Just as the scientist is he who practices science, the Greek citizen (polites) was the man who practiced politics, who participated in the affairs of the city-state (polis). Every citizen fulfilled deliberative and adjudicative functions. He was eligible for, and obliged to serve in, various public offices. He should be capable of ruling and being ruled. The polis constituted a space within which the citizen revealed who (as distinct from what) he was. The polis was a conventional web of relations which was sustained by the speaking and acting together of a plurality of people. Only a god or a beast could live outside the polis. Man could only live and act meaningfully within it. It is only there that his individuality could appear. The gods lived eternal lives, but mortal men could only gain a precarious kind of immortality, and thus escape meaninglessness, when their actions lived on in the organized remembrance that constituted the life of the polis.[1]

This Greek conception of citizenship was received into Western political thought, first in the middle ages, with the rediscovery of the works of Aristotle, in Christian terms, and then more fully, and in secular terms, in Renaissance Italy, as what came to be called the 'civic humanist' republican tradition. This tradition has been described in depth and at great length by J. G. A. Pocock. A central theme in his *The Machiavellian Moment* is that

> the revival of the republican ideal by civic humanists posed the problem of a society in which the political nature of man as described by Aristotle was to receive its fulfilment, seeking to exist in the framework of a Christian time-scheme which denied the possibility of any secular fulfilment.[2]

The civil humanists faced the problem of creating and maintaining a stable republic of virtuous citizens amidst a world of decay, unreliable fortune and particularity.

The civic humanist tradition was concerned with the role of the aristocracy. In this tradition Aristocratic striving for excellence and glory was to be transformed into service for the republic. Aristocrats should play an active part in government, curb the powers of the prince and give expression to the needs and wishes of the people. The civic humanist tradition emphasized the relation between military and civic virtue, the importance of military service for (and as) civil education.

It was, however, above all concerned with stability over time, and obsessed with fear of decay and corruption. The civic humanists wanted to preserve the moral stability of the human personality, which, they thought, could only be done by preserving a strong, virtuous and stable republic. This 'conservative' attitude made for a very different view of history than the modern one. History (fortune, the particular) was the enemy of secular fulfilment (the universal). It is only in later thought particularly in Hegel and Marx, that secular fulfilment and universality have been sought (and found?) in the particulars of history. For the civic humanists, history, both past and future, was an intractable problem. Past: how could a republic have been founded? Future: could history ever be anything but a movement away from the norms that define stability?

In this static view there is obviously little place for the dynamism of the bourgeois and of civil society. One could describe eighteenth century political thought as a struggle to carve out a place for the aspiring bourgeois inside the current language of civic humanist republicanism. In this class conflict at the level of political language what were earlier termed 'vices' or 'passions' came to be called 'interests.' The pursuance of particular interests was no longer seen as disruptive, but rather as contributing to the common good.[3]

The legal mode of understanding is another important strand in the tradition of discourse within which the enlightenment conception of citizenship developed. Here the Roman heritage, in particular that of Roman law, is dominant. Roman citizenship under the Imperium was hardly more than a status, defined and protected by law. Citizenship carried the privilege of enjoying the protection of the best legal system the world had known, but permitted complete inactivity in the public realm.

Apart from this specific influence of Roman law, one must remember that up to the Enlightenment the language of political theory itself had been characterized by legal concepts, expressions and modes of argument. The structure of political reality itself was often represented in terms of natural law. The central concepts of law — property and contract — had a central place in political theory — particularly in John Locke's work, which was very influential throughout the eighteenth century. The legal argument that those who had little or no property were legally irrelevant — non-persons — because they had nothing to make contracts about, only reinforced the commonplace idea that only those who had a stake in the commonwealth (property owners) qualified as citizens.

Enlightenment thought, then, had to operate within and upon these traditions of civic humanism and legal thought. In the attempt to universalize and rationalize them, the emphasis changed from military training to public education, from virtue to rationality, from property to interest as the qualification for citizenship, from concern with corruption of the ancient constitution to the possibility of 'making' history through the combined effects of rational individual actions. A characteristic product of this development was the political theory of Rousseau: people who were educated as citizens would all fully participate in the making of general laws which would provide equal protection to all citizens. However, particularity could not be done away with so easily. While it was being banned from the legal state it reappeared in civil society; 'private' inequalities re-invaded the public sphere.[4]

THE IMPASSE OF
VOLUNTARISTIC CITIZENSHIP

In the Enlightenment theory of citizenship, notions of tradition, rationality, universality and citizen 'choice' were closely connected and necessary to each other. The dissociation of these ideas from each other was concurrent with the degeneration of liberal theory into positivistic utilitarianism. The outcome was the emergence of a voluntaristic notion of citizenship: the term 'citizenship' was thought to refer to behaviour of individuals that expressed their individual, subjective, arbitrary 'will' or 'choice.' The theory of citizenship was divided into normative and empirical theories. In so called 'normative' theory citizenship was conceived as the exercise of will, of public choice, by individual members of a given political system. In 'empirical' theory this exercise of will was explained, unmasked, as an expression of individual attitudes and beliefs, that could be measured and moulded (e.g. by education, indoctrination, etc.). The relation between these two theories remained obscure, however. There was no theory within which the relation between 'choice' and its 'causation' could be understood. Let us consider this degeneration of the Enlightenment theory of citizenship in more detail.

The civic humanists wanted to preserve a given constitutional tradition. Enlightenment thinkers criticized tradition in order to transform it, but they never seriously thought that they could do without tradition. In modern liberal thought this bond between citizenship and tradition was obscured. The relation between citizenship and tradition became entirely contingent, arbitrary. In order to know whether the exercise of citizen will would aim at revolution (trying to create a completely new political order) or at continuation of the status quo, one had to look outside citizen theory, at prevailing attitudes and beliefs of individual citizens. But a collection of attitudes and beliefs is not a tradition. As we shall see, knowing a collection of attitudes and beliefs of individuals does not amount to an understanding of citizenship as a rational criticism of reworking of ongoing traditions.

After the Great French Revolution citizenship began to lose its universal aspirations. Romantic revolutionaries still expected that citizens, once they were freed from reactionary and oppressive powers, would spontaneously create a rational political order, but they believed that this would be a *national* political order, rooted in the unique history of a particular people. After the abortive revolutions of 1848, when politics came to be seen in realistic terms of power and will, citizenship lost its rational aspect as well.

In non-Marxist Western theory and practice citizenship and rationality have clearly parted company. Citizen action has come to be interpreted as voluntaristic, subjective, formalized, and non-rational (or even irrational when fear of the folly of the masses has gotten the upper hand). Rationality has been limited and instrumentalized. How has this come about?

First there is the problem of the increasing number of citizens. Until 1848 the illusion of a community of citizens who come together to discuss and decide about their common affairs could still be maintained, both in the limited circles of government and in revolutionary associations. With the appearance of the masses on the public stage things changed. It is impossible for thousands of people to come together to make decisions on the basis of rational discussions in which each citizen can speak his own mind. In the context of large states it is simply impossible for each citizen to make himself heard and be listened to, to appear in the public realm and reveal who he is. The Greek conception of citizenship, which had so strongly dominated political theorizing, seemed to have become inapplicable. At first it was hoped that new means of communication and transport and the concentration of people in cities would somehow result in spontaneous unity among citizens. But soon it appeared that where people had a free political say there was often irremediable discord, and that 'unity' was often not produced by the citizens themselves, but rather brought about by elites, who cleverly used the press, plebiscites (Napoleon III), the distribution of goodies (e.g. Bismarck's social insurance scheme), bribes, lies, and the frenzy of war. This manipulated fake-unity was found both in the wider political system and in other organizations. Characteristic examples of the futility of the liberal notion of politics as discussion between equals were the impotence of the Frankfurt Assembly (1848) and the successes of Bismarck's illiberal politics of power, realism and manoeuvre.

It would be mistaken, however, to see here a problem of numbers only. The number of bourgeois after all was considerable, and they had often been able to cooperate on the basis of discussion that seemed to be more or less rational and free. However, where those who thus far had been excluded from having a say in politics organized themselves as a class, conscious of its own economic and political position, it appeared that their rationality ran counter to that of capitalist production and of the state that provides no more than a protective framework for civil society. Their ideas of historical progress differed from those of the bourgeoisie. Now that contradictions and class conflict had become so pronounced that they could no longer be denied, bourgeois political thinkers could not put their trust in the rationality of history. In the realm of thought the close connections between historical progress, rationality and free citizenship were cut through.

German nineteenth- and early twentieth-century philosophy — historicism, 'Lebensphilosophie' (philosophies of life), Nietzsche, neo-Kantianism, Max Weber — can be read as a bourgeois response to the appearance of these contradictions at the level of ideology and philosophy (see Lukacs' *Die Zerstörung der Vernunft*). History now appeared as non- or ir-rational, as the working out of life-forces or the will to power, as the realization of a subjective myth or a unique culture. What first appeared as historial contradictions were now reinterpreted as eternal and tragic human conflicts (spontaneous life versus dead institutions, the culture of an elite versus the vulgar mentality of the masses). There was no rational progress in history. All civilizations (i.e., their elites) had to tackle the problem of how to give meaning to meaningless history, to rationalize the irrational.

Rationality was limited on the one hand to utilitarian means-ends calculations (rational means for non-rational ends), on the other to the logics of specialized sciences and techniques, which more and more came to dominate practical actions. The science(s) of society acquired a different character. In the first place a comprehensive understanding of society, as provided by liberal political economy or historical materialism, was abandoned in favour of a number of specialized disciplines, like sociology, economics, and psychology, which could avoid facing nasty problems by locating them outside their particular areas of competence. Thus a number of problems received no scientific analysis at all and were relegated to the domain of subjective values, intuition and choice. In the second place the notion of an emancipatory science of society was abandoned. Originally the emerging science of society aimed at two things, namely to understand the working of civil society and the creation of a 'civil' society, that is, of a society of citizens. This second aim was in many cases abandoned by the modern specialized disciplines. They tended to focus on non-rational factors that determine human behaviour, without indicating how these factors might be eliminated or rationally controlled. (I am speaking here of rational self-control of free individuals, not of elites who manipulate non-rational determinants of behaviour and thereby 'rationally' control other people.) Personally many social scientists were, and are, still committed to freedom and rational self-control, but these ideals could not find a logical place in their scientific constructions (Max Weber and Freud are exemplary here). Scientific rationality, in short, was no longer directly connected with societal, political or historical rationality. Politically speaking it became instrumental. It was used as a term in utilitarian calculations of how to reach non-rational, subjective ends or values. Rationality no longer provided a basic orientation in life.[5]

In politics too this separation between the rationality of means and calculations on the one hand and subjective, non-rational choice and action on the other, became more pronounced. The best known example of this trend is the separation between politics and administration. Here I am interested, however, in changes in citizenship that are less visible but equally important and fateful. Citizen activities were seen to belong in the so-called realm of subjective, non-rational, choice. Thus citizenship came more and more to be interpreted in voluntaristic terms. It was no longer substantially related to freedom and a rational ordering of society.

Such voluntaristic citizenship posed formidable difficulties and dangers. How could the expressions of millions of subjective wills be combined into meaningful political decisions that would guide the activities of the state? The Condorcet-Arrow voter's paradox showed that the majority principle provided an unsatisfactory solution to this problem. Apart from that, it was noticed that there was nothing in the rules of voluntaristic citizenship and democracy that could prevent the emergence of crazy or tyrannical majorities. It was clear to many leaders, and also to many theorists of democracy that voluntaristic citizenship should be controlled. It is here that the new specialized scientific disciplines proved helpful. They provided an understanding of the non-rational determinants of citizen behaviour. Some of these determinants could be manipulated. Ideological state apparatuses were developed and perfected. Political socialization replaced political education. Norms that were thought to be basic for social order were internalized. People were organized into political parties, interest groups and other pluralist associations. The vote was set up as the exclusive institution of direct citizen influence on the affairs of the state. Democracy became a method to maintain order, rather than a method to create rational policies. The random and irrational impulses of citizens were to be canalized by charismatic leadership, by narrowing down choices (between a small number of alternative general political programmes or teams of leaders), or by clever calculation (developing a social welfare function).

In sum, citizen participation was no longer rational and emancipatory, but acclamatory and dependent on the logic of order and domination. The ruling strata were clearly on the defensive.[6] They tried to remain in power by way of manipulated mass support and clever and aggressive government intervention in socio-economic life.

This state of affairs was acknowledged as the 'reality' of democracy by thinkers like Joseph Schumpeter and Robert Dahl. They tried to make it more palatable by pointing out that in liberal-democratic societies one finds a plurality of elites, programmes and groups, and that the citizen can exercise his democratic choice by shifting his allegiance (and vote) from one elite, programme or group to another.

In the old theory of rational citizenship rationality was not given but 'in the making.' Citizen participation was needed to rationalize authority. And rationalizing authority meant emancipation, the creation of a free society. Few people nowadays adhere to this view. The dominant ideas are that citizen activity is a rather futile act of will and that rationality can only be found in formalized sub-departments of life. Citizenship is now voluntaristic, rationality instrumental. In liberal-democratic states citizenship seems to be on the wane and the theory of citizenship is in an impasse.

CITIZEN AND CLASS: THE MARXIST CRITIQUE

The Enlightenment theory of citizenship has not only degenerated into empty voluntarism. It has also been criticized, both in its original and its degenerate versions, by Marxist thinkers. Very schematically one can distinguish three kinds of criticism.

1. The first is the one developed by Marx in *On the Jewish Question* (1844)

Drawing upon the distinction between state and civil society, between the public and the private, Marx points out that political emancipation is not enough to make man truly free. As a citizen he may enjoy (the illusion of) freedom, but as a member of civil society he remains as unfree, as much subject to the laws of the market and capitalism, as before. Human emancipation, true freedom, can only come about when emancipation is extended to all spheres of life, and to the sphere of production and exchange in particular.

As a criticism of the political democracies in Marx's own time this is correct. Does it also apply to the general Enlightenment theory of citizenship, and thereby to all its applications? And if so, in what way? There are, it seems, three ways in which Marx's analysis may, and has been, interpreted.

a. *Political emancipation is a condition for, and the instrument of, human emancipation.* A common imagery here is the upward spiral: political emancipation fosters emancipation in civil society, and this in turn allows for further political emancipation. This is the theory put forward by Eduard Bernstein and the revisionists (social democrats). Unfortunately it has not worked out as they hoped it would. Why? The most likely explanation, which needs more investigation than can be undertaken here, runs roughly as follows. The politically emancipated state can at best do no more than make minor corrections at the margins of civil society. It leaves its mode and relations of production basically unaffected. Conflict is built into this mode of production, and around it classes and class relations of dominance will inevitably tend to form, whatever formal equality there may be in the political sphere. One cannot move up in the spiral. Combating socio-economic inequality by way of political equality will remain a labour of Sisyphus as long as civil society's mode of production remains unaffected by the intervention of the democratic state.

Moreover, the structure of classes and power that is inherent in a given mode of production will in the long run (or, as the jargon has it, 'tendentially' or 'in the last instance') determine what actions the political state will be willing to undertake. The mechanics of this determination may vary in different times and places, from indirect financial constraints to direct threats, but the determination will always be there.

b. *The politically emancipated state is neutral with regard to human emancipation and changes in civil society.* This interpretation may hold true in particular situations where there is a precarious balance of forces. But as a general observation or theory it is mistaken. Simplistic liberal ideology, not Marxist analysis. It assumes that the spheres of the state and of civil society are completely separate, that whatever relations there are between them are purely external and contingent. The citizen as such could not do anything to increase human emancipation. He would have to wait for autonomous developments in civil society. What point would there be in his engaging in citizen activities?

c. *The political emancipated state that operates in bourgeois society* prevents *human emancipation.* The state tends to organize one class, the bourgeoisie, while it disorganizes another, the proletariat. It suppresses the identity of the agents of production in the political realm. It fosters the illusion that all citizens are equally free human agents, and thereby enables economic relations of dominance and exploitation to be produced, and be reinforced, in the political realm.

2. The second critique of citizenship

The second critique of citizenship, which is to be found in Marx's later writings and in Lenin, holds that all states, whether they are politically emancipated (democratic) or not, whether they operate in bourgeois society or not, are dictatorships of one class over another. The state itself is a class phenomenon. As long as there are classes, or more precisely, modes of production that tend to produce classes, there will be class dictatorships, that is, states. When classes disappear states will disappear as well.

According to this view the usual liberal understanding that sees dictatorship and democracy as opposites is mistaken. The idea that people can be emancipated by acting as citizens in the framework of the state is an illusion.

3. Most devastating of all is Louis Althusser's critique of theoretical humanism[7]

According to him men, either separately or democratically organized, do not make history. Man is a subject *in* history, not *of* history. History is to be understood in terms of class struggles, not in terms of interacting and freely choosing individuals. Any political theory that assumes that man makes history is in fact caught in the bourgeois legal ideology of individualism. It follows that a theory of citizenship is impossible. There are only ideologies of citizenship.

What can the theorist of citizenship reply to these three Marxist criticisms? As a first step he can try to determine what it exactly is that they criticize. At the beginning of this article we distinguished three levels at which citizenship may be analyzed: practical realization, institutions, theory. The first Marxist criticism, the argument of *On the Jewish Question*, operates mainly at the level of practical realization. The second criticism, that all states are dictatorships, mainly at the level of institutions. The third operates clearly at the level of theory — and by implication at the levels of institutions and of practical realization.

Now the first and second criticisms can be accepted at the level of practical realization and of institutions, while being countered at the level of theory by developing alternative institutional and practical possibilities or a revised theory of citizenship. The third criticism, however, seems to rule out any theory of citizenship, revised or not. In Althusser's view individual choice can never have theoretical status and explanatory value. What we call 'individual choice,' as well as the fact that we call it thus, must be explained in terms like class struggle, ideology, etc.

What are we to do with citizenship if Althusser's theoretical criticism is correct? We could do away with all theory, institutions and practices of citizenship, and forget about citizenship altogether. However, this would leave us with the problem of how to make sense of the reality of separately moving bodies, of individuals, and with the question of what place they have in political systems and political theories. One can also, while accepting Althusser's criticisms at the level of theory, continue to endorse certain institutions and practices of citizenship.[8] The problem of this position is that the relation of theory and practice becomes a very odd one. On the one hand, institutions and practices of citizenship without theoretical justification. Practices and institutions that are interpreted in terms that, once they are theoretically understood, are no longer acceptable. On the other hand a theory without direct practical implications.[9]

It is clear from these summary remarks that further investigation of the relation between Althusser's theoretical anti-humanism and the theory and practice of citizenship is needed. In particular one would have to ask what place there is, in theory and practice, for individual deviance and dissent under the dictatorship of the proletariat and in communist society. Our provisional conclusion can be that the Marxist critique of citizenship is appropriate at the levels of practical realization and of institutions, but that it leaves open the possibility of a revised theory of citizenship that takes Marxist criticisms into account.

THE CITIZEN AS
PRACTICING POLITICAL THEORIST

Let us now return to the impasse of voluntaristic citizenship and see whether a revised theory can help us get out of it.

What are citizen activities? The answer cannot be given by pointing to directly observable, naked facts. It must be in terms of a theory of citizenship, or at least of an interpretative framework. It is only from within such a perspective that one can observe the activities of citizens. Citizens and their activities are not 'given' in the same way that apples and stones are. (To be able to see apples we may also need a framework or theory, but the point is that it is of a different kind and less controversial than the theories that we need in order to observe the activities of citizens.)

Consider now the voluntaristic notion of citizenship according to which activities of citizens are defined as expressions of will (revealed preferences), in appropriate institutional form, by those who by law are defined as citizens. There seems to be little or no theory here, only factual description. This impression is misleading, however. The theory is there, but it is completely collapsed into the existing institutions. It says, in fact, that activities of citizens are those activities, and only those, that are defined as such by existing public institutions. The 'theory' of voluntarist citizenship consists of a mixture of crude utilitarianism and a bland acceptance of the institutional status quo. It collapses the liberal theory of citizenship into one of its historical institutional embodiments.

Questions about the formation of preferences, about the conditions for the rational exercise of free individual choice, about the legitimation and meaning of institutional arrangements, about the effects of citizen activities on policy, and about the relations between specific policies and justice, all these lie outside this theory. What this indicates is that with the advent of voluntarist utilitarianism *liberal notions and*

*theories of citizenship have become disengaged from more encom-
passing political theories.*

This isolation of citizenship theory is reflected in the focus of
current studies of citizenship. They are about the citizen's beliefs and
attitudes, about loyalty and socialization,[10] not about the influence of
citizen action on major policies and vice versa. Current studies of
citizenship recommend the practice of separate citizen activities ('the
more participation the better' seems to be the motto) that means extra
work for the already overloaded individual, instead of trying to interpret people's current activities in terms of citizenship. They focus on,
and glorify, direct democracy (of the neighbourhood-action type),
while virtually ignoring wider networks of dependency and dominance
within which individuals, including neighbours, have to act in the
modern state. Although of course not all studies have this focus, a fairly
extensive reading of the literature has convinced me that the micro-level
approach typifies the mainstream of current research into citizenship.

The thesis of this article is that this micro-level approach is detri-
mental to an adequate understanding of citizenship, and that the theory
of citizenship should be re-integrated into more encompassing political
theories.

As soon as one begins to reflect upon it, the insufficiency of the
voluntarist/institutional theory of citizenship will become clear. This
theory holds that *all* expressions of will that have the appropriate
institutional form are acts of citizens. But surely there are expressions
of will which, although they fulfil the formal institutional requirements, are too crazy, extravagant, odd, or harmful to be acceptable as
actions of citizens. In order to qualify as activities of citizens, activities
must be understandably related to some reasonable notion of the
common good, to the preservation and/or creation of a just society.
The will of citizens must be freely formed and aim at rational outcomes. That is, before we can qualify an expression of will as an act of
a citizen, we look not only at institutional requirements, but also at the
conditions under which it was formed and at the kind of outcomes it
understandably aims at.

This procedure, however, has its problems also. Terms like 'justice,'
'the common good,' 'freedom,' and 'rationality' are heavily contested
and highly ambiguous legacies of liberal theory. From a largely irrelevant micro-level we have moved to an intolerably vague and grand
level of analysis, which leaves us almost equally helpless. What I
propose, therefore, is to steer a middle course, by avoiding words like

'justice' etc. and asking instead what the minimal conditions are for considering actions as instances of citizenship, hoping that these will raise less disagreement. An answer to this question emerges when one remembers that citizenship and emancipation are inherently connected (the central thesis of the Enlightenment theory of citizenship) and that it sounds odd — almost a contradiction in terms — to call actions which tend to decrease the possibilities for future citizen action expressions of citizenship.

Actions of citizens are only those that tend to maintain, and where possible to enhance, the future exercise of citizenship. Assuming, for the sake of simplicity, that improvement is always possible, we can now formulate the minimal conditions for applying the term citizen. In order to qualify as actions of citizens, actions should at least either tend to improve (one of) the existing possibilities of citizen action, or help to develop new ones, or tend to make full citizenship available to more members of the polity.[11] With this central insight concerning the minimal requirements of citizenship, it seems to me one can hardly disagree. And it is not trivial either, because it enables one to break through the impasse of the currently dominant notion of voluntaristic citizenship. To sum up: citizen action cannot take for granted the conditions that make the effective expression of citizen will possible. These conditions can only persist when they are constantly sustained and transformed by concrete activities of citizens.

Of course we cannot do without institutions, but we should not hypostasize them as absolute definitions and guarantees of citizenship. It is in the light of the theoretical considerations that have been outlined here that the appropriateness of particular institutions of citizenship in particular historical contexts should be judged, criticized and worked upon. Thus for citizenship to flourish, there must always remain a tension between theory (the idea) and the institutions in which it is partially embodied.[12] This tension can only be maintained as long as the theory of citizenship remains part of (the movement towards) an encompassing political theory. It is by the very activities of citizens, who are rational individuals who have encompassing political theories (that are, to be sure, more or less developed), that this tension is realized. It is they, the citizens who are practicing political theorists, who work towards the free society by critically working upon existing institutions and traditions.[13]

Rational political theories do not exist in the abstract. They have historical roots, they are at home in specific forms of life. In social affairs there is a dialectic between rationality and tradition, or rather, between rationality as creativity and rationality as an available order. Social reason is not given, it is more than a merely becoming conscious of what was there already. But neither is it pure novelty. It is a creature of the order it creates.[14] Every rational political theory has its roots in history and tradition, but it ceases to be rational when it becomes identical with these. When on the other hand it cuts itself off from them, it becomes sterile or destructive, and is no longer able to increase actual human freedom. The Enlightenment progressed only as long as the tradition it was fighting against was still in existence and had to be worked upon. As an abstract and triumphant programme it has tended to become an empty ideology. Rational political theories are always critical of tradition but cannot do without it because it is in ongoing traditions that one must discover the seeds of transformation.

The liberal/Enlightenment theory of citizenship remains viable as long as it is not identified with one of its historical institutional embodiments. The area of citizenship that is provided by existing institutions is indeed an area of struggle, not only within institutions, but also *about* institutions. Citizenship is an essentially contested concept because the exercise of citizenship is always critical of the dominant institutional definition of citizenship.

What are the uses of this revised theory of citizenship? Can it be tested, and if so in what sense? Not in the strict sense in which a hypothesis can be tested. It is a basic perspective that provides orientation. In a weaker sense the adequacy of the revised theory of citizenship can be tested out by asking whether it helps people make more sense out of their political and individual lives, whether its basic perspective enables them to develop better situation-specific citizen strategies. (One would also have to inquire whether, and if so why, it serves some people and others not). The question whether acceptance of the revised theory of citizenship will serve emancipation (the practical critique and transformation of structures of interdependence and dominance) must in the last instance be answered by looking at, and by working in, specific historical practices. In this article I have tried to provide some theoretical groundwork for the practice of citizenship, without claiming to be able to predict or determine its outcomes.

In order to further clarify the meaning of the revised theory of citizenship, I shall present some thoughts about its implications for citizenship in the welfare state and for the relation between citizenship and class struggle.

CITIZENSHIP, BUREAUCRACY, AND PROFESSIONALISM IN THE WELFARE STATE

The welfare state is, or rather presents itself as, the amended liberal-democratic state. It recognizes, as T. H. Marshall has so eloquently pointed out, that effective citizenship does not only require a political say and a legally protected status, but also a certain level of socio-economic security.[15] Older theories of citizenship did not ignore this requirement. They solved the problem it posed by denying citizenship to those who did not have independent and secure socio-economic positions already. The welfare state accepts all its subjects as citizens and aims to guarantee to all and each of them the minimal socio-economic security that the free exercise of citizenship requires. It does so by providing them with access to arrangements of social security, health care, education, etc. and by legislating about the conditions of work, housing, etc. Thus it on the one hand poses fewer formal requirements of citizenship, but on the other greatly increases state intervention in the lives of citizens. It makes certain citizens, who because of their dependence formerly would not have qualified as citizens, dependent on bureaucratic arrangements of welfare, education, etc. It tries to transform these new dependencies into autonomy by formulating them as rights.

But (the threat of) legal redress works at best in some cases only. What the *clients* of the welfare state also need in order to function as *citizens* are strategies to combat and cope with bureaucracy and professionalism. The traditional institutions of the liberal-democratic state (parliaments, elections, political mass parties, courts, etc.), and the definitions of permissible citizen activities that they impose, do not sufficiently provide these. Bureaucratic and professional institutions need to be criticized, amended, and transformed by citizens who practice political theory in the sense outlined earlier in this article.[16]

I shall not develop a complete strategy to combat professionalism and bureaucracy, but consider only one requirement of it: equality between professional and citizen languages. The revised theory of citizenship invites a movement towards such equality, while the voluntaristic theory of citizenship has in fact no place for it.

Professional dominance rests not only on the possession of skills, but also on control over agenda-setting and over the language in which problems and their possible solutions will be conceived. In many cases the prevailing professional language severely limits the range of permissible arguments and answers. This professional control over agendas and language is also found in areas where citizens (or rather, clients) participate. Acting within such a setting, citizens will be hopelessly disadvantaged from the start. They will appear more unskilled and unknowledgeable than they are. Citizens will be dependent on the logic of bureaucratic professionalism and technical control. Issues will be debated in terms that are not those of their own working and living situations. They will have to adjust to an alien rationality. They will lack a language that can establish connections between their practical knowledge and the problems at hand.

Knowledge and skills always contain a considerable element of tacit knowledge, which cannot be formulated, but must be acquired in practice. Tacit knowledge is not readily accessible to outsiders. Although tacit knowledge cannot be explicitly formulated, it can be obliquely referred to in the language that is spoken by those who possess particular kinds of tacit knowledge and skills. When issues are framed in terms of professional and bureaucratic politics, citizens will remain outsiders. Because they are dominated by the languages of politicians, bureaucrats and other professionals, their practical knowledge and skills will remain largely inoperative. Self-government of citizens can only work if their tacit knowledge about their own life situations can enter into their political discussions. Thus they need not learn a lot of new things before they can begin to participate, but can learn while they participate. Citizen participation will not be a new activity alongside others, but rather a deeper awareness and grasp of what one was doing already.

Now the voluntaristic theory of citizenship seems to leave ample room for this equality between the languages of professionals and of citizens. But in fact it doesn't. Remember that the voluntaristic theory of citizenship defines permissible activities of citizens entirely in terms of dominant institutions. In the welfare state these institutions are the very embodiment of professional and bureaucratic dominance. Equality between the languages of professionals and of citizens is in fact ruled out from the start, because what people can say and do as citizens is being determined in professional terms. While the voluntaristic theory thus prevents effective citizen action, equality between the languages of citizens and professionals is a requirement in the revised theory of citizenship. This does not mean, of course, that such equality is easy to bring about. Accepting the revised theory of citizenship means removing one obstacle for the realization of the equality of languages of citizens and professionals, not the advent of full citizenship.

It is indeed very difficult not to be fooled by the logic of bureaucratic and professional control, which leads to dependent participation. Citizens are in a lost position already when they fail to insist on absolute equality between the rationality in terms of which they discuss their own life situations and other rationalities. Let me give three examples of how citizens are manoeuvred into a losing starting position by their own acceptance of an alien rationality of discussion: 1. The myth of the omnicompetent citizen; 2. the actor-audience image of politics; 3. the emphasis on the complexity of society.

Ad 1

Controlling society is a complicated affair for which a variety of professional skills is needed. Can the citizen who wants to participate in the governing of society possess all these skills? Obviously not. Once we accept the logic of the question that is being posed, the answer is obvious. However, it is the logic of the question that should be questioned. Why should we demand that citizens acquire skills they do not have, instead of finding out what they can accomplish with the skills that they do have. A citizen can begin to function properly when he has an awareness of his own life-situation and is prepared to discuss its relations to what other people do.

Ad 2

The ordinary citizen is not a spectator in a theatre who has stage fright because he must suddenly participate in the play and act out a role that is new to him. He is in it already and must become conscious of the part that he has been playing all along.

Ad 3

Experts like Niklas Luhmann are very persuasive when they present complexity as *the* problem of modern societies. Individual citizens, he insists, cannot adequately discuss and master societal complexity. Complexity is being reduced by a complex division of labour, in which individuals have specialized roles and training, and therefore only specialized (*parzelliert*) consciousness.[17] In response to this, it must be said that overwhelming complexity is not a given, a 'fact', but a construction of the theorist and a problem for the central ruler who wants to control the whole of society (surely a 'complex' task). Why should a direct understanding of daily life situations be a priori inferior to a 'sophisticated' view of complexity? Of course I do not say that citizens should not try to extend their understanding of their own position in society (on the contrary, this is precisely what discussion between citizens is about), but rather that self-government by citizens will certainly not develop if whatever existing skills and understanding they have are immediately brushed aside by so-called superior professional insight.

As I said earlier, what is presented here is not a complete strategy for citizen action in the welfare state. Whether full citizenship can indeed be realized in the context of the welfare state remains an open question, that needs careful comparative investigation.[18] Theory can remove some obstacles to the realization of citizenship, but not bring about its realization.

CLASS STRUGGLES AND THE
REVISED THEORY OF CITIZENSHIP

Finally what about citizenship and class struggles? The voluntaristic theory of citizenship is indeed incompatible with a Marxist perspective of class struggle. Does our revised theory do any better? Can it indeed do justice to the reality of class struggles? This question needs further investigation. My provisional answer is positive. The revised theory of citizenship does not only look at the individual expression of will, as defined by the dominant institutions, but also to the conditions of its formation and the kinds of outcomes it understandably aims at. It does not reify particular historical definitions and embodiments of individual autonomy. It sees the exercise of citizenship as always critical of dominant institutions. It conceives of citizenship as an area of struggle. It thus leaves ample room for class struggles at the level of citizenship. And most importantly, it enables us to develop notions and institutions of citizenship as an arena of struggle not only in the capitalist state, but also under the dictatorship of the proletariat (the socialist state) and possibly even under stateless communism. Thus we may conclude that the revised theory of citizenship seems to open up possibilities that were foreclosed by the too narrow identification of citizenship with the institutions of the liberal-democratic capitalist state. Further study and practice are required to find out whether these possibilities are real.

One important part of such a study would be to inquire into the formation of different languages of citizenship and their relations to different groups and classes. In particular one would have to ask under what circumstances attempts to develop a notion of citizenship that is viable for all members of the polity do in fact constitute an effort to make the exploited speak, think and act out the language of their class opponents. Does the quest for citizenship represent nothing but the old utopian wish of bourgeois socialists to have 'the life conditions of modern society without the struggles and dangers that necessarily follow from it?'[19] This article has posed the old question of the relation between citizenship and class in a slightly different, and I hope more fruitful way. It has not answered it.

NOTES

1. What I summarize here is, of course, the conception of Greek citizenship as it has been handed down to us by the Western intellectual tradition, as exemplified in the work of Hannah Arendt (see *The Human Condition* (New York, 1959)). The historical reality of Athenian citizenship is another matter.

2. J. G. A. Pocock, *The Machiavellian Moment* (Princeton, 1975), vii.

3. Recent scholarship has shown that in this battle political arguments for capitalism were often first formulated by aristocrats, and that the bourgeoisie was not as successful in developing its own ideology as many writers had assumed. (See Albert O. Hirschman, *The Passions and the Interests: Political Arguments for Capitalism before its Triumph* (Princeton, 1977), 4, 11, 12; Pocock, op. cit., 550.)

4. As an aside it must be noted that the conception of citizenship that has been outlined here was developed in major European states, where freely moving individuals (bourgeois), who were no longer tied to traditional communities and associations, confronted a centralized state power. Recently political thinkers have begun to pay attention to developments in countries where the context is different: the Netherlands with its tradition of *consociatio* and Raetia (Graubünden, Switzerland) with its autonomous village communities. In his beautiful book *The Death of Communal Liberty*, Benjamin Barber points out that the Raetian conception of freedom in the context of the independent local community constitutes an alternative to the dominating liberal-democratic idea of freedom. In Raetia there was neither a strong central authority, nor strong individual rights and alienation. There freedom was not defined in terms of sovereignty as central authority. According to Raetian political understanding sovereignty can only flourish when central authority is weak or absent. Freedom is 'collaborative self-reliance and community autonomy'

(171); it implies a unity of decision-makers and implementors, and a direct reciprocity of rights and duties. In Raetian villages the individual did not experience the atomization and alienation that are characteristic of bourgeois-citizenship. 'The sense of self given by his citizenship defined him as an autonomous man within the structure of his polity, not outside of it' (18).

5. The effort to ban rationality altogether from the so-called realm of meaning and values was not successful, because one cannot orient oneself without being rational in some sense. Rationality often re-entered the forbidden territory under the guise of a realistic politics of power and/or of technological necessity.

6. And they still are. Listen to Crozier, Huntington, and Watanuki in their 'Report on the Governability of Democracies to the Trilateral Commission.' In the Introduction they state: 'In some measure, the advanced industrial societies have spawned a stratum of value-oriented intellectuals who often devote themselves to the derogation of leadership, the challenging of authority, and the unmasking and delegitimation of established institutions, their behaviour contrasting with that of the also increasing numbers of technocratic and policy-oriented intellectuals. In an age of widespread secondary school and university education, the pervasiveness of the mass media, and the displacement of manual labour by clerical and professional employees, this development constitutes a challenge to democratic government which is, potentially at least, as serious as those posed in the past by the aristocratic cliques, fascist movements, and communist parties.' Michel Crozier, Samuel Huntington, Joji Watanuki *The Crisis of Democracy* (New York, 1975), 6-7.

7. See e.g. his *Essays in Self-Criticism* (London, 1976), 94-99 and passim.

8. Althusser has insisted that his anti-humanism is *theoretical*, apparently leaving room for individualist-humanist illusions at the level of practice.

9. Of course the temptation to draw practical consequences will always be there. Take the case of individuals whose activities deviate from what is normal, desired by the rulers, or predicted by non-individualistic social theories. Citizenship implies a *right* to deviate, within certain limits, as well as a right to criminal justice and punishment when going beyond these limits. A non-individualistic social theory, however, will invite one to see any deviance as a psychological problem. The deviant is not a normally functioning human being as supposed by the theory. He must be corrected.

10. A typical question that such studies address is what the effects of high school civics courses on beliefs and attitudes of citizens have been for a certain generation of students in a certain town.

11. Members being those who are part of the networks of interdependency and dominance and of the division of labour and care that form the polity.

12. See Pitkin on the tension between ideas and institutions of justice, Hanna Fenichel Pitkin, *Wittgenstein and Justice* (Berkeley, 1972), 186-92.

13. As Sheldon Wolin has recently written: 'If disillusionment is not to deepen into despair, political thinking and practical skill must turn to the task of finding new forms of living that will elicit the energies, competencies, and "moralism" of individuals. New forms would mean not only new relationships of cooperation, but new locations, ones that will be centered around places where people actually live, work and learn. They cannot be conceived administratively, that is, as decentralized "units"; they must be conceived politically, but not in the

outworn modes of elections, mass parties, or final decision-making authorities. It must be a politics grounded in everyday life, in the reality of working places, living places, and learning places, in the reality of people doing and depending.' Sheldon S. Wolin, 'The new conservatives' in *New York Review of Books*, 5, February, 1976: 10.

14. Paul Diesing, *Reason in Society: Five Types of Decision and their Social Conditions* (Urbana, I; 1962), ch. 6.

15. T. H. Marshall, *Class, Citizenship and Social Development* (New York, 1965).

16. Some readers will object that I paint a too benign picture of the welfare state as a good thing with some defects. The welfare state, they will say, tries to erect a barrier between the spheres of production and consumption, which in fact can never be separated. It thus masks exploitation that is inherent in the prevailing mode of production. On the one hand the welfare state facilitates, and is possibly even indispensable to, further capital accumulation. On the other hand it tries to keep those who are being exploited, the labour force, healthy and happy (or at least quiet, obedient and 'loyal') by welfare arrangements, education and other legitimizing devices. The welfare state is at best an unstable and contradictory reality: it tries to redress inequalities while leaving unaffected the mechanism that constantly reproduces them in the sphere of production.

I am not going to investigate these different interpretations here. My analysis aims at the development of citizen strategies to combat professionalism and bureaucracy. These are analyzed in the context of the welfare state, but their fate does not depend on that of the welfare state. I expect that they will at least facilitate the search for useful strategies in other contexts, socialist states for example, where bureaucracy and professionalism are found.

17. Niklas Luhmann, *Politische Planung: Aufsätze zur Soziologie von Politik und Verwaltung* (Opladen, 1971).

18. To me the differences between the US and The Netherlands are striking. Differences in traditions of participation, in levels of education, in civility, in general confidence in the functioning of society, and in the size of the country, seem to set limits to the kinds of citizen activities that can be effective in each particular country.

19. Marx/Engels, 'Manifest der Kommunistischen Partei', in: *Werke* (Berlin, 1974), band 4, 488.

2 Citizenship and Knowledge

Geraint Parry
University of Manchester, UK

The problem of reconciling the good man with the good citizen has been a recurrent theme in political thought ever since it was first raised by Aristotle. In raising it Aristotle examined two issues which have similarly recurred in discussions of citizenship, although sometimes in not such an overt form. These are the issues of political knowledge and of the self-control needed in the citizen who is expected in turn both to rule and to be ruled. The issues are interconnected but there are signs that the question of political knowledge has been neglected in recent years despite the continuing concern amongst theorists of liberal democracy with the citizen's roles as ruler and subject. In this chapter I wish to suggest that traditional political theory was correct in recognising the extent and source of political knowledge as an important problem. Political knowledge is a condition for effective citizenship. It therefore seems a topic worth reconsidering, even if its characterisation remains elusive.

As Aristotle saw it, the difficulty over the good man becoming the good citizen arose because, whereas the qualities of the good man were constant and universal, the qualities of the good citizen were related to the kind of state in which he lived.[1] Aristotle defines citizenship in terms of participation. A citizen is 'a man who shares in the administration of justice and in the holding of office' (1275a). He means by 'office' not only appointive or elective positions but membership of the popular assembly and the people's courts, and for our purposes we could regard anyone who is entitled to vote as the modern counterpart of the Aristotelian citizen. The good citizen will therefore be someone who excels in the administration of justice and in the duties appertaining to his office.

Political systems — 'constitutions' is the conventional translation — vary. They vary in their political objectives, in their political style, in the kinds of offices which are established, and in the duties of those offices. Since there may be specific requirements for office in one state which do not exist in another, the citizen of one state might not even qualify as a citizen in another. A person might fail a property or wealth qualification for the vote or might be excluded by a literacy or numeracy test or by belonging to the wrong sex. Similarly the person who would be a good citizen in one political system would not necessarily be a good citizen in another. Being a good citizen involves more than observance of the law. Even Hobbes acknowledged that there was a difference between the guiltless man and the just man. The good citizen has to be committed to upholding the principles on which the political system is based. This does not exclude reforming activities but these activities would be directed to realising more completely the political values of the community. Aristotle summarises it this way (1309a):

> Three qualifications are necessary in those who have to fill the sovereign offices. The first is loyalty to the established constitution. The second is a high degree of capacity for the duties of the office. The third is the quality of goodness and justice, in the particular form which suits the nature of each constitution. (If the *principle* of justice varies from constitution to constitution, the *quality* of justice must also have its corresponding varieties.)

The citizen of an oligarchy will therefore be expected to preserve the dominance of the ruling wealthy class (which may or may not involve, as Aristotle claimed, a policy of moderation). He should denounce those who press for political and economic equality. He should see to it that the citizens are constantly educated in the right oligarchical 'temper' (1310a). On the other side, the principle of democracy is equality of political rights. The good democrat will try to ensure that his fellow citizens make full use of the rights they possess. He would encourage political participation and guard against attempts to restrict access to government. If democracy is thought to entail majority decision he must not only obey such decisions himself but must help to ensure that others comply. In his citizen capacity he should defend even those decisions to which he is opposed, except perhaps those he believes to contradict basic constitutional principles. Since Aristotle also believed that democracy meant the rule of the poorer classes the good democrat would be expected to work strenuously for the implementation of class policies.

The duties attaching to the station of citizen thus bring one into conflict with what may be expected of one simply as a man. According to Aristotle it is only in special circumstances that there can be identity between the good man and the good citizen. Rousseau saw the problem in much the same way. To be a good citizen of an existing state involved a denial of oneself as a human being. Even the most representative of regimes required the alienation of the sovereign right of self-determination at periodic elections. Most contemporaneous regimes did not permit even so much of a right. They denied both humanity and citizenship. They treated their populations as objects to be administered. If there were anything which might remotely be described as citizen activity it was narrowly confined to a class and it involved playing roles which implied acceptance of the coercive basis of the state. At times Rousseau is more despairing than Aristotle of achieving any reconciliation between man and citizen. In *Emile* he declares that his purpose must be the education of man rather than the education of the citizen. He is nurturing man in the abstract. Nature called Emile to be a man before he was called to be a citizen. Educating the citizen, however, is shaping a man so that he is part of a whole, conscious only of the common life, the numerator of a fraction rather than being an independent unit. 'A citizen of Rome was neither Caius nor Lucius, he was a Roman.' Such education is not training a man for himself but for others, and where these are incompatible objects 'forced to combat either nature or society, you must make your choice between the man and the citizen, you cannot train both'. At the same time the vivid portrayal of citizen virtue in the very same passages indicate the underlying tension in Rousseau's thought.[2]

Such tension is very little evident in a writer like David Hume for whom citizen virtues are unquestionably artificial, but not the worse for being so. The citizen is the just man, but justice may require conduct quite opposed to what would be expected of a good man. Actions are only just if in accordance with a system of rules. These rules may require a benevolent and fair-minded man to return property to a miser or a 'seditious bigot'. Taken in isolation this would be an act both against private and public interest. But, forming one of a general set of rules, compliance with it becomes just and in the general interest. However, the reason why individuals in civilised societies comply is not a direct perception of their own or the public interest because this would be unreliable and uncertain. They obey because it is 'virtuous' to act justly. 'Virtue' is the name of conduct which is approved on account of the 'character and sentiments' of the person performing the action. As with so many British political thinkers from Locke onwards, public opinion is a crucial force. Men, Hume asserts, like to be esteemed virtuous by their fellow men. What is esteemed just and virtuous will vary (within broad limits) from society to society and hence the good citizen's conduct will vary. The standards of justice and virtue are shaped by education and the 'artifice of politicians', i.e. the process of socialisation.[3] The good citizen will be the one who has learned well the artificial conventions and expectations of his society. The good man may still act in private dealings according to such natural virtues as love and benevolence.

Although Hume does not worry overmuch about a conflict between the good man and the good citizen, he does agree with Aristotle and Rousseau in arguing that good citizenship requires education and knowledge. The citizen needs not merely a general education but a specifically political education. Following Aristotle's list of citizen qualifications he needs to understand enough of the established constitution to be able to appreciate what loyalty to it entails, he needs to know what duties are involved in the citizen office he holds, and he needs to recognise the principle of justice underlying the state if his conduct is to manifest the appropriate quality of justice. This is an education in 'knowing how' and 'knowing what'. The politically educated citizen knows how to move around in his society. He knows how to put forward a case for public action. He is sensitive to the possibilities of victory and defeat for his own proposals. This is the sort of practical knowledge which can generally only arise through political action. But such a citizen will also possess a considerable amount of factual knowledge about political rights, about the constitution and its various offices, and about the capacities and limits of government. Aristotle, Rousseau and Hume also agree that the citizen (as distinct from the good man) will need a knowledge of the attitudes and expectations of fellow citizens. He must learn how to fit in, how to appear but a fraction of the whole, how to win esteem.

All this knowledge has, Aristotle points out, to be applied to two roles in which the citizen finds himself. He must know how to rule and how to be ruled. In Rousseau's version he must know how to obey in his subject capacity the rules he has made in his sovereign citizen capacity. For both thinkers the good man and the good citizen are reconcilable only in the ideal condition where free men associate together for the fullest realisation of their capacities. The good man can only become good in and through co-operation and this, in turn, means that he must acquire the attributes of the good citizen. In an association of equally free men, however, citizenship cannot involve permanent dependence but either the concurrence or the alternation of ruling over and being ruled by one's equals.

The idea of citizenship as ruling and being ruled in turn has become a constant theme of democratic thought. It is variously described in modern political literature as the balance between the active and the passive, or the participant and the subject. At a certain level this distinction appears a truism. Democratic government has to be democratic and it has to be government. There must be a process by which citizens exert control over government and make it aware of their demands but there must also be a readiness to allow the government to enforce policies which it has arrived at. Participation for the sake of participating may have its attractions but most people participate in an activity which is expected to have some outcome.[4] What makes it more important to reassert is that in the first instance, as Sharpe has pointed out, it is a truism often forgotten. In the second instance there is a tendency for the active and the passive citizen roles, which in the 'classical' texts were played by each individual, to be given to different sectors of the population, which is altogether a different matter. Almond and Verba confusingly regard the theory of citizenship 'described in civics textbooks' as the 'rationality-activist' model, as if there were no room in such theory for the task of being ruled. They contrast it with their understanding of a civic culture and implicitly with the mixed subject-participant type. In this

> a substantial part of the population has acquired specialised input orientations and an activist set of self-orientations, while most of the remainder of the population continue to be oriented toward an authoritarian governmental structure and have a relatively passive set of self-orientations.[5]

Almond and Verba here express a view of politics which has become familiar. Modern democracies are characterised by what Schumpeter described as a 'division of labour' between the active leadership groups and the largely passive electorate. Instead of each person playing both parts, he is typecast as a full-time ruler (or at least an aspirant to ruling) or as a full-time subject. Stable moderate government, it is often suggested, depends on this division of labour being maintained, or, in fact, the traditional dual role of citizenship being abandoned in favour of specialisation.

It might be thought that the passive role of being ruled is not one that requires a high level of political education. Nevertheless, Aristotle believed that it was not an inconsiderable skill, and his view seems to be shared by some modern defenders of liberal democracies. Knowing when not to participate and when not to upset the division of labour between the political activist and the rest of the citizenry is something which does not come easily. As Schumpeter put it in his classic statement of this position: 'it takes a lot of self-control on the part of the citizen to refrain from political back-seat driving'.[6] Later writers increasingly came to conclude that a large part of the population lacked this kind of self-control. They did not 'know' how to be ruled. They were impatient and were uninterested in long-term perspectives. They did not understand the rules of the democratic game. The fact that nevertheless they did not upset the division of labour is to be explained by their apathy or at best by social deference, and not by any educated political choice. If men are accepted as not being political animals there is less occasion to worry about political education. It is only when in some crisis the elite attempts to mobilise the apolitical in a manner which requires some degree of knowledge and understanding that the problem of political education recurs. The predicament is comparable to that which Hannah Arendt found to be central in Plato's *Republic*:

> The trouble with coercion through reason . . . is that only the few are subject to it, so that the problem arises of how to assure that the many, the people who in their very multitude compose the body politic, can be submitted to the same truth.[7]

In other words it is difficult to appeal to the political knowledge of the population when no previous attempt has been made to encourage the population to educate itself politically. Force or fraud, as Arendt points out, then present themselves as the only alternatives.

Citizen education is therefore one way of ensuring that, in T. H. Green's famous phrase, 'will not force is the basis of the state'. It is no coincidence that so many of the major political philosophers have written on education. Plato, Aquinas, Locke, Rousseau, Bentham, James and John Stuart Mill down to Dewey and Oakeshott, in recent years, all wrote both on education and on politics. Education aims not merely at producing a learned person but at fitting someone out as a citizen of some particular kind of society. There is a sense in which all political thought is educational thought. There is a still stronger sense in which all educational thought is political thought.

Two objectives are pursued with varying degrees of emphasis in political education: the formation of political character and the provision of politically relevant knowledge.

Both aims are recognisable in Plato's *Republic* which, according to Rousseau, is the finest treatise on education ever written. Absolutely certain political knowledge was only attainable through a strenuous training designed to separate those with both capacity and determination from their natural inferiors. Plato did not of course draw the distinction between 'character' and intellectual achievement which is to be found in some of the English elite education which has yet owed much to him. Nevertheless, the guardian class could only effectively exercise its rule of reason if it also displayed the qualities of self-control and dedication which the arduous training had developed. The education was avowedly anti-democratic. Not only were both knowledge and character confined to a few but the absolutist character of Plato's conception of knowledge meant that his educational theory could no more admit the legitimacy of opposition than could his political theory. By contrast his Sophist opponents taught the art and logic of arguing a political policy or a legal case before the popular assembly or court where it was acknowledged that they would face similarly argued defences from the other side.

Locke and Rousseau directed their educational thought to a wider audience; Locke to the substantial propertied middle order and Rousseau to the mass of self-sufficient men who formed his political public. Education was, for both, a potentially liberating force raising the individual to self-awareness and also to an awareness of his obligations to others. Although Rousseau spoke of man being born free, his meaning was better expressed by Locke's argument that men were born free as they were born rational. Freedom and reason were both developed by age, experience, and education. Rousseau's remark that 'to renounce freedom is to renounce humanity' can be paralleled by Locke. For both, a man was only properly free when he acted from due deliberation and with an understanding of what he was doing. 'Without liberty', Locke states, 'the understanding would be to no purpose: and without understanding, liberty . . . would signify nothing.'[8]

Locke and Rousseau differ significantly over the implications of this connection between freedom and understanding for politics. Locke's emphasis is more on character and less on the specific content of political knowledge, on which he is more pluralistic than Rousseau. In both his writings on the education of children and in his *Conduct of the Understanding*, which is an intelligent adult's guide to clear thinking,

Locke expounds the habits and dispositions necessary to a rational individual who is to think for himself and to make his own way in the world. He reminds his reader of how to cultivate the distinctively human capacity of understanding. The individual is to employ his liberty of suspending judgement so as fully to consider all the circumstances of his situation and the likely consequences of future action and inaction. Failure to do this is a 'neglect of the understanding' which is morally reprehensible. Reasoning is a strenuous matter; the burdens of being a man are great. The individual must be as self-reliant as possible, avoiding partiality, prejudice, haste and inattention. He must strive to resist the almost overwhelming pressures of tradition and received opinion and examine its bases in reason. Those arguments which survive the test of reason thus become a kind of intellectual property of the individual to be developed and modified to the degree of which the individual is capable.[9] He must guard against the vested interests of parties, sects and groups, such as professors who do not like to see what they have taught for decades challenged, and their 'authority of forty years standing, wrought out of hard rock, Greek and Latin, with no small expense of time and candle' undermined by some 'upstart'.[10]

The constant theme of Locke's educational writings is the rejection of moral and intellectual authoritarianism. Each person must learn to take his own decisions over the handling of his 'property', understood in Locke's usual wide sense of life, liberty and possessions. 'By nature' no person could be better informed than any other as to how to make such decisions. Differences between individuals stemmed from the relative skill and industry with which they developed their God-given capacity of understanding, together with their opportunities for leisure. The far-seeing parent brings up his child to be able to make decisions for himself. He steadily relaxes his control as the child grows older and explains the basis of the decisions he makes on the child's behalf in such a way that the child can make them himself as he approaches the age of discretion.

But Locke says relatively little about the kinds of things a citizen must know. Admittedly he does provide reading lists on the laws and history of England, on the art of public speaking, on human character, and on political theory (recommending his own anonymous *Treatises*!).[11] But the true aim of education is, as Locke says, to make men familiar with the 'variety and stock of knowledge' as instances of the 'variety and freedom of *thinking*' and thereby to increase the 'power and activity of the mind'.[12] The good man and the good citizen is he who develops his understanding and sifts assiduously through his experience of the social, intellectual and political worlds so that he is equipped to tackle the central problem of both private and public life:

> In the whole conduct of the understanding there is nothing of more moment than to know when and where, and how far to give assent; and possibly there is nothing harder.[13]

Although Rousseau speaks in Lockean terms of 'thinking one's own thoughts', citizen education is specifically less pluralistic than in Locke. For Locke there was nothing inherently different in learning how to make decisions in political matters from learning to dispose of one's property. But for Rousseau the citizen must be educated for his place in the social order. Existing education, he believed, fell between all stools. It sought, as did Locke's, to preserve natural feelings in social life with the result that its product was inevitably

> at war with himself, hesitating between his wishes and his duties, he will be neither a man nor a citizen. He will be of no use to himself nor to others. He will be a man of our day, a Frenchman, an Englishman, one of the great middle class.[14]

Not only, as Lively points out,[15] does Rousseau share the common view of his period that all men of reason could discover a single moral truth, he also believes that there is a narrow set of values unique to particular states which the citizen of each state is to discover and make his own. His universalism is significantly restricted by the relativism he found in Montesquieu. The citizen learns not to be a man but to be a Spartan, a Roman, or a Carthaginian. So the citizen learns not merely how to reason; he also learns about the values of his own state. In this he receives a constant education from all the institutions of the state which should direct him in a single coherent, consistent manner. Rousseau cites Montesquieu with approval: 'At the birth of societies the rulers of Republics establish institutions, and afterwards the institutions mould the rulers.'[16] He then reiterates that the founding legislator must remake human nature giving each individual resources alien to him which force him to be dependent on his fellow men. Laws, civic religion, public theatre, and the arts instruct the citizen pupil in the particular civil spirit. Citizen participation then reaffirms these values in legislation. The citizen will express the general will in the assembly because the thoughts he has been thinking are not in fact 'his own'.

They should be the thoughts each would independently arrive at as a consequence of his public education. Not just character but knowledge is the object of such instruction.

J. S. Mill and Tocqueville sought to combine Rousseau's notion of government as a school with something of Locke's pluralism. What the pupil should learn at the school is 'responsibility'. This was a quality which could only properly be developed by exercising it. Governmental arrangements should therefore ideally be so constituted as to help and encourage men to play a part in decision-making. To take decisions which affected others as well as oneself moralised the individual and improved his 'character'. He found himself required to consider the aspirations and interests of others. He would find opposing aspirations supported by arguments which he must seek to understand and must appreciate that if they were to be rejected they must be defeated by superior arguments. In the process both sides would be mentally and spiritually educated.

Political knowledge for Mill and Tocqueville combined, as it did for Rousseau, both knowing 'how' and knowing 'that'. Participation in local government, voluntary associations, jury service and in the management of one's own work-place was an education in how to make decisions. But by drawing the person into decision-making in those matters with which he was most familiar — the area in which he lived, the voluntary associations to which he belonged, the place where he spent his working life — such participation drew on a person's wealth of substantive knowledge. Not only was such participation morally educative, it might be better informed. Moreover, it would harness such knowledge, whereas much of it might remain unexploited where a person was regarded as a mere object to be administered. Mill and Tocqueville differed sharply from Rousseau in a significant respect. This substantive knowledge was as varied as the experiences and stations of men. All became better citizens as a result of the plurality of life's experiments being made available as hypotheses for testing. As Locke had it, the 'variety and freedom of thinking' would increase the 'power and activity of the mind'.

The connection between citizenship and education was a major theme of the British Idealists. They recognised that, as K. B. Smellie succinctly put it, there was no longer

> any reason to suppose that the market value of any individual's services in a system of complex division of labour will be sufficient to secure him the goods and services which his development as a citizen requires.[17]

The degradation ensuing from the operation of the market must be counteracted by state-supported intervention of both a protective and developmental type so as to place the under-privileged in a position to develop their individuality by helping themselves. State limits to freedom of contract and on the sale of alcohol coupled with social work and above all the provision of education, formed a liberal programme which combined state and voluntary action to make freedom and individuality a reality and not a formal right.

They insisted that their programme was more than one of 'hindering hindrances' to citizenship. Individuality and citizenship was active and oriented to the community. Individuality involved separation from others in order to reunite consciously with others through art, science, society and religion, and thereby become 'a person in a world of responsive persons'.[18] This reunion must come through citizen activity. Men become citizens only when they use their rights. Rights are to be regarded not as rewards but as opportunities.[19] But opportunities could only be taken by the educated. With T. H. Green as their chief inspiration, philosophers such as Sir Henry Jones, Maccunn, Hetherington, Muirhead and Haldane flung themselves into the theoretical and practical questions of education. They acted on secondary school boards and were major figures in the establishment of university extension courses, the Workers' Educational Association, and other forms of adult education; some were involved in the development of teacher training.

They were, of course, much less suspicious of the state than Mill had been, but their objectives were far closer to his than they recognised. Muirhead's summary 'Character is everything' was not far from Mill in substance or language.[20] There is one further and possibly significant difference. I suggested that Mill's proposals for participation united practical knowledge with education in decision-making. The Idealists conceived of citizen education as 'generalist' (a view which has permeated political education in Britain). Schools should not attempt to train experts but to 'develop human personality', and both higher education and vocational training should include a substantial element of the humanities.[21] More than one displayed their personal or academic experience in commending the broad-based Scottish university degree. More importantly, unlike Mill they had no conception of reshaping society in a manner which would demand and encourage technical knowledge. Some were suspicious of both collective and co-operative socialism and felt, as Muirhead reports, that the removal of the degrading influence of low wages, unemployment and slums, aided by education, would suffice to establish the conditions in which citizenship might become a reality.

Although the connection between ruling, political activity and citizen education has been a constant theme of traditional political thought, it has been somewhat neglected by students of politics in more recent years. The revival of interest in schemes of wider popular participation has stimulated discussion of the social, economic and, more occasionally, the structural conditions for effective political activity. The political knowledge required for genuine citizenship has received little attention, although the lack of such knowledge is sometimes a half-concealed assumption in arguments which would seek to restrict participation in breadth and scope.

One of the few British political thinkers to discuss political education extensively has been Michael Oakeshott,[22] but 'citizen participation' is not exactly a prominent term in the Oakeshottian political vocabulary. As in the case of the earlier classics, Oakeshott's view of education coheres with his view of politics. Education is the inculcation of the student in an established discipline, craft or activity. The student is brought to appreciate, and to move about easily in, a complex of traditions and manners of doing a subject. He learns it from established masters and his graduation is a sign that he has been accepted by them as a fellow practitioner. Learning is a matter of apprenticeship. A political education (as distinct here from its academic study) consists in learning the political traditions and customs of one's country. There is something to know, but it is best learned on the job by taking part in the ordinary political arrangements of the community. Participation is important, then, but it need not be of the extensive nature assumed by many citizenship theorists. Whilst everyone in a society will receive some education in its traditions, there will be a few who apprentice themselves to the craft of ruling. Like most apprenticeships it will be long. It may need generations, which would seem to suggest that only the scions of political families can be expected to become masters. It is learned by imitating one's elders and is unsuited to the young who are particularly apt to confuse the activity of ruling with the management of an enterprise which is intended to produce something. It takes time to learn self-restraint. The examiners whom the candidates must satisfy (to use the appropriate British academic terminology) are the members of the existing political elite. Recruitment is a matter of sponsorship into the club, guild or mystery, the candidate having shown that he knows his parliamentary procedures and etiquette, or respects the anonymity of the civil service, or in other ways acknowledges the traditional procedures, even whilst being prepared for their modification.

The great virtue of the Oakeshottian approach is that it once again combines an education in the making of decisions with the acquisition of what is regarded as the relevant information – in this case *Lokalvernunft*, the knowledge of the local situation, as the eighteenth century conservative Justus Moeser termed it. Its drawback from the standpoint of citizenship theory would appear to be its full acceptance of a division of labour between the bulk of the population and an active elite, more interested in and more knowledgeable about the arts of ruling. Yet such a division does not seem to follow necessarily from this conception of education, but rather follows from Oakeshott's notion of the limited civil association. In a society characterised by a plurality of associations, all or many of which were involved in political activity, the variety of practical knowledge acquired by individuals in the course of their day-to-day activities might be more fully directed to the political realm.

Without some specification of the character and source of political knowledge discussions of political education verge on the truistic. Few would deny that the citizen should be better educated, and so educated as to develop his personality and, as Dennis Thompson rightly points out,[23] there can be no end to demands for further education in this generalised sense. To ask for a more precise set of requirements for an education in effective citizenship is, however, commonly dismissed as inappropriate. One reason is the view, stemming from post-war Anglo-American philosophy, that there can be no knowledge of moral and political ends. Bambrough's well-known critique of Plato's analogies argues that there is no skill of the sort Plato attributes to the guardians which would permit them to select political ends.[24] It is the passengers and not the captain who settle the destination of the ship. The implication is that there is in principle a political decision about ends distinct from the instrumental decisions about means on which expertise may be available. Most of us rather casually accept this and like to think that we may in some such way distinguish a political from an administrative matter. The fact that this distinction is often extraordinarily difficult to make does not appear to have led to an examination of the respective types of information required by political actors and administrators. Christopher Hood's outstanding study[25] reveals the ways in which administrative constraints may limit the implementation of political policies. It also shows the narrow line which divides the political from the administrative and the consequent difficulties in attaching responsibility for apparent governmental failures. Hood's study raises again the question as to what the political participant must know in order to be an effective decision-maker, or to make political demands which are translatable into action, or to issue praise or blame. One must also enquire about the circumstances in which a participant could acquire such knowledge and about the type of knowledge relevant to the participant's political objectives.

There appear to be three broad grounds for participation: instrumental, developmental and communitarian.[26] Each requires a different 'style' of participation differing in extent, in commitment, and in the character of the information it requires. The instrumentalist sees political participation as a means of promoting the interests of himself or of his group. Such a view presumes the actor to know what his interests are: 'The wearer best knows where the shoe pinches' is an often quoted adage. But in order to have something done about it does he need to know how and why it pinches? Or does he merely need to know where the shoe repairer is to be found? Certainly a good deal is still to be done in teaching people where the 'shoe repairer' is to be found – as Shelter, Help for the Aged and similar welfare organisations have shown in making the under-privileged aware of the benefits to which they are entitled. To know one's rights of recipience in law is important, but somewhat negative in terms of political activity. Other kinds of knowledge and experience are required if one is to press for changes in levels of benefits or, more radically, if the under-privileged are themselves to participate in determining and allocating aid. Decision-making of this sort must imply some degree of awareness of the revenues available for distribution, of the claims of possible beneficiaries, and of the options as to how benefits might be spread. It is knowledge, both political and administrative. The nature of such knowledge and the means of its acquisition are clearly matters of some practical significance if the participation movement is to spread and become established.

Participation on developmental grounds may face fewer questions. Although advocates, such as Mill, presumed that educative participation would, by improving individual character, promote the general good, it can, paradoxically, be a rather self-regarding form of participation. Most forms of citizen activity could be construed as educative and the participant need only have some expectation that he will find himself improved or 'stretched'. There must indeed be some instrumental element in such activity. Although some appear attracted to it, participation in political participation is of limited value. For the most part one receives a political education in the process of achieving some goal.

The third 'style' of participation is community oriented. Here the object is neither the promotion of one's immediate interests nor the search for self-education. The citizen participates in order to further the good of his community which may or may not be in his particular interests, and which may or may not be justified in terms of his own development. The extent and nature of his participation will be related to his estimate of what he can contribute to the community at any juncture. Self-esteem may lead some to believe that they invariably have something to contribute, but to justify participation on these grounds should involve knowledge of communal need and of the abilities of oneself and of fellow citizens. The citizen — and it could be argued that only someone participating for these reasons is a genuine citizen — might reasonably decide in a particular case that another is better suited to act. Inaction would imply rational deference, not apathy.

Such reasoned deference does mean that the citizen must know something of the task in hand — what levels of expertise it requires, and the further consequences likely from a decision in this particular case. It requires a knowledge of the other likely participants. In a large society this is almost impossible to acquire at an individual level. In a society of strangers the instrumentalist attitude of Bentham may seem more convincing.[27] Lacking knowledge of others, the best policy is to mistrust them — 'minimise confidence and maximise control'. Whether or not such distrust reflects an alienated condition, it can be a workable policy for constitutional democrats. It involves sets of checks and balances which reduce discretionary power and, by their automatic operation, also reduce somewhat the burden of information the citizen will require.

From the standpoint of citizenship theory another drawback to the reasoned deference which may be implicit in the idea of communal participation is that reasoned deference may readily degenerate into habitual deference. The counterpart to the 'vainglorious' participant, mentioned earlier, is the 'diffident' citizen who assumes his own incompetence and the relative competence of others. Most surveys conclude that a sense of citizen competence is positively correlated with education and social class. It is part of the argument of developmental theories that a sense of competence feeds on successful participation. The sense of incompetence of the diffident citizen is equally likely to be fed the longer he defers to others. One explanation of the sense of incompetence is that it reflects a 'fear of freedom'.[28] I am suggesting that an additional explanation may lie in the lack of relevant political knowledge, or perhaps in not knowing what knowledge is relevant.

The problem can appear in practical form when a government or political elite attempts in a crisis to mobilise a population by calling upon it to perform citizen duties which they have not been expected habitually to perform. The United Kingdom has experienced several attempts in the last decade or so by political leaders to invoke the 'Dunkirk spirit'. Leading articles in the press have as regularly complained that these appeals have fallen on deaf ears and have lamented a decline in morality, patriotism, or civic spirit amongst the British. It is, no doubt, possible that this is the explanation and that the country is full of rational economic men who have worked out the benefits of being free riders. But another possibility is not that ears are deaf to the call but that subjects do not *know* what to do. Appeals in general terms are seldom translated into terms to which the individual can respond. Where they are translated the appeal is trivial – to save on hot water. Injunctions to 'work harder' may not carry weight to a worker who has never been responsible for deciding the rate of an assembly line, or calls to 'harness the inventive power of the nation' to someone whose inventive powers have never been stimulated by the necessity of solving a major problem of production, distribution or government.

On the other hand there is an increasing feeling amongst citizens and politicians – reflected as usual by political scientists – that the traditional methods of central government cannot handle the tasks they have assumed or had thrust upon them. Government has ever more been called upon to rectify the injustices of the market. To do so the centre has demanded the means of control and has become cumulatively more suspicious of 'self-government' at the local level or the periphery, lest deviant decisions upset some general plan. More recently, however, governmental regulation has proved less successful and we have had the unaccustomed sight of politicians pleading with their electorates not to ask too much of them. It has become fashionable for political scientists and economists to search for the point at which governments may become 'overloaded'. One sign may be that the centre lacks, or cannot process, the knowledge required to understand how to satisfy the demands upon it. As Herman van Gunsteren puts it, 'the learning capacity of a system of rational central government is simply too small'.[29]

Various reactions to this may be detected. One is to strengthen the centre still further, expand its regulative powers, feed in more information through reports and commissions, and streamline the civil service. The second course is to advocate government's withdrawal as far as possible to the task of maintaining and umpiring general rules. Hayek has been among the most consistent advocates of this course and the undoubted resurgence of interest in his work in the last few years almost certainly reflects the growing disillusionment with interventionist government. The problem of political knowledge does not exist as such for Hayek. Indeed, a legal order is founded on the necessary ignorance of men concerning the bulk of the particular facts which determine the working of society.[30] Individuals employ their particular knowledge for their own particular purposes. Government, necessarily ignorant both of the knowledge and the purposes of its subjects, should content itself with framing abstract rules which would be likely to 'enhance the chances that the efforts of unknown individuals towards equally unknown aims will be successful'.[31]

Dispersed knowledge becomes public, it would seem, only as a result of its employment by each individual in pursuit of his own goals. It might equally be to the private advantage of any individual or group to conceal knowledge. The communitarian pooling of knowledge of the citizen participant, whilst nowhere rejected, is not encouraged by Hayek's individualism.

The third reaction to 'overloaded' government is devolutionary and has traditionally been favoured by developmentalists and communitarians. *Lokalvernunft* is set against the alleged relative ignorance of the centre. It is the failure of understanding which is among the most frequent complaints against control government and this, it is claimed, may be most effectively remedied by devolving or transferring authority to the locality or to a group or profession. Local self-government should encourage the otherwise deferential to come forward into the public domain, confident that they know something of the matter in hand or, at least, that they can assess the quality of others' contributions. Much has been written lately of citizen trust in government. For the communitarian what local self-government would imply is government trust in the citizen. It involves recognising the citizen as a mature agent, knowledgeable, and capable of exercising discretion.[32] Advantages of instrumental, developmental and communitarian characters are widely anticipated. A benefit, often regarded ambivalently, may be an enhanced sense of commitment to the whole of which the locality is a part. This tends to be what employers have in mind when they support a degree of industrial democracy.

The other side of the coin is the particularism, either aggressive or defensive, which local self-government may also encourage. Will knowledge of one's own community develop sympathy for the plight of others? Many political and moral creeds strive instead to overcome the prejudices of parochialism. The siting of nuclear power stations may be a case in point. It is easy for a community to have enough knowledge of the dangers to wish that the station be not placed within its boundaries, and enough awareness of its advantages to wish it to be sited somewhere else. Umpirage seems to be called for in the form of some central state body. Nuclear power indeed raises in a fascinating form the general issue of the extent of knowledge required in a citizen. In many countries there have been campaigns to secure some voice for the citizen in the development of nuclear power. Some communities have held referenda. Here is a pressing moral and political issue over ends, which yet appears to require a level of knowledge well beyond that which most of those called upon to participate can possess – an issue which divides those on whom the citizen might expect to call as experts. It is unclear as to how the relevant knowledge might be generated. Both Hayekian individuals and local communities or professional bodies can have an interest in limiting knowledge, and the uncommitted citizen must rely on what slips out in the course of conflict of interests. This appears to be the argument of John Plamenatz who, in one of the few recent discussions of the question, dismisses the whole issue of citizen knowledge as a non-problem.[33] Plamenatz's case is that although political leaders are better informed than the ordinary citizen about some political matters, it does not follow that the citizen knows much less than he needs to know in order to perform his tasks adequately. The argument rests on the familiar division of labour thesis. The citizen does not need the politician's information because it is not his job to take the political decisions: 'The voter, when he casts his vote, does not take incompetently a kind of decision that the expert or the political leader takes more competently; he takes a decision of a different kind.'[34]

Plamenatz acknowledges that this different kind of decision should be an informed one, but he is not at all precise as to what this means or where the voter acquires the appropriate information. He is supposed to 'understand the significance of what he is doing when he casts his vote', know that the alternatives he is offered are real ones, and 'understand the rights and obligations peculiar to democracy'. But this would appear to be a limited knowledge that accrues to the individual in the ordinary course of his affairs. Democracy is a matter of reposing confidence and authority in political leaders for limited periods. In a complex society the amount of knowledge potentially relevant to politics is immense and the problems it raises are ones of distribution. Democracy must try to ensure that the information is directed to the appropriate decision-makers.

But even in the form of democracy which Plamenatz discusses the problem may be more than one of distribution. In a society geared to only instrumental participation will information be gathered and stored in a form suited to communal decisions? There is also the problem of persons within a community recognising as citizens the political and social relevance and implications of their knowledge, e.g. of architects and planners acquiring and distributing the knowledge, not only of how to build high-rise flats but of their likely social consequences.[35]

A more participant democracy than envisaged by Plamenatz where citizens came nearer to ruling and being ruled in turn would, at the very least, require a different pattern of distribution of information — one in which it was more rapidly and evenly circulated. But it also requires an education in ruling. Taking one's turn at being ruled requires some knowledge, especially about the acceptance of authority. Ruling, however, is an experience which few can acquire unless society, economy and government is reconstructed in a radically decentralised fashion. Government of the little platoon with which one is familiar is a training for taking a more significant part in the government at the level of the state. There the tasks may be more complex, although some who argue for decentralisation see the state as returning to a role of umpire. More importantly the politics of a state are inherently more general. The particularity latent in theories of decentralisation remains a problem, not entirely overcome by the faith of many of its advocates that self-government is inherently an education in respecting the rights and aspirations of others. Mill rightly saw the need for adding to the state the role of disseminator of information. The British government's action in publishing and distributing literature on both sides of the question during the EEC referendum is an interesting precedent which might usefully be followed in the case of the development of nuclear power. However, only if government were not itself a party to the dispute would this be a truly fair test of Mill's proposal. Mill here recognises what Aristotle had recognised: that the many can become effective citizens and surpass the 'experts' only when their separate sources of knowledge 'meet together'. Aristotle's solution to the problem he set of reconciling good men with good citizens, of combining knowing how to rule and how to be ruled, was to find a form of association in which they could become one person 'who − as he has many feet, many hands, and many senses − may also have many qualities of character and intelligence' (*Politics*, 1281b).

NOTES

1. *Politics*, 1276b-1277a, Oxford University Press edition, trans. E. Barker.
2. J. J. Rousseau, *Emile*, Book I, trans. Cole (London, 1957), 6-10.
3. David Hume, *Treatise of Human Nature* (Oxford, 1958), Book III, Part II, Section II.
4. For an outstanding criticism of American democratic theory on these lines see L. J. Sharpe, 'American democracy reconsidered', *British Journal of Political Science,* 3 (1), 1973: 1-28; and 3 (2), 1973: 129-67 and in particular the discussion of 'functional effectiveness', pp. 130-44.
5. G. Almond and S. Verba, *The Civic Culture* (Boston and Toronto, 1965), 24-25.
6. J. A. Schumpeter, *Capitalism, Socialism and Democracy,* 4th edn. (London, 1954), ch. 23, 295.
7. H. Arendt, 'What is authority?', in: *Between Past and Future* (London, 1961), 108.
8. J. Locke, in: J. W. Yolton (ed.), *Essay Concerning Human Understanding* Vol. II (London, 1965), xxi, 68.
9. Lockean man, rather than being the abstract, isolated non-social individual he is so often portrayed as being [e.g. by Steven Lukes, *Individualism* (Oxford, 1973), ch. 19], is constantly faced by the force of public opinion.
10. *Essay*, Vol. IV, xx, 11.
11. J. Locke, 'Some thoughts concerning reading and study for a gentleman', in: J. Axtell (ed.), *John Locke: Educational Writings* (Cambridge, 1968), 400.
12. J. Locke, *Conduct of the Understanding, Works,* Vol. 3 (London, 1823), section 19.
13. *Conduct,* section 33.
14. *Emile,* 8.
15. Jack Lively, *Democracy* (Oxford, 1975), 137.
16. J. J. Rousseau, *Social Contract* (London, 1952), Bk II, ch. vii.

17. K. B. Smellie, *A Hundred Years of English Government* (London, 1950), 94.

18. H. Hetherington and J. H. Muirhead, *Social Purpose: A Contribution to a Philosophy of Civic Society* (London, 1918), 106.

19. J. Maccunn, *Ethics of Citizenship* (Glasgow, 1894), 70.

20. J. H. Muirhead, *Reflections by a Journeyman in Philosophy* (London, 1945), 95.

21. E.g. Hetherington and Muirhead, *Social Purpose,* 213-16.

22. M. Oakeshott, *Rationalism in Politics* (London, 1962).

23. D. Thompson, *The Democratic Citizen* (Cambridge, 1970), 22.

24. R. Bambrough, 'Plato's political analogies', in: P. Laslett (ed.), *Philosophy, Politics and Society,* 1st series (Oxford, 1965), 98-115.

25. C. Hood, *The Limits of Administration* (London, 1976).

26. I have discussed these further in 'Participation and political styles', in: B. Chapman and A. Potter (eds.), *W.J.M.M: Political Questions, Essays in Honour of W. J. M. Mackenzie* (Manchester, 1974), 190-204.

27. For a discussion of Bentham's theory as suited to a world in which men are strangers to one another see David Manning, *The Mind of Jeremy Bentham* (London, 1968), Introduction.

28. See not only the work of Erich Fromm but also the notion of the individual *manqué* in Oakeshott's work.

29. H. van Gunsteren *The Quest for Control* (London, 1976), 152.

30. E. g. F. A. Hayek, *Law, Legislation and Liberty,* Vol. I, ch. 1; and Vol. II, ch. 7 (London, 1973 and 1976).

31. Ibid., Vol. II, 11.

32. For a discussion of trust and discretion within the context of industrial relations see A. Fox, *Beyond Contract* (London, 1974).

34. J. Plamenatz, *Democracy and Illusion* (London, 1973), 195.

35. For some thoughts on this issue in political science see Jean Blondel, 'Plea for problem-oriented research in political science', *Political Studies,* xxiii, 1975: 232-43.

3 Comments on some Radical Critiques of Liberal-Democratic Theory

Graeme Duncan
University of East Anglia, UK

It is possible to counterpose, very broadly, two ways of thinking about man and society, the one 'individualist', seeing men as isolated, self-sufficient and perhaps egotistic entities and the political order as a means — albeit a necessary one — of maintaining peaceful or tolerable relations between them, and the other 'communitarian', perceiving men as intimately connected with each other, mutually dependent in a psychological and not merely an economic sense, brothers and sisters rather than competitors and foes, with the political and social order as their organic being, both reflecting their true natures and sustaining them as human creatures. However, even if this passes as a clear scheme or line of division — which it is not, needing closer definition and amplification, but it will do rough service — it would take a crude and dogmatic historian of ideas to cut the cloth of his subject according to it. Social and political theorists may hold what is — from any particular point of view — the most curious combinations of ideas; 'individualism' and 'communitarianism' take various forms in both abstract or general definitions and in actuality; and the historian and critic of con-temporary forms of individualism, which he may see as false, shallow or unreal, is often the advocate of a truer or fuller individualism in the future. As Ellen Wood notes, in the course of a history of ideas whose purpose is to urge the claims of 'dialectical' as against 'liberal' or 'metaphysical' individualism, individuality is taken properly to mean not simply 'atomism or privatisation, but the impulse towards self-activity, creativity and self-development'.[1] Abstract counterpositions of individuality to collectivism or socialism already imply questionable theories about the content of individuality, which *may* be realisable only in socialism, its highest form. The meaning of individuality is no more uncontested than that of sociality or community: our views of both the existing and the truest relationships between them depend upon values, theories of human nature, philosophies of history, and epistemologies. These will give a particular flavour and content to our accounts of 'individual and society', and will also decide the ways in which we (mis)interpret the notions of others. There are different versions of liberal and of socialist or Marxist individualism, and there are also positive and negative accounts of each.

Such general claims should not be used to blur the fact that there are real and substantial differences between social thinkers, and that in democratic theory one of the crucial lines of division occurs over a species of individualism which is, according to its critics, morally inadequate and sociologically obtuse. This form of liberal or 'possessive' individualism is condemned as too narrow, constricting and selfish, as untrue to the facts about men (untrue perhaps to their actual desires and claims, certainly to their needs and capacities) and about societies (which both create individuals and, as they are, destroy the chances of most people becoming individuals in any substantial sense).

Liberal individualism was subjected to sustained critical examination in the period between the French Revolution and the middle of the nineteenth century, by which time the liberal state in Britain presided over industrial expansion which was rapid, unique and, apparently, socially devastating. To critics of the liberal industrial order, whether backward-looking or forward-looking, it seemed that Burke's age of 'sophists, economists and calculators', the new-world of Jews, jobbers and the commercial spirit, had suddenly arrived. Burke's question — 'Is every landmark of the country to be done away with in favour of a geometrical and arithmetical constitution?'[2] — and his charge that his opponents were 'so taken up with their theories about the rights of man, that they have totally forgotten his nature',[3] struck responsive chords in many who were far from accepting his view of the good society, and who focused upon the economic rather than the ideological roots of contemporary evils. The powerful image of man's separation from his fellows, of a decomposed or disbanded people, reduced to 'elementary principles', to 'the dust and powder of individuality', seemed to catch the essence of the modern, contractual state. Contract was a dirty word: the democratic contract spelt social dissolution, the loss of individual identity and substance, rather than the emancipation of mankind. It belonged to bourgeois market society, idealised in the *Gesellschaft*, whereas subjectivity, the personal, the human, 'real and organic life', 'all intimate, private and exclusive living together', belonged with the contrasting social model, the *Gemein-*

schaft.[4] Later historians and sociologists have perceived an historical process whereby a rich and productive cluster of tight primary groupings and associations were destroyed, with their destruction leaving nothing but 'the fluid mass of individuals'.[5] Often they succumbed, as did Burke himself, to the danger of attaching romantic images of discrete social types to concrete historical eras, as if neat and clear dichotomies fit the tangle and untidiness of reality. It is clear why the various victims of nostalgia should have imaginatively reconstructed shattered or threatened institutions as a back-drop to what they saw as contemporary demoralisation. But, while Gemeinschaft and Gesellschaft and their fellows might serve useful purposes as ideal types, they are less useful if not downright misleading when they are paraded as actual types of society — feudal and capitalist, or pre-industrial and industrial — and may be dangerously narrow if presented as complete moral visions of the world, as if we should or must choose one or the other. Each has its costs and limitations.

The critique of liberal individualism moved forward from Burke — though not as a development of his ideas or as a logical progression — in the writings of the youthful Marx on representative government and the rights of man, which Marx took to be the appropriate political forms of capitalism. Marx rejected both the antagonism between the free man and society posited in liberalism, and its treatment of the isolated or asocial individual as the starting-point of analysis, as in social contract theory or the classical political economy. Political economy subordinated the citizen to the 'egoistic man', the narrow wealth-seeker and the labouring instrument. Alienated and egoistic man was conceived to be man as such: 'it is man as a bourgeois and not man as a citizen who is considered the true and authentic man'.[6] Liberal political institutions and attitudes to society expressed both the narrowness of men and their separation from each other, which were existing facts and not mere illusions. Society was perceived as external to the individual, and an encroaching force against which barriers had to be erected. Assuming an antithesis between society and the individual, which made sense in terms of man's actual, alienated relationships under capitalism, democratic theory reduced the realm of citizenship — the political community — to a mere means of preserving the rights of man, and reduced men themselves to self-sufficient entities. The rights of man are founded upon the separation of man from man: they are the rights of the circumscribed, self-interested individual, withdrawn into himself and protecting himself against others. 'Security is the supreme social concept of civil society, the concept of the police. The whole society exists only in order to guarantee for each of its members the preservation of his person, his rights and his property.'[7] In the circumstances, the market-place was an appropriate image of human relationships. Men were restricted, impoverished, and isolated, while appearing ideologically as sovereign individuals, while society was perceived as a commercial enterprise – an appropriate sphere for their 'free' activity. Rejecting, though not as a Utopian visionary, liberalism's false opposition of the individual being to society, as abstract categories, Marx envisaged a change of circumstances and of men which was to introduce a true individualism, possible only – conceptually as well as practically – with a rich and satisfying communal life.

C. B. Macpherson may be described fairly as a Utopian Marxist – highly critical of possessive (liberal) individualism in terms often reminiscent of Marx's early and middle writings, hostile to the economics and the politics of the market, yet virtually silent about class struggle and revolutionary change, craving only a moral transformation of the shallow democratic consciousness. Possessive individualism, which he associates especially with the English empiricists, perceives man as a possessor of his own capacities (and potentially of other things as well), so that men become self-interested individuals possessing faculties or resources which are saleable; it sees market relations as the fundamental relations of society – society is 'a lot of free equal individuals related to each other through their possessions',[8] and political society is conceived as a rational device, a set of contractual arrangements, for the protection of property, including capacities – it is 'a human contrivance for the protection of the individual's property in his person and goods'.[9] To Macpherson this narrow, possessive liberal doctrine determined and limited the particular form of democracy which developed in liberal states. Extensions of the franchise were demanded and admitted 'on competitive liberal grounds',[10] too logically to complete the competitive market society.[11] The liberal state 'simply opened the competitive political system to all individuals who had been created by the competitive market society',[12] while continuing its essential co-ordinative and exploitative functions. So democracy was accommodated to the competitive individualist market society and the liberal state, and in the process was divested of its participatory and communal potentialities.

Ellen Wood's account of liberal-empiricism – Hobbes, Locke, Bentham, parts of J. S. Mill – also indicts it for its possessive character.

In her view it virtually equates ego and individuality with egoism and egocentricity. It sees active egoism as 'the immutable essence of man'.[13] In her model liberalism is characterised by a conception of community as 'externalised, perhaps enforced co-existence, assuming atomistic relationships among individuals, and insofar as individuality tends to be equated with atomism and privatisation, an essential antagonism between individuality and sociality'.[14] It has a conception of liberty 'in which human freedom is not incompatible with subjection *even* to objective forces external to the individual'.[15] It takes for granted the antagonism between public and private, individual and community. In contrast with its virtual equation of egotistic atomism with individuality, the relationship between individuality and community is seen as reciprocal in dialectical individualism. The dialectical, unlike the 'metaphysical', approach, 'emphasises the dynamic unity, the reciprocity, of individual and society, the ways in which individuality of sociality are mutually reinforcing rather than antagonistic. It also conceives of individuality and sociality as evolving through a dialectical interaction in which the nature of self-consciousness and the sense of community develop and mutually change each other in a dynamic process'.[16] Two different principles of society might be based on the contrasting individualisms: 'civil society' might be the society of metaphysical individualism, 'human society' that of dialectical individualism'.[17] Co-operation and true sociality are associated with dialectical individualism, while 'it would not be unfair to say that the very premise of empiricist-liberal individualism, as anticipated by Hobbes and reflected, *in diluted form*, by his liberal successors, is that ego is by very definition anti-social'.[18]

These attacks upon liberal-democratic theory and practice are scattered and sometimes sloppy. At times liberal-democratic practice as a whole is seen — and dismissed — too indiscriminately, and particular thinkers are pressed into ideological frameworks which are much too constricted.[19] Many traditions — Marxism hard and Marxism soft, populism, therapeutic psychiatry, anarchism, existentialism — flow into what I have called, far too baldly and with too little comprehensiveness, the critique. Yet there are firm and discernible participatory and communitarian democratic traditions, even though these are rarely articulated with sufficient clarity or fullness. Within these overlapping traditions there is considerable diversity — communitarianism, for example, has strongly conservative as well as socialist and libertarian forms — but this can be ignored here. The main general lines of attack on liberal democracy are that liberal possessive theory[20] and practice effectively limit the political and other choices and powers of the great mass of subjects, and that it rests upon an historically limited, unworthy and socially destructive conception of man. The first, which is familiar and correct though incomplete, is summed up in Macpherson's complaint that liberal society fails to satisfy his basic criterion of democracy, which is 'the equal effective right of individuals to live as fully as they may wish' — loose, perhaps, but clearly incompatible with the existence of the capitalist market as it actually works or, more broadly, with the substantial inequality of resources characterising all capitalist — perhaps all — states. Inequalities of (extractive) power gives a small fraction of men control over the rest. People have vastly differential access — sometimes no access — to the things necessary to develop human qualities. Whatever else it achieves, freedom of enterprise and acquisition clearly does preclude 'equal access to the means of labour' and hence the widespread possibility of 'a fully human life'.[21] The structure of power and the distribution of wealth, with their associated exclusions, oppressions and inequalities, may be linked by critics with the corruption or emasculation of the ordinary citizen. Psychological forces thus help to maintain social stability. The socialised individual is regarded as void, lacking a firm sense of self — lacking genuine individuality or autonomy. He is seen as an isolated but subservient member of the crowd, his self-expression manufactured, his actual choices manipulated. Men are not self-determining, the sovereigns of circumstances but, in Marcuse's well-known phrase, 'manipulated and indoctrinated individuals who parrot, as their own, the opinion of their masters'.[22] Given that the liberal's prized autonomy is false, that men are in fact left incapable of autonomy, it may even be urged that they are unable to answer for themselves the question of what are false and what are true needs.[23] Hence, democracy — if it is presented as the society in which basic goals are to be realised, or the conceptual ragbag into which we thrust all that we value — is vastly different from a means of registering wants as (generally ill-informed and impotent) political consumers.

But the other side of the story remains to be told. The ideal standard which, by implication, may be reached by some non-capitalist states or societies, needs to be specified as its concrete manifestations or approximations noted. Particular notions of individuality, sociality, etc. inevitably have implications, though these are rarely clear or direct, for concrete social institutions. Radical theory must go beyond showing how particular institutions and arrangements in our own time violate human possibilities, to tackle questions concerning the institutional arrangements and the social distributions which are most compatible with the honourable values it proclaims. It is far too easy to indicate the oppression or unfreedom associated historically — and perhaps systematically — with private property, free enterprise, free contract and the free market and to leap suddenly, without touching this earth, to a grandiose conception of freedom as 'the transcendence of objective determination' or 'the conscious and rational transendance of objective forces'.[24] Society also tends to be perceived, grandiosely, as a prison or a lunatic asylum, as one thing, to be characterised simply. If the inferior model of man is linked systematically with certain historical conditions, for example to a class and a market society, then clearly the new order must abolish at least classes and the market.

That both human nature as it was and theories of human nature were linked systematically with particular historical conditions, Marx and his followers have had no doubt. Macpherson, for example, compliments Bentham and his empiricist predecessors for offering 'a penetrating analysis of the human nature which had been produced by the society they know'.[25] However, the limits of the bourgeois vision in political theory were revealed in the assumption 'that bourgeois human nature is the final form (or, more usually, the universal form except for some supposed primitive age) of human nature'.[26] Macpherson himself does not appear to believe in a final form of human nature, but he does counterpose an image of the productive and active man to that presented in what is seen, somewhat harshly, as capitalist political theory and political science.[27] There, man is passive, reactive, seeking material satisfactions, egotistic yet allowing his interests to be safeguarded or represented by others, generally apolitical and apathetic — except in crisis situations when he erupts devastatingly onto the historical stage. Macpherson's own image of human nature is of man 'as at least potentially a doer, an exerter and developer and enjoyer of his human capacities, rather than merely a consumer of utilities'.[28] Pursuit of the egalitarian principle of democracy — conceived as a form of society and not merely as a system of government — requires 'one man, one equal effective right to live as fully humanly as he may wish'.[29] Existing democracies are to be tried against a standard of the development of human capacities, indeed, they are already being so tried, as 'bourgeois individualism is in retreat, pressed by socialist and other humanisms'.[30] Indeed, so impressed was Macpherson by the demand of blacks and students to become controllers instead of controlled — as in revolutionary Third World movements — that he argued that any realistic political science must now incorporate the 'developmental' or 'positive' conception of power.[31]

While the critics of liberal-democracy from the Left are committed, in general, to participatory and communitarian values, it is clear that these values rest differently in different theories, and are seen to be expressed in a variety of institutional forms. To some, politics can create community, whereas to others community is far deeper than mere politics, and cannot be created by political means, nor expressed in a political form. Politics may even be deemed incompatible with community, which requires or presupposes the withering away of the state. Again, the fragmentation of community is subject to socialist, conservative and other interpretations and resolutions. But, to create a rough type of radical critique, man is ideally and possibly — though perhaps not in fact — a participant, actively determining his own fate or future. An active, informed, democratic citizenry exerts itself politically, thereby governing itself, realising 'the untapped potentials of men' and creating 'the foundations of a genuine human community'.[32] Man is also seen as a communal being, free of egotism, freed from the carefully drawn lines and the historically constructed but unnatural divisions and barriers which cut him off from his fellows. Analytically, however, man the participant and man the communal being are not necessarily the same thing — the active participant might be selfish or separated from his fellows, or might trample over them (the Stirner model), while the communal and altruistic being may not be alive in all his faculties, making his own world. But within the broadly Marxist and the anarchist theoretical traditions the two are seen as linked closely, as man participates *with* rather than simply participates *in*, and as a community free of destructive differentiation is seen as a necessary condition of truly human activity and the necessary setting of human individuality. Self-government and community — both notoriously absent in liberal democracy — are married, theoretically, in participatory democracy, which thereby resolves Rousseau's problem. The 'politics of authenticity', as it is labelled by one student of Rousseau, is 'a dream of an ideal community in which individuality will not be subsumed and sacrificed, but fully developed and expressed'.[33]

The communitarian assumptions underlying many of the contemporary attacks upon the liberal, contractual state are brought out well by Eugene Kamenka and Alice Erh-Soon Tay, in an article con-

cerned with the continuing appeal of the forceful contrast of Gesellschaft and Gemeinschaft as social types:

> Much of the revulsion from the individualistic, liberal democratic concept of
> the rule of law presents itself as a conscious demand for a return to the
> face-to-face society, the organic community of living social bonds and
> commonly-shared ideologies and interests.[34]

Gesellschaft law, they continue,

> Is seen by many in Western societies today as impersonal, inhuman, abstract,
> itself a form of alienation that tears man out of his context, fails to see him as
> a man but recognizes him only as a debtor, a criminal, a rate-payer, a
> contracting party, in short, as the holder or owner of specific and limited legal
> rights or duties vis-a-vis another, rights or duties that are external to his
> personality.[35]

These concluding comments are intended to offer a critical and con-
structive evaluation of a generalised participatory and communitarian
critique of liberal individualism. From my own perspective, the critique
is convincing in much of its characterisation and indictment of liberal
individualism. That body of theory has accepted, without sufficient
anxiety, political apathy as a central feature of normal life, and the
compatibility of the market as it is with the free development of all
individuals. It has accepted too easily its pluralist self-image. 'The
politics of pressure groups is the essential feature of the politics of
democracy. The only alternative to the politics of pressure groups is
government that rules over isolated and rootless individuals who have
no groups other than the government to protect them, and no autonomous social power of their own.'[36] The democratic communitarian
critic may emphasise a representational argument – the inability of the
pressure group system to adequately represent all proper claims and
interests in the society – but the centre of his concern will be the
inability of a liberal-democratic order to satisfy the needs of individuals
for fellowship or intimacy. Stressing that political orders are to be
evaluated against conceptions of human possibilities (e.g. active participation and autonomy) and needs (e.g. community), he will deny that
existing human nature is explained adequately, even if its features are
described correctly. But the steps from an account of potentialities and
needs and of the historical and social forces which currently obstruct
them, to strategies of change and exemplifications of the new, freer,
more communal order are difficult, and are rarely made convincingly.

In the first place, participatory theory offers a much broader notion of the political than does liberalism; or, alternatively, it holds a different view of the relations between social and political. More areas of life are deemed political, not merely as a form of analysis, a reconceptualisation of things, but as a design for change. It is a way of saying that more areas of life should be subject to accountability or popular control, and are proper spheres for participation and self-development. In addition, they are seen as congenial to it, given their immediate proximity to individual lives and destinies. It is at once the power which is exercised within the traditionally non-political parts of life and the particular role which they can play in developing potentialities which draws them to the attention of the participatory democrat. The image of isolated self and his property separated from the larger society naturally seems arbitrary, and a ground for irresponsibility, at a time when continuity and correctedness are being stressed.[37] The insistence on the work-place as the area of major relevance for democracy, and the related demands to democratise corporations, etc. is merely one aspect of a broad movement.

As yet a mass of questions remain unanswered. How is the relationship between the specific enterprises and the immediate communities in which the individual works and lives and the total society to be understood? How does participation in smaller units tie in with the larger world of politics? Might the worker be master of the factory and both slave of the state and fierce rival of competing enterprises? Might the democratic participants fall out very badly? Can participation flourish in scattered enterprises when major decisions are made still in the remote and traditional political realm? If face-to-face societies, organic communities carefully bounded in numerical and geographical ways, are the thing, must not they either be severely limited in the decisions which they can make alone and directly, or be separated again from major (nation-wide) decisions by some kind of representative system? Examples of such 'practical experiments in living' as kibbutzim or hippie communes or free schools or worker's co-operatives, do not really show what is feasible in large, complex, modern societies, as they are either set within very specific material and cultural contexts, or are random or privileged. This leads immediately on to the question of whether the Gemeinschaft model has any relevance at a national level. Certainly the image of an undifferentiated, structureless total community links Marx and many of the more openly Romantic rebels of the post-war years. The dream is to transcend bourgeois freedom, bourgeois political institutions, the arrangements and values of the pluralist state, which nurture privilege and conflict, and to attain a unity where all are free and equal. John Passmore finds that Nietzsche's description of the Dionysians admirably sums up the ideal of the Romantic rebels.

> Now the slave is free; now all the stubborn, hostile barriers, which necessity, caprice or shameless fashion have erected between man and man, are broken down. Now, with the gospel of universal harmony, each one feels himself not only united, reconciled, blended with his neighbour, but as one with him; he feels as if the veil of Maya had been torn aside and were now merely fluttering in tatters before the mysterious Primordial Unity.[38]

In my own view, the ideal of a national community, or of direct democracy at a national level, is possible only in a formal and diluted form, or at terrible costs which would amount to its deformation. But this is quite different from saying that those who have had such an ideal, e.g. Rousseau or Marx (with question marks after the 'national'), were committed in any sense either to an abstract community or to a regime of plebiscites and permanent mobilisation.[39] The natural scepticism with which most Western social scientists and social theorists greet the notion of the undivided, whole man as a model for the contemporary world is often expressed in very questionable ways, as when Cuba or the People's Republic of China are presented as the actual social approximations to any image of wholeness and community. But what does remain true is that communitarian theorists, while properly criticising the atomisation and loneliness of their own societies, defending values which many of us find preferable to those of liberal individualism, and representing a yearning for community (if not salvation) which has appeared frequently throughout history, offer accounts of a truly human society that are both evasive (perhaps on principle) and fail to take sufficient account of the assumptions about power which pushed liberals towards representative government and civil liberties.

We may share Passmore's preference for the complex ideal of 'a plurality of intersecting communities' over 'the old perfectibilist, and in the end tyrannical ideal of a total unity',[40] and yet fear that the diversity and choice which he clearly values face new and serious threats in the present. Many of those who believe that we now face a desperate ecological crisis hold that the necessary countermeasures include a strengthening of attitudes receptive to authority and community. Robert Heilbroner argues in *An Inquiry into The Human Prospect* that it is doubtful whether the freedoms and delights of self-expression will survive the intense pressures which are growing steadily. If we are to survive, he insists, we must reckon with the need for 'welcomed hierarchies of power and strongly felt bonds of people-hood', with the claims of authority and ideology having priority over the liberation of the individual. China becomes the model of a society which blends a 'religious' orientation and a 'military' discipline, which contains certain paradigmatic elements of the future — 'a careful control over industrialisation; an economic policy calculated to restrain rather than to whet individual appetites; and, above all, an organising religiosity expressed through the credos of a socialist "church" '.[41] In the British publication *A Blueprint for Survival*, a village-based society is envisaged, with the population of Britain reduced to twenty million through 'subtle cultural controls', and with 'the best means of in-culcating the values of the stable society incorporated into the educational systems'. Friendships and activity are confined within a very narrow compass. These visions of new, defensive communities do not reject the liberal's valued privacy and individualism as in themselves inferior or bad, but as luxuries which can be afforded no longer in a harsh, anxiety-ridden world.

In his last work, John Plamenatz argued that the impersonality commonly condemned in modern industrial societies is not only 'inevitable in economically advanced societies . . . but also desirable, to the extent that it contributes to the proper functioning of institutions on which the dispensing of justice, the protection and enlargement of freedom, and the efficient provision of indispensable services in vast and highly diversified communities depends'.[42] Yet it is also un-desirable to the extent to which it isolates men and makes them lose all sense of political efficacy or significance. The communitarian and participatory side of democratic theory is a vital part of the democratic tradition, resting upon a generous and optimistic moral theory, upon the supposed needs of individuals and groups, and upon social impera-tives which may be increasing in urgency. But it alone is not a com-prehensive theoretical foundation for democratic practice. The cramped or closed house of community needs to be opened up, and to be made more sensitive to the diversity of actual selves and to conflicts of interest, belief and value. That means taking account of the liberties, the rule of law and the contractualism which remain achievements of the liberal state, however defective even these may be in practice.

NOTES

1. E. M. Wood, *Mind and Politics. An Approach to the Meaning of Liberal and Socialist Individualism* (Berkeley, 1972), p. 14. Distinctions are sometimes made between *individualism*, implying anarchy and social atomisation, and *individualité* or *individuality*, implying personal independence and self-realisation. See S. Lukes, *Individualism* (Oxford, 1973), 8 and 18. I will not be dwelling on the different terms, but accept that there is such a distinction.

2. E. Burke, *Reflections on the Revolution in France* (London, 1955), 52.

3. Ibid., 62.

4. The phrases are those of Tönnies, writing in the late nineteenth century.

5. The telling phrase is Durkheim's. Peter Laslett stresses 'the minute scale of life, the small size of human groups before the coming of industry'. *The World We Have Lost* (London, 1965), 51.

6. *On the Jewish Question,* see T. B. Bottomore (ed.), *Karl Marx, Early Writings* (London, 1963), 26.

7. Ibid., 25-26.

8. C. B. Macpherson, 'The deceptive task of political theory', *Democratic Theory* (London, 1973), 199.

9. C. B. Macpherson, *The Political Theory of Possessive Individualism* (Oxford, 1962), 264.

10. C. B. Macpherson, *The Real World of Democracy* (Oxford, 1966), 6.

11. Ibid., 10.

12. Ibid., 11.

13. E. M. Wood, op. cit., 49. This paragraph and the one on Marx are taken virtually unchanged from an unpublished paper, '*The Left against Mill*', which I presented with John Gray to the 1975 Annual Meeting of the Amerian Political Science Association.

14. Ibid., 13. Cf. again, p. 123: according to the liberal conception of the relationship between individuality and sociality, 'the two are antagonistic and individuality is self-annihilating in the sense that it demands a sociality ultimately inimical to it. In short, this is a concept in which there is an eternal tension inherent in individuality and between individuality and sociality, and neither the one nor the other can ever be fully realized.'

15. Ibid., 13.

16. Ibid., 10.

17. Ibid., 18.

18. Ibid., 62.

19. It is outside my scope — and, in most cases, beyond my ability — to defend each liberal (possessive) individualist against such portrayals of them. Along with John Gray, I did offer a defence of J. S. Mill against 'the Left' in the paper referred to in note 13, and I have also defended Mill against the egoism charge in *Marx and Mill: Two Views of Social Conflict and Social Harmony* (Cambridge, 1973).

20. The point has been made strongly by Christian Bay in respect to democratic mythology as a whole.

> Of all the myths that serve to pacify and depoliticise citizens in our modern world, including political theorists, none has been more effective, I believe, than the illusion of democratic government: the assertion that we all have equal political rights, and that, consequently, the ultimate power in society rests with the majority.'

He stresses the need to destroy 'the submissiveness-producing effectiveness of the democratic myth'. 'Foundations of the liberal make-believe', *Inquiry*, 14 (3) August 1971: 214-15.

21. C. B. Macpherson, *The Real World of Democracy*, op. cit., 60 and 62. This applies especially when the relations of production are invasive, i.e. when some have the labour of others under their control.

22. H. Marcuse, 'Repressive tolerance', in: Wolff, Moore and Marcuse (eds.), *A Critique of Pure Tolerance* (Boston, 1969), 90.

23. Marcuse's claim, in *One Dimensional Man* (London, 1972), 6. A. S. Kaufman, in 'Wants, needs and liberalism', *Inquiry*, 14 (3) Autumn 1971, argues that 'different theories of the good life will generate different catalogues of human and false needs' (p. 194), and asserts that only 'when our very "desires and impulses" are shaped in ways that make for commitment to an autonomous existence, can we be reasonably sure that our lives are lived in accordance with our own natures' (p. 199). He finds that, although 'there are dangers in forcing people to be free, they are less than those inherent in uncritically accepting the modes of socialization that happen to prevail' (pp. 201-2).

24. E. M. Wood, op. cit., 14 and 45.

25. C. B. Macpherson, *Democratic Theory*, op. cit., 202. However, their successors seem to have been guilty of a kind of bad faith, screening out class when they should have seen it, for they — including J. S. Mill, Bagehot and T. H. Green — wrote at a time when 'the market had clearly created a dominant and a subservient class, and freedom for the former was domination over the latter', p. 200.

26. Ibid., 198.

27. The list of political scientists normally includes Berelson, Dahl and Lipset.

28. C. B. Macpherson, 'Problems of a non-market theory of democracy', *Democratic Theory*, op. cit., 51.

29. Ibid.

30. 'Progress of the Locke industry', *Canadian Journal of Political Science*, 3 (2) June 1970: 326.

31. *Democratic Theory*, op. cit., 50.

32. J. L. Walker, 'A critique of the elitist theory of democracy', in: McCoy and Playford (eds.), *Apolitical Politics* (New York, 1967), 205. Walker is here seeking to identify the most distinctive feature of classical democratic theory.

33. M. Berman, *The Politics of Authenticity* (London, 1971), vii. Cf. H. Marcuse, 'Socialist solidarity is autonomy', *An Essay on Liberation* (Pelican, 1972), 90.

34. 'Participation, authenticity and the contemporary vision of man, law and society', in: Cohen, Feyerabend and Wartofsky (eds.), *Essays in Memory of Imre Lakatos* (Dordrecht, 1976), 336.

35. Ibid., 337.

36. C. Frankel, *The Democratic Prospect*, pp. 46-7.

37. This point is also made by Kamenka and Tay, op. cit., 355.

38. *The Birth of Tragedy from the Spirit of Music,* quoted J. Passmore, *The Perfectibility of Man* (London, 1972), 309.

39. As J. L. Talmon argues in the case of Rousseau — presenting a misleading account of Rousseau's ideals, he then adds his own causal theory (psychological and sociological) of what would be required to implement them, and then implies that Rousseau was somehow committed to these methods. See J. L. Talmon, *The Origins of Totalitarian Democracy* (London, 1952).

40. Passmore, op. cit., 310.

41. 'Learning to live with the future', *The Observer*, 29 December 1974.

42. J. Plamenatz, *Karl Marx's Philosophy of Man* 426.

4 Democracy and Social Justice

David Miller
University of East Anglia, UK

The principles that we use to evaluate social and political institutions have affinities for one another whose precise nature is hard to establish. We sense that a person who holds a particular principle of freedom, for example, ought for consistency's sake to hold corresponding principles of authority, equality and so forth, but we are hard put to it to explain what 'corresponding' means here. My intention in this chapter is to examine what kind of connections may exist between the principle of democracy and various principles of social justice, and in doing so to throw some light on the evolution of liberal thinking from the classical liberalism of the seventeenth and eighteenth centuries to the modified form of that doctrine that is prevalent in the West today. I shall try to show that changes in the liberal theory of social justice have been intimately connected to changing attitudes towards democracy as a form of government.

The separation between social and political institutions which characterises the modern state allows us to make an analytical distinction between questions about the distribution of political power and questions about the distribution of property, income and other benefits in society. I stress that this is an analytical distinction only, because my case will be that the answer we give to one kind of question influences the answer we give to the other. The distinction is nonetheless important, because it shows that holding a principle of social justice does not logically entail holding any particular principle for distributing

This paper first appeared in the *British Journal of Political Science*, Vol. 8, No. 1, 1978, and is reprinted here by permission of the Cambridge University Press.

political power, such as the principle of democracy, and vice versa. Unfortunately, this point becomes blurred when 'democracy' is used to refer to social arrangements like equality of opportunity or public ownership of the means of production (this is the sense in which it is sometimes claimed that the Soviet Union is more 'democratic' than the US or the United Kingdom). In this chapter the term will be used exclusively to refer to a form of government, namely one in which ultimate control rests in the hands of the people rather than in the hands of a single man or a small minority.

If the principle of democracy is not *logically* related to any principle of social justice, what other kind of affinity might exist? First, an empirical connection may be postulated between democracy and a principle of social justice. Democracy may be thought necessary to realize a certain conception of social justice or, on the other hand, it may be thought to prevent such a conception from being realised. Again, a particular distribution of goods in society may be held to be a necessary condition of democracy — if, for instance, it is claimed that democracy requires the private ownership of the means of production, or a levelling of economic inequalities. Claims of this kind clearly purport to be empirical in nature, but they are so wide-ranging that they resist decisive testing, and tend in practice to be held as articles of faith.

Often, however, we have to do with connections that are not empirical even in form but are instead analogical. Principles of social justice and principles for distributing political power rest on supporting assumptions about the nature of society and the state, about human motivation, and so forth.[1] Now it is possible to begin from one set of assumptions when discussing social questions and another set when discussing political questions — possible, but difficult. It is more natural, and more convenient, to use assumptions that are identical or at least closely analogous. For instance we may use a social institution whose workings we think we understand as a model for understanding the state. One person may conceive of the state on the model of a joint stock company, complete with articles of association, shareholders and so forth, and thus derive political principles which correspond to the operating principles of such a company. Another may regard the state as an enlarged family. Equally, political analogies may be used in thinking about social institutions — for instance when demands for industrial democracy are supported by presenting the work-place as a state in miniature. However, the analogical connection may not be as well developed as this. It may simply consist, for example, in a view about human equality or inequality, which forms the basis for thinking about both state and society. If a person considers inequalities of merit to be of central importance in discussing economic distribution, he is likely to think they are relevant to political questions as well. There is, however, no way in which connections of this kind can be validated, either logically or empirically. They depend upon a psychological need that people have for order and simplicity in their thinking about politics and society, an area in which strictly logical arguments is of limited use.

For this reason, I shall speak of principles of democracy and social justice as being consonant or dissonant with one another, rather than as logically connected or incompatible, borrowing a term from psychology to emphasize that the connections in question are largely psychological in nature. Two principles will be described as consonant with one another when they are empirically and/or analogically related — that is, when the implementation of one is held to require the implementation of the other, or when they rest on analogous justifying assumptions. Principles will be described as dissonant when the implementation of one is held to prevent the implementation of the other, or when they rest on disanalogous justifying assumptions. Specifically, I shall argue that the liberal-democratic tradition conceals a dissonance between the principle of democracy and the classical liberal conception of social justice, which may be removed in either of two ways: by abandoning the democratic principle (this was the solution favoured by the earlier liberals) or by modifying the conception of social justice (this is the solution favoured by modern liberals). In short, the liberal-democratic position is less internally coherent than its supporters usually realise, and there is a strong tendency for one or other of its constituent elements (liberalism or democracy) to become predominant.

To show how the dissonance between democracy and the liberal conception of social justice arises, we must begin with some definitions. The notion of democracy includes a number of elements, but for our purposes the crucial element is political equality. Each member of the society whose political institutions are in question is to have an equal share in political power. Precisely how that power is to be exercised — whether directly as in a Greek-style democracy or indirectly through the election of representatives — is immaterial here. For convenience we may assume a representative system, in which case the notion of political equality resolves itself into two parts: first, each person is to have an equal say in the election of representatives; secondly, the representatives thus chosen are to carry out, in broad terms, the wishes of those they represent. The first requirement means in practice that everyone shall have one, and only one, vote and that electoral con- stituencies shall be equal in size. It is this requirement that distinguishes most clearly between democratic and anti-democratic positions, and it will feature largely in the subsequent discussion.

The conception of social justice in classical liberalism combines egalitarian and inegalitarian elements. Its basic principle is the distribu- tion of social benefits according to desert, which is inegalitarian since men's deserts are taken to be unequal. But to implement this principle a framework of formal equality is required. Each man is ascribed the same set of rights (which are often referred to as 'natural'): freedom of thought and expression, the right to own property, freedom of con- tract, freedom of association, equality before the law, and equality of opportunity (understood as the absence of formal barriers to prevent a man entering the occupation of his choice). By exercising these rights each man is enabled to gain the substantial benefits — wealth, prestige, etc. — which he deserves. If formal rights were not equal, some men would start from a position of undeserved advantage, and rewards could not possibly correspond to deserts. If, on the other hand, there were to be substantial equality — equality of property, income, etc. — then of course desert would go unrewarded. The liberal conception of justice is opposed both to the feudal conception, which demands an inequality of formal rights according to the status of each person, and to the communist conception, which makes substantial rights equal in order to distribute benefits according to need.[2]

We may therefore sum up the classical liberal conception of justice in the following terms: an equality of formal rights, coupled with an inequality of substantial rights, which are distributed according to the deserts of each individual. Each man is to have an equal (formal) right to own property, for example, but the amount of property he owns (his substantial right) should depend on his deserts — his capacities, efforts, etc. Whether such a combination of equality and inequality was success- fully realised in the kind of society favoured by liberals is a question outside the scope of this paper. The issue we must take up is how the democratic principle — the principle of political equality — is related to this conception of social justice. To put the question in a nutshell: are political rights to be conceived of as analogous to the formal rights in the liberal conception, and therefore incorporated into the framework of equality? Or are they to be considered along with the substantial rights, and therefore distributed unequally, according to the deserts of each recipient?

When the question is posed in this form, the answer may seem obvious to the modern liberal. Political rights are to be distributed equally because they are based on the same premise of human equality as the other rights in the liberal catalogue. Just as every man is to have freedom of thought, the right to own property, etc., so he is to have an equal right to the vote. Was this right not written into the various Declarations of Rights which form the classic political statements of liberalism? In fact this response reads back into the history of liberalism an assumption that has only more recently become commonly accepted, and I shall try to show that the classical liberals did not take it for granted that political rights were to be equal. These older liberals did not conceive of political rights as closely analogous to civil rights like freedom of speech and association; they saw that political rights were different in kind from civil rights, have a different justification and different implications for the workings of society; and they were much more inclined to regard a share in political power as a privilege, to be distributed only to those who had earned it, in the same way as other benefits like wealth and prestige.

One part of my argument, therefore, is that if we begin from the liberal conception of social justice and its underlying assumptions we arrive not at democracy but at a political meritocracy in which power is awarded to those who possess the relevant kind of merit. The sense of human equality contained in classical liberalism is sufficient to sustain equal civil rights, but not to sustain equal political rights, which require a stronger justification. How this comes about, and how 'political merit' is to be understood, will emerge in the course of the discussion.

But my argument can also be turned in the opposite direction. If we begin from the premise of political equality, if we assume, in other words, that each man is entitled to an equal share of political power, we shall be led to challenge the liberal conception of social justice. This comes about because equality of political rights relies upon a stronger sense of human equality than is contained in classical liberalism. I shall refer to this stronger sense of equality as equality of citizenship. Equal citizenship grounds equal political rights, but it also grounds social and economic claims which are incompatible with the notion of social justice held by the classical liberals. These are claims for a level of material provision which allows each person to acquire the full status of a citizen. To achieve this level of provision, the notion of social justice must be altered to give weight to considerations of need, which were ignored by the earlier liberals. Citizenship does not necessarily require that all social benefits should be distributed according to need, but needs must at least be satisfied up to the social minimum that secures the citizen's status. In this way modern liberals have been led to revise their conception of social justice so that it becomes consonant with their assumption of political equality.[3] In place of a distribution of benefits on the basis of desert alone, the modern view recommends a balance between the claims of desert and the claims of need – needs being satisfied up to the social minimum, deserts being rewarded with the social wealth that remains and with 'intangible' goods such as prestige.

I shall therefore try to demonstrate that the standard liberal-democratic position, which prescribes a distribution of social benefits according to desert together with an equality of political rights, is internally dissonant. I do not mean that such a position is wholly untenable, or that no liberal has ever actually held it, but that it contains strong internal pressures towards greater consonance, which may be achieved either by abandoning the principle of political equality or by modifying the conception of social justice. We shall see how the earlier liberals were driven in the former direction, while later liberals have taken the latter course. Let us start, then, by looking at the reasons why the classical liberals rejected democracy as a form of government.

SOCIAL JUSTICE AND POLITICAL INEQUALITY IN CLASSICAL LIBERALISM

A rapid survey of liberal thinking about government between about 1650 and 1900 reveals that virtually none of the classical liberals believed in political equality, in the sense of universal and equal suffrage. Almost all of them wished to see the vote restricted to a part of the population only, using various criteria – property, education and so on – to limit the extent of the franchise.[4] This fact would be more apparent were it not for our natural tendency to interpret earlier liberal thinking in the light of modern democratic liberalism. Thus, we misread liberal claims about 'government by the people', for example, taking it for granted that 'the people' means 'all the members of society', whereas for earlier liberals 'the people' was more often a deliberately ambiguous phrase, referring to those who were not members of the aristocracy, but having no clearly defined scope beyond that.[5] Again, when we come across explicit exclusions from the franchise in liberal writing, we tend to put them down to timidity or conservatism on the part of the thinker concerned rather than regarding them as intrinsic to the liberal position. In this way the Levellers, or Locke, or J. S. Mill, are read as democrats, even by those who recognise that all of them wished to exclude substantial portions of the population from the exercise of political rights. It is felt that the exclusions are extrinsic to the main arguments being advanced.

In this section we shall reverse the usual procedure, take the restrictions on the franchise seriously and see how they form an essential part of the liberal position. How is a restricted or an unequal franchise connected to the liberal view of social justice? Following the outline in the previous section, we may distinguish empirical from analogical connections, and consider each in turn.

Empirically, liberals did not believe that a just society was compatible with an unrestricted franchise. Social justice meant, as we have seen, the distribution of material rewards according to desert, within a framework of formal equality. As essential means to this end, the liberals defended private property, freedom of contract and limited government. But would property be safe and government remain limited if political rights were extended to the whole population, including the propertyless masses? Few liberals thought so; somehow a line had to be drawn so that those who might threaten the property system were excluded. The drawing of the line was controversial: in the debates during the English Civil War, for example, Independents and Levellers disagreed over whether only those with a 'permanent, fixed interest' in the country — landowners and some members of trading corporations — should be eligible to vote, or whether the franchise might be extended to everyone who was not a servant or in receipt of alms.[6] Both sides agreed, however, that political rights should not be extended beyond the point at which property might be endangered. 'All the main thing that I speak for, is because I would have an eye to property', argued Ireton, the leading Independent, and the Levellers did not challenge the argument.

There is a paradox in this position, however. If the liberal regime of private property and free contract produces social justice and general prosperity, as the liberals claimed, how can it be dangerous to extend the suffrage universally? Why should anyone wish to disturb the system? The answer given was that the benefits of the regime were not properly understood by those who lacked property themselves. The propertyless were liable to put the short-term benefits of confiscating property before the long-term benefits of maintaining it: greed would blind them to their own true interests. The liberal Whig Macaulay, for instance — a champion of reform in 1832, but opposed to universal suffrage under British conditions — maintained that, although the interests of the middle and working classes were really the same, only the middle class had *immediate* interests which were identical with the general interest. The working class, Macaulay argued, had an immediate interest in plundering the rich and distributing the proceeds; the long-term results of this policy would not be felt until the second generation, which would have to begin producing without the benefits of accumulated capital. For that reason, 'the higher and middling orders are the natural representatives of the human race. Their interest may be opposed in some things to that of their poorer contemporaries; but it is identical with that of the innumerable generations which are to follow.'[7]

Herbert Spencer produced a subtler version of this argument when he claimed that the working class, although unlikely to destroy property outright if given power, were liable to want property taxed at an intolerably high level to finance public works and social services. The reason was that the benefits of a public park or a free library were immediately obvious to everyone, while the effects of taxation were only felt directly by those who paid it. Spencer's solution, reversing the old slogan, was that there should be no representation without (direct) taxation.[8]

The weakness of the empirical argument connecting social justice with a limited franchise is that it fails whenever it can plausibly be claimed that the lower classes have a 'stake' in the country — whether through owning small amounts of property, paying taxes or simply earning enough to make violent change unacceptably risky. Both Macaulay and Spencer had to admit that, according to the terms of their argument, it might one day be possible for the franchise to be extended safely to the working class. This is why the analogical arguments really weighed more strongly in the liberal mind; these sought to show that political equality was *in principle* wrong on liberal premises.

To argue for political inequality by analogy with social inequality, it was first necessary to destroy a counter-analogy between political rights and the natural rights to life, liberty and property. If the right to take part in government could be shown to be natural in the same sense as, say, the right to free speech, then it would be difficult for a liberal to argue against political equality. It was not hard to defeat this claim, however. First, political rights could plainly only be exercised within the context of a civil society, and not in a 'state of nature', which liberals were wont to use as a device for justifying lists of natural rights. It was difficult to see, then, how these rights could be regarded as natural; they were social creations, and, as such, society was entitled to regulate them in its own interests. Secondly, whereas the natural rights were all rights to be protected in various ways (against assault, confinement, etc.), and so essentially negative in their content, political rights were rights to *do* something – to participate in politics and thus to affect other people's interests. It therefore appeared that the correct analogy was not with the equal formal rights, such as the formal right to acquire property, but with the unequal substantial rights that resulted from the exercise of these formal rights – for instance people's rights to the property they had appropriated, which were bound to be unequal given differences of effort and ability. Ireton combined both of these points when he argued that to grant a natural status to political rights would logically imply an equal right to material goods as well.

> Now I wish we may all consider of what right you will challenge that all the people should have right to elections. Is it by the right of nature? If you will hold forth that as your ground, then I think you must deny all property too, and this is my reason. For thus: by that same right to nature (whatever it be) that you pretend, by which you can say, one man hath an equal right with another to the choosing of him that shall govern him – by the same right of nature, he hath the same [equal] right in any goods he sees – meat, drink, clothes – to take and use them for his sustenance.[9]

The same logic lay behind the thinking of the French revolutionaries when they distinguished between the rights of man, which belonged to every human being as such, and the rights of the citizen, which were conferred upon those members of a particular society who were judged worthy to exercise them. The Abbé Sieyès, for example, argued that the members of a society should be divided into two groups: passive citizens, who should simply enjoy their natural rights in a legally protected form, and active citizens, who should also possess political rights.

All the inhabitants of a country should enjoy therein the rights of a *passive citizen*; all have a right to the protection of their persons, their property, their liberty, etc., but all have not the right to take part in the formation of public authority; all are not *active citizens*. Women – at least in the present state of things – children, foreigners, and, again, those who in no way contribute to the public establishment, should not have any active influence in public matters.[10]

If political rights were not natural rights, and therefore not be to granted to everyone on an equal basis, how should they be distributed? To preserve the analogy with the liberal theory of social justice it was necessary to find a criterion of merit that would correspond to criteria like effort and achievement, which were used to justify the unequal distribution of economic rewards. Here we can detect an evolution in liberal thinking as we move forward in time. For the early liberals, such as the radical Puritans in the Civil War, the main criterion was personal independence. To be eligible to vote a man must be shown to have a will of his own, which meant that he must not be dependent on a master, or on the charity of other people. To cite Ireton again, 'If there be anything at all that is a foundation of liberty it is this, that those who shall choose the law-makers shall be men freed from dependence upon others.'[11] Petty explained the Levellers' willingness to exclude servants and alms-takers from the franchise in the same terms: 'I conceive the reason why we would exclude apprentices, or servants, or those that take alms, is because they depend upon the will of other men and should be afraid to displease [them]. For servants and apprentices, they are included in their masters, and so for those that receive alms from door to door . . .'[12]

The exact logic of this criterion is hard to make out. Petty's explanation suggests that the reason for excluding dependent men is that they are liable to vote simply as their masters tell them, and therefore to have nothing to contribute to political decision-making in their own right. But this appears to make the vote of retainers simply redundant, rather than to be a positive reason for excluding them, unless of course it is argued that their presence in the ballot distorts the result by giving undue influence to masters with a large number of retainers. There is, however, a further element in Puritan thinking which if accepted does give positive grounds for excluding dependents. This is the view that those who have fallen into dependency have 'forfeited their birthrights' as Englishmen, i.e. have lost those rights which would otherwise belong to them as part of their heritage through a voluntary and culpable act. Loss of political rights is therefore a kind of penalty for the blameworthy action of becoming dependent on a master or on charity, rather than in the same way as criminals are often held to have forfeited their political rights by their illegal acts; conversely those who have maintained their status as 'free-born Englishmen' deserve to exercise the rights of Englishmen (many of the Levellers believed that they were demanding the restoration of ancestral rights that had been eroded over the centuries).

With the passing of time, however, independence as a condition for political rights became steadily less relevant, as contractual wage-relationships came to replace master-servant relationships in both agriculture and industry. Liberals began to emphasise a different criterion for admission to the franchise, namely the political knowledge and ability which would allow the voter to make an intelligent use of his vote. Since ability could not be measured directly, a property qualification was usually suggested as a rough-and-ready test of political 'merit'. Consider, for example, the argument of the French revolutionary Barnave, made in a speech to the National Assembly:

> Representative government has but one snare to fear – that of corruption. In order that it should be essentially sound, it is necessary to guarantee the purity and incorruptibility of the electoral body, which should, therefore, be protected by three fundamental guarantees: the first, knowledge, and it cannot be denied that the possession of a certain amount of wealth is the most certain measure of a better education and a more extended knowledge; the second, an interest in affairs . . . and the third, independence of fortune, which places the elector above corruption.[13]

We find a similar argument being used by nineteenth-century liberals in England to justify excluding a substantial part of the population from the vote. 'It is not by mere numbers, but by property and intelligence, that the nation ought to be governed', Macaulay asserted, and he proceeded to argue that, in the case of the working class, lack of education coupled with physical hardship made the members of this class unlikely to vote in a rational way:

> It is therefore no reflection on the poorer class of Englishmen, who are not and who cannot in the nature of things be, highly educated, to say that distress produces on them its natural effects . . . that it blinds their judgement, that it inflames their passions, that it makes them prone to believe those who flatter them, and to distrust those who would serve them.[14]

Likewise Bagehot, having argued that 'every person has a right to so much political power as he can exercise without impeding any other person who would more fitly exercise such power', went on to contend that property was the most realistic test of a person's fitness to exercise power: 'Property is, indeed, a very imperfect test of intelligence; but it is some test. If it has been inherited, it guarantees education; if acquired, it guarantees ability. Either way it assures us of something.'[15]

A slightly different line of thought underlay the demand made by some liberals that the vote should be conditional, not on property ownership, but on the payment of a certain level of taxation. Paying taxes was not, of course, thought to be a sign of intelligence, but it was held (by, for instance, J. S. Mill and Spencer) to provide a guarantee that the voter would behave responsibly, and in particular would not support extravagant proposals for public expenditure. However, the same demand was sometimes interpreted somewhat differently, by drawing an explicit analogy between the state and a private association. The argument in this case was that only paid-up members of the association – those who contributed to its funds – had a right to decide what its policy should be. Consider again Sieyès, distinguishing between active and passive citizens. 'All the inhabitants of a country . . . may enjoy the advantages of society; but only those who contribute to the public establishment are, as it were, true shareholders in the great social undertaking. These alone are truly *active citizens,* true members of the association'.[16] We shall later see how Mill used a similar analogy as part of his argument for inequality of voting rights.

To summarize, we have examined three ways in which liberal opposition to political equality was connected with the liberal view of social justice. First, liberals believed a government based on universal suffrage would disrupt the kind of social order that they favoured by giving excessive power to those with no (immediate) interest in the preservation of the system. Secondly, instead of regarding the vote as a natural right which a person possessed simply by virtue of belonging to a given society, they saw it as a privilege which had to be earned by displaying proof of one's competence to take part in government – and in this respect it was analogous to social and economic benefits which were to be distributed according to the respective deserts of the recipients. Thirdly, some liberals made an explicit comparison between the state and a private company, arguing that only those who made a financial contribution to the state's revenue should take part in making political decisions.

These arguments received their most sophisticated statement in the mature writings of J. S. Mill, and we may end this section by considering Mill's view of government in somewhat greater detail. A few prefatory remarks on Mill's theory of social justice are necessary. Despite his utilitarianism, and despite his occasionally expressed sympathy for communism as a higher form of society than capitalism, Mill clung in his social and economic writings to the liberal view of justice. He argued in favour of economic competition and against the state's using its powers of taxation to redistribute benefits to those in need. His principle of justice was one of contribution: benefits should go to those who had earned them by labour or by 'abstinence' (in the case of capitalists) rather than to those who had acquired them merely by inheritance or − one of Mill's chief convictions − by belonging to the male sex.

> No rational person will maintain it to be abstractedly just that a small minority of mankind should be born to the enjoyment of all the external advantages which life can give, without earning them by any merit or acquiring them by any exertion of their own, while the immense majority are condemned from their birth to a life of never-ending, never-intermitting toil, required by a bare and, in general, a precarious subsistence.[17]

Thus, Mill did not regard the capitalist society of his time uncritically. The inheritance of wealth meant that a minority of men began life with undeserved advantages; there was discrimination against women; and even capitalists who made their own fortunes earned higher rewards than could be justified by 'abstinence' and the labour of superintendence. He therefore proposed that the inheritance system should be modified, that women should be given equal opportunities with men, and that workers should be encouraged to form their own co-operatives instead of working for capitalists. But he nevertheless continued to adhere to the basic social ideals of liberalism: unequal rewards, free competition in the market, a general policy of *laissez-faire* (with specific exceptions). We have now to see how this conception of justice is related to Mill's attitude towards democracy, as it is revealed in his mature writings.[18]

Mill argued that forms of government should be judged by two fundamental criteria: the extent to which they promoted the virtue and intelligence of the people, and the extent to which they made use of existing virtue and intelligence to produce socially beneficial policies. The implications of the first criterion are relatively straightforward. Given Mill's views about the educative functions of political participation,[19] it meant that everyone should if possible take part in politics. Ideally, there should be universal suffrage. But the second criterion did not necessarily point to the same conclusion. For government to function well, it was necessary first that the officers of government should be of suitable calibre, and second that the body which controlled the government (i.e. the electorate) should be adequate to its task. It might be inadequate either through 'general ignorance and incapacity' or through 'being under the influence of interests not identical with the general welfare of the community'. Mill saw both possibilities as very real, and accordingly took steps to compose his electorate in such a way that they were avoided.

The first possibility was obviated (in *Considerations on Representative Government*) by removing from the electorate those persons who were demonstrably unfit to vote. Mill had earlier prepared the ground for these exclusions by denying that there was any fundamental right to vote. 'We must never lose sight of the truth, that the suffrage for a member of Parliament is power over others, and that to power over others no *right* can possibly exist. Whoever wishes to exercise it, is bound to acquire the necessary qualifications ...'[20] The classes excluded were: first, those who were unable to pass a simple literacy test; secondly, those who paid no taxes (it being argued that such people would be irresponsible in their financial views); thirdly, those who lived off public charity ('He who cannot by his labour suffice for his own support has no claim to the privilege of helping himself to the money of others'[21]). Mill then argued that these exclusions were not permanent, and expressed himself in favour of the social reforms which would bring the suffrage within reach of 'all who are in the normal condition of a human being'.

The second possibility — that the electorate might be controlled by sinister interests — was harder to deal with. Mill's particular fear was of an electorate dominated by the working class. Like Macaulay, he believed that this class had immediate interests which were incompatible with the permanent interests of society. Given political power, it might be tempted to overtax property, for example, or to level incomes. But Mill did not entirely share Macaulay's optimistic estimate of the middle class. Instead, he preferred to construct an electorate in which working class and middle class were approximately balanced, thus (Mill hoped) leaving the deciding voice with those who were moved by a concern for 'reason, justice, and the good of the whole'.[22]

The shaping of the electorate had, however, to follow principles of justice rather than explicit class criteria, and for that reason Mill opposed a property qualification for the vote, arguing that the possession of wealth was more often a result of accident than of merit. His first proposal was that minorities should be fairly represented through a system of proportional representation. (The details of the rather elaborate scheme recommended in *Representative Government* are beside the point here.) However, this scheme would not by itself prevent the working class from having a preponderance of votes, if the suffrage were universal or nearly so. It was therefore necessary to distribute votes unequally. Mill argued that, on grounds of justice, the weight of any opinion ought to be proportional to its worth.

> When two persons who have a joint interest in any business differ in opinion, does justice require that both opinions should be held of exactly equal value? If, with equal virtue, one is superior to the other in knowledge and intelligence – or if, with equal intelligence, one excels the other in virtue – the opinion, the judgement, of the higher moral or intellectual being is worth more than that of the inferior: and if the institutions of the country actually assert that they are of the same value, they assert a thing which is not.[23]

But how were intelligence and virtue to be measured? Mill thought that ideally there should be a direct educational test, but in default of this occupation seemed a rough and ready guide to intellectual quality. In *Thoughts on Parliamentary Reform* he proposed a graduated scale of votes, running from the manual labourer with a single vote to the university graduate with five or more; and a similar scheme is outlined (less explicitly) in *Representative Government.* He added that everyone should be able to qualify for extra votes by voluntary examination. In this way the vote would become, not a right, but a 'just privilege', i.e. one gained on the basis of recognised criteria of merit.

Mill's opposition to democracy (in the sense of political equality) is therefore perfectly clear:

> I do not look upon equal voting as among the things which are good in themselves, provided they can be guarded against inconveniences. I look upon it as only relatively good; less objectionable than inequality of privilege grounded on irrelevant or adventitious circumstances, but in principle wrong, because recognising a wrong standard, and exercising a bad influence on the voter's mind. It is not useful, but hurtful, that the constitution of the country should declare ignorance to be entitled to as much political power as knowledge.[24]

The connection between this political outlook and his conception of social justice is also clear. Mill opposes advantages that are gained through 'adventitious circumstances'; he does not oppose unequal advantages when they correspond to relevant inequalities of desert. In the social sphere, the relevant basis of desert is social contribution; in the political sphere, it is intellectual and moral contribution – the 'worth' of an opinion. The underlying assumption is the same in both spheres, though its working out is naturally different in each.

Mill's proposals, as he records,[25] won no support among his contemporaries – partly, no doubt, because democratic ideas were gaining strength in progressive circles (with consequences that we shall trace in the following section), but partly because there seemed no way of implementing the proposals without drawing arbitrary distinctions. This problem bedevilled liberal thinking about government. The theoretical case for an unequal franchise could be cogently stated on liberal premises, but it was impossible to find a test of political merit that would work equitably in practice as a basis for legislation. However the line between voters and non-voters was drawn, anomalies could always be pointed out. Thus, when liberals were faced with pressure from the excluded classes for a share of power, it was difficult for them to present a case for a restricted franchise which did not seem to be a mere defence of vested interests; eventually democracy was conceded less for reasons of pure principle than because of the practical difficulties of having anything else.

The fact that the liberal position was eroded by the course of events in this way does not of course mean that it has been theoretically rebutted. One question that we shall have to answer in the next section is whether a principled defence of democracy can be given; whether, in other words, political equality can be shown to have a value in itself, quite apart from the practical objections to an unequal or a restricted franchise.

POLITICAL EQUALITY AND CITIZENSHIP IN MODERN LIBERALISM

In the previous section we traced the way in which the liberal belief in justice as the reward of desert was used to argue that inequalities in political rights should correspond to differences in men's competence to take part in government. We must now examine the argument in the reverse direction. If one begins from the premise of political equality — if one believes as a matter of principle that each person should have an equal right to participate in government — what consequences follow for the notion of social justice? It is again necessary to emphasise that the consequences in question cannot be strictly logical ones. There is no logical inconsistency between the principle of political equality and the liberal conception of social justice. My claim, however, is that the two ideas are dissonant, in the sense explained above. It will again be useful to distinguish empirical from analogical arguments and to consider each in turn.

The empirical case for holding that political equality requires the modification of liberal notions of justice is really the mirror image of a liberal argument considered earlier. The liberals maintained that men who were not independent, and therefore had no wills of their own, had no right to take part in government. The democratic converse is that everyone has a right to take part in government and that therefore society must be ordered in such a way that every citizen is guaranteed an independent status. Rousseau is probably the best exemplar of this position. The general will, he argued, could only be expressed if each person took part in debating and voting in the assembly, and furthermore each person must voice his own authentic opinion on political matters. This was impossible where some members of the community were personally dependent on others for their livelihood. It was therefore necessary for the state to use its powers of legislation to protect equality. Note, however, that

> By equality, we should understand, not that the degrees of power and riches are to be absolutely identical for everybody; but that power shall never be great enough for violence, and shall always be exercised by virtue of rank and law; and that in respect of riches, no citizen shall ever be wealthy enough to buy another, and none poor enough to be forced to sell himself . . .[26]

Rousseau certainly did not intend the state to eliminate all differences in wealth. He believed strongly in private property and in rewarding those who contributed to the community in proportion to their deserts. The measures that he proposed to secure equality (modification of the inheritance laws, progressive taxation) hardly match up to the modern welfare state. We should recognise, however, that Rousseau had in mind a society composed mainly of independent farmers and artisans, and in this context the problem was to prevent the concentration of resources in a few hands, in order that everyone should have easy access to the means of production and not be obliged to sell his labour on unfavourable terms. What matters to us is less the practical proposals than the general logic of Rousseau's argument. The logic is that, where social inequality threatens the political independence of the poorer citizens, the state should step in to compress the extremes of inequality and to provide everyone with an independent means of livelihood. Such a view conflicts with the liberal conception of justice as the reward of desert realised through a free market which rewards the deserving and penalises the undeserving. The classical liberals acknowledged that this might imply the creation of a dependent class — servants, paupers, etc. — who would therefore be unfit to vote. Rousseau's argument, on the other hand, anticipates the modern idea of a guaranteed minimum standard of living, which eliminates the extreme of poverty if not the extreme of wealth. One modern liberal has noted how widely accepted Rousseau's view now is:

> It is everywhere agreed that men do not get the equality which is a condition of freedom merely by being given the vote; they must also have the security which enables them to use that vote independently and responsibly. If they are to count politically, if they are to have a mind of their own which makers of policy cannot afford to neglect, they must be so placed economically that they are not much more dependent on others than others are on them . . . These are principles which liberals and democrats in the West, whose thinking, whatever their party allegiance, has been deeply affected by socialist doctrines, share with Rousseau . . .[27]

The more powerful argument linking political and social equality is, however, analogical in form and consists in deriving both kinds of equality from a more fundamental notion of human equality. I aim to show that in modern societies political equality has come to symbolise the basic human equality between the members of a given community in such a way that everyone who is excluded from, or treated unequally in, the political realm will suffer a loss of self-respect. He will feel that his equal worth as a human being has been denied. However, this same notion of human equality also provides the justification for a certain measure of social equality; there are degrees of social and economic deprivation which will bring about a loss of self-respect in the same way as exclusion from the political realm. Thus, anyone who accepts the justification of political equality in terms of self-respect ought to accept a social policy that aims to remedy serious cases of deprivation and that may thus conflict with the liberal view of social justice; need has to replace desert as the basis for distributing at least a part of society's resources.

Another way of arriving at this position is to see both political equality and a degree of social equality as part of the broader notion of equal citizenship. This approach has been associated particularly with T. H. Marshall, who defines citizenship as follows:

> Citizenship is a status bestowed on those who are full members of a community. All who possess the status are equal with respect to the rights and duties with which the status is endowed. There is no universal principle that determines what those rights and duties shall be, but societies in which citizenship is a developing institution create an image of an ideal citizenship against which achievement can be measured and towards which aspiration can be directed.[28]

According to Marshall, the rights of citizenships fall into three broad categories: civil rights, such as free speech, property, etc.; political rights; and social rights, such as the rights to education, housing and welfare. Marshall gives a historical account of the way in which these different categories of rights were successively won in liberal societies. Consequently, although Marshall shows the social importance of the status of citizenship in offsetting the economic inequalities of capitalist society, he does not explain why the different kinds of rights should all be necessary to citizenship as a fully developed institution. To do so it is necessary to examine the values that underlie political citizenship and then to show that these values justify an extension of citizenship into the social sphere. I shall undertake the first task in a rather roundabout way, by showing that a number of arguments which are often held to justify political equality do not in fact do so. The argument which *does* justify political equality also justifies a degree of social equality and thus connects the political rights of citizenship to the social rights – or so I hope to show.

We may begin by eliminating merely pragmatic arguments for political equality, such as the argument that equality of political rights is the only arrangement that people in modern liberal societies are likely to accept in practice, or the argument that no principle for limiting the franchise can be found that does not turn out to be arbitrary in its practical application. Both of these arguments are probably sound, but they do not constitute principled justifications of political equality and can on that account be passed over by the political philosopher (though not of course by the politician).

One principled justification which we have already discussed is that political rights are simply natural rights; they belong to man as such. The objections to this have also been expounded. Probably the simplest and most cogent is Mill's point that the vote gives a man power over other men and hence cannot be a (natural) right. A variant on this theme is to derive the right to participate in government from the right of self-government. Since we each have the right to order our individual lives, it is said, we have the collective right to order our common affairs. The difficulty here is that democratic government is not self-government, in a literal sense, since the decisions that are made will not reflect the wishes of every person in the community (except in the rare case of unanimity of opinion). If this difficulty is avoided by saying that the decisions nevertheless represent everyone's 'real will', one is entitled to ask whether universal and equal participation is necessary for the 'real will' to emerge. If the 'real will' is characterised by its intrinsic rationality, for example, then the need for political equality is far from obvious.

A less metaphysical argument is provided by the utilitarian justification of democracy. Only by placing control in the hands of the people as a whole, it is said, can we ensure that government will promote the general interest as opposed to any sectional interest. All that the utilitarian argument strictly requires, however, is that control be placed in the hands of a body of people whose interest is identical with the general interest. The people as a whole obviously form such a body, but there are so many subclasses of the people. James Mill, who developed the utilitarian argument with the greatest rigour in his *Essay on Government*, thought it permissible to exclude women and males under 40 from the vote on these grounds (the excluded groups being assumed to have interests which were identical with those given the vote). We shall probably demur at Mill's actual exclusions, but the principle on which they were made was perfectly sound for a utilitarian. Suppose we were to restrict the vote to 10 percent of the adult population chosen at random, the utilitarian requirement would be fully met (since the interests of 10 percent of a large population must be insignificantly different from those of the whole). The utilitarian argument does not justify political equality, therefore, but simply justifies having a representative electorate.

Another argument which fails to give a strict justification of political equality concerns the benefits of political participation.

Participation, it is said, is intellectually and morally educative. It encourages the citizen to inform himself about public affairs and obliges him to consider the interests of people remote from himself before coming to a decision. Leaving aside empirical objections to this claim, the argument fails because it justifies universal participation but not necessarily *equal* participation. It is satisfied by a system in which everyone has a vote but some people have two or more. Indeed one of the most eloquent exponents of the case for participation, J. S. Mill, also argued, as we have seen, for a plural voting system. Like the previous argument, the participation argument justifies a family of electoral systems of which political equality is one member, but it does not justify political equality in particular.

Suppose, however, that we employ both arguments together. Does not this provide a watertight case for political equality? The participation argument shows why everyone should have a vote; the utilitarian argument provides reasons against giving any group a plurality of votes (such a group will be liable to control policy in its sectional interests). But is the case really watertight even now? John Stuart Mill believed that a plural voting system could be justified on utilitarian grounds, since an evenly weighted vote would effectively place power in the hands of the educated working class, whose (short-term) interests were by no means identical with the general interests of society. This points to a logical weakness in the utilitarian justification of democracy. The justification only succeeds if the interests of the majority in the community are assumed to coincide with the general interest. Remove this assumption and no determinate distribution of votes can be derived from considerations of utility.

In maintaining that neither the utilitarian argument nor the participation argument (nor both together) justifies political equality, I do not mean to imply that they are irrelevant to the general justification of democracy. The temple of democracy is supported by many pillars, and these are two of the most important. But neither pillar strictly supports that element in the general notion of democracy with which we are concerned, namely political equality. To support that element, it is necessary to explore the connection between political equality and equality in a broader sense.

What I wish to suggest is that in modern liberal societies an equal right to participate in government has become an essential expression of the basic equality between the members of each state. For practical purposes the state is the most inclusive community to which a person belongs, and it is therefore important that he should possess an equal status in that community, to offset the inequalities of economic and social life. In wealth, prestige, etc. individuals are visibly unequal, but political equality allows each person to consider that he is as worthy and important as every other member of the community, and this enhances his self-respect. Putting it the other way round, if the political system incorporates overt inequalities – by denying some people the vote or by distributing votes unequally – those who are deprived are likely to feel that they have been branded as inferiors in a quite general way, in a way that denies their fundamental equality with other members of the community. This can perhaps best be seen by considering the case that is made to justify extending the vote to sections of the community that have hitherto lacked it – women, young people, criminals. In each instance the crux of the argument is not that the deprived group have special interests which can only be protected by giving them the vote, but that the members of these groups ought to be recognised as full members of the community. The claim is essentially a claim for status, and testifies to the symbolic role which equal voting rights have come to play in modern societies: it is impossible to create political inequalities without damaging the self-respect of those who are placed in an inferior position.

Among modern liberals, Rawls has most clearly seen the connection between self-respect and political equality.

> The basis for self-esteem in a just society is not then one's income share but the publicly affirmed distribution of fundamental rights and liberties. And this distribution being equal, everyone has a similar and secure status when they meet to conduct the common affairs of the wider society. No one is inclined to look beyond the constitutional affirmation of equality for further political ways of securing his status. Nor, on the other hand, are men disposed to acknowledge a lesser than equal liberty. For one thing, doing this would put them at a disadvantage and weaken their political position from a strategic point of view. It would also have the effect of publicly establishing their inferiority as defined by the basic structure of society. This subordinate ranking in the public forum, experienced in the attempt to take part in political and economic life, and felt in dealing with those who have a greater liberty, would indeed be humiliating and destructive of self-esteem.[29]

What Rawls fails to see, however, is that economic inequalities may themselves threaten the self-respect of those who occupy the lower positions in society. This is partly a matter of actual levels of poverty, and partly a matter of relative deprivation by comparison with those who are better off. At any given stage of economic development there exists a rough consensus on what constitutes a minimum standard of living, and anyone who falls below that standard will not feel that he is really the equal of someone who is comfortably above it. Poverty is not only painful, it is also ignominious. The same may be said about social and economic inequalities in themselves, though the point at which the size of an inequality begins to undermine the self-respect of the worse-off cannot be fixed with any precision. It seems to depend on psychological factors such as the visibility of the inequality to those at the bottom, which in turn depends on how conspicuously the better-off display their wealth, and so on. But although the practical implications for social policy of a concern for self-respect are for this reason difficult to state precisely, the general principle is fairly clear. In so far as the size of inequalities weakens the self-respect of the worse-off members of society, it will be necessary to redistribute resources from the better-off to the worse-off. The aim will be to bring each person up to the accepted minimum standard of living by providing him with the necessary goods and services, and to reduce inequalities by progressive taxation.[30]

This in turn requires a new notion of social justice. The kind of social policy which is necessary to protect self-respect is incompatible with the liberal view of justice as the reward of desert. To some extent the rewards of the able and the hard-working have to be reduced to provide for the sick, the unemployed, and so on. The new criterion of justice that is introduced is one of need. Indeed unless the redistribution of resources to the needy is seen as a matter of justice, it will fail in its object of preserving the self-respect of the recipients.[31] It is therefore important both that there exists a general social conviction that the relief of need is a matter of justice, and that the institutions which serve this function work in such a way that the recipients of relief are not stigmatised.

Thus, the same considerations of human equality and the need for self-respect that underlie the case for political equality support a view of social justice that incorporates distribution according to need. To understand why equal voting rights are important, we must refer to the sense of equality that is violated if these rights are denied to some. But this same sense of equality is violated if a society with ample resources allows some of its members to live in poverty, or if it permits extreme differences in wealth or status. Citizenship is denied as much by these factors as by the removal of a person's right to participate in government. It is undoubtedly more difficult to lay down the conditions of citizenship in the social realm than in the political realm, but that there should be some provision for need is not in question. We have therefore discovered a further sense in which political equality and the liberal view of justice are dissonant doctrines. The assumptions that support political equality also support a view of justice different from that of the classical liberals.

To conclude, we have found that the ideas of democracy and social justice are more closely related than appears at first glance. This is because both ideas depend on assumptions about human equality and inequality. If we take as the central fact about human beings their unequal deserts, we arrive at the classical liberal conception of social justice, but by the same consideration we are led to make political rights depend on desert as well. If, on the other hand, we begin from the conviction that each man is equally entitled to self-respect, irrespective of desert, we can justify political equality, but we must also alter our conception of social justice to take account of need. We cannot consonantly use inegalitarian assumptions in our social thinking and egalitarian assumptions in our political thinking. This introduces a bifurcation between man as social agent and man as political agent which is ultimately unsupportable.

NOTES

1. See my 'The ideological backgrounds to conceptions of social justice', *Political Studies,* 21, 1974: 387-99; and *Social Justice* (Oxford: 1976).

2. For an expansion of this contrast see the works cited in note 1.

3. I do not suggest that this is the only reason for the change in conceptions of social justice, but it has certainly weighed heavily with some liberals, as we shall see later.

4. I shall not even consider the exclusion of women, taken for granted by almost all liberals until quite recently, since this raises special problems of its own.

5. See, for example, J. Hamburger, *Intellectuals in Politics: John Stuart Mill and the Philosophic Radicals* (New Haven and London, 1961), ch. 2 on the philosophical radicals' view of 'the people'.

6. See A. S. P. Woodhouse (ed.), *Puritanism and Liberty* (London, 1951); C. B. Macpherson, *The Political Theory of Possessive Individualism* (Oxford, 1962), ch. 3.

7. T. B. Macaulay, *Speeches on Politics and Literature* (London, n.d.) 430.

8. H. Spencer, 'Parliamentary reform: the dangers and the safeguards', in: *Essays: Scientific, Political and Speculative*, Vol. II (London, 1883).

9. Woodhouse, op. cit., 58.

10. Cited in F. V. A. Aulard, *The French Revolution,* Vol. I (London, 1910), 181.

11. Woodhouse, op. cit., 82.

12. Woodhouse, op. cit., 83. There has been a lively dispute both over the Levellers' consistency in excluding various categories of people from the franchise, and over the meaning they attached to the term 'servant'. See especially Macpherson, *The Political Theory of Possessive Individualism,* ch. 3, and 'Servants and labourers in seventeenth-century England' in his *Democratic Theory: Essays in Retrieval* (Oxford, 1973), 207-23; P. Laslett, 'Market society and political theory', *Historical Journal,* 7, (1964): 150-54; K. Thomas, 'The Levellers and the franchise', in: G. E. Aylmer (ed.), *The Interregnum: The Quest for Settlement 1646-1660* (London, 1972).

13. Cited in E. Thompson, *Popular Sovereignty and the French Constituent Assembly 1789-91* (Manchester, 1952), 57. On Barnave more generally, see R. Miliband, 'Barnave: a case of bourgeois class consciousness', in: I. Meszaros (ed.), *Aspects of History and Class Consciousness* (London, 1971), 22-48.

14. Macaulay, *Speeches,* op. cit., 3.

15. W. Bagehot, 'Parliamentary reform', in: *The Collected Works of Walter Bagehot,* Vol. VI (London, 1974), 208-9.

16. Cited in Aulard, *The French Revolution,* op. cit., Vol. I, 181.

17. Cited in H. Spiegelberg, 'Accident of birth: a non-utilitarian motif in J. S. Mill's philosophy', *Journal of the History of Ideas,* 22, 1961: 489. Several other relevant passages from Mill are cited in this article.

18. On the development of Mill's attitude towards democracy, see J. H. Burns, 'J. S. Mill and democracy, 1829-61', in: J. B. Schneewind (ed.), *Mill: a Collection of Critical Essays* (London, 1969), 280-328.

19. See J. S. Mill, *Utilitarianism: Liberty: Representative Government* (London, 1964), 215-17.

20. J. S. Mill, 'Thoughts on parliamentary reform', in: G. Himmelfarb (ed.), *Essays on Politics and Culture* (New York, 1963), p. 319.

21. Mill, *Utilitarianism,* op. cit., 282.

22. On Mill's view of the political role of the classless intelligentsia, see further G. Duncan, *Marx and Mill: Two Views of Social Conflict and Social Harmony* (Cambridge, 1973), ch. 8.

23. Mill, *Utilitarianism,* op. cit., 283. Note that Mill here uses the analogy between a private business and the state to make his point.

24. Mill, *Utilitarianism,* op. cit., 288.

25. J. S. Mill, *Autobiography,* J. Stillinger (ed.), (London, 1971), 153.

26. J. J. Rousseau, *The Social Contract and Discourses* (London, 1968), 42.

27. J. Plamenatz, *Man and Society,* Vol. I (London, 1963), 431.

28. T. H. Marshall, 'Citizenship and social class', in: *Sociology at the Crossroads and Other Essays* (London, 1963), 87.

29. J. Rawls, *A Theory of Justice* (Oxford, 1972), 544-45.

30. This is one of the important conditions of preserving self-respect, but it is not by itself sufficient, since self-respect may be undermined by degrading working conditions, racial prejudice and other such factors. Once the value of self-respect is admitted into political argument, it has ramifications that are far wider than at first appears.

31. Cf. the position advanced in T. D. Campbell, 'Humanity before justice', *British Journal of Political Science,* 4, 1974: 1-16. I have discussed Campbell's arguments in a forthcoming paper, 'Social justice and the principle of need'.

5 The Rationality of the 'Social Treaty'

Pierre Favre
University of Clermont-Ferrand, France

Up to the present day the interpretation of Jean Jacques Rousseau's *Social Contract* has undoubtedly centred on the concept which gives the title to his book, and which he also refers to as the *social pact*. This has caused neglect of the terms of a second contract, the *social treaty* which, at first, might seem of minor importance but, when analysed in depth, appears so bound up with the contract that the very existence of the latter depends on it. In our opinion this neglect of the social treaty prevents any understanding of the fundamental enigma of Rousseau's political theory. Thus, we have been deprived of the insights which the work — in its very failure to link the social treaty and the social contract — contributes to political thinking.

However, Rousseau's reasoning, as expressed in the famous Chapter VI of Book I[1], seems sufficiently explicit as to his conception of the social treaty. It is said that 'the fundamental problem is to find a form of association which will defend and protect with the whole common force the person and goods of each associate, and in which each, while uniting himself with all, may still obey himself alone, and remain as free as before'. The solution to this problem is provided in a twofold contract. The first, the social contract proper, also referred to as the social pact, can be stated in the following words: 'Each of us puts his person and all his power in common under the supreme direction of the general will, and, in our corporate capacity, we receive each member as an indivisible part of the whole.' The second contract, that is the social treaty, is stated in the next sentence: from the moment when it is concluded, the pact of association 'creates a moral and collective body made up of as many members as the assembly has votes. By this same act, the body is given its unity, its common ego, its life and its will.' Owing to the conditions of its creation, the civil society is a deliberative body capable of taking collective decisions. Thus, the collective decision-making process is far from being a technical arrangement of secondary importance: it is the most important part of the social treaty and thereby indissolubly linked with the social pact. Moreover, Rousseau is aware of this: in *The Social Contract* he continually returns, from one point of view or another, to problems of collective decision-making, regarding both unanimous and majority decisions.

In conformity with Rousseau's posing of the problem, we shall try to tackle the question of the social treaty, which can be re-stated as follows: 'What method of collective decision-making must be adopted if I am to accept the loss of the freedom to decide which I used to have, and if I am to accept obedience to a decision made in common?' Is there a rational answer to such a question? To begin with, we shall seek to clarify the terms of the problem by studying a fictitious example. Then we shall see how Rousseau thinks he has solved the problem. In fact, neither the analysis of our example, nor the study of Rousseau's work will bring any answers to our questions. So we shall have to draw conclusions from this.

Having raised the question of collective decision-making, let us begin by disregarding Rousseau's own response. To be more precise, let us try to build a simple and logical model in order to find a complete answer.

Our method will be to construct an example, as is customary when you wish to cast light on a difficult theoretical problem. This is the approach adopted by game-theory specialists or economists and sociologists who favour methodological individualism. Let us imagine ten men of different origins and character who are brought together by circumstances and wish to form a society. For the moment, it does not matter whether these men are ten house-owners setting up an interest-group, or ten crack international swindlers creating a kind of Mafia, or ten doctors founding a hospital, or ten friends launching a club. What matters is that they should be considered as being capable of rational behaviour: they can size up a situation, envisage its potential developments, rank their preferences, settle on their goals and choose the strategies best suited to their attainment.[2] One can imagine these ten men asking themselves Rousseau's question about the social treaty given above: 'What method of collective decision-making must be adopted if I am to accept the loss of the freedom to decide which I used to have, and if I am to accept obedience to a decision made in common?'

Our ten men will probably agree quite quickly on one point: the different levels of collective choice between which they will have to choose. The most classical level is that of unanimity: a decision becomes the general will only if all the members of the society agree to it. But they will also think of majority rule and its variants: a straight majority (six 'ayes' and four 'noes'), a 'reinforced' or 'qualified' majority (7 votes to 3, 8 votes to 2, or 9 votes to 1). But, logically, one must go further.[3] Cases in which some members abstain and where members are not able to vote must be examined. The 'majority' can then be even lower: 5 votes to 4 if there is an absentee or an abstentionist, 4 to 3 if there are three, etc. Moreover, a group may well decide to give one, two, or three men the power to decide without referring to the others, for example in order to avoid the unwieldiness of meetings and debates attended by all group members.[4] To simplify,[5] each member, when thinking over his membership of a society, must therefore decide what his position will be as to each of the ten possible decision-making rules: unanimity, agreement between nine members, agreement between eight members, seven members, six members, an efficient coalition[6] of five, four, three and two members, and one man's decision. Finally, as much for the sake of convenience (the graphs will require a zero point) as to raise the problems it poses, we shall discuss the situation symmetrical with unanimity in which the decision imposed upon the group is not made by *any* member of the group either because it is arbitrary (recourse to chance, as in certain ancient decision processes), or because the decision is imposed by some external authority (which can be impersonal, such as market forces for economists) or even because, by a precedent decision, unanimous decisions are not carried out.[7]

Each of the ten men in our example will thus be situated on the following scale which will be the x-axis of our graphs (see Figure 1).

Figure 1

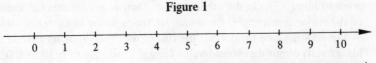

Number of persons whose agreement is required and sufficient for a collective decision to be made

Each of the ten future 'citizens' of the new society is confronted with a scale of possible decision-making procedures, one of which must be chosen by the group. Two stages have then to be covered. In the first, which is the longest to mark out, each of the ten citizens must say upon which decision-making procedure his entry into the society depends. In the second stage, the ten individual choices being known, they will have to be combined and aggregated so as to discover the common decision-making process which will finally be selected.

How will the ten men choose amongst the possible collective decision-making procedures? In accordance with the individualist methodology which we have adopted for the moment, one can answer by treating these ten men in the same way as *economic man*, for example, by working out utility curves.[8]

First of all, in evaluating the decision-making processes, each man will consider the *risk* of having to obey unacceptable decisions under different procedures. Of course, this risk is a function of the number of people whose agreement is necessary for a decision to become a mandatory rule. But there is no reason to suppose that this risk varies in the same way for all. On the contrary, these ten dissimilar men, precisely because they are dissimilar, will assess this risk differently. To understand this better, let us draw a graph. On the x-axis we measure the sequence of decisive fractions (0/10, 1/10 ... 10/10). On the y-axis, we measure the risk taken from 0 (zero risk) to 1 (maximum risk) — any scale of measurement would have sufficed. How then does the risk vary according to the possible decision-making processes? Let us imagine that the first of our ten men is a democrat. His estimate of the risk could be expressed as shown in Figure 2. The risk seems to him to be at its greatest when the decision is made independently of the group (point a). The risk remains very great when the decision is left to a minority (a decision made by two persons, risk 0.9, point b; a decision made by four people, risk 0.8, point c). Even when five people manage to win acceptance for their choice (point d), the risk seems great to him (0.7). On the other hand, as soon as one reaches the shores of the majority principle, the democrat trusts in the enlightened views of the majority and thinks that the risk of the decision being adverse to his interests diminishes considerably (straight majority of 6/10, risk 0.2, point e; reinforced majority of 8/10, risk 0.1, point f). In the case of unanimity the risk naturally is nil (point g). All ten members of the group (including the person at issue) vote in the same way, and the decision cannot be unacceptable.[9]

The second man is timorous. Before committing himself to the society, he is afraid of often being in the minority and of having to face an oppressive majority. The curve that expresses this fear is characteristic (curve 2 of Figure 3, where the democrat's curve 1 is traced). The

Figure 2

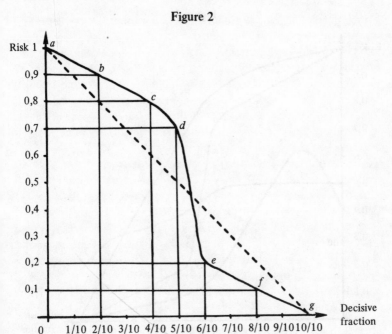

timorous person cannot bring himself to let minorities take decisions or even simple majorities. In his view, a 6 votes to 4 majority is very risky (0.7). The risk seems to him to diminish when decisions are voted by majorities. But the risk is still at 0.4 for a four-fifths majority. It is at 0.2 for a majority of 9/10, and at zero in the case of unanimity.

The third person is a misanthropist. He has faith neither in men, nor in himself. His curve (curve 3, Figure 3) tends sceptically to the horizontal. The risks of a decision taken by 1, 2, 3 or 4 people only seem average to him (0.5), for a small group of people has as much chance of making a good decision as a bad one. In his view these risks are neither greater nor lesser than those of a decision imposed on the group from outside; such a decision could be salutary or not. When the number of people whose agreements are sought grows, the risks seem slightly less serious to the misanthropist (0.4 risk for a 6/10 majority, 0.3 for a 9/10 one). The risk is not even nil when the group is unanimous, because he and others can be mistaken and a unanimous decision can quickly appear unacceptable.

The fourth man is cunning (the schemer). He considers himself to be

Figure 3

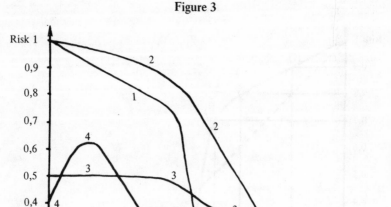

sufficiently cunning to think that, whatever the decision-making procedure, he will often be able to master and exploit it to his advantage (curve 4 of Figure 3). He is particularly worried about the monopolisation of the decision process by competitors — for he cannot foresee if he will or will not be elected — and over whom his tactics of seduction would perhaps have little effect. The schemer is more afraid of a decision made by a minority of the group than by an outside authority (risk 0.4): it is better to have a leader from outside than a leader among one's peers. The schemer thinks that a really collective decision does not risk being unacceptable. This risk is already weak for a 'majority' of 5/10. Then it decreases regularly.

We shall not present the curves of the last five men. The reader can imagine other graphs that correlate the decision-making process and the risks run, and justify them by dominant character traits. The reader could even try to work out his own curve! But it must not be forgotten that each curve can, quite legitimately, have a different plotting. This is so even when the graphs have the same overall orientation linked with the growing probability (in inverse ratio to the risk) of each person's being a member of the efficient coalition as the coalition's size grows. As each curve can be different, the conditions laid down by each person under which he or she accepts to enter the society will themselves be very different. For example, what is the risk-evaluation of the straight majority (6/10)? The democrat sees a 0.2 risk, the timorous a 0.7 risk, the misanthropist a 0.4 risk and the schemer a 0.1 risk. Study of the figure shows that no decision-making process — not even the unanimity rule — seems capable of being the object of a preliminary agreement which would be indispensable to society's formation.

The potential risk of a future decision being unacceptable is not, however, the only factor to be taken into account when deliberating; the second element is the *cost* that each person will have to endure to get the community to make a decision favourable to his or her interests. This second aspect is often neglected: one usually thinks in terms of protecting the individual from social oppression. In fact, an individual must also evaluate how much it will cost him to get a favourable decision. These costs are easy to imagine: there is the time 'spent' in meeting partners and in convincing them to approve of one's proposal, and of course this time depends on the number of people whose agreement is required to form an efficient coalition. To gain support, one might have to do someone a good turn, or offer presents. One might also have to mortgage the future, if it is necessary to bargain, by promising to approve a future proposal by the person whose agreement you require today. The evaluation of these costs obviously affects the choice of collective decision-making processes. If one takes the case of a reinforced majority, a high cost will probably have to be endured by a person who wishes to obtain a decision, as he or she will have to convince many people. If one or two persons decide for the group, the applicant or petitioner can concentrate on them. But, once again, the costs which each individual might want to endure to get a decision made will vary greatly from one person to another.[10] One person will have confidence in his powers of persuasion, another will be aware of the fact that he will not have enough time to meet those people whose votes he cannot do without, etc.

Once again, a graph will be of some help to us, but its plotting raises two problems. First, the costs can be calculated in more or less arbitrary units (the number of hours spent in convincing other associates, monetary equivalents of the sacrifices made to obtain support, etc.). We shall do this simply by speaking of *units* of cost. But what scale should we choose? Logically, there is no reason why one should limit the anticipated costs to a finite number of units. These costs can normally vary between zero and infinity. An individual might never manage to convince his nine associates, and thus might never get a unanimous backing for his proposal. However, let us simplify matters, and the future comparison of curves, by supposing that the costs will be represented within a scale of ten units, even if in some cases the 'expenditure' of these ten units of cost is not sufficient (or on the contrary is not necessary) for someone to convince the whole of the group. The second problem is where should one place the starting-points of the curves; at the point of intersection of both axes, or along the x-axis at point 1/10? The answer is not simple. If we make the curve start at the point of intersection, we have to suppose that, for the person whose costs we are calculating, a decision which fails to gain the support of a single member of the group costs nothing. This would be true if we decided only to take account of the decision-making costs within the group, and if we thus decided to ignore the fact that a person can act to obtain a favourable decision from outside the group, thereby incurring costs.[11] On the other hand, originating the curve on the x-axis at point 1/10 would imply that the person endures no costs when he 'decides for himself', and when he thinks about the decision which he is going to ask the group to make.[12] In reality, this is not true. Whoever wishes to organise a collective action must collect information and think, and thereby incur costs. Furthermore, the very fact that a collective decision is necessary increases the costs that are to be borne by each person, as each member of the community has to anticipate the group's possible reactions, and has to consider various alternative strategies, etc. Our answer to the second problem is therefore to state that it is not too illogical to situate the origins of the curves at the point of intersection of both axes.

Therefore, we can now try to plot the cost curves of the four types of persons described above: the democrat, the timorous man, the misanthropist and the schemer. But first, as before, let us plot a reference curve. If the increase in costs were purely arithmetical, that is if, for example, I needed one hour to make a decision, and one hour to convince you, and another to convince your neighbour, and so on, then the cost curve would be elementary, as shown in Figure 4. Obviously, this is only a theoretical figure: the cost curve can differ considerably according to individuals.

First of all, what about our democrat? His cost curve is comfortably average (Figure 5). He is thoughtful: he needs a unit and a half to make

Figure 4

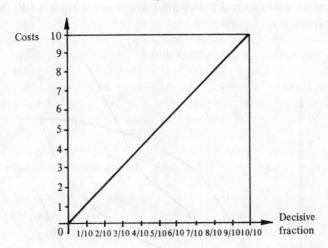

Figure 5

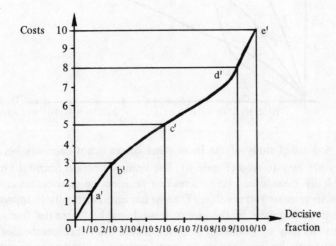

a decision (point a'). He will use another unit and a half to convince the first person (point b'), then he will accelerate: for example, the 'expense' of two more units will enable him to get the support of three other persons (point c'). He will go on just as regularly, having diffi-

culties only with the last two persons: eight units will be used to gain
the ninth man (point d'). Two more will be needed to win over the last
one (point e').

Figure 6

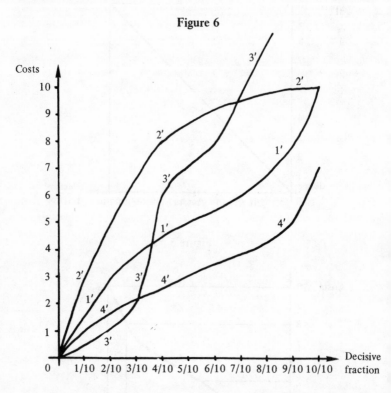

A detailed study of the three other curves is not necessary because
they are easy to read (Figure 6). The timorous person (curve $2'$) quite
naturally takes a long time to make a decision: he equivocates and he
uses three units to take sides. Then he has much difficulty in approaching three members of the group: in so doing, he 'burns up' five more
units. As may be imagined, he could 'seduce' the other members of the
group with his two remaining units owing to a 'gathering snowball'
effect and to the earnestness and modesty of his proposal. The misanthropist requires a more sinuous line (curve $3'$). Because he is self-
willed, he makes his own decision very quickly and has little difficulty
in enlisting the support of two other members. But, from that moment
everything goes wrong. He invests four units in convincing the fourth

person. The three following members make him use up the four remaining units. He would therefore influence the last three persons only if he could spend more than the ten units decided upon. His curve goes outside the graph because his character causes unshakable hostility. Finally, the schemer (curve $4'$) acts craftily. He thinks quite fast, and is convincing, even though the last two persons do resist him a little. However, he has no need of his ten units to make a decision and to convince everyone: seven units are enough.

At this point, how do we stand? Ten people are considering what collective decision-making process to adopt in order to accept setting up a community. To this end each individual has quantified two elements which will influence his choice. First, in terms of various possible decision-making procedures, how much risk is there of a 'majority' to which an individual does not belong imposing an unacceptable decision? Secondly, in terms of the chosen decision-making procedure, how much would it cost an individual to obtain the group's support for a plan favourable to his or her interests? At this stage the problem to be solved collectively, that is the problem of the social treaty, has been only partially solved.

The first question, which we shall immediately dispose of: are other elements to be taken account of in addition to risks and costs? Obviously, the answer is 'yes'. For example, one could think of plotting

Figure 7

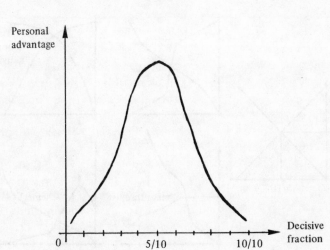

a curve which would show the *personal* advantages[13] each invididual expects to obtain from living together with other people according to various decision-making processes. The curves would probably reveal a familiar figure such as that shown in Figure 7. If one person alone decides, there is every chance that my personal advantage will be small unless I am the one who decides. If all decide unanimously, my relative advantage compared with the others will probably be equally small as everyone will benefit from the situation. If half a community is opposed to the other half, the winning coalition should consolidate its interests to the detriment of the defeated coalition.[14] However, we shall not multiply the number of individual curves. It would be fun, but the difficulties would be out of proportion to the satisfaction of adding variables to the two initial variables. Thus, for the sake of clarity, we shall keep to the risks and costs curves.

But there is another question: how is each of the ten persons — or at least each of the four whose curves we have plotted — going to determine the collective decision-making process which conditions his entry into the community? The best method seems to be a comparison between the risks and costs for each possible decision-making process. In practice, the superposition of curves (Figure 8) gives a direct reading.[15]

Figure 8

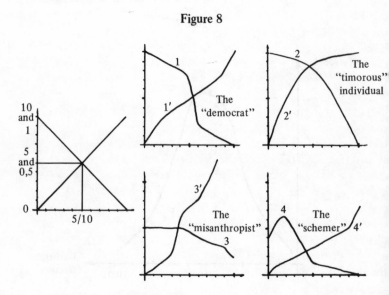

Not surprisingly, the democrat will want to keep to the rule of the majority (6/10). According to him the risk is slight, and the cost reasonable. He will hesitate to let only five members decide: for him, the cost of obtaining a decision decreases very slightly, whereas the risk grows a lot. The timorous person is in a dramatic position. If he accepts majority rule (6/10), he accumulates all the drawbacks: the risk is very great, and the cost of the decision is unbearably high. All this means that he will not get any agreement on a proposal which is favourable to his interests and that the decisions taken will probably be unacceptable to him. The question cannot be settled, and our man will have to grade both necessities: if he is looking for security, he will call for near-unanimity (the risk diminishes considerably whereas the costs hardly increase). If he is looking for efficiency, he will accept the decision to be taken by two persons, or even by one person. The misanthropist is in an easier position. He will reject unanimous and majority decisions, because the costs he might incur are nullifying, and because he takes risks easily. He agrees only with minority decisions and with their dissymetrical logic: he will have everything to gain if he gathers the minority around him; if not, he will not lose much more than if he waited for an unobtainable majority! Finally, the schemer has every advantage. He can afford to accept a 4/10 'majority', but might even favour 7/10 or 8/10 majorities because they are less risky and do not make him incur high costs. Being the only person in this situation, one can expect him to make the most of his advantage and plead in favour of a reinforced majority which would give him a clearly superior position within the association. Each person has thus been able to choose a course of action for the debate which will settle the choice of possible collective decision-making processes.

Two remarks can be made at this point.

(1) Our comparison between risks and costs can be criticised for presupposing these phenomena to be comparable by means of almost identical qualification (from 0 to 10 and from 0 to 1) and of the superposition of graphs. In reality, 'risks' and 'costs' have nothing in common and, as shown by Pareto, any comparison between these phenomena can only be subjective. Some can fear risks more than the rest, others think above all of costs: nothing can enable us to settle the question and the results of a decision-making process can be very different (as we saw in the extreme case of the timorous person). Let us acknowledge this criticism without studying it in depth so as to finish the chapter and to judge its findings as a whole.

(2) We know that the described functions could receive complex mathematical treatment.[16] But, so long as one has not put the stated hypotheses to the test, it does not seem necessary to find the equations of the fictitious behaviour analysed in this chapter, and to work with those equations at the risk of forgetting the very nature of what they express. Before all that, we need to know, with the help of workable examples, if the (mathematical) game is worth the candle.

On the sole strength of the simple examples given above, we can now draw three conclusions. The first compels recognition: the rule of unanimity does not enjoy the prerogative traditionally associated with it. The democrat lays no claim to it, nor does the timorous individual, the misanthropist, and the schemer. Why is this so? Because the very logic of unanimity is contradictory. On the one hand, it guarantees that no measure will be adopted without the individual's consent (this being the universally recognized characteristic of unanimity). But on the other hand, unanimity requires an individual to obtain the consent of all his associates.[17] Unanimity is thus unacceptable seeing that one has to take into consideration not only what one rejects, but also what one wishes to accomplish. The second conclusion also contradicts generally accepted ideas: the majority principle cannot logically be presumed superior. For some, it can lead to a fairly good balance between the risks incurred and the costs borne; for some, it leads both to great risks and to high costs; and for others, it is too risky in terms of the costs incurred. The significance of majority rule varies considerably according to the characteristics of individuals who want to found a community. It is thus a highly uncertain rule the legitimacy of which depends on each individual's situation. The third conclusion is merely a development of the second: no rule of decision-making has identical properties in the eyes of each individual concerned. This is the case both of the various qualified majorities one can think of, and of less democratic decision-making rules such as a decision being made by one member of a group, or by a triumvirate, etc.

The situation of our ten potential associates therefore seems specially hard to appreciate. Now what about the last stage of our line of argument? Let us accept that each of the ten men has made his choice and knows what decision-making process he would like to see adopted before agreeing to form an association. How can one deduce the general will from ten individual preferences? Well, there simply is no solution to this problem.

(1) In the first place one cannot conclude a social treaty based on a

unanimous decision. As we have shown, our ten men are obviously not unanimous. And we have pointed out the rational obstacles to unanimous rule (unanimous adoption of a decision-making process can only be changed unanimously — therein lies the difficulty). Unanimity is thus impossible, and yet everyone wants his choice of decision-making process to be adopted before joining the association!

(2) Secondly, one cannot put the choice of decision-making process to the vote and adopt the one chosen by the majority, precisely because no agreement has yet been reached concerning the legitimacy of majority-rule. Similarly, it is unthinkable to seek a graphic or statistical mean taken from individual preferences, since the mean would appear to be a substitute for the majority principle.

(3) In fact, any method of aggregating individual choices would be rejected if each of the ten individuals were to draw up, in order of preference, a list of the ten decision-making processes which are set before him. There are two reasons for this: on the one hand, such a method would itself have to be agreed to and one wonders how (see the circle described above); on the other hand, any attempt to determine the general will by aggregating the graded series of individual preferences would come within the terms of Arrow's Impossibility Theorem according to which any collective order could turn out to be intransitive. In other words, there are conformations of individual preferences which are said to be intransitive even when one cannot foresee what these conformations are and without sure knowledge of being able formally to prove this intransitivity.[18]

Let us summarise. Our question was: what collective decision-making rule ought to be adopted to bring a rational individual to give up his independence and accept participation in the life of the community. Our answer is: this is an impossibility. Equally rational individuals can lay down very different conditions of entry to the association regarding the choice of decision-making process and, prior to their entry into the social order, no procedure can lead to an agreement on this interlocutory point.

Although it may be surprising, we should like to say immediately that this conclusion is too premature, and that our line of argument is to be rejected. Yet the formal scheme which we have indulged in ought not to appear useless, for it has two functions. On the one hand, it is like J. J. Rousseau's paradigm in the *Social Contract*: what we consider as Rousseau's failure rationally to lay the foundations of the legitimate society is due to the same contradictions contained in the above reasoning. On the other hand, the reasoning, having reached its conclusions, is to be subjected to criticism. In our view this criticism is useful to the extent that the scheme perhaps reflects a category of theoretical reasoning one frequently comes across[19] and which often turns out to be the foundation of highly elaborate constructions.

To be more precise, our reasoning has shown the rational impossibility of concluding the social treaty, and more widely, the social compact itself. Rousseau perceived all the elements of this reasoning which is deducible from the *Social Contract*, and that is why the book does not manage to lay the foundations of a legitimate order. Thus, the failure of our reasoning is also Rousseau's. But both these failures in no way prove that a social treaty cannot have a legitimate foundation; but it is the way the question has been put that is erroneous. The reasoning has shown how Rousseau came up against an impossibility. But the reasoning to which Rousseau fell victim (albeit implicity and subconsciously) has led his thinking astray.

As ours is not the generally accepted interpretation, we have to show that Rousseau confines his thinking within the bounds of the diabolical logic which we described above. We shall not take the trouble to give details, but we shall summarise an article published in French in which we systematically pointed out relevant textual references and which the reader can look up if he requires further development of the argument.[20]

(1) Rousseau's reasoning is based on the principles of methodological individualism. Each individual must turn the contract over in his mind before entering into the association which he has every right to refuse: 'Civil association is the most voluntary act in the world; every man being born free and master of himself, no one can, under any pretext whatever, enslave him without his assent' (Book IV, ch. II, para. 326). Each individual should evaluate the contract by the yard-stick of his personal interest. As Rousseau says in the first sentence of the *Social Contract*, one has 'to take men as they are' (para. 2). And man is legitimately selfish. He lives on self-love. Each 'thinks of himself', 'gives preference to himself' (Book II, ch. IV, para. 83). Each must pledge himself to society 'without injuring himself, and without neglecting the cares which he owes to himself' (Book I, ch. VI, para. 39), etc. Finally, each will be equal to all: 'Let us suppose that the State is composed of ten thousand Citizens . . ., each member of the State has as his share

only one ten-thousandth part of the sovereign authority' (Book III, ch.
I, para. 157).

(2) An individual who consents to the social compact must estimate
the risks incurred. A society that originated in a contract is an artificial
construction, whose fate cannot be foreseen with certainty and which
can, of course, either succeed or fail. By the contract, 'man is deprived
of many advantages that he derives from nature' (Book I, ch. VIII, para.
55) — in particular, he loses the freedom and independence he had in
the state of nature — and what he gains is risky. Man must therefore
decide if he is willing in future to accept the general will. Thus, in a
contracting society, 'the Citizen is not a judge of the peril to which the
law requires that he should expose himself; and when the prince has
said to him:"It is expedient for the State that you should die", he ought
to die' (Book II, ch. V, para. 90).

(3) Rousseau is then faced with the social treaty, that is with the
two methods of consent whose legitimacy he wishes to establish:
unanimous consent and majority consent. This is where the *Social
Contract* is at stake and where begins the reasoning analysed above. In
fact, Rousseau confines himself to a choice which dooms his theoretical
construction to failure and which he cannot unravel. First proposition:
the general will is acceptable to an individual only by unanimous
consent which, in practice, is impossible. Second proposition: the
collective will necessarily will emerge from a majority decision yet
nothing guarantees that this decision expresses the general will which
alone is legitimate. The co-existence of these two propositions — which
we shall now study in detail — leads to the very deadlock we came up
against above, although in a different way.

(4) Rousseau obstinately hunts down any dissension that might
appear within the legitimate society established by the contract. He
obstinately describes the unanimous consent upon which the society is
based, knowing full well that only unanimous consent can justify entry
into the society. Rousseau believes he proves that it is possible to
establish such unanimous consent. In reality, the unanimous consent
which he thinks he has revealed is never meaningful.

We shall not dwell on the first form of unanimous consent, that
which should exist when the social contract itself is concluded and
interpreted. This form of unanimous consent necessarily follows from
Rousseau's own definitions. Thus, although the social contract 'by its
nature requires unanimous consent' (Book IV, ch. II, para. 326) such a
consent only expresses the fact that those who disapprove of the

contract are not a party to it. 'If, then, at the time of the social compact, there are opponents of it, their opposition does not invalidate the contract, but only prevents them from being included in it: they are foreigners among citizens' (ibid). This unanimous consent is upheld in the interpretation of the contract itself which can be summed up in a single clause, 'the total alienation to the whole community of each associate with all his rights' (Book I, ch. VI, para. 42). The clarity of this single clause guarantees its entire interpretation. Each will always be aware of the obligations contained in the contract as the clause means that each renounces in advance any claim to rights whatever they might be. 'The alienation being made without reserve' (ibid.), and as the parties to the contract give up all their rights, no-one will ever be authorised to defend his prerogative as an individual, 'no individual associate has anything more to claim'. The unanimous consent upon which the contract is based is therefore perfect, and logically unquestionable, but meaningless because of its purely definitional character.

The second form of unanimous consent more directly involves Rousseau's line of argument: it is a legitimate society's consent to its laws. In this case, Rousseau manages to establish unanimous consent only by accepting a logical circle even though he resorts to subterfuge to hide it. This is the circle: Rousseau lays down the principle of universal suffrage, the right to vote being 'a right which nothing can take away from the Citizens' (Book IV, ch. I, para. 321), 'all votes should be counted' (Book II, ch. II), etc. Yet he understands perfectly well that, in any free society, the citizens' vote obviously cannot be unanimous. As he needs to prove that laws are based on unanimous consent, he either defines a contracting society as a society without dissent, thereby making the right to vote useless, or he modifies the conditions under which the vote takes place so that the popular decision appears to be unanimous. A number of well-known quotations from Rousseau show his longing for a contractual association without dissent. For a people to be 'adapted for legislation' (Book II, ch. X, para. 133), (a) there must be a high degree of consensus; (b) the people must be sufficiently few 'for every member to be known by all' (ibid.); (c) there must be 'good sense, justice and integrity ... common to all the citizens' (Book IV, ch. III, para. 340); (d) and finally the people 'should enjoy abundance and peace' (Book II, ch. X, para. 131), an abundance which should be distributed such that 'no citizens should be rich enough to be able to buy another, and none poor enough to be forced to sell himself' (Book II, ch. XI, para. 136). It is obvious that all these conditions converge: where they exist there is no need of legislation. And if by chance a few laws needed to be promulgated there would be no doubt regarding general assent to them. 'A State thus governed needs very few laws' (Book IV, ch. I, para. 316). 'The necessity of these laws is universally recognized. The first man to propose them only gives expression to what all have previously felt' (ibid.). Rousseau thus imagines a society without dissent in which all polls are unanimous.[21] Even where there is dissent, Rousseau does not dispense with unanimous polls, for he supposes them to be unanimous or interprets them as such. He presupposes unanimous ballots, because in order to attain unanimous consent, which is impossible in the counting of votes, Rousseau accepts that in some cases the people should not vote. He accepts tacit consent which could be considered as unanimous: 'the orders of the chiefs cannot pass for decisions of the general will, so long as the Sovereign, free to oppose them, refrains from doing so. In such a case the consent of the people should be inferred from the universal silence' (Book II, ch. I, para. 69). Later, Rousseau re-states this possibility: 'tacit consent is presumed from silence and the Sovereign is supposed to confirm continually the laws which it does not abrogate when able to do so' (Book III, ch. XI, para. 262). More often, Rousseau interprets majority decisions as signifying unanimous consent. Rousseau's line of argument is well known: he refuses to justify the majority principle as being autonomous or as having any specific value. Majority decisions are of value only to the extent that they are surrogates for a higher unanimous consent. As Rousseau says: 'When a law is proposed in the assembly of the People, what is asked of them is not exactly whether they approve the proposition or reject it, but whether it is conformable or not to the general will, which is their own; each one in giving his votes expresses his opinion thereupon; and from the counting of the votes is obtained the declaration of the general will. When, therefore, the opinion opposed to my own prevails, that simply shows that I was mistaken, and that what I considered to be the general will was not so' (Book IV, ch. II, para. 329). In other words, if the majority decision were to be put to a second vote, the minority, having been enlightened by the first expression of the general will, would vote in favour of the proposition adopted in the first ballot by the majority. The second ballot would reveal unanimous consent. The trouble is, Rousseau dispenses with a second ballot. The second ballot is fictitious, it is only a part of his reasoning. Unanimous consent is implied a posteriori: Rousseau lays this down in principle by means of a theoretical artifice.

Rousseau's attitude, in another form, is traceable to the doubtful concept of unanimous consent analysed above. Legitimate institutions depend on unanimous consent, but this is an impossibility. Although non-existent, it is a theoretical reference-point. It supersedes all reasoning in proportion as the line of argument develops.[22]

(5) Rousseau is not a slave to his justification of the majority principle by an underlying unanimity. On the contrary, his thinking delves deeply into the fundamental problem of collective decision-making, and uncovers the discrepancies which are at the heart of the majority principle.

First contradiction: majority rule deprives a citizen of his autonomy by enclosing his action within a succession of collective decisions. If we accept that an individual is both egotistical and rational, we have to believe that his vote will not express the general will but his self-interest. He could adopt a strategy whereby he would vote for a decision whose costs will fall equally on all but from which he will derive more benefit than others. Another somewhat more perverse strategy would be to vote for a measure whose benefits he would share with others but whose obligations and constraints he would elude and disregard. Such are the results of M. Olson's study of collective action in certain groups:[23] in extreme cases the decision itself will be non-existent, for if all the members of a community follow the same process of reasoning, no one will bring to the decision any intention of realising it (except under external coercion). In other words, Rousseau describes the contradiction that undermines the very logic of the majority principle. He says that a citizen could try 'to enjoy the rights of a citizen without being willing to fulfil the duties of a subject' (Book I, ch. VII, para. 53). His egotism 'may make him regard what he owes to the common cause as a gratuitous contribution, the loss of which will be less harmful to others than that payment of it will be burdensome to him' (ibid.). Knowing how little he contributes to the general will, and observing that he necessarily benefits from the services provided by society for all its members, 'his share in the injury done to the State will appear to him as nothing' (Book IV, ch. I, para. 320), whereas his self-interest will be satisfied. It is thus clear that to situate the origin of the general will in the self-interest of each man is to introduce into the very theory of the general will the contradiction that normally will make it collapse.

The starting-point of the second contradiction is simple. Majority decision, because it is made collectively, requires each associate to place himself in relation to the others in a *vote-bargaining situation*. The associate can no longer make up his mind alone, he has to obtain a majority decision. He thus has to convince a sufficient number of associates, each of whom behaves in accordance with his self-interest. Therefore, each will agree to vote for the proposition of another only if there is a promise of reciprocity. To begin with, deficient balances will be achieved as the bargaining will lead the community to take decisions which will not be rational either for the community or for the individual.[24] Later, stable alliances will be entered into, as associates who are used to bargaining together profitably will coalesce, and these coalitions will finally be institutionalised in the form of political parties (in the same way as competition engenders oligopoly). According to Rousseau's logic, an egalitarian democratic society gives rise to 'partial associations'. Rousseau's line of argument is purely arithmetical. Within society as a whole the citizen is acutely aware of the limits to his influence: if the State is composed of a million voters, the individual's share of the general will is negligible as it represents one-millionth of the whole. The citizen thus tends to join organisations that are closer to him and in which his influence is greater (a hundredth in an association of a hundred members). Partial associations will thereby necessarily multiply. But the influence of the arithmetical factor does not stop there: owing to an equally mechanical evolution, the State will split into two and only two partial associations – a majority and a minority. For Rousseau, once such a situation is reached, the collective decision ceases to give expression to the general will. The majority vote only expresses the will of the majority part. 'It would be ridiculous in such a case to wish to refer the matter for an express decision of the general will, which can only be the decision of one of the parties, and which, consequently, is for the other party only a will that is foreign, partial, and inclined on such an occasion to injustice as well as liable to error' (Book II, ch. IV, para. 84).[25]

Thus, because majority rule naturally divides a society it can give rise to a permanent split between two 'partial associations'. The division into majority and minority reflects the opposition between organised groups and prohibits the majority from the right legitimately to express the general will.

We shall not develop the final contradiction, the elements of which appear in the *Social Contract*, because it is of a different nature.

Rousseau is led in effect to distinguish between the people — an association of equal and independent citizens — holders of the general will, who 'desire what is good' (Book II, ch. VI, para. 105), who 'are never corrupted' (Book II, ch. III, para. 75), and the masses, an assemblage of individuals, 'a blind multitude, which often knows not what it wishes because it rarely knows what is good for it' (Book II, ch. VI, para. 105), and who are 'often deceived' (Book II, ch. III, para. 75). There are 'a thousand kinds of ideas which it is impossible to translate into [its] language'. 'Views very general and objects very remote are alike beyond their reach' (Book II, ch. VII, para. 114). How can one consult the people, but not the masses? How can one bring the masses to become a people? Rousseau here introduces two major difficulties in his theory based on the predominance of the general will. On the one hand, he casts a permanent suspicion on collective decision-making: how can one distinguish between cases where the majority really expresses the people as holders of the general will, and those where the majority is only the unworthy clamour of the masses? On the other hand, he is induced to giving the people a master: the legislator who 'must make the people see objects as they are, sometimes as they ought to appear' (Book II, ch. VI, para. 105). The legislator is dedicated to being a useful leader who if needs be has recourse to 'divine authority (to lead) those whom human prudence could not move' (Book II, ch. VII, para. 116). But nobody can guarantee that the legislator, whose job it is to convince the majority of what is good for it, will give advice that conforms to the general will which has become dumb.

(6) At this stage of our study of the *Social Contract*, it must be pointed out that Rousseau has not yet taken the decisive step. One must not deduce from the existence of the above contradictions that the majority decision never reflects the general interest. In reality, there are two possibilities: either the majority is an arithmetical accident that barely hides unanimous consent, or the majority is usurping the general interest and leading it astray. Up to now, Rousseau has merely shifted the problem, but this was necessary in order to find an objective solution. The problem is no longer, 'is a majority decision consistent with the general interest?', as we know that such a decision can be unassailable in some cases and valueless in others. The question we should ask is: 'Under what conditions can majority rule function in accordance with the general interest?' The answer to this is of decisive importance. For Rousseau, it is impossible to answer the question, and this impossibility, and it alone, is what leads to condemnation of the

majority principle. In some cases the majority decision will be right, in others it will be usurpatory, but *we shall never be able to know with certainty* which is the case. In other words, some majority decisions are acceptable, but the *principle* of majority rule is unacceptable. It cannot be a fundamental political principle because it is so uncertain. Rousseau does not want to say that the principle of majority rule causes only wrong decisions to be made; such would be the trivial opinion of all opponents of democracy. The strength of Rousseau's reasoning lies simply in his observation of the fact that one will never know and one will never have the means of knowing whether a majority decision expresses the general will or not.[26]

Let us turn to Rousseau's text. A political system which gives the majority the right to take decisions on behalf of the community as a whole is legitimate if 'all the marks of the general will are still in the majority; when they cease to be so, whatever side we take, there is no longer any liberty' (Book IV, ch. II, para. 330). Rousseau warns against majority decisions which appear legitimate and right and which seem to express the general will only because it is impossible to 'distinguish a regular and legitimate act from a seditious tumult, and the will of a whole people from the clamors of a faction' (Book III, ch. XVIII, para. 309), but also because it is impossible to foresee 'that the general will will not prevail' (Book III, ch. XV, para. 282). Unfortunately, it is impossible to know when 'the general will becomes dumb' (Book IV, ch. I, para. 319). The existence of a majority is then a symptom of social decay: 'all, under the guidance of secret motives, no more express their opinions as Citizens than if the State had never existed; and, under the name of Laws, they deceitfully pass unjust decrees which have only private interest as their end' (ibid.).

Rousseau's democratic pessimism[28] is thereby justified. Rousseau cannot rationally guarantee the validity of a democratic decision. If a majority were still to possess all the marks of unanimous consent, nothing could prevent it from governing. But this is unrealistic: the majority will never act as the guarantor of its own legitimacy.

The social treaty has taken its revenge on the social compact, the predominance of which was only apparent and not real. The impossibility of concluding a social compact originates in the contradictions which are at the heart of the social treaty.

The example developed in the first pages was an attempt to find a rational answer to a simple question. It only showed the absence of such an answer: no collective decision-making process is compatible with the great variety of individual aspirations. In the *Social Contract* Rousseau wanted to answer the same question according to the same logic. He succeeded no better and, in our view, the most interesting reason for reading Rousseau today is to interpret this failure.

Having thus brought twice to light the contradictions inherent in the mode of collective decision-making, we hope that by our reasoning we have drawn up a complete set of propositions of which five need developing: (1) no mode of decision-making is collectively rational; (2) unanimous consent is a theoretical concept which is only meaningful as an end reference-point in a scale of decision-making processes; (3) a collective decision may be legitimate or illegitimate according to the distribution of individual preferences without this proving the legitimacy of the decision-making process which gave rise to it; (4) no collective decision-making rule has identical properties in the eyes of the individuals who make up the community; and (5) no collective decision-making rule can avoid the paradoxes of collective action which invalidate the principle upon which the decision is made, without the community realising it.

These five propositions do appeal to the imagination, and it is true that further reflection on them might enrich political analysis and provide conclusive proof of the validity of such intuitions. But there are dangers, and each of the above propositions requires confrontation with more empirical reasoning. One could easily contradict these propositions by stating that some decision-making processes are in fact considered as rational by the societies which use them to express collective preferences; that individuals do in fact agree on the properties they attribute to such a decision or such a decision-making rule, that individuals do in fact recognise the legitimacy of certain decisions and decision-making processes even if their rationale is not founded in logic, etc. One could add that this alone is of importance.

Yet the answer cannot be convincing unless it is directed at the crucial point where the reasoning ceases to be valid. That is our present task.

It is tempting to reason like a mathematician and try to save the reasoning by criticising it from within. The logical conclusions of the reasoning are not convincing? Then let us start again from different premises and we shall come safer into port! For example, a good way of justifying the principle of majority-rule would be to multiply the curves comparable to those plotted above: by superimposing them, we would probably find a *mean point* which would apparently legitimise majority rule. In fact, we would only have materialised the purely arithmetical centre of gravity of the figure.[29] We could also adopt other assumptions, modify the quantities, calculate more precisely, etc. But we shall do nothing of the kind. All these methods pay too much attention to a theoretical construction the function of which is merely illustrative. It is useless to invest vast reserves of ingenuity in perfecting a scheme based on purely fictitious data. A rational model is useful only if it helps one to think about what it is composed of and what it presupposes. One must not build on sand.

Therefore the really decisive criticisms of the proof are those of external origin which, in the name of sociological realism, state that our reasoning itself has no profound meaning.

A group of men wishes to coalesce and form an association? So be it! But these men are not abstractions that have appeared from nowhere and whose behaviour is commanded by academic rationality. In the first place, they have social affiliations. This is not to say that it would suffice to stick a label onto each of the four characters chosen in our example above; it would not be of much interest to say that the democrat belongs to the middle class, the timorous individual to the lower class, the misanthropist to an upper class under attack and the schemer to an up-and-coming class. What is important is to point out that the curves can no longer be plotted arbitrarily, but will have to be plotted according to a social logic that needs to be explained. As we have already said, the notions of risk and cost do not have the same meaning for each individual, and could be graded or ranked in different ways. It must now be said that these curves are not distributed according to chance as our methodological individualism implicitly assumed. The curves are influenced by social relations, and these social relations are interrelated in a determinate way. The curves will therefore form a group or cluster according to these social relations; they will not be scattered over the span of the graph. The relations between the curves and different social origins will be variable: proximate or remote, direct or like the reversed image of a mirror. For example, it would be useful to show how an individual's strategy might consist in exploiting a collective decision for personal gain. This is the case of those who obtain state subsidies and yet refuse to pay their taxes. It would be even more useful to find out in what social situation this strategy may or may not be used, to discover how these strategies are arranged and how they are hidden from view, etc. Similarly, it would be interesting to know how collective decision-making processes are perceived, to study the different ways in which the social classes react to the principle of majority rule, to establish how much the various decision-making processes are accepted by different social circles, to describe how each individual rationalises his participation in collective decision-making, etc.

But that is not all. These men who wish to form an association do so at a particular historical moment. Nowadays, as majority principle is a social practice known for eight centuries, this basic rule of the social treaty will naturally compel recognition or, at least, will act as a reference, in the same way as unanimous consent whose paradox will not always be spontaneously perceived. All curves will certainly register a horizontal reading at majority-rule level. Social factors will operate within the bounds imposed by the mode of decision-making decided on by history, the system of majority decision being put to better use by some citizens than others, according to the social influence which they can wield. In the thirteenth century, in answer to the same question, the curves plotted by the ten future associates would have been just as diverse as those we plotted, but for different reasons. The rationality at work would have been of a different order: thus, rule by a majority of two-thirds has often preceded acceptance of simple majority rule, because it resulted from the physical superiority of two men against one. Moreover, at a particular period in the history of the Church the majority (*maior pars*) was not deemed to be the better or saner party (*sanior pars*). On the contrary, the minority party, because of its very nature, was considered as endowed with sounder judgement and was to be obeyed.[30] It is of no use to prove that a social treaty cannot be concluded rationally if the rationality to which one refers owes its existence to certain specific circumstances.

We do not wish to develop these thoughts any further, although we realise that we have presented them in rather abstract form. One would patiently have to go back over the elements of the proof described above so as to re-state our line of argument in a completely new perspective. But if we tried we would discover that the proof of our reasoning would fall apart. We said that the ten potential associates 'were gathered under the influence of certain circumstances'. But what circumstances? Why do they want to form an association? To which social order do they belong? What rules and regulations will they have to obey?[31] What form of education have they had? What experience have they had of other associations? How do they see themselves and how do they perceive others? etc. Our approach is quite different from the more theoretical one adopted at the beginning of this chapter, and it must now be quite clear that the choice of decision-making process by each group is not free but determined by a series of social forces (even if this determinism cannot easily be isolated and analysed).

Finally, we should like to draw a few provisional methodological conclusions from our consideration of the problem of the social contract.

(1) Reducing problems to a simple logical pattern can be a useful way of analysing concepts on condition that this is not an a priori exercise, and on the understanding that, by means of simple logical combinations of fictitious data, one can prove almost any proposition.

(2) The rationality upon which most societies are based is quite different from the logical reasoning by deduction in terms of which one is always tempted to explain society. This is not to say that social rationality cannot be analysed by means of formal reasoning nor that formal reasoning does not influence social rationality, nor that the relative importance of formal reasoning is constant. This simply means that a social situation exists or does not exist for social and historical reasons, few of which are under the sole command of the rationality of social actors. The social treaty has substance, even though this substance does not appear to be rational: those who, like Rousseau, have proved the fundamental irrationality of the treaty have nonetheless contributed historically to its legitimisation.

(3) Methodological individualism leads exclusively to a formal reasoning process and will therefore prevent any understanding of social rationality. We realise that this has not been proved in this article: our aim has merely been to illustrate the deadlock to which such an approach leads.

NOTES

1. We shall only indicate the book, chapter and paragraph-number of quotations, which all come from Jean-Jacques Rousseau, *The Social Contract or Principles of Political Right* 1, revised translation edited with an introduction and notes by Charles M. Sherover (New York, 1974).

2. Cf. R. Boudon's description of *homo sociologicus*: 'he is a self-willed actor with a set of preferences who looks for acceptable ways of achieving his aims, who is more or less conscious of the degree of control he has over the situation in which he finds himself (in other words, who is conscious of the structural constraints which limit his freedom of action), and who acts according to a limited amount of information and in conditions of uncertainty (Raymond Boudon, *Effets pervers et ordre social* (Paris, 1977), 14).

3. We shall not dwell on the case of an even score: five 'ayes' and five 'noes'. Traditionally, at least in France except when otherwise stipulated, preference is given in such a case to those who favour the status quo: those who oppose the adoption of a new measure are therefore the winners.

4. This can be justified in a variety of ways. In Rousseau's legitimate society, 'the common good is perceivable by all and only requires common sense', to such an extent that 'whoever first proposes (a new law) only states what all the others have already felt' (Book IV, ch. I): a single person, chosen at random, could decide for all. Without being so angelic, the ten crack international swindlers may decide not to take the risk of meeting and choose to let each one of them take turns to manage their common interests.

5. Many other decision-making processes could be studied, either refinements of voting techniques (successive debates with different majorities, quorum rules, etc.), or the *logical* possibilities of aggregating ten individual choices. Unfortunately, the number of logical methods of aggregating choices is increasing so rapidly that it is impossible to study them all: there are 16 possible methods for two voters, 256 for three voters, 65,536 for four voters, etc. Cf. G. T. Guilbaud, 'Theories of the general interest and the logical problem of aggregation', *Economie appliquée, ISEA*, 5, 1952: 552-55; and Jean Piaget, *Essai sur les Transformations des opérations logiques: les 256 opérations ternaires de la logique bivalente des propositions* (Paris, 1952).

6. By 'efficient coalition', we mean any combination of individual preferences which, by virtue of a specific rule, is victorious. The rule can be practical (thus, one could stipulate that if there is an even balance of votes, the efficient coalition is the one which has the support of the most senior member of the assembly). Or a coalition can be efficient in a purely logical sense (three votes can be victorious over seven if they are given pre-eminence). Even the term 'majority' is sometimes used in this case. Thus, Guilbaud (see above) points out that 'a decision has been taken by a majority, in the wide sense of the word, when a community has come to a prior agreement as to what efficient coalitions are, that is, has determined in the case of each *partition* (division or separation into two sets for counting votes) which is the victorious party'.

7. Unanimous consent can appear to be suspect and dangerous. In an article in *Le Monde*, Michel Cicurel describes the existence 'in the Hebraic tradition of a

judicial rule according to which a Rabbinical Tribunal has to discharge a defendant it had unanimously condemned to death. This rule has been the object of much talmudic comment. Here is the essential explanation: before the carrying out of the sentence, the tribunal has to think it over for one night to reflect, if need be, on its judgement. The Rabbis were of the opinion that in cases of unanimous judgement reflection lost all its value. This distrust of unanimity is exemplary.' (*Le Monde*, 2 August 1977: 10).

8. Much contemporary political research is based on the application of economic theories to the study of social behaviour, competition between political parties, etc. For more details concerning the example developed here see James M. Buchanan and Gordon Tullock, *The Calculus of Consent, Logical Foundations of Constitutional Democracy*, (Ann Arbor paperbacks, 1962).

9. There must be no ambiguity. Two elements are taken into account by risk calculation. First, the purely statistical probability is that the person who is thinking about the decision-making processes will be a member of the group which will take the decision. If unanimous consent is required, such a probability will be equal to 1 ('I shall necessarily be in the group'). If a 9/10th majority is imposed, the rate of probability will be 0.9 ('I have nine chances out of ten of being in the decisive group'), etc. The probability curve is then simply the straight dotted line from a to g in the above graph. Any consideration of the risk incurred takes this probability into account. But, secondly, the risks are also evaluated in terms of many other factors. ('The decision taken by a majority remains acceptable even if I have voted against this decision', 'A minority can take a decision which is to my advantage even if I have little chance of being a member of that minority', etc.).

10. We are not considering *real* costs, but the *prediction* of probable costs, despite our avoidance of the conditional tense for stylistic reasons.

11. This argument does not completely eliminate the ambiguity of the zero point on graphs and scales which it is always necessary and often enriching to discuss. If the decision which no one supports is the object of an individual's strategy to impose a change, it is because such a decision has the support of the very person who intervenes in its making.

12. We wish to point out a difference in the construction of the second graph compared with the first, and also another ambiguity concerning the x-axis points. In the graph concerning risks, whatever the curve, each point simply indicates the number of people whose agreement is required, without individualising them. When the agreement of two persons out of ten is 'efficient', these two can be the democrat and the misanthropist, or the timorous individual and the schemer, or such and such a person, or you and me, or others, without my knowing beforehand if I shall be a member of the decisive group. But this is not true as regards the costs curve, at least for point 1/10. This point alone is individualised for each of the curves: it represents the person whose curve is being traced. For example, in the case of my curve I necessarily begin to incur a cost by deciding for myself; then I shall have to convince the others, that is, depending on circumstances, you, or such and such a person, etc. Points 2/10, 3/10, 4/10, etc. therefore have the same significance as in the preceding graph and indicate a proportion of other members of the group.

13. We remind readers that the man who is thinking of joining an association is here considered to be perfectly 'rational' and selfish: the interests of the group as a whole (which at this stage does not exist) are indifferent to him except if they coincide with his own. Only self-interest can bring him to coalesce with others. This assumption, which is also Rousseau's, cannot be refuted by logical reasoning, as we shall see.

14. In the same way as in a two-party system, marginal voters or swing-vote minority parties acquire an importance which is out of all proportion to their numbers. Cf. William Riker, *The Theory of Political Coalitions* (New Haven, 1962).

15. But we shall not give any particular importance to the point of *intersection* of both curves, as one would probably do spontaneously, because both of them have different ordinates and share only the x-axis.

16. Cf., for example, the articles on 'Participation, coalitions, vote trading', in *American Political Science Review*, 69 (3) September 1975.

17. The aporia (false reasoning) upon which the concept of majority rule is based has often been exposed, but in a different way. In *La Démocratie, sa nature, sa valeur* (Paris, 1932) Kelsen states that it is wrong to consider the rule of unanimous consent only from the point of view of someone who wants to get a norm changed or a new law adopted. This means that almost all the members of the group will have to live 'within a different social order from the one they would like ... Such a situation is a far cry from real individual autonomy' Charles Eisenmann, *Cours de droit constitutionnel comparé* (Paris, 1950-51), 99.

18. Cf. Kenneth J. Arrow, *Social Choice and Individual Values*, 2nd edn. (New York, London, Sydney, 1963). The great number of articles, etc. in French concerning Arrow's book are listed in the French version (Paris, 1974, 219-30). For a more political rather than economic presentation of Arrow's theorem cf. my book *La Décision de Majorité* (Paris, 1976).

19. Cf., for example, among other books, that of John Rawls, *A Theory of Justice* (Cambridge, Mass., 1971). For a critical evaluation of Rawls's book, cf. in particular the series of articles published in *The American Political Science Review*, 69 (2), June 1975: 'Justice: a spectrum of responses to John Rawls's theory'; and Raymond Boudon, 'Effets pervers et philosophie sociale. La théorie de Rawls', in *Effets pervers et ordre social*, op. cit.

20. 'Unanimité et majorité dans le *Contrat Social* de Jean-Jacques Rousseau', *Revue de Droit public et de la Science politique*, Janvier-Février 1976: 111-86.

21. Another method by which Rousseau achieves the same aims is to give laws such a general function that everyone agrees to something that does not affect anyone's individual interest.

22. One can summarise the line of argument as follows: there must be unanimous consent for majority rule to be legitimate, but where there is unanimous consent, the principle majority rule will never be applied precisely because there is unanimity . . ..

23. Cf. Mancur Olson *The Logic of Collective Action* (Cambridge, Mass., 1965).

24. Deficient balance is well illustrated by the prisoners' dilemma. Here is an example that is related to collective decisions. Let us imagine an association in which it would be right on grounds of the common interest for its five members

to decide to share the burden of a special tax to finance a subsidy for one of them. But this would be incompatible with the logic of majority rule. The associate who asks for a subsidy will obtain it only if he gains the support of two other associates. These will certainly trade their vote by asking for reciprocity. Three subsidies will be decided upon by a majority vote in a hypothetical case where only one subsidy was required. This perverse result will often be hidden by the fact that the bargaining will be different and the reciprocal vote will be given much later on another occasion.

25. However, it must not be forgotten that Rousseau has already justified the existence of a majority by the latent unanimous consent which it possesses. To make his line of reasoning coherent, Rousseau has to distinguish two cases, but he can only suggest this distinction since its formalisation would only reveal the problematics upon which the *Social Contract* is based. On the one hand, the existence of a majority party within a body politic can simply reveal an accidental difference of opinion as yet too innocuous to warrant the disintegration of the group. The general will remains unaffected. 'When the whole people decree concerning the whole people, they consider themselves alone; and if a relation is then constituted, it is between the whole object under one point of view and the whole object under another point of view, without any division at all' (Book II, ch. VI, para. 100). On the other hand, the existence of a majority party may indicate that 'the will of one party' has prevailed and in this case, the will is not general but is a 'particular will' (Book II, ch. II). However Rousseau is unable, as we shall see, to specify the criteria by which one may differentiate situations where a majority party 'divides the whole' of society and those where the majority does not indicate 'any division of the whole'.

26. It is striking how Rousseau's reasoning is close here (by the recital of the conditions required to achieve a particular state) to that of the neo-classical school of economics. In an article by Howard R. Bowen, 'The interpretation of voting in the allocation of economic resources', *The Quarterly Journal of Economics*, 58, November 1943: 27-48, the author, without referring to Rousseau, manages to determine optimum collective conditions of economic production which correspond exactly to the (necessary but insufficient) political conditions described in the *Social Contract*.

27. As was usual at that time, Rousseau uses the term 'plurality'.

28. 'Taking the term in its strict sense, there never has existed, and never will exist, any true Democracy'; 'If there were a people who were Gods they would govern themselves democratically. A government so perfect is unsuited to men' (Book III, ch. IV, paras. 192, 197).

29. This is the sort of problem that appears when one uses Black's orders as defined in Duncan Black, *The Theory of Committees and Elections* (Cambridge, 1958).

30. Cf. A. Esmein, 'L'unanimité et la majorité dans les élections canoniques', in: *Mélanges Fitting*, T.2 (Montpellier, 1907), 354-82.

31. In France, for example, doctors' associations – in order to protect the freedom of medical practice – have to function according to the principle of unanimous consent. But this does not prove that the decisions made within these associations have unanimous support.

6 Social Contract and Social Breakdown

Kenneth R. Minogue
London School of Economics, UK

The recent spectacular revival of interest in the idea of the social contract is an excellent illustration of the fact that old theories never die; they merely bide their time. They are never, of course, revived in their old form: Rawls and Nozick are very different from Hobbes and Locke. Nor do they always bring back their old sparring partners with them: it does not seem likely that we need brace ourselves for a revival of the theory of divine right. An explicit claim to divinity is decisively out of fashion, even if the exercise of powers much more absolute than even a Louis XIV dreamed of is very much à la mode. These few remarks about intellectual continuities are intended to introduce a short exploratory chapter the purpose of which is to consider what the idea of the social contract signifies in the wider context of the history of European politics.

First, we may note how very recent this revival is. Acceptance of the notion of the social contract, we were told in a suggestive argument not so long ago,

> was comparatively short lived. Within the context of the history of social thought, it occupied a position intermediate between two deterministic theories of society. The former of these was the belief that society had been created, and was directed, by God . . . . By the XIXth century man was again being considered subordinate to more powerful forces, no longer a free agent capable of creating a world according to his own wishes.[1]

This judgement was published no more than a decade ago, and corresponded to the general opinion dominant from textbook level upwards to the effect that the social contract theory had been given the coup de grâce by Hume, and had succumbed to a more historically sophisticated manner of thinking. Yet Hume's famous essay on the subject attacks the contractarians for not answering the question that interested Hume (how did society in fact come into existence?) rather than the question which had interested them (how is a sovereign power rightfully or rationally constructed?)

This latter contractarian question about the nature of obligation is not a perennial concern of social life. In many eras and in many societies, it seems never to have arisen at all. Nevertheless, it certainly had arisen in the Middle Ages, and wherever individualist assumptions about life are current, it is never very far from the surface of thought. It is curious, therefore, that we should all have believed until recently that the social contract theory was dead. One extraneous reason for this, no doubt, is that political theorists hunger for refutations. They hunger, that is to say, to possess a completely dead past, full of theories of purely historical interest, such as scientists have. A more direct reason is that the historical décor of the contract was thought to have been decisively exposed as unrealistic. It had been widely recognised, of course, that the history *was* peripheral to an argument about obligation, but even as such, the supposedly historical element of the contract was an affront to our newly acquired sense of historical density. The main reason why a change in fashion had been taken for an intellectual extinction, however, lay elsewhere. It seemed no longer possible to believe that men could spin a society out of nothing other than their own wills, guided by a form of instrumental reason alone. It was the circularity argument which had most seriously damaged the reputation of the contract: namely, the argument that a social contract must be the consequence of existing social arrangements rather than their cause. The grand structures of Hobbes and Locke had collapsed into the dust of a petitio principi.[2]

But wise in our hindsight, we may now see that the supposed refutation of the social contract was one of those comedies of mis-understanding with which the history of political thought is so lavishly adorned. No doubt it is true that men could not generate a language and a set of sophisticated legal concepts without a basis of existing social experience, and it was to this that the rationalistic element of the contract sometimes seemed to point. But if we put to one side the rationalist apparatus of origins, the social contract doctrine is obviously about the relapse of political life into a situation of social breakdown, as when Hobbes speaks of 'those men that are so remissly governed, that they dare take up arms to defend, or introduce an opinion, are still in war; and their condition not peace, but only a cessation of arms for fear of one another; and they live, as it were, in the precincts of battle continually.'[3] The argument of this paper is that the social contract doctrine is a reliable sign that the fundamental arrangements of social life have come into question, and that fears of a complete social breakdown are appearing. This seems to me true both of the popular and the philosophical versions of the doctrine, and it is striking that the current revival has seen the reappearance of both versions.[4] Such a conjunction might just be coincidence, or (since the thing called 'the social contract' in modern British politics is very different indeed from either the currently philosophical version or from earlier versions of contract) it may just be an appropriation merely of the name to cover something fundamentally dissimilar. My argument is that there is a genuine structural connection between the two versions of the current contract doctrine.

By a popular version of the social contract, I mean the doctrine that 'government is nothing more than a mutual compact between the people and their kings' to quote George Buchanan's *History of Scotland*.[5] This doctrine was used by Buchanan to justify the deposition of Mary Queen of Scots, and eventually provoked, of course, a strong reply from James VI of Scotland who had the misfortune to have Mary for a mother and Buchanan for a tutor. Buchanan's doctrine involves Calvinist beliefs about the rights of inferior magistrates and is, no doubt, a revision to meet new circumstances of mediaeval beliefs about the rights of the baronage to call a delinquent ruler to book. James stated precisely what is intellectually deficient in such a doctrine: namely, that a contract involves not only the two contracting parties, but also an impartial judge; and, in the absence of such an impartial third party, one of the parties cannot rightfully be brought to book by the unsubstantiated conviction of the other party to the contract.

John Locke supplied some sort of answer to this difficulty in Section 223 of the *Second Treatise:* 'People are not so easily got out of their old Forms, as some are apt to suggest . . .. This slowness and aversion in the People to quit their old constitutions . . .', etc. This is not much of an answer, and is very much a hostage to changing times and circumstances. But Locke did not really need an answer because, although the *Second Treatise* is notoriously an occasional work, and pretty inadvertent in some of its reasoning, Locke had seen with a philosopher's practised eye that the popular version was vulnerable to the criticism of James I, and had supplied, in at least this respect, a variation typical of the philosophical versions of the contract. The people, in Locke's argument, are related to their rulers by way of trust and not contract, and hence the rulers cannot break the contract. Similarly, rulers are not morally exposed to the charge of breach of contract in Hobbes, Spinoza or Rousseau. Popular and philosophical versions of the contract are clearly distinguished on at least this point. They correspond to different requirements and have different structures.

It is understandable, then, that philosophers might have wanted to revive the idea of the contract in discussing obligations: or alternatively that some new twist of contemporary politics should have led people to revive the idea of government as a bargain struck between rulers and their peoples. It is odd, however, that the two versions of contract theory should have been recently revived both independently and virtually simultaneously. And this, I take it, is the case. Rawls had been working at his theory of justice for many years before its publication in 1971. But this date must count as the moment of the reappearance of the philosophical version. The popular version became current in Britain in 1974 as the result of special circumstances, and may well, for all I know, owe its *name* to the Rawlsian philosophical revival. Both Rawls and the British Labour Party were concerned with the distribution of goods (in a very wide sense of 'goods'). But Rawls was concerned with rules and individuals, whereas the Labour Party was concerned with government and corporations.

The two kinds of theory serve different though related functions. The philosophical version is concerned to elaborate the principles of what is currently called, rather eccentrically, 'distributive justice'. Over the last century, modern states have come to be thought of as 'public households', that is to say, single productive units faced with the *political* problem of how the product should be distributed. Distribution in earlier times (and to some extent, even to the present) was left to individual action in conjunction with the laws of economics, as subject to regulation by the state. In more recent times the inegalitarian consequences of such an arrangement have seemed undesirable, and liberals and socialists have argued about the appropriate place of desert on the one hand and need on the other in the distribution of the product. Such a controversy has meant that questions of principles of distribution and issues of 'social inequality' have become of increasing interest to political philosophers.

This preoccupation, by being described as a matter of 'distributive justice', has been linked to Aristotle and the tradition of political philosophy, but this link appears to be significantly anachronistic. In

Politics, Vol. III, p. ix, Aristotle is concerned with the constitution of a polis, and his argument is glossed by Barker as: 'Aristotle is here enunciating a theory of distributive justice which goes on the basis of proportionate equality. As A and B have given to the state, in the way of personal merit and personal contribution to its well-being, so A and B should receive from the state, in the way of office and honour.'[6] The last words are crucial in indicating that Aristotle is not talking of the distribution of substantive goods. It would be surprising if he had been, since the Greeks did not regard a *polis* as a productive association, and drew a vital distinction between an *oikos* or household (which was productive, and despotically ruled) and a *polis* or city-state (which was a political association and politically ruled).

We have here, then, a second oddity in the present situation of social contract theory. Our first oddity was the simultaneous *and* independent revival of both popular and philosophical versions of the contract from the museum of antiquities to which they have been so long confined. A second oddity is the association almost universally made between this revival and an Aristotelian argument with which it has no other connection than the accident of a name. Political philosophers, we may guess, prefer their work to have the resonance which comes from association with the constantly replicable problems of the classical writers; and it is perhaps also true that associating the present question of distribution with an intellectual problem about justice which was successfully dealt with in the past gives reassurance that the difficulties of the present situation will also turn out to be manageable. This reassurance is badly needed because there is at present no sign that the present problem of who should draw what rewards from the productive endeavours of the community is in sight of being solved, nor even that it is solvable at all.[7] The problem of distribution, as currently construed, arises from the collapse of belief in the validity of the laws of economics which seemed in the past to provide a realistic, if limited, connection between the input of effort and the outcome in reward. Over the last century, the economy has been subject to greater and greater control by governments, and the point has now been reached where neither the traditional beliefs inherited from the past about distribution (such as that doctors and other educated men should get more than dustmen and street sweepers) nor the economic consequences of a free market (tending to benefit the risk-takers, the quick-witted and, up to a point, the industrious) can stand against the immediate desires of political demand as expressed by trade unions and in the democratic success of governments promising to manage the economy in such a way as to guarantee full employment and other benefits. At least in the short run, prices and wages can be determined by political *fiat*. This situation has produced dramatic effects upon British life in the last decade, and I am taking it for granted that the same problem exists elsewhere. Indeed, my suggestion is that it is a problem which is eventually unavoidable given the combination of industrialism and democracy.

These are problems never contemplated by Aristotle; he was talking about constitutional arrangements, not about the distribution of goods. The modification of constitutions is classically a central part of the activity of politics, while the question of who gets what raises a host of problems much less amenable to rational discussion, and quite capable of provoking the most violent and destructive frenzies. I propose to develop this argument by distinguishing between *situations of social breakdown* on the one hand, and *situations of constitutional revision* on the other. The Dark Ages of Europe are the most celebrated instance of the breakdown of an entire social order. In such a situation the instabilities of life dissolve all social arrangements into bargains or contracts entered into by men according to the power they have available to them. Natural characteristics such as intelligence, physical strength, culture and cultivation, count for nothing in themselves by contrast with the immediate accidents of power and combination. In such desperate straits men and communities resort to 'commendation' and acquire 'masters' or 'lords' on a variety of conditions, not excluding that of slavery, which is, of course, a bargain in which the slave secures his life, but little or nothing else besides. A social structure can be built upon this slender basis because commendatory relations become hier-archical as happened in the Dark Ages, and because the higher authorities make the intermediate lords responsible for the obedience of their subordinates, as was done by the Carolingians and others at that time.[8] A 'masterless man' becomes an outlaw. But once a society of this kind has been built up, it develops constitutional regularities of its own which transform the situation, and political life takes place in what I call a 'situation of constitutional revision'. The element of bargain or contract by which the society was constituted in its extremity falls into the background and the minds of men are more impressed by the naturalness of arrangements to which they have now become accustomed. The politics of such a time are more orderly and revolve around questions like the respective constitutional powers of

Pope and Emperor, or of Pope and Council of the Church.

A similar sequence of events took place in ancient Greece, which also, of course, had its own 'dark ages'. After the development of the *polis*, the Greek cities moved into a situation of constitutional revision announced by the appearance of the great lawgivers of Greek thought — Solon, Lycurgus, Dracon and their lesser brethren. If constitutional conflicts should become so fierce that they seem to threaten the whole social order, recognition of the bargaining element in social conventions and political life will once more come to the forefront of political discussion, and this is what happened during the Peloponnesian War. But Aristotle's discussion of distributive justice is found within a firm context of political life being understood as a natural rather than an artificial thing, and what he has to say about distributive justice, to the extent that it is a practical question of distribution at all, related to a situation of constitutional revision rather than to a situation of social breakdown.

It would be obvious from what I have said that I take the beginning of the modern period, the time when social contract theories abounded, to have been a situation of social breakdown. It was clearly very far from being the same kind of desperate breakdown of human association that took place in the Dark Ages, but the emergence of a centralised state and the problems of religious confession were clearly felt by the men of that time to be of fundamental significance, matters going well beyond mere matters of constitutional revision. Besides, the growth of individualism meant that an emerging disposition of behaviour brought the choosing or bargaining element of life to the forefront with a result at least similar to what had been produced by the necessities of the Dark Ages. The commonest and most visible cause of social breakdown is the incursion of new people into an already weakened area. No such nomads disturbed the early modern period, but the loosening of feudal ties and the growth of urban opportunity produced a similar effect.

The social contract theory in its heyday in the seventeenth and eighteenth centuries was, then, a response to a sense of breakdown. Such is, of course, the accepted view, but it is one we may generalise further than is usually done. Whenever the social contract appears, we may diagnose a sensitivity to the threat of breakdown, because that is what the social contract theory is about, especially in its popular versions. By contrast, the philosophical version *may* be provoked by social conditions, and perhaps usually is, but like all philosophical theories it can lead an autonomous life of its own and there is no reason why it might not come into currency at a particular time purely as the result of what has happened in the world of the free play of speculation. Either version of the theory is a sign that men want to rethink their social arrangements in terms of fundamentals, but fundamentals, of course, come in all shapes and sizes. Aquinas can hardly be thought a superficial writer, but he gives an Aristotelian account of political life in terms of the nature rather than the choices of men. The fundamentals chosen by the classical writers on the social contract, by contrast, were dictated partly by their sense of breakdown (which led them to give a bargaining account of political life) and partly by the growing historical awareness of the period.

It is necessary to recall this element of historical awareness, because the social contract theory in its heyday is commonly thought to have been the triumph of rationalist speculation over empirical likelihood. But social contract arguments were cultivated cheek by jowl with an even greater volume of historical discussion of the questions of the day. This historical discussion concerned itself with both the classical and the mediaeval past. The classical past, it may be schematically ventured, inspired an idea of republicanism and civic humanism, and was usually cultivated in an idiom inspired by Machiavelli. The mediaeval past, on the other hand, was more useful in supplying material for arguing out a variety of more immediate local conflicts, particularly those concerned with the rights and powers of the sovereign. Sacred history was the most influential of all appeals to the past. If we remember, as we should, the range and extent of this literature, we shall not be satisfied with the superficial opinion that the social contract theory succumbed to a growth of historical awareness. For if we are talking simply of consciousness of the *past*, then it was abundantly present throughout the early modern period. This consciousness was more that of the lawyer and the antiquarian than what we shall call the historian. But then it is also true to say that the historical awareness of the eighteenth century was often more that of the developmental sociologist than that of a historian in the modern sense.

So far as the attempt to influence political life is concerned, this array of arguments, both speculative and historical, may be convincingly seen as rhetorical variations upon the same set of preoccupations. That is to say the popular contract is but a version of constitutional argument such as will appeal to the philosophically minded. What it inevitably lost in the way of direct relevance to the question in hand, it might well gain by its claim to rational demonstrability. But in fact the two kinds of argument are usually found mixed up together and the argumentative steps of a social contract are illustrated and developed in terms of the Old Testament, Greece and Rome, the mediaeval period, and travellers' tales of the primitive world. It is plausible to suggest, then, that the social contract doctrine is a stylised account of some earlier version of political experience, and that what is a precedent in one idiom becomes an essence in the other. Seen from this point of view, the striking feature of the social contract is that the popular versions seem to refer back to the high Middle Ages of the twelfth and thirteenth centuries, while the more philosophical versions appear to go further back to the Dark Ages themselves.

John Milton, for example, tells us that 'since the King or Magistrate holds his authority of the people, both originally and naturally for their good in the first place, and not his own, then may the people as oft as they shall judge it for the best, either choose him or reject him, retain him or depose him though no Tyrant, merely by the liberty and right of free-born Men, to be governed as seems to them best.'[9] This is evidently a compound of contemporary beliefs about tyrannicide and deposition on the one hand, and mediaeval political experience on the other, and indeed Milton does go on, among a host of biblical and historical examples, to cite the powers of the barons of England to bring an erring king to book. The considerable prominence of Magna Carta in the discussions of the time cannot but have kept such episodes before the minds of social contract writers. 'It is also affirmed', Milton tells us, 'from diligent search made in our ancient books of Law, that the Peers and Barons of England had a legal right to judge the King.'[10]

It is a striking fact that if we think in terms of the dominant currents of political development in the seventeenth century, this version of the contract might well be presented as a reactionary and anachronistic attempt to impede the obvious evolution of a modern state towards absolute monarchy. John Hampden and his like were men of the past seeking to sustain and entrench mediaeval ideas of consent which had become outmoded by the appearance of a form of sovereign monarchy in which the dispersed powers of a mediaeval realm — Church, king and baronage — were rationally consolidated into a single coherent organ.

Some at least of the philosophical versions of the contract — most notably those of Hobbes and Spinoza — clearly recognise this. Furthermore, they reached this point by taking the difficulties of getting out of the state of nature more seriously than was done in popular versions of the contract. And in taking this particular component of the contract more seriously, they were evidently concerned far more with the problem of social breakdown than with that of constitutional revision. If there is a historical model to be found for this variation of emphasis, it is certainly not the comparative stability of the High Middle Ages but the total instability of the Dark Ages, when political communities were actually being built up out of the arrangements made by invading barbarians and a weakened indigenous populace, bargains which were indeed made in the complete absence of any superior power who could enforce their terms. The state of nature is often taken to refer to such contemporary events as the Huguenot wars in France, the Thirty Years War in Germany, and the English Civil War. No doubt it did. But these were circumstances of violence and instability somewhat short of the total social collapse that occurred in many places at the end of the Roman empire in the West. The philosophical version of the contract is not only more profound than the popular; it also refers to a different, and a different type of, historical experience.

In time, of course, things settled down again, as things usually do. A stable and entrenched oligarchy appeared all over Europe and America, and it has been plausibly argued that conflict between this oligarchy, which saw itself as the guardian of liberty, and strong, enlightened monarchs, often enthusiastic about equality, was the subject matter of politics in the eighteenth century.[11] Alexander Pope's *Essay on Man* could, after the turbulence of civil and religious wars, revive in a new form the stabilities of the Great Chain of Being. But what concerns us is the intellectual form in which this stability was understood. We are confronted with two forms of it: economics, and history.

Increasing attention has been given in recent decades to Bernard de Mandeville's *Fable of the Bees* as the work that explored a new conception of social stability based paradoxically upon an extreme individualism. The secret of society was that men who pursued their own private and selfish ends were nonetheless indirectly facilitating prosperity and contentment. Half a century later, in the work of Adam Smith, this paradox has become fully matured in the idea of the invisible hand which co-ordinates the actions of men to the benefit of their greater prosperity. In time, this idea was taken up by Hegel and was further transformed by Marx. In Mandeville's early version, there remained a voluntarist element: 'Private Vices by the dextrous Management of a skilful Politician may be turn'd into Publick Benefits', Mandeville remarks at the end of his 'Search into the Nature of

Society'.[12] But what if skilful management were lacking? This question could be settled by theorising the actions of politicians in such a way that they expressed blindly but determinately the plan of Providence which, in the hands of the Scots and the Germans, became an elaborate theory of historical evolution from stage to stage in an ascending spiral. The invisible hand became the cunning of reason, and the wounds of social breakdown left behind nothing but the scars of transition.

With the return of stability came the resuscitated conviction that human life was orderly so long as reason could penetrate the fog of human contingencies.

> ORDER is Heav'n's first law; and this confest,
> Some rich are, and must be, greater than the rest,
> More rich, more wise; but who infers from hence
> That such are happier, shocks all common sense . . ..

Pope wrote in the *Essay of Man,*[13] and the prestige of Newtonian science helped to spread the view that human life was no less law-governed than the heavens above. No doubt we had not yet got the laws right; there remained plenty of scope for constitutional revision. The strength of this opinion can be measured in the work of the man who certainly diagnosed correctly both the cause of the next threat to social stability, and the direction from which it would come. Marx saw clearly that any civilisation which was both increasingly democratic, and increasingly dependent upon the co-operation of the labouring poor, was moving inexorably towards a crisis. But his primary concern was neither with constitutional revision nor with social breakdown, but with an intermediate idea called revolution. A revolution is, in Marx, a law-governed crisis with a determinate outcome, called communism. There was no question of society largely going back into the melting pot and requiring a completely new and unpredictable mould. In retrospect, this appears as a supreme measure of his nineteenth century optimism.

If this reading of the past is correct, then the currency of social contract theories is a litmus paper indicating the fear of a social breakdown. This means, among other things, that any connection with Aristotle is delusory, for he is concerned not with breakdown but with the very different situation of constitutional revision. It is delusory in another sense too, for Aristotle was concerned, as were the social contract theorists of the early modern period, with the distribution of political power and the conditions of political office. These are formal questions, and the very stuff of politics as it has been understood until recent times. But the present issue is how to distribute not formal powers but substantial goods — services, and levels of income. There is a limit to formal rights, but there is no limit at all to the goods and services we may demand. Because the issue is of this kind, the crisis has been long delayed in the coming by rising expectations flowing from technological advance. It is that very experience of past success which gives the present threat of breakdown its special character.[14]

NOTES

1. Michael Levin, 'Use of the social contract method: Vaughan's interpretation of Rousseau', *Journal of the History of Ideas,* 38, October-December, 1967: 4.

2. The more elaborate form of this criticism is to be found in Henry Maine's influential *Ancient Law.* He pointed out in Chapter IX 'That which the law arms with its sanctions is not a promise, but a promise accompanied with a solemn ceremonial . . . No pledge is enforced if a single form be omitted or misplaced, but, on the other hand, if the forms can be shown to have been accurately proceeded with, it is of no avail to plead that the promise was made under duress or deception.' It is only as ancient law had become rationalised that the 'nucleus of a Contract' was able to 'break away the external shell of form and ceremony'. Here was a detailed and erudite embodiment of the principle that what is prior in reason is not at all necessarily prior in time. See the World's Classics edition, 1931, 260-61.

3. Hobbes, *Leviathan,* (Oxford, 1955), ch. 18.

4. Cf. the distinction between the 'significant' and the 'professional' element in the work of Rawls. The distinction was made by Ronald Dworkin and is quoted by Norman Daniels (ed.), *Reading Rawls* (Oxford, 1975), xii.

5. Quoted in J. W. Gough, *The Social Contract* (Oxford, 1957), 64.

6. *Politics,* 1946, 120-21.

7. Thus F. A. Hayek who discusses the problem in terms of Social Justice, is emphatic that there is no rational way of distributing goods to individuals in a society. See *Law, Legislation and Liberty,* Vol. II (London, 1976), subtitled 'The Mirage of Social Justice'. For another view, see David Miller, *Social Justice* (Oxford, 1976).

8. See Marc Bloch, *Feudal Society* (London, 1961), ch. XI.

9. 'The tenure of kings and magistrates', *Selected Prose of John Milton* (Oxford, 1949), 336.

10. Ibid., 341.

11. See R. R. Palmer, *The Age of Democratic Revolution,* Vol. I (Princeton, 1961).

12. B. de Mandeville, *Fable of the Bees* (Harmondsworth, 1970), 371.

13. IV, 49-52.

14. For one treatment of this question, see E. Gellner, 'A social contract in search of an idiom: the demise of the Danegeld state?' *Political Quarterly,* 46, 1974: 127-52.

II Democracy and Consensus Today

7 Democracy and Self-determination

Elias Berg
University of Stockholm, Sweden

I. DEFINING DEMOCRACY

A. Criteria for a Definition of Democracy

There are certain general adequacy criteria that any definition should satisfy. Some of them are conceptual: a definition should be so inclusive that it does not exclude any of the things to be defined, and it should distinguish between the things to be defined and those left outside of the definition.[1] Others are terminological: a definition should not be incompatible with all the common usages in the field in which it is to be used. (This criterion does not prescribe that the definition be couched in terms of common usage, but only that it is not incompatible with the use of such terms.)

'Democracy' is a value-laden term. It is reasonable to assume that most people in today's world think of democracy as something valuable (if they bother to think of it at all). They do not regard it as the only value in social life, nor do they necessarily regard it as the highest value, which can never be circumscribed in favour of other values (nor need they regard it as intrinsically valuable). Yet, if the denotation of the

Author's Note: The present chapter is intended to be part of a more extensive study in democratic theory. It is based on my papers 'Democracy and self-determination', prepared for the ECPR annual meeting in 1976 (Louvain-la-Neuve, Belgium), and 'Democratic community', prepared for the ECPR annual meeting in 1977 (West Berlin); these papers have been re-written in the process of being merged. For criticism and suggestions on these papers, I am indebted to Jack Lively (Warwick), Lorentz Lyttkens (Stockholm), Hans Mathlein (Stockholm), Hans Oscarsson (Stockholm), Geraint Parry (Manchester), Kaj Sköldberg (Stockholm), Palle Svensson (Aarhus), Jan-Axel Swartling (Stockholm), and Björn Wittrock (Stockholm).

term democracy according to a given definition consisted wholly of things repugnant to these people, the definition would be incompatible with common usages. Now, a proposal for re-defining the value-laden term democracy may produce what has been called a 'persuasive definition', whose

> purport − is to alter the descriptive meaning of the term, usually by giving it greater precision within the boundaries of its customary vagueness; but the definition does *not* make any substantial change in the term's emotive [evaluative] meaning. And the definition is used, consciously or unconsciously, in an effort to secure, by this interplay between emotive and descriptive meaning, a redirection of people's attitudes.[2]

Yet democracy also seems to be what has been called an 'essentially contested concept', which is the subject of debate without any fixed terminal point,[3] and a definition of a term which stands for a concept[4] that is subject to constant revision could hardly avoid being 'persuasive'. Moreover, the solution of emerging social and/or scientific problems may call for successive re-definitions of terms, which may thus mark stages in conceptual development.[5] It should also be emphasised that a currently dominant definition, which fits best into the most widely spread usage, is no more politically neutral than is a deviant definition: while the latter may be 'radical', by questioning existing social arrangements, the former may be 'conservative', by tending to prevent the rise and dissemination of 'subversive' ideas.[6]

How, then, should we define democracy? What are the criteria for an adequate definition of democracy? I suggest the following four criteria of adequacy.

(1) There has been in the last decades a lively discussion about the concepts of 'power' and 'influence'. It seems obvious that this discussion is closely related to the discussion of democracy so that, in fact, the discussion of power and influence, on the one hand, and the discussion of democracy, on the other, are largely, if not wholly, overlapping. A definition of democracy should therefore enable us to link − conceptually and not merely empirically − the concept of democracy as used in theoretical discussions with the concepts of power and influence, as used in such discussions; I shall call this requirement the criterion of *theoretical adequacy*.

(2) There have also been in recent years a great many political actions and movements based on demands for a more equal sharing of power in society. Some of these actions and movements have originated

on the local level (in neighbourhoods or municipalities), in occupational organisations (for example trade unions), among university students, or within industrial plants ('industrial democracy'); others have focused on the national electoral and parliamentary levels. Yet individuals are 'whole' human beings, and one cannot, by compartmentalising them into different roles, make decisions in one role-area less important to them than decisions made in another. Actions and movements on local, organisational, academic or industrial levels are no less 'political', no less oriented toward democracy, than are such actions and movements that refer to national elections or parliaments. A definition of democracy should therefore enable us to link — conceptually and not merely empirically — the concept to demands by participants in actual conflicts over the distribution of power in society; I shall call this requirement the criterion of *political adequacy*.

(3) One important purpose of a definition of democracy is to enable us to compare the democratic character of different social institutions or groups; I shall call this requirement the criterion of *comparability adequacy*.

(4) Like other definitions, a definition must be compatible with at least one common usage in the field in which it is to be used. This means that it must be compatible with usage among participants in and/or discussants of conflicts over power distribution in society; I shall call this requirement the criterion of *parlance adequacy*.

B. Democracy as Popular Rule

(1) A Preliminary Definition

A natural point of departure for a definition of democracy is its meaning in Greek: popular rule. But this is no more than a point of departure: neither 'rule' nor 'popular' should be left unexamined. Moreover, it does not indicate what kind of definition we want, which brings us back to the above criteria of definition.

(2) Absolute or Relative Approach: Descriptive or Ideal-Type Definition?

There are two major ways of defining democracy. One is to specify certain characteristics of real-world phenomena (existing now, formerly and/or in the future); this is a descriptive definition. The other is to specify certain characteristics of a pure type; this is an ideal-type definition. One of the above criteria for defining democracy is comparability adequacy. Which of these two ways is, then, better suited to comparing different social institutions or groups from the point of view of democracy? If we use a descriptive definition, we shall end up with statements that a given set of social arrangements either is or is not a democracy. Such statements would often seem to presuppose rather arbitrary dividing lines between democratic and non-democratic social arrangements.[7] On the basis of ideal-type definitions, statements of comparison are couched in relative terms: one set of social arrangements is closer than another to an ideal type of democracy, i.e. the two sets are more or less democratic. Comparisons in relative terms appear to be less arbitrary than are comparisons in absolute terms.[8] Comparability adequacy thus suggests that we choose an ideal-type definition of democracy.

(3) Rule: Procedural or Substantive?

(a) 'Government by the People' vs. 'Government for the People'. Lincoln's famous phrase makes a distinction between 'government by the people' and 'government for the people' (for the expression 'government of the people', see below). The former is procedural and refers to how one decides, to forms of decision-making, while the latter is substantive and refers to what one decides, to the content of decisions. It is customary among political scientists[9] and among many non-socialists to define democracy in exclusively procedural terms, while socialists often include substantive elements in the definition.[10] Now, while it may seem more reasonable to interpret (popular) rule as a procedural concept, this interpretation must be qualified. In the first place, the substance (content) of decisions may — explicitly or implicitly, intentionally or unintentionally — include procedural matters. A decision may create (or abolish, or modify) a set of rules for decision-making. If this qualification is disregarded, one easily jumps to the conclusion that whatever is brought about by democratic decision-making must itself be democratic. Yet it is possible, for example, to abolish democracy by democratic decision-making (and, conversely, to introduce democracy by dictatorial fiat); similarly, the content of a decision to retain monarchy is not made democratic by the fact that it is supported by a majority. In the second place (and more importantly, since the previous qualification does not refer to genuinely substantive elements), a definition of democracy calls for some substantive specification of matters subject to popular rule.

(b) Popular Rule and Individual Self-Determination. The reason why a substantive specification is a necessary ingredient in a definition of democracy can be found in the meaning of popular rule. A 'people' consists of individuals, and popular rule thus implies rule by those individuals who are members of the people. In some sense popular rule must therefore be related to individual self-determination. As I shall try to show, self-determination necessarily includes a substantive element, which can be integrated with a procedural element into a consolidated concept of democracy (see below, section II). Such a substantive element refers to matters that are important to the individual.

(4) Two Dimensions of Popular Rule: Efficacy and Scope of Democracy

If we move from the individual level to the societal level, an individual's ability to control the making of decisions on matters that are important to him corresponds to a people's ability to control decision-making on matters that are important to its members. An individual's ability effectively to control the making of decisions (which will, in section II, be called 'self-choice') corresponds to the people's ability effectively to control decision-making; it corresponds to the *efficacy* of democracy. Similarly, the importance to the individual of matters subject to decision-making (which will, in section II, be called 'self-relevance') corresponds to the importance to the people of matters that are important to its members; it corresponds to the *scope* of democracy. Efficacy and scope can accordingly be seen as two dimensions of popular rule.

The introduction of the scope dimension thus implies letting substantive elements into the largely procedural concept of democracy. Of the above definitional criteria, the criterion of theoretical adequacy as well as the criterion of political adequacy seem to require a scope dimension: they both emphasise that it is the importance to the citizens, not the governmental character, of popular decision-making which should be the basis for judgements about degrees of democracy. Democracy, in other words, involves non-governmental as well as governmental decision-making; it is popular self-determination, not merely popular government.

(5) The Third Dimension of Popular Rule: Base of Democracy

(a) 'Government of the People'. Whatever Lincoln may have had in mind (if anything) when he used the expression 'government of the people', it could be interpreted as referring to the diffusion of governing, or ruling, among the citizenry. It would thus indicate a third dimension of popular rule.[11] This is the *base* of democracy, i.e. the spread of participation in decision-making among members of the people.

(b) Popular Rule: Majoritarian or Egalitarian? While the second part of 'popular rule' has been examined above, the meaning of the first part, popular, remains unclear. Popular refers to the base of democracy, but how do we judge the democratic quality of this base? There seem to be two possible approaches. One is by way of majority rule, i.e. to regard majority support for a society's decisions as sufficient evidence of a democratic base. The other approach is by way of equality, i.e. to estimate the approximation to an equal distribution of self-determination among the people and to use that the closeness of such approximation as a basis for assigning degrees of democracy. According to the former approach, it is, in principle, only the majority — however large — which counts, and (practically always) some members of 'the people' do not really belong to it: at least temporarily, perhaps permanently, some individuals are left outside of the membership. According to the latter approach, everybody is, in principle, a full member of 'the people'. To be sure, very young children cannot take part in ruling, but above some minimum age (and, possibly, some minimum mental capacity), everybody must be given an equal share in the ruling. While the majority principle is probably an inevitable decision technique, more enduring exclusion of some citizens from the rule (whether by formal regulations or simply as a matter of fact) is incompatible with democracy. Popular rule does not imply maximising the number of rulers but equal sharing in the rule.[12]

(6) The Unit of Application of Democracy

There is still something missing in our discussion of the definition of democracy. What does the term democracy denote, i.e. to what is it supposed to be applied? To a sewing circle? To a neighbourhood skating club? To a local church group? To a town? To a trade-union federation? To a political party? To a country? To a multi-national corporation? To the world? All these and innumerable others are candidates for being the unit of application of democracy.

According to the above discussion, democracy refers to some kind of collectivity of individuals. This collectivity forms the basis of common decision-making which, in turn, presupposes communication among the members of the collectivity and thereby some common language. (This language is not necessarily identical with the mother tongue of any of the members; cf. the use of English in India.) The collectivity thus constitutes (to some minimum degree) a common focus of attention, and it is therefore no mere categorical grouping, such as red-heads or 77-year-olds. The collectivity is also delimited from other collectivities by formal or informal rules of membership.

Such collectivities can be geographical or functional. The former are territorially based, for example nation-states or municipalities of various types. The latter are based on social positions (employers' organisations, trade unions, etc.) or on individual attitudes, whether they are oriented toward public or private, toward work-time or leisure activities (political parties, temperance associations, bridge clubs, etc.).

If democracy is to be 'applied' to a collectivity, it must be possible to attain a reasonable degree of approximation to the ideal of democracy within the confines of such a collectivity. The efficacy and base dimensions of democracy seem to permit a functional collectivity to be its unit of application: all its members can have equally efficacious control of decision-making in the collectivity. The scope dimension, however, appears to exclude this possibility. Since individuals are 'whole' human beings,[13] decision-making in many different fields is relevant to their lives and thus cannot be denied to them if they are to be self-determining. Consequently, self-determination presupposes a multifunctional collectivity. The unifying element of such a collectivity could conceivably be a complex 'super-function' that includes different sub-functions. Yet a super-functional collectivity would probably be geographically based. Among highly self-relevant decisions, many refer to the individual's residence[14] and thereby have an obviously spatial aspect. Furthermore, inter-individual communication very largely takes place among neighbours or among work-mates, and the great majority of persons with whom any one individual has regular contacts tend to live within the borders of that individual's own country. Democracy's unit of application should therefore be a geographical collectivity.

What, then, can we say about the size of the collectivity to which democracy is to be applied? The efficacy dimension indicates that such a collectivity be small, although modern techniques of telecommunication may have made this requirement somewhat less urgent. The base dimension does not seem to indicate any particular size of the collectivity: the members of a very small collectivity might be genuine equals, but above this mini-community level the number of members need not be related to a collectivity's approximation to equality of self-determination. The scope dimension, however, seems to suggest a numerically large collectivity in which many different interests could be satisfied. Moreover, in order to be able to bring about and/or maintain approximate equality of self-determination, a collectivity must be relatively independent of decisions made outside of its borders; it must be comparatively safe from intervention into its own affairs. While no geographical collectivity (not even the US or the Soviet Union) is completely sovereign, the alternatives − either a world of equally powerful geographical (or functional) sub-divisions or a single global community − are out of reach within the foreseeable future. In today's world, most of the decisions that are important to the average individual, as well as most of the decisions that he can realistically hope to influence, are made within the confines of the nation-state. We thus seem to be left with the nation-state as democracy's unit of application. Decision-making within this unit, however, takes place on many levels, nation-wide and sub-national (public or private), and is to some extent a conveyor of decisions on the super-national, cross-national (e.g. multinational-corporation) and international levels. On each of these levels decision-making contributes more or less to (or deducts from) the democratic character of the national system as a whole.

(7) Democracy Re-Defined

On the basis of the preceding discussion, we can now re-define *democracy* as an ideal type of national decision-making system whose members (above some minimum age level) enjoy equality of self-determination. This definition satisfies the criteria of theoretical and political adequacy as well as the criterion of comparability adequacy (see above). It also satisfies the criterion of parlance adequacy: it is compatible with one common usage (among several common usages) in theoretical and/or political discourse.

II SELF-DETERMINATION

A. The Meaning of Determination

The verb 'to determine' and its derivatives will here refer exclusively to relations between human beings. No doubt man-made things and natural phenomena and events always play a mediating part in such relations, but only in so far as both sides of them include human beings will these relations be regarded as examples of 'determination'. Since democracy is a decision-making system, determination will be discussed in terms of ability to affect decision-making. By *decision*, I mean a deliberate choice among two or more alternative actions or courses of action.[15] A 'course of action' may involve one or more decisions, and thus one decision may imply a choice of another decision (other decisions). To effect the making of a decision, i.e. to *determine* the decision, is to produce one or more empirical conditions of its occurrence. Such conditions may be necessary and/or sufficient or merely facilitating:

(1) If, and only if, a, then x.

(2) If, and only if, a and b, then x.

(3) If a or b, then x.

(4) If a and b or c and d, then x.

With respect to x, a is in sentence (1) a necessary and sufficient condition; in sentence (2) a necessary but not sufficient condition; in sentence (3) a sufficient but not necessary condition, and in sentence (4) a neither necessary nor sufficient but facilitating condition.

Now, any one individual's ability to determine decisions is limited. A single person can usually produce only facilitating conditions of even a decision made by himself alone: according to sentence (4) above, that person's contribution *(a)* in a given situation *(b)* could be replaced by another person's contribution *(c)* in another situation *(d)* without change of the resulting decision *(x)*. Furthermore, a collective decision (i.e. a decision made by more than one individual) does not necessarily conform to the intentions of any one of the participants in its making. In addition, while determination here refers to relations between human beings and to decision-making, a decision may be largely shaped by existing social structures. Finally, it is usually not any single decision but a whole *process of decision-making* involving a series of decisions that is important.

In a decision-making process several *stages* can be distinguished. After the *initial* stage, where the first decision is made, and one or several *intermediary* stages, given individuals are formally authorised, at the *authorising* stage, to carry out general decisions by more specific decisions at one or more *implementing* stages, including the *terminal* stage, immediately before the final action(s). Among these stages one or more may be *crucial*, i.e. may be stages where the controlling decisions are made. We cannot predict with certainty what stages will be crucial, and we may remain uncertain about that even after the completion of the decision-making process; the authorising stage may often be crucial, but prior commitments at the initial or intermediary stages and/or specifying decisions at the implementing stages can sometimes be more important than formal authorisation. Whenever a decision-making process includes an authorising stage − and in practice it would seem incomplete without one − the process must take place on two or more hierarchical *levels*: what is decided on a higher level is regarded by those on a lower level as a formally rule-based, normative premise of their own decision-making.

The number of stages varies greatly from one decision-making process to another. At the apex of the political hierarchy, for example, a foreign government may be recognised by a decision process involving only a few stages; similarly − nearer the base of the political hierarchy − decisions about a minor intra-plant labour-management issue may be made within a short span of stages. Nation-wide traffic regulation, on the other hand, or national health insurance, probably requires a far greater number of decision stages.

B. The Problem of Self-Determination

An individual's self-determination may be circumscribed in many different ways. He may be subjected to physical compulsion (for example by being dragged away from his house) or to negative or positive sanctions (threats of reprisals or promises of rewards). In addition to such, as it were, 'external' pressures, he may be exposed to subtler, 'internal' domination, which takes the form of shaping his general outlook. Such *perceptual distortion* may affect his view of himself and his basic values and thus create *false consciousness* (i.e. a distorted view of 'self'); it may also affect his view of the world, his factual and/or logical assumptions about ways to realise his value preferences, and thereby create *instrumental ignorance* (i.e. a distorted view of 'determination'). False consciousness and instrumental ignorance may result from *manipulation*, i.e. deliberate action by other individuals, and/or from *structural mystification*, i.e. from existing structural arrangements in the society (cf. Figure 1).

(Two comments should be made on this discussion of perceptual

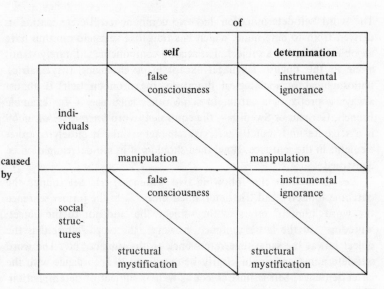

Figure 1

distortion. In the first place, a situation without any perceptual distortion is an ideal extreme, which can only be approximated in real life. In the second place, my discussion of perceptual distortion is incomplete, and the above figure therefore slightly misleading, since there may be cases of such distortion that are examples of neither manipulation nor structural mystification. False consciousness and/or instrumental ignorance may be due to real complexities in the problems and/or to intellectual deficiencies in the individuals that are faced with these problems. Perceptual distortion is relevant to self-determination only to the extent that it facilitates control of the self by other people, but it need not be the result of deliberate individual effort or of structural arrangements in society.)

While the establishment may cement its rule by distorting the common citizens' perceptions, opponents of the establishment may pretend to know these citizens' 'true' will and thus justify a claim to decide on the latter's behalf. In either case, their self-determination seems to fall by the wayside. How, then, can self-determination be re-defined so as to eliminate perceptual distortion?

C. The Reflexive Character of Self-Determination

The word 'self-determination' has two components. 'Determination' is derived from to determine, which is a transitive verb and can thus have an object as well as a subject. The second component 'self' rarely stands alone in the English language: except in psychological (psychiatric), philosophical or sociological literature, the pronoun 'self' is almost always a prefix or a suffix. In some other languages — for example French, German or Swedish — the equivalent word *(même, selbst, själv)* is a separate unit, but its reflexive character links it closely to other elements in the sentence. How, then should self in self-determination be construed?

Let us look at the following two sentences: 'He determined the outcome himself', and 'He determined himself'. In the former sentence the word 'himself' refers to the subject, 'he' and not to the object, 'outcome'. In the latter sentence, however, the word 'himself' is the object but at the same time refers back to the subject, 'he'. The word self-determination should clearly be construed in accordance with the latter sentence. Self is thus object as well as subject of determination. This may indicate a way to re-define self-determination.

D. Self as Subject of Determination: Self-Choice

(1) Conceptual Components of Self-Choice

Like determination, self-determination is defined here in terms of decision-making. An individual has *self-choice* to the extent that he makes or effectively participates in the making of decisions. Such deciding or effective participation presupposes that he has access to — i.e. he is able to decide or take part at — crucial decision stages; that he *actually decides or participates* at these stages, and that his deciding or participation has some *weight* in affecting the outcome of the decision-making. Deciding or participation does not necessarily imply physical presence: an individual can decide or participate by oral or written communication from a distance (telephone, telegraph, mail). Weight is measured in terms of a decider's or participant's ability to affect the content of decisions in accordance with his intentions.

(2) Some Empirical Conditions of Self-Choice

In order to identify the conditions of self-choice in the real world, we should focus our attention on the above three components: access, actual deciding or participation, and weight. In addition, certain background factors should be taken into account. The following conditions are vague, and some of them may overlap. The list is not necessarily exhaustive and the order of enumeration does not indicate priority. Yet, on the whole, self-choice is more likely to exist the more of these conditions are fulfilled. (It should be emphasised that the conditions refer to one given individual's self-choice and do not state anything about equality of self-choice or self-determination.)

A person, *P*, is likely to have self-choice if

Background:

1. *P* is legally protected against the use and threats of violence and blackmail as well as against different types of bribery.
2. *P* is economically well off. (The satisfaction of conditions 1 and 2 tends to prevent and/or make ineffective undue pressure on decision-making by way of threats or promises.)
3. *P* is well educated and well informed. (This tends to give him general knowledge and 'good judgement' as well as particular knowledge about the issues to be decided; it also helps him find out when and where decisions are to be made.) This presupposes that *P* is able to acquire information about matters that pertain to his decision-making. To the extent that such matters include the views of other individuals, their freedom of expression is also presupposed. (Since equality of self-choice is not discussed here, no further assumptions about general freedom of information are necessary.)
4. *P* has ample time to rest. (The satisfaction of this condition − as well as of condition 2 − tends to preserve *P*'s health and to prevent him from being exhausted and thereby increases his ability to decide or participate in decision-making.)
5. *P* has ample time for leisure. (*P*'s leisure enables him to increase his general and particular knowledge, which tends to produce the results indicated under condition 3 above; it also helps him establish contacts with, and to get support from, other individuals inside and outside of the decision-making group.)

Access:

6. *P* has access to authorising stages of decision-making.
7. *P* has access to a large number of initial, intermediary and implementing stages on different levels of decision-making.

Actual deciding or participation:
>   8. Deciding or participation in decision-making takes little (if any) time away from *P*'s leisure hours.

P believes that it makes a difference to him if one rather than another of the alternatives is chosen in a given decision and/or that the weight of his own contribution is considerable (see below, conditions 11-13), because he is well-informed (see above, condition 3) and because

>   9. The issue(s) to be decided is (are) closely related to *P*'s daily life (cf. below).
>   10. *P* derives immediate personal benefits from one particular decision outcome (which may, for example, increase his pay or improve his working conditions).[16]

Weight:
>   11. *P* has a large personal sphere of decision-making, which is legally protected from interference by others. (This tends to increase the number of *P*'s one-man decisions. While demands for such a personal sphere of decision-making may seem unrealistic in today's industrial world, the 'rights'-approach is not yet out-moded.[17])
>   12. Much of *P*'s participation in collective decision-making takes place in groups with a small number of members. (This tends, other things being equal, to increase *P*'s contribution to decision-making.)[18]
>   13. *P* possesses material (e.g. economic) and mental (e.g. prestige) resources to which other members of the decision-making group pay great attention when they take their stands on the issue(s) to be decided. (They may for example, be economically dependent on *P*. The fulfilment of condition 3 may also give *P* a reputation for general knowledge and 'good judgement'.)

E. Self as Object of Determination: Self-Relevance

(1) Conceptual Components of Self-Relevance

That a person himself (rather than somebody else) decides does not necessarily mean that his decision is significant to him. A state tax inspector, for example, may make a simple and uncontroversial decision about the tax assessment of another person whose life has no bearing whatsoever (except for the cursory acquaintance with his tax records) on his own. From the inspector's point of view, his decision is an expression of self-choice but not of self-relevance. Conversely, a decision may be significant to a person, even if it is made by somebody else. In the example just given, the inspector's decision is surely significant to the assessed person: from the latter's point of view it is self-relevant but not an expression of self-choice.

Self-relevance means relevance to the self as object. What is relevant to an individual is that which is important to himself. The definition of self-relevance must therefore somehow identify such important matters. A decision is *self-relevant* to the extent that it affects — positively or negatively — (a) the interests of and/or (b) the disinterested causes supported by the self.

(a) The above definition implies that interests are of importance to the self. If interests are defined in terms of expressed wants, anything which a person happens to want, at least if he wants it strongly, is his interest. This means that he cannot be mistaken about what his interests are (even though he may change his wants, and thereby his interests, from time to time). Since, as has been said above, any serious analysis of self-determination must come to grips with the problem of perceptual distortion, this way of defining that problem out of existence cannot be accepted. Instead, we must conceive of interests in a different manner and focus our attention on real (objective) and not on merely supposed (subjective) interests. An *interest*, then, is what is conducive to satisfying the needs of the self.[19] A *need* points out what is empirically necessary to the self, i.e. that without which the self either cannot exist at all or is somehow 'incomplete', not fully developed. Among such needs some are wholly or largely physiological or physical, and without some minimum satisfaction of these needs the self cannot exist at all:

(1) the need for nutrition (food and drink);
(2) the need for rest (sleep, relaxation);
(3) the need for protection from the climate (too cold or too hot);
(4) the need for sexual gratification;[20] and
(5) the need for bodily safety (absence of physical threats).

Once these needs have been (minimally) satisfied, the development of the self calls for the satisfaction of certain psychological needs, such as:

(6) the need for love;
(7) the need for self-esteem; and
(8) the need for self-actualisation.[21]

While the possession of means for satisfying these needs varies with social position, the needs themselves refer to persons ('whole' human beings), not to positions (roles). In another sense, however, needs are affected by the social context. The first five needs are in themselves largely independent of social arrangements, but the last three are in themselves socially determined, i.e. their underlying assumptions about a fully developed human being may not be accepted in all societies. Moreover, the particular form of any of these needs is certainly dependent on the society in which it is expressed.

Needs may be more or less satisfied. A person may, for example, be well fed but over-worked, i.e. one of his needs (1) is satisfied to a high degree, while another (2) is satisfied to a very low degree. More importantly, there may be conflicts in the satisfaction of needs. An individual's work may provide him with an income that covers far more than his expenses for food, clothing and housing, but it may at the same time severely circumscribe his creative abilities, conversely, a more creative kind of work may pay an income on or below the subsistence level. Satisfying one of this individual's needs (8) is thus incompatible with satisfying some of his other needs (1, 3, and perhaps others); he is exposed to a conflict among his own interests. In resolving such interest conflicts the individual himself is the sole arbiter.

The satisfaction of a need does not necessarily involve deliberately aiming at satisfying it. Quite often needs – in particular the last three – are satisfied in the process of trying to realise aims which are not oriented to the self at all. An individual may, for example, satisfy his need for self-actualisation (as well as his need for love and his need for self-esteem) by working for an altruistic cause, such as aid to political prisoners at home and/or abroad.

To be able to satisfy many of his needs (in particular 4, 6 and 7), an individual must count upon the health and friendly reactions of other people, whose interests are therefore to some extent also his own. The interests of members of one's immediate family, for example, are thus largely one's own interests, too. This can also be expressed by saying that a person's self is not wholly delimited by that person's physical body.

(b) The above definitions imply that any aim (in decision-making) which affects an individual's interests – whether positively or negatively (for example by being in conflict with them) – is relevant to him. (Self-relevance is thus not the same thing as self-satisfaction.) Yet relevant to an individual is not only what affects his interests but also what affects his *disinterested causes*. Such causes are those whose realisation he favours even when, and to the extent that, it is unrelated to his own interests. It should be emphasised that the present discussion is about what is 'relevant' to a person, not about what furthers his interests: even the negative effects on the latter are relevant to him. A person may, for example, consciously sacrifice one or more of his interests to promote a disinterested cause; in this case he has self-choice in making a decision that is relevant to him. It should also be emphasised that a cause is 'disinterested' if, and only if, it is in fact unrelated to his interests. This means that an individual may very well be mistaken about what his disinterested causes are. He may genuinely believe that the success of the cause he supports has no bearing on his interests, while in fact it does; in this case the cause is not disinterested. Conversely, he may support a cause in the belief that its success will further his interests, while in fact it has no effect on them at all, in this case the cause is disinterested. For a teetotaller, prohibition of the sale of alcoholic beverages may be a disinterested cause in this sense: provided that he favours prohibition for its own sake — and does not merely derive the satisfaction of certain psychological needs (8 and, perhaps 6 and/or 7) from working for it — its realisation does not necessarily have a bearing on his interests.

Self-relevance is thus defined largely in terms of interests, either (a) directly or (b) indirectly, by way of 'disinterest'. Now, no person is likely to be able to identify any significant number of another person's interests and, in any case, an individual must himself resolve conflicts and assign priorities among his own interests. Yet to some extent, *areas of interest* can be identified from the 'outside', i.e. without eliciting answers from (or reading the minds of) the people having the interests. On the assumption that people 'normally' (disregarding, for example, extreme masochists) have certain needs — in particular, but by no means only, the first five on the above list — an observer could, in principle, identify some of the areas of interest of another person.[22] A person's disinterested causes, on the other hand, would seem almost inaccessible to an outside observer. We thus arrive at a somewhat paradoxical conclusion: the relevance of an individual's immediately self-oriented aims can to some extent he established independently of his own expressions of preference, while the relevance of his more altruistic aims can only be established by himself. Interests accordingly constitute the conceptual and empirical core of self-relevance: they are conceptually dominant (by being present in both parts of the definition), and they are more easily amenable to empirical observation. By their largely residual and essentially 'subjective' character, disinterested causes (while genuinely relevant to the self) are far less important to democratic theory.

Demarcating areas of interest is likely to reduce perceptual distortion, in particular false consciousness: at least it tends to prevent the individual's attention from being diverted from his primary concerns. If the theoretical possibility of demarcating interest areas can be translated into practice a way will thus have been found to curtail manipulation and structural mystification. Such demarcation requires empirical criteria for recognising those areas.

(2) Some Empirical Criteria of Self-Relevance

In order to discover an individual's areas of interest we must ask where he satisfies his needs. The answer is fairly simple: an individual normally satisfies his needs where he earns his living and where he spends his daily life, i.e. in his work-place and in his home. In addition, any area where decisions affecting his personal security are made is relevant to him:

(1) Obviously relevant to an individual are decisions about his income and working conditions: amount of pay, form of remuneration (piece-rate; hourly, daily, weekly or monthly payment; profit from private business or farm; etc.), kind and organisation of work (manual or intellectual; individual or collective; degree of mechanisation or compartmentalisation; etc.), work time (working hours; leisure; vacations; etc.), etc.

(2) Likewise relevant to the individual are decisions affecting his residence: type and quality of living quarters (apartment or private house, in good or bad condition), type and quality of location (urban, suburban, country; slum or 'nice neighbourhood'; distance to shopping areas; etc.) etc.

(3) Furthermore, it can be safely assumed that the individual wants to preserve (or improve) his own health, which means that decisions about health care, for example about the costs and standards of medical treatment (doctors', dentists' and psychiatrists' fees, hospital bills, outlays for medicine, etc.) and — somewhat less directly — medical research, are relevant to him.

(4) Finally, an individual wants protection from physical violence, whether illegal (hooliganism), semi-legal (police brutality) or

legal (to which he may be exposed in the course of military combat service), and decisions affecting internal disorder or external war are therefore clearly relevant to him. (Such decisions are no less relevant to him if he wants to overthrow the existing 'law and order' and/or supports an 'enemy' country.) It should be borne in mind that an individual's areas of interest often do not coincide with areas of his own decision-making, which is merely another way of saying that self-relevance is not the same thing as self-choice.

F. Self-Determination Restated

Self-determination is a combination of self-choice and self-relevance. An individual has *self-determination* to the extent that he is not excluded from making decisions that are relevant to him and to the extent that he makes or effectively participates in the making of such decisions.

Several comments should be made about this definition. First, it implies that self-determination (like determination and self-choice) is actual exercise of an ability to decide, not only the possession of this ability. This makes self-determination more 'tangible', more easily amenable to observation. Since any one individual's self-determination can only be measured over a fairly long period of time, and since it is not limited to any particular area of decision-making, the risk of overlooking the importance of 'non-decisions'[23] does not seem to be very great.

Secondly, self-determination is a matter of degree: a person can have more or less of it. It is in fact doubly relative, since a person can have more or less self-choice by taking part in the making of decisions that are more or less relevant to him.

Thirdly, self-choice is a procedural concept, referring to how decisions are made, while self-relevance is a substantive concept, referring to what decisions are made. Since self-relevance as well as self-choice is included in the concept of self-determination, and since self-determination, in turn, is included in the concept of democracy, the latter concept contains – as has been pointed out above – a substantive element, too.

Fourthly, while self-determination thus includes a substantive element, it is not the same thing as self-satisfaction. One may be satisfied without having self-choice: other people's decisions may realise one's own aims. Conversely, that one decides what is relevant to one's self does not necessarily mean that one's decisions bring about the desired result: one may take care of one's business well or badly.

G. 'Negative' Liberty, 'Positive' Liberty, and Self-Determination

In a recent anthology on social work the meaning of self-determination has been illustrated by a study of the 'negative' and 'positive' concepts of liberty. The former is there said to be the absence of external restraints on an individual's activity, while the latter is said to be the individual's ability to develop his potentialities as a human being. According to that study, both concepts are liable to being misused but, historically, positive liberty has tended to give more support to efforts at manipulating individuals.[24]

There are certain differences between the two concepts of liberty and the 'subjective' and 'objective' components of self-determination. The definition of negative liberty often excludes participation in collective decision-making,[25] which makes it a narrower concept than self-choice. Positive liberty expresses more of a tendency to action than does self-relevance, which merely points to matters of importance to the self. Moreover, 'liberty' usually connotes the ability to decide rather than the actual making of decisions, while self-determination is here defined in terms of actual decision-making.

In spite of these differences there is a rough correspondence between negative liberty and self-choice and between positive liberty and self-relevance. As defined here, self-determination explicitly relates the elements of the two liberties to each other and integrates them into a new compound.[26] Self-determination also seems to obviate positive liberty's liability to manipulative misuse: fulfilling the hope expressed above, the definition eliminates perceptual distortion. While such definitional elimination cannot, of course, exclude perceptual distortion from the real world, the new 'purified' concept of self-determination is a better instrument for revealing its presence. Moreover, by indicating areas of interest, empirical criteria of relevance suggest ways of structuring decision-making so as to reduce the scope and effects of perceptual distortion. In this sense, self-determination gives some hints about construction sites for the building of democratic institutions.

III. SUMMARY AND CONCLUSIONS:
A RE-EXAMINATION OF DEMOCRACY

Starting from certain criteria of adequacy, we have defined democracy as an ideal type of national decision-making system whose members enjoy equality of self-determination have been analysed, and its reflexive character has been made the basis for subdividing it into the procedural element of self-choice and the substantive element of self-relevance. The meaning of each of these two concepts has been examined, and certain common-sense empirical conditions for realising self-choice and criteria for identifying self-relevance have been suggested.

A main purpose of the preceding analysis – as has been pointed out above – has been to integrate the substantive element of democracy with its procedural element into a consolidated whole. This integration has not taken the form of specifying substantive policies to be realised in decision-making: in a democracy, one cannot pretend to know the people's 'true' will before it has been expressed (see above, section II). Instead, the procedural element of decision-making has been combined with the substantive element of interest areas (delimited on the basis of certain assumptions about human needs), which indicate the subject-matter, but not the direction, of such decision-making.

Now, if we look only at democracy – and disregard other societal values (whose realisation we may conceivably sometimes regard as more important, in case of conflict, than the attainment of a very high degree of democracy) – can we see any political implications of the above analysis? The analysis is mainly conceptual, but it contains a number of empirical assumptions. Unless these are very wrong, one major political conclusion emerges. In order to provide the incentive and insight necessary for self-determination, *decision-making must be closely related to the citizen's daily life* (cf. empirical self-choice conditions 8-10 and empirical self-relevance criteria 1 and 2). This means that decisions about conditions within industrial plants, farms, business offices, public administration departments, etc. should be emphasised in the building of democratic institutions. Decisions at the work-place may therefore be important, but they are not necessarily crucial stages in decision-making processes: decisions on a lower level are often co-ordinated – and thereby usually altered – or set aside on a higher level. On the other hand, authorising stages are not always crucial either. Decision-making should be structured so as to avoid both merely passive ritualised participation at authorising stages and active participation in mere pseudo-control nearer terminal stages. While decisions *at* the work-place thus need not be very significant, decisions *about* the work place — or the home — (almost) always are.

Our analysis thus seems to call for a re-examination of democracy.[27] Instead of discussing it mainly in terms of traditional forms of parliamentary (or presidential) elections and legislative control of the national executive, we should start 'from below',[28] from the citizen's immediate daily experience, and discuss how lower levels of decision-making could be linked to higher levels without too much loss of 'immediacy'.

This interpretation implies that it is misleading to talk of 'direct democracy' *or* 'representative democracy': any reasonably close approximation to the ideal type of democracy necessarily contains both 'direct' *and* 'representative' elements.

Another implication is that the citizen's right to decide must not be stopped by private ownership of the means of production (if, indeed, such ownership is compatible with any significant approximation to equal self-determination). In addition, democracy requires vigorous debate of local and intra-organizational issues which, in turn, seems to indicate that campaigning and voting on such issues — and perhaps on national issues, too — should be conducted during paid time at the work place.

A discussion of the complicated questions raised by the above political implications[29] would take us far beyond the confines of the present chapter.

NOTES

1. For a discussion of such criteria, see Giovanni Sartori, 'Concept misformation in comparative politics', *The American Political Science Review,* 64, December, 1970: 1033-53.

2. Charles L. Stephenson, *Ethics and Language* (New Haven, [1944] 1947), 210.

3. W. B. Gallie, 'Essentially contested concepts', *Proceedings of the Aristotelian Society*, New Series, 56 (1955-56): 167-98; cf. Ernest Gellner, *Contemporary Thought and Politics* (London and Boston, 1974), 95-112.

4. Henceforth, the word 'define' and its derivatives will refer to concepts as well as to terms.

5. Cf. Quentin Skinner, 'Some problems in the analysis of political thought and action', *Political Theory*, 2, August, 1974: 277-303, in particular 294-99.

6. Cf. Åke Sandberg, *The Limits to Democratic Planning* (Stockholm, 1976), 200-1.

7. For a recent example of efforts at drawing such arbitrary dividing lines, see Leif Lewin, *Hur styrs facket?* (Stockholm, 1977), 177-80.

8. ' "Democracy" is a noun, but should be an adjective . . . And the most important thing to do is not to think of there being some one system which exemplifies true democracy, but rather to distinguish different aspects of each system, and consider which aspects are, and which are not, democratic.' J. R. Lucas, *Democracy and Participation* (Harmondsworth, 1976), 9.

9. For recent examples, see Nils Elvander, 'Dags för en seriös debatt om demokratins problem' and 'Vänstern vacklar i synen pa demokratin', in: Nils Elvander (ed.), *Socialism och demokrati* (Stockholm, 1975) 18-23 and 33-38, and Lewin, op. cit., 60, 229; cf. however, ibid., 203, 241-42, where a slightly more substantive view is suggested.

10. Cf. Bengt Abrahamsson, *Exemplet Jugoslavien* (Stockholm, 1976), 120.

11. For somewhat similar discussions of dimensions of democracy, see Alf Ross, *Hvorfor Demokrati?* (Copenhagen, 1946), 175-78, and Carl Cohen, *Democracy* (Athens, Georgia, 1971), 8-28. Cf. also Harold D. Lasswell and Abraham Kaplan, *Power and Society* (New Haven, 1950), 73.

12. Cf. Elias Berg, *Democracy and the Majority Principle* (Stockholm, 1965), 128-59. In my future study in democratic theory I plan to examine more elaborately the problem of equality of self-determination.

13. See the discussion of the criterion of political adequacy, above, section I.

14. See below, section II.

15. Cf. Harald Ofstad, *An Inquiry into the Freedom of Decision* (Oslo, 1961), 15-17.

16. Cf. the discussion of 'concern over the election outcome' and of 'sense of political efficacy' in Angus Campbell, Philip E. Converse, Warren E. Miller and Donald E. Stokes, *The American Voter* (New York, 1960), 103-5. Cf. also Mancur Olson, Jr, *The Logic of Collective Action* (New York, 1971), passim.

17. Cf. for example, Christian Bay, *The Structure of Freedom* (Stanford, 1958), 371-90, and D. D. Raphael (ed.), *Political Theory and the Rights of Man* (London, 1967), passim.

18. Cf. the discussion of the 'degree of exclusiveness of power', in: Malcolm Hamilton, 'An analysis and typology of social power', Part I, *Philosophy of the Social Sciences*, Vol. 6 (1976), 312.

19. In his article, 'On "interests" in Politics', in: Ira Katznelson, Gordon Adams, Philip Brenner and Alan Wolfe (eds.), *The Politics & Society Reader* (New York, 1974), 259-77, William Connolly rejects the definition of 'interest' in terms of needs (ibid., pp. 268-71). His own definition is: 'Policy x is more in A's interest than policy y if A, were he to experience the results of both x and y, would

choose x as the result he would rather have for himself' (ibid., p. 272; italics omitted). This definition seems to be empty – we have no idea *what A* would choose – until it is given some empirical content. When Connolly subsequently appears to give a (negative) hint about the nature of such content, he at the same time seems to presuppose certain assumptions about human needs: 'any current choice the implications of which deeply impair one's capacity to make future choices – such as the agreement to accept enslavement – always weighs heavily against one's interests', and 'reflection about interest-regarding choices is part of the process of deliberation into what it means to be a person' (ibid., pp. 274-75).

20. It may or may not be true that sexual needs, instead of being satisfied, can be 'sublimated' into cultural or religious activities (cf. the celibacy rules in the Catholic church).

21. Needs 5-8 are taken from Stanley Allen Renshon, *Psychological Needs and Political Behavior* (New York, 1974) 65, 73. The list of needs given here should be regarded as exemplifying rather than definitive and exhaustive. While the substitution and/or addition of other needs would to some extent affect the empirical content of self-relevance, the latter's need-oriented character would remain.

22. Cf. Lucas, op. cit., 87-88, 92, 106-7.

23. See, for example, Peter Bachrach and Morton S. Baratz, 'Two faces of Power', *The American Political Science Review,* 56, December, 1962: 947-52, and 'Decisions and nondecisions', ibid., 57, September, 1963: 632-42. See also many other discussions of this issue, for example by Richard M. Merelman, ibid., 62, June, 1968: 451-60; Raymond E. Wolfinger, ibid., 65, December, 1971: 1063-80 and 1102-4; Frederick W. Frey, ibid., 65, December, 1971: 1081-1101; Geoffrey Debnam, ibid., 69, September, 1975: 889-99 and 905-7; Peter Bachrach and Morton S. Baratz, ibid., 69, September, 1975: 900-4.

24. Isaiah Berlin, 'Two concepts of liberty', as reprinted in F. E. McDermott (ed.), *Self-Determination in Social Work* (London and Boston, 1975), 141-53. Cf. the critical analysis of this study in C. B. Macpherson, *Democratic Theory* (Oxford, 1973), 95-119.

25. Cf. ibid., p. 109.

26. For a somewhat different way of integrating these elements, see ibid., 118-19; cf. ibid., pp. 41-42.

27. For examples of such re-examination, see Peter Bachrach, *The Theory of Democratic Elitism* (Boston, 1967); Macpherson, op. cit.; Kenneth A. Megill, *The New Democratic Theory* (New York, 1970); Carole Pateman, *Participation and Democratic Theory* (Cambridge, 1970); Anton Pelinka, *Dynamische Demokratie* (Stuttgart, 1974).

28. Cf. Sandberg, op. cit., 287-317.

29. Cf. Geraint Parry (ed.), *Participation in Politics* (Manchester, 1972), passim, and Ulrich von Alemann (ed.), *Partizipation – Demokratisierung – Mitbestimmung* (Opladen, 1975), passim.

8 Consensus and Depoliticisation in Contemporary Political Theory

Pierre Birnbaum
University of Paris I, France

During the sixties a number of writers emphasised the emergence over the second half of the twentieth century of political models which in one way or another diverged considerably from classical models of democracy.[1] The latter rested on a deep confidence in man and asserted the specifically political character of human nature: political power should in consequence spring from the choice of citizens themselves. From this point of view, and despite profound differences in other aspects,[2] theories of direct democracy (Rousseau) agreed with those of representative democracy (Bentham, Locke, etc.) in affirming the necessity of the participation of citizens in the government of their society.[3] Since man was considered as a rational being, educational development should facilitate his participation in the political life of the community.

However, in the decade following the Second World War, extensive research into electoral sociology and studies of political behaviour revealed generally the existence of fairly extensive depoliticisation affecting American society most particularly. These findings led a considerable number of writers to reconsider the political vocation of man, asserting at the same time that the stability and smooth functioning of a democratic system would be the better assured, the less citizens, only slightly affected in the aggregate by politics, participated in the direction of communal affairs (Berelson, Dahl, McClosky, Stouffer, etc.). Such a depoliticisation, empirically established and accepted as empirical reality, led to a notion of consensus through apathy that differed radically from the classical theory of 'consent': henceforward dependent more on mechanisms of social control, consensus takes on a strong ideological colouring which strengthens the status quo and forestalls questioning. This chapter attempts to show how, in most of the dominant models of contemporary political theory, there can be found, stated overtly or implied covertly, a profoundly biased conception of consensus which is based on the one side on the political apathy of citizens and on the other on the supposed competence and expertise of their rulers.

THE DEPOLITICISATION OF CITIZENS

Besides the present empirical actuality of the depoliticisation of citizens, the theory of consensus through apathy and the absence of political convictions results from the use of organicist analogies and, at the present time, from the 'rediscovery' of primary groups and communal forms of social organisation. These are important features, for example, of the models of Talcott Parsons, David Easton or still more, Robert Dahl.

From Organicist Analogies to Primary Groups

Without dwelling at great length on the point, it can be said that, since the nineteenth century, organicist theories such as those propounded by De Bonald and De Maistre have confronted and opposed the political individualism born of the French Revolution which endangered the natural organisation of society. For these writers, just as for August Comte, the whole possesses a specific nature; it follows its own laws fixed for all eternity, each of its parts performing a particular function. On this questionable basis, consensus becomes identified with the simple functioning of the whole: it is stripped of any rational character and seems to be indistinguishable from nature itself.

Society is thus no longer built on an agreement about rules and values, it is a given. In this sense, De Bonald can claim, 'Our misfortune is to have wished to constitute society with the metaphysic of men of imagination'.[4] In the same way, De Maistre remarks that 'the more human reason trusts itself and seeks to derive all its resources from itself, the more absurd it becomes and demonstrates its powerlessness. This is why the world's greatest scourge has always been, in every age, what is called philosophy.'[5]

The authorities now being supposed to speak for the whole, they will identify themselves with their functions and consequently will not exercise any power. The division of labour and the functional allocation of powers will thus sustain a natural organisation of society requiring no rational participation of citizens. In a way, organicist metaphors exclude the very notion of consensus.

In our own day, it will be held here, the movement towards the 'rediscovery' of primary groups also arises from an apolitical conception of society which serves only to buttress the idea of a natural harmony at the expense of a rationally elaborated consensus. Just as previously the biological analogy, with its elaboration by the proponents of absolute organicism, undermined the notion of consensus based on reason, so the primary group as 'a fusion of individualities in a common whole', that is to say 'a we',[6] seems to give rise to a society that emerges through aggregation and remains indifferent to great metaphysical and philosophic questions, such as the idea of legitimacy or still more the concept of popular sovereignty, since it does not presuppose a rational commitment of citizens to principles which could govern social life.

Fears about the disappearance of primary groups in an industrialised and urbanised society, dissolving social links and atomising social relations, could be countered, and the inadequacy of the concept of mass society[7] demonstrated, by revealing the permanence of those primary groups. Their survival[8] at once strengthened the communal character of society and made less plausible the ideological extremes apparently so inescapable in a mass society. The rediscovery of primary groups allows in this way the exclusion of certain kinds of conflict and most especially those which might encourage class conflict.

This is clearly demonstrated by the way in which Elton Mayo and his colleagues interpret the solidarity which they consider purely affective and which seems to develop spontaneously in the work group of Western Electric. According to Mayo, this solidarity 'depended for its perpetuation upon the evolution of a nonlogical social code'[9] and shows no 'political' character;[10] these workers 'constitute a group within which individuals have developed routines of relationship to each other',[11] impervious to changes in the social policies of management. Harmony is thus linked to technological proximity arising from the division of labour and creative of common social norms; it is not the product of conscious reflection taking as its base the social identity of workers and so leading to a specific consensus. In parallel, Shils and Janowitz emphasise the lack of political concern amongst the vast majority of German soldiers in the Third Reich; integrated in their primary group, these soldiers became indifferent to any preoccupation of an ideological nature. According to these authors, the unity of the German army was to only a small extent maintained by the Nazi convictions of its members. Essentially it was the regular satisfaction of certain elementary personality needs which motivated the high morale of the German soldier.[12] So, once again, affectivity replaces reason. The classical studies of Lazarsfeld and his associates can be cited as further evidence. They too show the absence of rational determination of citizens, integrated in their primary group and voting more for their group than as a result of a rational choice. Again, the affective and quasi-biological dimension is decisive, and consensus is reduced to pure and simple affectivity.[13]

Many other works could be cited all ending in similar conclusions; mention may be made of the research of Almond and Verba and that of Eckstein which present us with a model of democracy based on a communal civic culture, 'parochial' and integrated, which allows little room for rational choice.[14] Very significantly, in these theories from those of De Bonald and De Maistre to those of Shils and Janowitz, Almond and Verba, Lazarsfeld, Mayo and Eckstein, natural and affective consensus goes hand in hand with the disappearance of conflict and power, the signs of rupture and dissension. A similar problematic has exercised a considerable influence on an important part of contemporary political theory.

Political Apathy in Parsons, Easton and Dahl

The general orientation of the Parsonian model relies on the very classical notion of 'support' because in the end it is that which secures the application of the principle formulated by T. H. Marshall, 'one man, one vote', which Parsons uses to resolve the equality-inequality contradiction. For him, those holding positions of authority and power are able to legitimise this inequality by invoking the elective principle thanks to which they occupy these positions.[15] Election must be able to secure the solidarity of all members of the political system, strengthening adherence to collective norms and consequently the stability of the legitimate order;[16] so, for Parsons, 'voting is an exercise of power'.[17] Emanating from citizens, the power of those in authority rests on their 'trust'; consequently they feel obliged to fulfil their legitimate obligations by conforming to the wishes of citizens.

Put in this way, Parsons' theory seems like a simple illustration of the classical model of representative democracy; decisions taken by rulers are always affixed with the seal of legitimacy and consensus appears to be secured by being grounded in rational consent. However, in a fundamental article 'Voting and the equilibrium of the American political system', since he is concerned with American society itself and abandons at the same time his purely normative preoccupations, Parsons moves completely away from the classical model, which has just been evoked, by adopting the theses defended by the Lazarsfeld team. As has just been mentioned, Lazarsfeld and his associates give a decisive role to primary groups in the determination of the electoral choice of citizens. Consequently, the vote reflects rather group values than the more or less rational adherence of the citizen to a vision of the real world. Parsons declares himself 'impressed' by this discovery which accounts for integration and stability.[18] Now, the analyses of *Voting* run counter to Parsons' normative model; by accepting their conclusions, Parsons modifies radically his general model to the extent that rulers can no longer take advantage of the 'trust' which citizens might rationally place in them. Since primary groups are organic quasi-groups very little concerned with politics, the whole classical thesis of consensus is, in consequence, brought into question at the very centre of the Parsonian model.[19]

If we turn to the works of Robert Dahl, we can again see there that political apathy plays an essential role in the elaboration of a general model of democracy. His thesis is well known; it centres on his presentation of the polyarchic model, the nearest approximation to democracy, that is 'a system of decision-making in which leaders are more or less responsible to the preferences of non-leaders' and which 'does seem to operate with a relatively low level of citizen participation'.[20] Abandoning in this way both classical models of direct democracy and those of representative democracy, Dahl goes so far as to main that 'by their propensity for political passivity the poor and uneducated disfranchise themselves'.[21] Rather than holding to the basically rational character of man and asking himself why political apathy should now be prevalent, Dahl claims that 'it would clear the air of a good deal of cant' if we abandoned the assumption 'that politics is a normal and natural concern of human beings'.[22] Consequently, it is not surprising for him that family and professional life should so commonly divert Americans from politics.[23]

As he too acknowledges the essential role of primary groups,[24] Dahl reaches the same conclusion as Parsons — and uses the same language — that elections are 'a ritual'.[25] The apolitical consensus to which Dahl's argument leads thus prompts him to pour scorn on 'the dogma that democracy would not work if citizens were not concerned with public affairs'.[26] This illustrates the degree to which classical theories of consensus have been degraded.[27]

Political conflict, therefore, no longer stands at the 'centre' of the political system.[28] Harmony through apathy and the absence of all controversy in the end strengthens the existing power structure which benefits from the various processes of socialisation and internalisation of values: in a society such as that Dahl describes, it is difficult to perceive the means by which citizens might participate rationally in the governance of their community.

In conclusion it should be noticed briefly that organicist metaphors together with the general systems theory and cybernetics which draw inspiration from them, whatever David Easton and Karl Deutsch may say, leads them to favour the whole at the expense of the parts, justifying in this way a supposedly natural and harmonious functioning of a political system directed by authorities themselves acting in a functional manner. It is understandable that for Deutsch this new political theory has nothing in common with 'political ideologies and philosophies'![29] The application of the science of servo-mechanics in fact, in the last resort, makes the rational participation of citizens useless: the system can manage to function without them. Communication replaces rational consensus. But, since social structures nonetheless persist, the process of communication involves different sections of the population very unequally. This is recognised by David Easton himself when, in the last edition of *The Political System*, referring explicitly to the work of Bachrach and Baratz, he admits that non-decisions thrust into 'political silence' those social groups who have not the ear of the authorities.[30] Paradoxically, Easton agrees that

> class, status or caste differences between authorities and sections of the membership may give birth to divergent psychological sets characterised by different ideological, ethical and perceptual predispositions. Authorities may be relatively incapable of becoming aware of and responsive to cues fed back from members other than those who resemble their own class, status or caste categories or with whom they identify.[31]

Here Easton shows himself as one of the few theorists who recognise the limits of systems analysis: all the same he does not modify his general model. Again, we are very far from participatory democracy.

KNOWLEDGE, THE PROFESSIONALISATION OF POLITICS AND POWER

Organisational Theory and Professionalisation

Sheldon Wolin was the first to remark how far the age of organisation has led to the 'sublimation of politics'.[32] For Saint-Simon as for August Comte, organic philosophy was certainly about to succeed critical philosophy and to be clearly embodied in the positivist structuring of social organisation. So knowledge would necessarily open the way for the suppression of metaphysical errors; it rendered politics itself almost useless. The organicist metaphors of De Maistre and De Bonald already mentioned were now reconciled with science and industrial progress in joint opposition to every ideology and political practice which might make dysfunctional the good administration of the social whole. Once again, consensus is linked to the technological necessities of the division of labour: in consequence, the kind of opposition to such an organisation which is, from the nineteenth century on, to be found in most social theories was to be regarded as an intolerable expression of dissent. We can recognise the truth of Wolin's claim that the science of organised systems was to lead to the exclusion of great political debates concerning the principles on which citizens should reach agreement.

An attempt will now be made to show how, in organisational theory, the idea of competence tends to act against the idea of universal participation, at the same time perverting the notion of consensus. The principle of the allocation of functions according to competence is in fact subscribed to as much by organisational theory (the rational basis of bureaucracy) as by those who insist on the growing importance of professionalisation in modern industrial societies. The theory of professionalisation is linked to organisational models which are based, in Max Weber's phrase, on the progressive rationalisation of the world. Attached to their duties, actors are supposed to identify themselves with them and to act according to universalist and not particularist criteria, their competence, guaranteed by educational qualifications, ensuring an impartial exercise of their responsibilities favourable to collective interests. A rational utilisation of skills results in the neutrality of those in authority and consequently strengthens their legitimacy: according to Parsons, 'the professional complex has already not only come into prominence but has even begun to dominate the contemporary scene in such a way as to render obsolescent the primacy of the old issues of political authoritarianism and capitalistic exploitation'.[33]

This theory of professionalisation has already been subjected to numerous criticisms;[34] the important point here is that it contradicts the classical theory of democracy, emptying of all significance any recourse to a universal suffrage, for example. This is very clear if we turn to the notion of professionalisation put forward by Schumpeter. This notion leads him to construct a new model of democracy in which functional elites struggle for power. According to Schumpeter, 'personal success in politics . . . will imply concentration of the professional kind';[35] in modern societies, in his view, the citizen 'becomes a primitive again' once he leaves a personal sphere and becomes involved in political problems: 'in modern democracies of any type other than the Swiss, politics will unavoidably be a career'.[36] If politics becomes 'a career', it is clear that citizens can no longer participate in the direction of their own affairs. In the final analysis, professionalisation founded on knowledge monopolised by the elites undermines, in the models of Parsons, Easton and Dahl, the notion of consensus.

Professionalisation, the Power of Elites and Consensus

In his 'mature' writings, Parsons offers us a definition of power that excludes any conflictual or hierarchical dimension. Modifying the theses defended in *The Structure of Social Action*, Parsons now puts the emphasis on the collective ends which power realises by acting in the name of the whole society and not in terms of a particular social group only.[37] Power therefore becomes functional and tends to become identified henceforward solely with rationally exercised authority: according to Parsons, 'while in earlier civilizations, political responsibility has tended to be institutionalized in the hands of general upper classes or aristocracies, in modern Western society, at least the trend has been in the direction of its coming into the hands of groups with more or less of an occupational character, e.g. politicians and civil and military servants.'[38] Possessed of considerable skill and specialised know-how, the professionals will conform, in Parsons' view, to the ethic of responsibility (Weber) in order to realise collective ends.

By legitimising the work of the professionals, knowledge can only at the same time strengthen the depoliticisation of citizens, who take on the character of amateurs.[39] Inevitably the contradiction is posed between equality and the rights to authority of the skilled few. For Parsons, education justifies these necessary inequalities from a functional point of view. He thus admits that the 'gap difference' makes the idea of self-government,[40] like that of elective democracy, inapplicable to large industrial enterprises as inimical to efficiency. Parsons stands by the elective principle only in the political domain since he continues to appeal to classical models of democracy and to the principles posed by T. H. Marshall.[41] Yet, starting from the problem posed by Parsons, it is difficult to see the reason why the ideas of competence and professionalisation should be inapplicable to politics which would, it follows, be the only sphere left to election and so to inefficiency. If Parsons were ready to follow his reasoning through to the end, he would have to revive the question of the elective principle in the political sphere since, in the name of efficiency, he refuses to apply it to industry. Willy-nilly, Parsons' argument moves away from classical models of democracy because it renders illusory citizen participation.

David Easton's political system is also governed by authorities who should be skilled and act in terms of universal and legitimate norms. According to Easton, 'the professionalisation of political roles'[42] is the straightforward consequence of a minimal division of political labour. For him, 'the capacity for the performance of political tasks is assured by some minimal differentiation of political from other social roles . . .. Where there is no specialization of political roles at all, as compared to general social roles, the capacity of a system for handling political matters is quite restricted. The need to feed, house and clothe the members of a society imposes firm and inescapable limits on the time that can be devoted to politics.'[43] So Easton, in his turn, accepts as inescapable the professionalisation of political authorities who perform their duties at the expense of the participation of amateurish and depoliticised citizens. However, continual insistence on the idea of competence necessarily, as Easton himself admits, draws us away from 'a discussion of the way in which the political pie is cut and how it happened to get cut in one way rather than another'.[44] This is tantamount to claiming that citizens should rely on the competence of the authorities and not question the power structure itself, which is the basic determinant of the particular organisation of the system. Once again, those essential questions that ought to concern citizens are nonetheless seen as beyond their competence. In this situation, professionalisation very often appears as an ideology justifying a power whose strength derives from resources other than competence. To the degree that such questions are not raised in public debate, knowledge and competence serve as alibis which hide a particular power structure: the role given to them can again only lead to a false consensus.

The theme of the professionalisation of rulers plays an equally important part in the model offered by Robert Dahl; indeed, he stresses that 'the members of the political stratum are the main bearers of political skills'.[45] For these professionals, politics is consequently a 'career', a 'vocation'.[46] Like Weber, Schumpeter, Parsons and Easton, Dahl holds that expertise and professional know-how give rise to a specific power exercised in a technical manner and according to legitimate norms. However, in the same way as Easton, Dahl shows himself aware of the fact that political professionals most often restrict themselves to anticipating the 'expected' desires of business leaders, who thereby possess a power of indirect control.[47]

The latter can moreover rely on a consensus largely favourable to them, shaped as it is by an educational system and a press preaching a credo that wholly legitimises their power.[48] Again, the notion of professionalism and purely neutral action in political leaders loses all meaning since, in reality, they bend to the desires of business whose power is justified by universally held values internalised by various integrative mechanisms. Finally, on Dahl's own admission, there exists in New Haven no consensus founded on the rational participation of citizens.

In the models of Parsons, Easton and Dahl, an empirically established political apathy is explained by the survival of primary groups and of communal or organic forms of social organisation: this depoliticisation, contrary to classical models of democracy, is then accepted and justified by the assertion of the inevitable character of the division of labour which requires entrusting the regulation of the social system to professionals who will exercise this power in a neutral and legitimate fashion. The political apathy of citizens devoted to their private life, the professionalisation of elites accepting as their duty the organisation of the social system, these should be the bases of a new consensus which is quite compatible with the absence of citizen participation.[49] But this consensus, already unacceptable from the point of view of classical theories of democracy, loses all reality once the permanence of the structures of domination and cultural hegemony are recognised. As

Parsons, Easton and Dahl themselves paradoxically admit, still today knowledge cannot claim to be used as the basis of a new legitimacy in contemporary societies: it should not then be used as the basis for a new type of consensus.

NOTES

1. See, for example, C. McCoy and J. Playford (eds.) *Apolitical Politics* (New York, 1967). P. Bachrach *The Theory of Democratic Elitism* (Boston, 1967).

2. Carole Pateman stresses these differences in *Participation and Democractic Theory* (Cambridge, 1970) 18-32. A. Ryan lays stress on the particular position of J. S. Mill who can be situated in both of these traditions: *J. S. Mill* (London, 1974) 215-17.

3. See G. Parry, 'The idea of political participation', in: G. Parry (ed.) *Participation in Politics* (Manchester, 1972).

4. De Bonald, *Essai analytique sur les lois naturelles de l'ordre social* (Paris, 1800), 19-20.

5. De Maistre, *Etudes sur la souveraineté*, Oeuvres complètes (Lyon, 1884), t.i, 357-8. See Judith Schlanger, *Les métaphores de l'organisme* (Paris, 1971).

6. Charles Cooley, *Social Organization* (New York, 1962), 23.

7. William Kornhauser, *The Politics of Mass Society* (London, 1965).

8. Edward Shils, 'The study of the primary group', in: H. Lasswell and Daniel Lerner (eds.) *The Policy Sciences in the United States* (California, 1951).

9. E. Mayo, *The Human Problems of an Industrial Society* (New York, 1966), 116.

10. Ibid., 174.

11. Ibid., 111.

12. E. Shils and M. Janowitz, 'Cohesion and distintegration in the Wehrmacht in World War II, in: *Public Opinion Quarterly*, 12, 1948: 280.

13. E. Katz and P. Lazarsfeld, *Personal Influence*, (Glencoe, 1955).

14. G. Almond and S. Verba, *The Civic Culture* (Boston, 1965), 17, 339. H. Eckstein, *Division and Cohesion in Democracy* (New Jersey, 1966).

15. T. Parsons, 'Equality and inequality in modern society', *Sociological Inquiry*, Summer 1970: 27.

16. T. Parsons, 'On the concept of political power', in: *Politics and Social Structure* (Glencoe, 1969), 378-79.

17. T. Parsons, 'The political aspects of social structure and process', in *Politics and Social Structure*, 337.

18. T. Parsons, 'Voting and the equilibrium of the American political system', in: *Politics and Social Structure*, 233.

19. In a recent article, Thomas Lewis fails to notice this fundamental change that separates Parsons from the classical model of democracy with which Lewis connects him. See 'Parsons' and Easton's analyses of the support system', *Revue Canadienne de Science Politique*, January 1975: 682.

20. R. Dahl, 'Hierarchy, democracy and bargaining in politics and economics', in: H. Eulau (ed.) *Political Behaviour,* (Glencoe, 1956), 87.

21. R. Dahl, *A Preface to democratic Theory* (Chicago, 1956), 81.

22. R. Dahl, *Who Governs?* (New Haven, 1961), 279.

23. Ibid., 71, 279.

24. Ibid., 323.

25. Ibid., 108, 159.

26. Ibid., 280. See also R. Dahl, *Modern Political Analysis* (New Jersey, 1970), 58-59; *Polyarchy* (New Haven, 1971), 203.

27. P. H. Partridge, *Consent and Consensus*, (London, 1971), 32-33.

28. E. Shils, *Le Consensus*, Association Internationale de Science Politique. 7è Congrès (1967), 13.

29. K. Deutsch, *The Nerves of Government* (New York, 1966), 26.

30. D. Easton, *The Political System* (New York, 1971), 373.

31. D. Easton, *A Systems Analysis of Political Life* (New York, 1965), 438.

32. S. Wolin, *Politics and Vision* (Boston, 1960), 352.

33. T. Parsons, 'Professions', in: *International Encyclopedia of the Social Sciences*, Vol. 12 (Macmillan, 1968), 546.

34. See, for example, D. Rueschemeyer 'Doctors and lawyers: a comment on the theory of the professions', *Canadian Review of Sociology and Anthropology*, February 1964; and T. Johnson, *Professions and Power* (London, 1972), ch. 2.

35. J. Schumpeter, *Capitalism, Socialism and Democracy* (New York, 1956), 285.

36. Ibid.

37. T. Parsons, 'On the concept of political power', op. cit., 361.

38. T. Parsons, 'Authority, legitimation and political action', in: *Structure and Process in Modern Society,* Glencoe, 1960), 184.

39. Jürgen Habermas has examined the contribution of Weber and Parsons to this 'ideology' which constitutes, in his eyes, technocracy and the faith in science. *La Technique et la science comme 'ideologie'* (Paris, 1973).

40. T. Parsons, 'Equality and inequality in modern society: or social stratification revisited', *Sociological Inquiry*, Summer 1970: 38.

41. Ibid., 27.

42. D. Easton, *A Systems Analysis of Political Life*, 127.

43. Ibid., 124.

44. Ibid., 475.

45. R. Dahl, *Who Governs?* , 90.

46. Ibid., 305-6.

47. Ibid., 137.

48. Ibid., 84, 257, 316-17.

49. See Pierre Birnbaum, *La fin du politique* (Paris, 1975).

9 Pluralism and Consensus

Jack Lively
University of Warwick, UK

CONFLICT AND CONSENSUS IN CONTEMPORARY THEORY

Consensus, so often taken as a desirable objective in politics and as a means of explaining the unity of the body politic, has declined in both its normative and its descriptive appeal. Holding once a prominent position both in high theory and in ordinary political discourse, concepts such as the general will and popular sovereignty have degenerated into clichés of the more tired political rhetoric. Most dominant political perspectives now lay a contrary stress on conflict and competition. This is no less true of pluralism than of Marxism. If Marxist theory presses the centrality of class conflict and the determination of state structures by such social confrontation, so too does pluralism, at least in its contemporary forms, accept the ubiquity of social division and the necessary reflection of that division in political alignments and arrangements. It differs from Marxism, of course, in making a virtue of those necessities. It asserts as a happy achievement of a pluralist system that it facilitates an adequate and accurate representation in the political sphere of social, economic, ideological and cultural cleavages.

Yet the banishment of consensus from political theory is by no means either total or unequivocal. In Marxism the banishment is for a fixed term, and consensus is talked of in the future perfect rather than the present or the past imperfect tenses. Once a truly universal 'universal class' has emerged, consensual agreement, hitherto either impossible or possible only through a widespread false consciousness, will become a reality, and political conflict, in its historical form, will wither away. In no less decisive a manner, pluralist theory has to resort to notions of consensus; and it is led to do so primarily in order to bring some coherence to its theory of the state. In the pluralist scheme of things the political system should ideally both represent the divisions within society and resolve those differences. It is, I shall argue, in order to sustain this second requirement that pluralist theory is forced back on the notion of consensus. It is only by appealing to this notion that its implicit or explicit portrayal of the role of the state — the impartial adjudication between or compromise of group claims — can be rendered convincing.

MONISM, ANARCHISM AND PLURALISM

Since the emergence in the sixteenth century of the nation-state in anything recognisably like its modern form, political thinking has been dominated by the problem of defining the extent of central state power. For the most part, the problem has been tackled either by seeking the justification, and thus by inference the extent, of state power or by determining the countervailing rights of individuals and groups. In the first enterprise the justification has increasingly been posed in secular and instrumental terms as the resolution of social conflict. This view that the prime role of the state is to establish and maintain social coherence amongst individuals and groups in some sense naturally in conflict has had its rivals — that the state should promote the greater glory of God, or the progress of humanity, or the moralising of individuals, or the realisation of the Rational in history, and so on — but it has nonetheless dominated in modern theories of state.

Three paradigmatic responses to this interrelated problem of the extent of power and its justification in terms of conflict-resolution may be distinguished: monism, anarchism and pluralism. At the heart of the monist response is the belief that social coherence is vitally if not solely dependent on political discipline. Two basic assumptions inform this belief: first, that interpersonal or intergroup conflict is an ineradicable feature of social life either because of rooted traits of human nature (greed, pride, aggression, insecurity or whatever) or because of fixed aspects of the human condition (the necessary scarcity of desired resources); and secondly that this socially and perhaps also psychologically destructive conflict can only be contained if there exists some single, unified and overriding power in society with the capacity to impose settlements on contending parties. Clearly this monist position has taken shape in the concept of state sovereignty as it has developed in the hands of Bodin, Hobbes and Austin. But the limited concern of such writers with law and order issues is not a necessary part of the monist response. What is central is the notion that the state can claim a monopoly in whatever means are needed to ensure social unity; and if these means are thought to include, for example, economic or ideological control as well as physical coercion and legal regulation, then from the monist standpoint the state can properly monopolise these resources also.

At the opposite pole lies the anarchist response, in many ways a flat rejection of the central assumption of monist thought, that social harmony depends ultimately on a politically imposed order. The central concern of anarchist thought has been to depict the actual or potential sources of social integration that lie beyond and could supersede entirely the coercive power of the state. How then is social harmony to be reached without coercion? One answer has been through the elimination of the causes of conflict. In the Hobbesian paradigm, of course, such a hope lies outside the bounds of reasonable ambition. If, however, conflict is not rooted in the human *persona* but is caused by distorted institutions or the maldistribution of desired resources or the insufficiency of desired resources, then new-model institutions or equality or abundance will secure its demise. Another answer has been through the inculcation or development of a shared community of values. The routes to this value consensus have been variously mapped; for some the perfecting of innate rationality, for others the benevolent manipulation of conditioned responses. But whether it is Godwin's schoolmaster or Skinner's 'operant conditioner' who is abroad, the objective has been a process of socialisation rigorous enough to exclude social division and persistent anti-social behaviour. A third and final answer has stressed that social co-ordination may be achieved not only through coercion or the sharing of objectives but as a by-product of men's pursuit of their own interests and purposes. Through bargaining, the mutual proferring of advantages, individuals and groups willingly adapt their behaviour to the desires of others. The intellectual construct embodying these ideas is of course the notion of the market. Their most enduring monument is laissez-faire economic theory, but the desire to replace coercive by contractual relations also enters main-line anarchist thought in the ideas of Proudhon, and has been resurrected in recent rethinking on anarchism.

Pluralism lies between these monist and anarchist poles. With monism, it accepts the need for a political mechanism to ensure social cohesion, but it insists too that the state is not the sole guarantor of social order and, partly in consequence, has no need to monopolise social control to achieve that end. On the contrary, it is essential for power in society to be divided and diffused. This response has a long genealogy, stretching back at least to Locke and Montesquieu and Tocqueville, but its central axiom has been restated recently and succinctly by Robert Dahl. 'Instead of a single centre of power, there must be multiple centres of power, none of which is or can be wholly sovereign.'[1] The exploration of the force of 'must' in this quotation would be a long task. For the claimed virtues of the division of power are various and complex and have been long debated. On one view, it is the only means of establishing effective checks on power, the only realistic answer to the question, *quis custodiet ipsos custodes?* On another, it is a way of achieving mixed government, the supposedly desirable blend of government by the one, the few and the many. On yet another, it provides for the extension of popular political participation by creating a multiplicity of power centres accessible, in a way which central national governments supposedly cannot be, to the communal energies of an active citizenry. Or, lastly, it has been seen as the political frame in which all group interests in society can best be represented and through which they can best be reconciled.

It is on this last justification of pluralism that I shall concentrate, not because it provides necessarily its most secure defence, but because it is that most characteristically stressed in recent pluralist theory.

THE ASSUMPTIONS OF CONTEMPORARY PLURALISM

In recent years pluralism has been revived particularly in the United States as the major defence of political practice in Western democracies. What are the salient features of this pluralist position? They can, I think, be summarised in six general propositions.

The first is that society is, and must necessarily be, an arena of diverse and conflicting interests. An historical dimension has now been added to this timeless assertion: the increasing division of labour in industrial society makes more precise and specific the articulation of group interests and gives wider groups the organizational and educational capacity to press their interests. In contrast to the Marxist prognosis of a progressive consolidation and bifurcation of the lines of social conflict, what strikes the pluralist is the cumulative fragmentation and diversification of interests in modern society.

The second proposition is that all interests have some claim to be heard and taken into account in the formulation of public policy. The actual impossibility and undesirability of extending toleration to all conceivable groups and of taking seriously into account all conceivable wants, needs or claims, presents an immediate objection to such an assertion and, in consequence, it is usually narrowed to the demand that all 'legitimate' interests have a claim to be heard.

The third position is that each individual's group affiliations and interests are likely to outweigh in scope and intensity those interests he may hold in common with all other members of society. Or, to modify this a little, the only common interest is likely to be in maintaining a system which maximises the capacity of each individual to pursue and protect his own peculiar interests.

The fourth proposition is that, although state intervention will not always be necessary to the resolution of conflicts between social groups, it will often and increasingly be so. As the socio-economic system becomes more complex and interdependent and as the state itself becomes a major consumer of human and material resources, so the state will be drawn more and more into previously apolitical areas mainly in order to regulate and contain the external costs of private settlements. So questions such as wage-bargaining or price-fixing, previously settled by trade unions and employers, manufacturers and customers, move within the ambit of political decision.

The fifth proposition is that such intervention should be geared to the reconciliation of group claims, whether these are contradictory demands on each other or contradictory demands on government itself. The major tasks of government thus emerge as conciliation or accommodation, the strengthening of those bargaining processes through which groups can come to mutually satisfactory agreements or the formulation of public policies so as to equilibrate group claims.

The sixth and last proposition is that governments are most likely to attend to their proper task of reconciling sectional claims if all groups possess some effective means of pressurising governments. In other words, it is within a pluralist context of diffused power that the primary duty of government will best be served, for in that context this obligation of government is transformed into a functional necessity. This is the point at which pluralist theory turns into a defence of Western democracies for, it is claimed, the electoral sensitivity of democratic politicians to intense minorities, the extensive coverage of interests by group organisations and the considerable access to decision-making these organisations have, all lead to a sufficient diffusion of power to ensure a more-or-less adequate representation of interests.

These then seem to be the main strands of recent pluralist thought – the necessary diversity of interests, the right of groups to self-protection, men's attachment to group rather than general interests, the necessity for the state to intervene in a conciliatory or accommodating role and the need for power to be diffused amongst social groups. Many debatable issues are raised in this cluster of ideas. One, which has attracted a good deal of attention recently, is the notion of interests and the general interest implicit in them. What I wish to examine particularly here is the putative relationship established between the state and organised groups. There is, I would claim, a dilemma for pluralist theory in this relationship. Governments, if they are to perform adequately their tasks of conciliation and accommodation, must be impartial and not be over-identifiable with particular groups in the community. At the same time, in pluralist democracy they must be responsive to the demands of groups whose powers are independent of government itself. For the monist there is no problem; the state must be independent enough of pressures from below to be impartial and it must have sufficient power, at least in the last resort, to impose what the general interest requires despite sectional resistance. The pluralist, however, wishes to assert the crucial role of government in the impartial resolution of conflicts whilst at the same time refusing to attribute to the state any clear hegemony in the group complex. The escape from this dilemma involves a resort to the notion of consensus. Governments can be subject to group pressures yet act independently and impartially because, in doing so, they in one way or another reflect and draw strength from a general and fundamental agreement on values in society.

THE ARBITER THEORY

To explore these ambiguities in the pluralist theory of the state further,

I will rephrase and utilise a distinction, made in other terms by William E. Connolly and Robert Paul Wolff, between the arbiter and arena theories.[2] Broadly the distinction is this. The arbiter theory envisages government as standing above the group battle, settling the ground rules for the conflict (particularly those determining what groups and what modes of action are 'legitimate'), ensuring the enforcement of those rules, and perhaps correcting imbalances if there is danger of particular groups growing into over-mighty subjects. The arena theory, in contrast, sees politicians as merely co-equal participants in the group battle. As state intervention in social and economic arrangements becomes more extensive and more crucial, so group conflicts are increasingly enacted within the political system and resolved by public policy decisions. Although these decisions remain nominally those of political leaders, they are the end-products of a process in which politicians are merely one group of political actors in contest with other political actors.

The most obvious and in many ways the most powerful objection to the arbiter theory is that, in any clash of major social interests, governments cannot and do not seek or achieve impartiality but must necessarily be partisan in their decisions. This objection, that the state does not stand above the conflicts of 'civil society' but is a product of them, was of course raised by Marx in his critique of Hegel, reiterated by Lenin in his critique of revisionism and has been restated recently by Miliband in an explicit rebuttal of contemporary pluralist theory.[3] The pluralist answer to this objection is that it is precisely the pluralist diffusion of power that creates the demand for and the possibility of impartial government arbitration. Where some sort of balance of power between social groups has been struck, where combatants possess a real capacity for mutual harm, an arbiter will be welcome; mutual deterrence is the condition of détente. Not only does the diffusion of power create the disposition to appeal to arbitration, it also ensures that governments will arbitrate impartially, since otherwise groups will refuse to accept their decisions. What is concealed within this response to the Marxist objection is an appeal to value consensus. Arbitration is not arbitrary, or at least the 'arbitrary' element in arbitration is simply that the arbiter is not bound, as is the judge, by settled and authoritative rules and precedents; arbitration nevertheless implies a decision on the merits of the case, requires reference to some principles of justice or equity or appropriateness. And, if these principles are not commonly accepted by those appealing to arbitration, the decisions of the arbiter cannot be seen as impartial. In this light, the possibility of impartial government is conditional on, not just a sufficient diffusion of power for each group to protect its interests, but on a common agreement on what constitutes impartiality.

However, the arbiter theory goes beyond asserting the possibility of impartial government arbitration. It sees the role of government as determining what groups are legitimate, how they may legitimately act and what is a proper balance between their powers. The difficulty here from the point of view of contemporary pluralist theory is how to reconcile two objectives for government which might in many instances be contradictory, on the one side that government policy should be the product of the interplay of actual sectional demands and on the other that government should regulate group activity on some general standards of justice or the general interest. Governments which must, according to the theory of democratic pluralism, be sensitive to group pressures both to win office and to carry through policies effectively, must at the same time act as independent regulators of group activity. Commonly, a reconciliation between these two potentially in-compatible requirements is attempted by appealing to public opinion. In its role as a regulator of group activity, government represents a general consensus on values, it tells the groups what the public will not accept; and it is precisely from its representation of a consensual viewpoint that government can derive the authority to overawe and restrain groups. What is implied here is a view of the man-in-the-street as schizophrenic; he is both a citizen, pressing governments and groups to conform to general social principles and general norms of behaviour, and a competitive consumer of government policies, pressing his own sectional interests. And, on this argument, the man-in-the-street as citizen must be the ultimate restraint on the man-in-the-street as com-petitive consumer.

Some of the difficulties of this appeal to consensus are empirical. Does such a consensus exist in Western democracies? If there is such a consensus, is it independent of political manipulation? And, if there is such a consensus, how durable is it likely to be? First, is there really sufficient general agreement on sufficiently concrete principles to form a guide-line to rulers in their putative role of arbitrating between and restraining groups? The evidence suggests otherwise.[4] Agreement on values, if it exists, is likely to be at such a level of generality that it is compatible with quite radical disagreement on attitudes towards public policy or institutional structure.

Even supposing the existence of some consensus on the rules of the game or the principles to be applied in assessing priorities between group claims, it is possible that this consensus is not independent. It is possible, in other words, that such agreement is manufactured. If the general will is, as has been suggested by theorists as politically divergent as Schumpeter and Marcuse, not so much a generator of the political process as a product of it, not so much the master as the subject of politicians, it cannot be posed as the fount of political ground rules.

A last point can be made on the reality of consensus. It is an implicit assumption in many studies of political culture that there are value perceptions which are not only widely spread and commonly held in a community but are also deep-rooted, fundamental, unchanging or at any rate alter only slowly and under massive historical pressure. However, the second assumption is no more beyond question than the first. For any general consensus may be historically fragile and liable to break under the impact of circumstances. How far, for example, is any consensus which may exist on the rules of the political game in Western democracies likely to survive extensive economic dislocation, high unemployment or very rapid inflation? It would at the least seem foolhardy to insist on the survival capacity of consensual agreement without knowing more about the effect of crisis situations on opinions than we do.

Apart from these empirical difficulties, it is doubtful if the appeal to shared values is compatible with pluralist assumptions. For it is difficult to see what is or could be, within pluralist assumptions, the democratic mechanism for translating consensual views into policy decisions. An attempt was made some time ago by David Truman to explain such a mechanism.[5] His general thesis is a statement of the theory of group pluralism; public policy is the equilibrium point between the pressures exerted by organised groups. However, Truman adds an additional dimension to the argument with his notion of 'potential groups', by which he attempts to explain the intrusion into the process of policy formulation of generally held values. Groups are constrained in their tactics and their objectives by the fear that potential groups will actually organise themselves if those tactics or objectives flout general norms. Governments too must take into account the covert wishes of potential groups in their efforts at compromising group demands. The ambiguities of Truman's argument reflect the ambiguities of the arbiter theory generally. As theories of collective action suggest, and as the relative weakness of public issue pressure groups as against sectional interest groups confirms, the likelihood of strong organised groups arising to protect widely held values, even if they are clearly flouted, is small. Nor, within a pluralist context, can it be assumed that the democratic process will ensure that such values will be taken into account by governments. There can be no resort to the simple majoritarian position that democratic politicians must act on what most people want or believe to be right on pain of electoral reprisal. For the electoral mechanism is depicted as a means of conveying intense wishes to government; and it is assumed that this must be a route to 'minorities rule' since it is accepted that the individual's sectional attachments will in any but the most extreme circumstances outweigh his communal attachments.[6] Men as citizens can only be brought in to redress the excesses of men as economic agents in the (on the theory) unlikely circumstances of their feeling more strongly about general issues than sectional interests.

The theoretical dilemma facing the arbiter theory stems from its desire to avoid presenting the state as at least *primus inter pares*, as having purposes different in kind from those of partial groups. This leads of necessity to theoretical incoherence. To avoid the conclusion, apparently exhortatory and incompatible with pluralist premises, that governments should act on general principles and appraise group demands rather than just bending to them, the theory is led to present the claimed concern of democratic governments with general principles of equity not as a moral obligation but as a course forced on them by public opinion. If government buckles to its task of impartial arbitration, this must be because it is yielding to some demand upon it, which in this case must proceed from the whole community. So the resort to consensus is crucial, but the theory does not show how a consensus, even if it exists, could in practice be politically effective.

THE ARENA THEORY

The alternative formulation of pluralism, the arena theory, is a more radical and tougher version; but again it involves an ultimate appeal to the notion of consensus. On this formulation politicians are stripped of the lonely eminence of arbiters. They constitute one group amongst many, merely co-equal participants in the process of conflict and accommodation lying behind public policy decisions. The political structure itself is not the eminent domain of politicians, nor have they a peculiar capacity or obligation to speak for principles different from and morally superior to those of other groups. The political structure is simply the most important arena within which the competitive life of groups is played out. Clearly encapsulated within this argument is a particular view of the general interest. Public policy is in fact a function of balancing group forces, the end-product of the bargaining process. And this fact should cause no alarm, for the 'general interest' cannot be understood as anything other than the summation of group interests. In this way the theory substitutes a procedure for a standard; the 'general interest' becomes a phrase descriptive of what actually emerges from the bargaining process and ceases to be a criterion for appraising the claims made by various groups.

Two questions immediately present themselves. What interests do politicians, and particularly governing politicians, serve? What groups do they represent? The traditional if obscure answers — the general interest and the whole community — are theoretically unavailable since there is no general interest that can be set against group interests and since the pluralist depiction of the electoral process precludes the possibility of politicians acting habitually in this way. The escape from this dilemma is in many ways daring if not particularly novel (bearing in mind the utilitarian defence of democracy). The answer to the question, 'what interests do politicians serve?', is 'their own'. Their concern is essentially with their own accession to or hold on office. However, we should not, we are assured, be dismayed at this for, in the political as in the economic market, public benefits are not the object but a by-product of entrepreneurial actions. Pre-eminent amongst the benefits gained from the politicians' pursuit of political self-interest is that they must in consequence undertake the role of honest brokers between all those seeking to influence governmental decisions. The electoral road to political fortune lies in their attempting to aggregate, harmonise or accommodate different group demands.

The arena theory is much less immediately vulnerable than the arbiter theory. The attacks upon it, particularly by American writers, have been empirical in emphasis, their main burden being the charge that the facts of American political life do not measure up to the requirements of the theory. The battleground is too well known to need much further mapping. First on the field were those flatly denying that pluralist dispersion rather than élite domination was characteristic of the American political system. More recently, critics have concentrated on the alleged bias of American pluralism, a bias which, by restricting entry to the political market and limiting the issues on the political agenda, reinforces and conserves the position of already socially advantaged and organised groups. If this is war, it seems to be civil war, for the attack is not upon pluralist values as such but on the assertion that they are realised in the United States.

A different critique of the arena theory may be mounted by questioning the internal coherence of its implicit view of the state. The main question at issue here is whether or not the state does or could perform only the limited role allotted to it by the theory. How far is it feasible to depict governors as having only a brokerage function? An answer to this question may be suggested by looking at two more limited questions: the problem of the legal status of groups and the notion of bargaining implicit in the arena theory.

Hidden within the theory there is an assumption that groups are in one sense of an ambiguous phrase 'natural', an assumption that communities of interest arise, find organisational expression and seek satisfaction of their claims independently of political support or direction. They are natural social products not political artifacts. The role of government is then essentially passive; it can respond to or attempt to frustrate pressures from groups but it cannot fundamentally determine the pattern of group behaviour. This assumption is necessary to the coherence of the theory. For if the emergence of organised groups, the relative resources they can muster, and the directions in which they can develop are in any significant way dependent on political decision or legal status, it becomes less plausible to talk of those holding political authority as being merely one of the partners in the group quadrille.

The point has been made in different ways. Much of the discussion of pluralism in England early in this century centred on the notion of the 'real personality' of groups. Whilst this was in part simply a way of pressing for the acceptance of corporations as legal persons, it did, so far as it set out a Realist rather than a Fictional theory of corporations, assert a sociological fact as well as a legal aspiration, the fact that groups are organisms with real wills of their own. The theoretical difficulty is obvious enough — how to reconcile the pluralists' attack on the theory of the monistic state as conflicting with social reality with their equally insistent assertion that the legal status of groups is decisive to their development.

The terminology has changed in recent pluralist discussion but the root problem remains – the unwillingness to accept the extent to which political decision may affect group activity and relative group powers. In general terms this may be seen in attempts to extend group analysis to political systems other than Western democracies. Whilst it may appear obvious that group politics as generally understood can flourish only in a specific legal climate (guaranteeing freedom of association for instance) and that the necessary socio-economic conditions of group articulation are not necessarily sufficient conditions for these legal provisions, these are obvious facts ignored in the 'convergence thesis' and in the application of group analysis to Soviet politics. More particularly, the unwillingness to face the possible impact of political decision on group behaviour may be seen in recent discussion of entrepreneurship in group organisation. As in earlier talk of the 'real personality' of groups, the main thrust is towards establishing that group organisation is self-generating since, it is argued, in the political market shared felt needs will be automatically translated into effective political demands through the intermediary of the organisational entrepreneur. This claim is seriously undermined by the free-rider problem as outlined by Olson.[7] That a collection of individuals has an interest in common is no guarantee of its organising to pursue that interest. For it is only if the individual's acceptance of the costs of participation is both a necessary and a sufficient condition of his receiving benefits (and benefits outweighing the costs) that the economically rational individual will voluntarily fund group organisation. And only in special circumstances will these conditions be met – where the group is small and each member's participation is necessary to any benefits being received by anyone, or where the organisation can offer 'selective incentives', benefits which, unlike the common benefits, can be enjoyed only by those who participate in the organisation. The damage that this does to the pluralist position is clear, and has perhaps been a stimulus to recent (and to my mind unsuccessful) attempts to overcome the free-rider problem.[8] It is damaging in two ways. By breaking the assumed link between need and effective demand, it raises the same charge of injustice as can be brought against the economic market. More pertinently here, it brings up the possibility that group leaders may pursue an alternative 'political' strategy. Where 'entrepreneurs' have no or insufficient selective incentives to induce voluntary participation, they may seek to exclude free-riders by forcing all those receiving general benefits to join the organisation. The efforts of professional associations to restrict entry into the profession and the parallel efforts of trade unions to establish the closed shop are illustrations of this strategy at work. One of the most effective and in some instances the only way of achieving this objective is by making membership of the organisation legally enforceable. This at once brings political decision into the process of group formation and maintenance; and, to the degree that governments alter the relative bargaining resources of groups and do not merely facilitate compromise between organisations whose powers are independently determined, the arena theory's depiction of the role of the state becomes inappropriate.

The notion of bargaining involved in the arena theory presents parallel theoretical difficulties. Obviously enough, the politics of accommodation depends on the willingness of groups to accommodate one to another. The assumption that such a willingness exists is fundamental to the arena theory. Basically it is assumed that for every group conflict there is at least one settlement that is mutually satisfactory, one settlement which all parties can agree is preferable to any other feasible outcomes, even if it is not for any one party the most preferred outcome. In other words, the assumption is that political conflicts are non-zero-sum rather than zero-sum.

The first and most apparent objection is that many political conflicts are zero-sum. Even if we assume that economic conflicts are generally reconcilable, it is a common experience that the move from cash to principle exacerbates conflict and depressingly obvious that racial or religious differences may be irreconcilable. In situations of such raw conflict, it may not be possible for politicians to act the honest broker. Indeed, in terms of their own political interests this may be undesirable. Where political cleavages are deep and cumulative, political fortunes are likely to be made in the exaggeration and exploitation of differences rather than the aggregation of interests. The point is well illustrated by the contrast between the pessimism (from a democratic viewpoint) of theorists of 'plural' societies and the optimism of 'pluralist' theorists.[9] In societies divided by deep cultural chasms, any attempt by politicians to compromise and aggregate interests either within the party or in government policy is likely to lose them support in their natural or major constituencies.

The pluralist could quite legitimately shrug aside this objection by confining himself to the claim that the politics of accommodation is only possible where most conflicts are non-zero-sum. But this is immediately to delimit the circumstances in which a pluralist dispersion of power is appropriate and to emphasise consensual agreement, if only on the range of claims made and the range of methods used to realise them, as a necessary precondition of a viable pluralist democracy.

I would not wish to dispute the assertion that consensual agreement is highly supportive of exchange politics. It does seem likely that a disposition to accommodate will lead to accommodation. However, it does not follow that the existence of such agreement can be deduced from the fact of exchange politics and the fact that accommodation between groups is normally achieved. The point can best be made by looking more closely at the distinction between non-zero-sum and zero-sum conflicts. The distinction holds in fact only if the preferences of the protagonists are abstracted from the relative power resources they bring to the conflict or bargaining situation. If, to take the simplest situation, A has a unilateral capacity to harm B, then that must be taken into account by B in his determination of his preference ordering. He may agree to A's demands for fear of the harm that might otherwise be inflicted upon him. Although, as speakers of ordinary language, we might be tempted to talk of his being coerced, the settlement is still non-zero-sum since, whilst for A the outcome is presumably the most-preferred, for B the outcome is not the least-preferred. The fact of accommodation, of agreement on a settlement in a conflict situation, does not necessarily imply that the settlement is in any real sense satisfactory to all protagonists, unless either power resources (capacities to harm) are roughly equal or there is common agreement on the propriety of the given distribution of power resources. It is assumed in the arena theory that both these conditions hold in Western systems. It is not of course necessary for the theory to deny that many conflicts are about the redistribution of some good or another. But, since the theory postulates that decisions on these matters are reached (and properly reached) through the interaction of independent power groups, it is forced to claim that there is rough parity of power resources and/or that the power distribution is generally acceptable.

The first claim is tentative but overt. For perhaps obvious reasons, pluralists have not claimed equality in organisational resources as a necessary condition for pluralism; rather they pose non-cumulative inequalities as the base. Many different sorts of resource, it is argued, are of value both in creating an organisation and in securing its political effectiveness; numbers, wealth, organisational skills, expert knowledge, intensity of feeling, access to the media and to decision-makers, the occupation of a strategically crucial electoral position or position within the productive system, a favourable public image — all these and other factors affect a group's capacity to organise and its bargaining strength. Where the inequalities are cumulative, where, that is, a favourable position in one distribution is accompanied by favourable positions in many others, a pluralist system is untenable. It can be sustained, however, if all groups have some resource peculiarly available to them, some distribution in which they are favourably placed. Whether or not this holds true for Western systems in general and the United States in particular is the main focus of the argument between American pluralists and their critics.

The second assumption — that the given distribution of power resources is generally acceptable — is more implicit in the arena theory. This theory, like laissez-faire economic theory before it, concerns itself largely with the strategies of exchange between market units and ignores the pattern of distribution determining what advantages and disadvantages individuals or groups may possess in the market exchange. The political, like the economic, market is claimed to be neutral, but only in the sense that none are excluded from entry to it, none are refused the possibility of bargaining for what they want with what they have. The snag is that the market will only appear neutral to market participants themselves if the initial distribution of resources is to them acceptable (and of course equality of distribution might be unacceptable to many). Here again the arena theory is forced back to the assumption of consensual agreement; for it is only if there is such agreement on the legitimacy of the existing distribution of power resources that the claimed virtue of the pluralist diaspora, the achievement of a neutral political evaluation of competitive group claims, will be practised or practicable.

This assumption is the weakest link in the arena theory's chain of argument. For the pattern of power distribution is not usually uncontentious and may be precisely what is at issue in political dispute. Given the possibility of attempts to alter the existing distribution and given also the effect that governmental decisions can have on the power distribution, it is unlikely that politicians can stick consistently to the brokerage role allotted to them by the theory (although partisanship might be less clearly visible if their commitment is to preserving the status quo).

CONCLUSION

Despite the pluralist emphasis on conflict, competition and division of power, contemporary pluralism in both its formulations must fall back on an appeal to consensus. It is forced to do so by its dual desire to present the state as politically neutral and at the same time to resist assigning to it any functions morally superior to those of other forms of social organisation. To avoid the monist conclusions to which the first desire might lead, it resorts to anarchist premises. If the state is depicted as arbitrating between groups, it is merely representative of a shared community of values. If the state structure is simply a mechanism for facilitating bargaining between groups and politicians simply agents in this process, the neutrality of the political market and consequently the general acceptability of existing power distributions is assumed. In both instances the fall back on consensus is necessary to maintaining the coherence of the theory of the state.

NOTES

1. Robert A. Dahl, *Pluralist Democracy in the United States* (Chicago, 1967), ch. 1.

2. Connolly distinguishes between the umpire and the arena theories; see William E. Connolly, 'The Challenge to Pluralist Theory', in: William E. Connolly (ed.), *The Bias of Pluralism* (New York, 1969), 30-34. Wolff distinguishes between the referee and the vector-sum theories; see *The Poverty of Liberalism* (Boston, 1969), ch. 4, 122-61.

3. Ralph Miliband, *The State in Capitalist Society* (London, 1969).

4. See James W. Prothro and Charles M. Grigg, 'Fundamental principles of democracy: bases of agreement and disagreement', *Journal of Politics,* May 1960; Herbert McClosky, 'Consensus and ideology in American politics', *American Political Science Review,* June 1964; Robert A. Dahl, *Polyarchy* (Yale, 1971), 124-88.

5. David B. Truman, *The Governmental Process* (New York, 1951).

6. Robert A. Dahl, *A Preface to Democratic Theory* (Chicago & London, 1963), 133.

7. Mancur Olson, *The Logic of Collective Action* (Harvard, 1965), ch. VI.

8. Cf. Robert H. Salisbury, 'An exchange theory of interest groups', in: Robert H. Salisbury (ed.), *Interest Group Politics in America* (New York, 1970), 32-67; Norman Frohlich, Joe A. Oppenheimer and Oran R. Young, *Political Leadership and Collective Goods* (Princeton, 1971), ch. I.

9. Cf. Alvin Rabushka and Kenneth A. Shepsle, *Politics in Plural Societies. A Theory of Democratic Instability* (Columbus, 1972).

10 Ideology: Key to Power

Uli Windisch
University of Geneva, Switzerland

Contrary to what is generally claimed in the human sciences, we maintain that little is yet known about the actual nature of ideology, such as its properties, its potential, its functions and its effects. In addition to this lack of knowledge, the principal sociological approaches are reductionist in character. These approaches are very narrow and tend to distort the issues, and in the long run make it impossible to grasp the specificity of ideological reality.

Two major approaches illustrate these shortcomings. The first type groups approaches which may be called *determinist*. They have a structuralist orientation and aim at defining the links between ideological argument and social conditions, i.e. which social conditions give rise to ideologies. Comparative structures or 'structural homologies' are analysed by correlating, corresponding and reinforcing them. One aspect of this analysis is the search for internal coherence within these structures, but more important (for all social phenomena are structured) is the unity and degree of this coherence. It is well known in structuralist research that even when the content is different the structures are isomorphous.

Another axis of research of this first approach lies in relating an ideological trend to a class or segment of a social class. The points which are generally discussed: the nature of this relation as simple reinforcement, as a degree of distortion, and as a type of interpretation, theorisation and 'rationalisation' by certain agents who have 'the highest degree of possible consciousness' (L. Goldmann) in a situation within a given social group.

Although this is a determinist approach, it has nothing in common with the famous 'mechanist theory of reflection' which we see no point in discussing as this theory has few supporters. Everyone agrees that ideology has a certain amount of 'relative autonomy'; however there is disagreement as to the degree of this autonomy.

Why then is the determinist approach unsatisfactory today? It is clear that no study of ideology can ignore this perspective. An ideology is always essentially related to the social conditions in which it appears. The determinist approach is unsatisfactory because it stops halfway, because it only acknowledges and admits certain elements of ideology. It fails to recognise some essential aspects. Instead of merely mentioning 'relative autonomy', it should be examined, analysed and its components revealed. Too often this convenient little term merely serves to indicate that ideology is not being discussed according to mechanist principles. What then is 'relative autonomy' in practice?

We shall attempt to show that ideological autonomy can be far more extensive than is generally admitted, even in the most 'autonomist' approaches. Two concrete examples drawn from the Swiss social reality (an example of local power and the phenomenon of xenophobia) show how ideology can have its own dynamic force (an autodynamism), how it can play an active and transformative role, and that while it is subject to social conditions, it may, in turn, affect social relations and, in some extreme cases, lead to a complete restructuring of social and political relations in a given society.

Instead of using the term ideology, a process of *ideologisation* has the advantage of stressing this dynamic, active and transformative aspect which we consider fundamental. This change of perspective inevitably brings us back to certain *intrinsic* characteristics of ideology.[1] Surely any sociological study must ask itself the primordial questions: who is speaking (which group or class)? to whom? for what purpose? with what results? The interpretation of an ideology demands a constant interchange between its content and situations, stand-points and given social conflicts. However, such an approach is only the first step and as yet says nothing about the specificity of the ideological level and its possible determining power. Here we will briefly point out some of the essential features of ideology: its *ubiquity*, its omnipresence. Ideology is, in fact, always present, in all fields and at all levels of a given society. For this reason we reject the 'end of ideologies' argument; no society exists without ideologies.

In pluralist societies the *multiplicity* and wide *diversity* of the transmission of ideological messages are an added factor. The reason why it is so difficult to measure the *impact* of these messages is precisely because of their multiplicity and extremely variable and contradictory content.

It is undoubtedly partly because studies in ideology concentrate primarily on extreme ideologies that the ubiquity of ideology is seldom realised. Elements of ideological nature always and inevitably underlie all collective action. Without an ideological argument or point of reference, neither collective action nor political or social mobilisation exists. Ideology is the element which acts as a mediator for the desires, aspirations and plans of social groups. How can one conceive of collective mobilisation without ideological arguments?

At an even more basic level, the very existence of ideologies can be explained by the *incomplete* nature of all human society. This aspect of incompleteness may be interpreted in a number of different ways: as a mere lack or shortcoming; as arising from social inequality, alienation, domination and the exploitation of certain social classes by others, etc. Whichever way we look at it, however, ideology is always seeking to overcome the incomplete nature of all human society. With certain ideologies, words suffice for this. In others, the argument is only the first stage; it must lead to action and bring the social incompleteness to the final stage of the argument.

However, for an ideology to lead to collective action, it must necessarily simplify social reality. Such *simplification* is the most basic characteristic of any ideology. It is, in fact, impossible within the context of any given ideology to be aware of all the nuances, of the immense complexity, diversity, and the manifold contradictory aspects of a given social reality. The comprehension of a given social reality inevitably comes about by means of its simplification. The indispensable operation of simplification contradicts the determinist approach to ideology. While a given ideology is obviously always in relation to the social reality in which it appears, it does nonetheless *reconstruct* this reality and in doing so, *transforms*, corrects and *rectifies* it.

Another intrinsic characteristic of ideology also contradicts the strictly determinist approach. Even if an ideology is applicable to the situation of certain social groups or classes, it still nevertheless aims at reaching different groups, or classes or a much larger public. The situation then arises where antagonistic social groups adhere to the same ideology. Perfect harmony between ideology and social classes can never be attained. A given ideology can never succeed in grouping together all the members of the social groups or classes from which it has evolved. At the same time, it attracts members of other social groups or classes. In other words, ideology creates its own specific momentum. If ideology were only understood by means of the determinist approach, it would not be possible to explain certain intense collective impulses.

Yet another contradictory aspect of ideology is that it always aspires to the truth, but, by simplifying, it inevitably obscures and distorts issues. Yet, in order entirely to fulfil its functions, an ideology must never appear to be an ideology, as such.

Ideology is elaborated and based on a number of general axes which make comprehension of an entire society possible. These axes must be general and simple enough to include *all* present and future phenomena and cover all imaginable deductions and projections. In short, ideology must have an answer to everything. It must be able to give a meaning to everything and an identity to everyone, particularly in times of crisis. Nationalist ideologies and the related phenomenon of hero identification have the essential function of overcoming uncertainties as to the self and restoring a weakened or 'lost identity'.

Ideology is often contrasted to science. However, verification, which is indispensable in science, does not concern ideology. Ideology is an affirmative, apodictic certainty and its basic principles are, or should be, beyond the scope of verification. The problem of verification does not even arise with ideology but, if it ever did, it would be made to appear just that – an ideology. Where science advances by degrees, ideology either affirms or denies absolutely. It knows no doubts. The features of ideology are simplicity and systematisation as opposed to the multiple nuances, reservations and precautions of science, common sense as opposed to facts, coherence as opposed to the contradictory aspects of reality, generalisations as opposed to precision, repetition of basic certitudes as opposed to control, and evocative words and emotionally charged ideas as opposed to the cold terminology of science. Ideological language is connotative and non-analytic. Its vocabulary is evocative, suggestive, prestigious and emotional.

Two other features of ideology are its sacred nature and moral aspect.

Where science tackles the unknown, ideology breaks it down into sections. Ideology works according to the system of right and wrong, Good and Evil, Self and Other, with the Other as necessarily inferior or even immoral. It is the moral aspect of ideology which allows it to both praise and condemn simultaneously. Ideology goes beyond reality and transcends it. It even draws on the realm of the imagination. It is precisely because it deals with *all* aspects of individual and group life that ideology can have such powerful impact and attract such total and fanatical adherence.

This last feature of ideology concerns our criticism of the second approach to ideology, i.e. analyses which focus on its *occultative* function. From this point of view ideology obscures, disguises and occults: it is unconsciousness, lack of consciousness, false consciousness – the 'irrational', phantasmic aspect of certain ideologies, of 'spontaneous representations' (as opposed to 'true' and 'objective' knowledge), of false consciousness and of alienation. In certain cases it is even described as stupidity. It must be recalled that no ideology is pure phantasmagoria. An ideology is always to some extent founded on a number of true elements, even if the latter are sometimes drastically changed (distorted) by argument. Moreoever, science is never entirely stripped of all ideological elements.

Once again, we feel that this type of approach tends to be very narrow and leads nowhere. To insist on or stigmatise the 'non-logical', 'irrational' or such like aspects of an ideology is pointless and shows a misunderstanding of certain intrinsic and fundamental characteristics of ideology.

Terms such as alienation, false consciousness, spontaneous representations, non-logic seem to us far too convenient. Furthermore, they evade some important ideological aspects. To speak of false consciousness, for example, implies that a true consciousness exists. All ideologies cause a certain amount of distortion although not all do so to the same degree, nor on the same objects, nor with the same results. Rather than attaching such concepts (which undoubtedly have a significant heuristic value but are far from explaining all its aspects) to what are very different forms of distortion, the *conditions* from which they originate should be analysed. In order to do this – and this is one of our main theses – we must look beyond our capitalist mode of production. However interesting theses on the fetishism of goods and on reification may be, they fail to understand or explain the different and multiple contemporary forms of alienation. It is certainly not by chance that, among the growing number of current studies devoted to the more determining and deeper characteristics of our Western civilisation, the most interesting have a strong historical emphasis. To determine the deep nature and origin of a given basic feature, studies now go back not just a few decades but several centuries or even thousands of years in the course of our history. While this historical depth is becoming increasingly frequent, it is worth recalling that a few decades ago an author such as W. Reich, in an attempt to explain the origins of fascism, had already realised the necessity of referring back several thousand years through our civilisation.[2]

It seems, in fact, that no theory based solely on characteristics of a capitalist way of production can ever provide a satisfactory explanation to the most derealising contemporary ideologies (for example fascist ideologies).

A far more general theory and approach are necessary — a kind of historical anthropo-sociology. Capitalism is only one of the innumerable successive layers of the sedimentation of our collective mental structures. Holding up the theory of reification as the answer to everything may have involuntarily caused a reification within the realm of the perception of ideology, its nature and basic properties. Despite their unquestionable contribution, ideological analyses in terms of class consciousness and objective class interests seem to contain striking shortcomings.

Let us take as an example the very large proportion of workers throughout the world who vote against their 'objective interest' by supporting Right-wing or extreme Right-wing political parties. Different theories have been advanced to explain this phenomenon: lack of class consciousness, the inculcation of a dominant ideology precisely because it is dominant, alienation, embourgeoisement, etc. These different elements certainly go some way towards explaining the problem, but it seems to us that a great deal more research is necessary to reveal various other factors which defy the logic of the alignment of the different social classes or strata with certain political parties and ideologies.

In a study carried out on the local politics of a small community, we found that the analysis of factors which defy this logic entailed looking back several centuries and even tens of centuries in the history of this community and of the surrounding region.[3]

Analyses in terms of class consciousness and objective class interest also lack another fundamental aspect. Let us try to define it by comparing *collective consciousness* and *class consciousness*. It appears that the objective interests and the class consciousness of a given social class only constitute a small part of the daily preoccupations of the members of such a class. These preoccupations as a whole are called collective consciousness. One of the reasons why an analysis in terms of class consciousness has so little impact on the masses could perhaps be because it tends to limit collective consciousness to solely objective interests. It is nevertheless agreed that the impact of an ideology depends on the extent to which it is related to the daily preoccupations of the masses as a whole (collective consciousness). Gramsci defended this thesis throughout his works.[4] He showed by means of numerous concrete examples that an ideology must have something in common with both the theorists and the masses. We also quote W. Reich on this problem:

> theory must be created from the life of the masses and returned to them in the form of practice.[5]

> The class consciousness of the masses does not consist in knowledge of the historical or economic laws governing human life, but in knowledge:
> 1. of the essential needs of each in every sphere. . . .[6]

> If one attributes one's own wishes to the masses and fails to judge the actual situation independently of one's own desires, one neglects those wishes which would be the easiest to satisfy (the projection on to the masses of the situation as it is seen by a minute group)[7].

Broadly speaking we consider W. Reich's theses as being important for several reasons.

(a) He indicates in a very effective way the distinction we make between class consciousness and collective consciousness. He even distinguishes between two types of class consciousness, one elaborated by theorists and politicians and the other from amidst the popular masses. The former aims at evolving objective economic and historical laws and mechanisms whereas the latter is far from this concept and these wide perspectives: 'it arises from the small, the daily, the banal'.[8] It deals with the many trivial matters of daily life.

(b) Reich seems to have understood the profound nature, scope and power of ideology and the dynamic forces it may release.

(c) This leads to an essential generality: the same need can as easily be orientated and politicised for reactionary purposes as for progressive ones. And, since the masses are concerned with the most immediate problems (which theorists consider small, trivial and secondary), the importance of an ideological intervention at the most elementary, but for the masses the most basic, level, is clearly understood. Such a situation could indirectly reveal the limitations of concepts such as false consciousness and alienation.

(d) Finally, we advance a thesis which should be apparent from the evidence: conservative forces understand the deep nature and power of ideology far better and use it far more skilfully (though obviously for conservative purposes) than any other force.

Conservative and reactionary ideologies are often criticised by progressive theorists for their 'illogical' or 'contradictory' nature. Indeed, another of the characteristics of ideology is that is is to a certain degree contradictory and yet these contradictory aspects seldom appear as contradictions to the masses. Adherence to an ideology does not only depend on logical and rational criteria. The Nazis *played* on this point. They succeeded in using all the elements of revolutionary ideology for reactionary purposes. This explains why a progressive ideology must continually distinguish between reactionary and progressive manifestations among the preoccupations of the masses. A general abstract denunciation of fascism is useless unless it is based on the daily preoccupations of the masses.

It does seem to be a feature of Left-wing political parties to underestimate political intervention at an ideological level. An ideology has not the slightest chance of success unless it is formulated on the basis of the most every-day preoccupations of the masses, and, therefore, it is useless to try to impose an ideology merely because of the so-called *objective interests* of a class. Such a concept shows a misunderstanding of both the popular masses (of the collective consciousness) and of the true nature and power of ideology.

THE POWER OF IDEOLOGY ILLUSTRATED BY TWO CONCRETE EXAMPLES

An Example of Local Politics

In our studies carried out on the political life of local communities we came across an apparently peculiar case: a mountain community (Chermignon) in Valais (a canton in the French-speaking part of Switzerland) which at present has a population of some 2,000 inhabitants. Originally a rural community (in 1920 80 percent of the active population was still employed in agriculture), within a very short time it became a large internationally known tourist resort (Crans-sur-Sierre) receiving several tens of thousands of tourists annually for winter sports. Although this community experienced explosive *economic* development, its political system hardly changed and exhibits a number of specific features. It is a system which is still founded on clans (essentially, though not exclusively, based on family ties). Two traditional clans (a third one appeared about ten years ago) are committed to a pitiless struggle for local power. This struggle between clans in no way corresponds to a class struggle on a local level. On the contrary, and this is the essential detail, all socio-political categories and all social classes are represented within each clan and in almost the same ratio. In each clan there are employers, white- and blue-collar workers and members of the major cantonal and national parties (from Right-wing to extreme Left.) The clans therefore cut across class and ideology.[9]

Members of the same clan have an extremely deep and intense 'us' consciousness. It is a kind of *clan consciousness* which transcends by a long way class consciousness, at least at the level of local politics. Moreover, this clan antagonism, the interclan struggle, affects nearly all other levels of the social reality, notably economic, social and cultural. Each clan has its own entrepreneurs, its bank, its cafés, its food shops, its band, its meeting places, etc.

Local power itself, the 'power structure', on the contrary, cuts across neither class nor ideology. Whichever clan they belong to, those who hold the economic power also hold the political power. A very small privileged minority, the descendants of six autochthonous families, exclusively retain the political offices handed down from father to son and from generation to generation for over a century.

The coexistence of an exclusive *class power* and an extremely strong *clan consciousness* deeply ingrained into the mental structure of the population, is the 'non-logical' element which needs to be explained.

At the time of local elections, the blue- and white-collar workers of each clan vote and campaign keenly for the most economically privileged people in their clan. Thus, they also struggle against other blue- and white-collar workers of the rival clan as well as against any individuals who may nevertheless have the same 'objective interests'.

Each clan has a very rich symbolism which makes it possible for each member to identify himself closely with the group to which he belongs and, equally important, to oppose members of the rival clan. Each individual lives and expresses his clan identity constantly with arrogant pride and in all aspects of daily life.

The origin of these clans should no doubt be explained since they appeared in the context of another type of economy, but that is not the object of this very short chapter. We will limit ourselves to proposing a brief interpretation of the present situation. There is obviously a great temptation to describe this political situation in terms such as false consciousness, alienation, generalised and collective politics and absence of class consciousness, since the workers in the community fail to vote according to their 'objective interests'. Not only are they politically disunited but they support their respective employers ('the class enemy'). Certain political militants, from outside, do not hesitate to describe this political situation as 'political backwardness', 'political underdevelopment', 'irrationality' and even 'stupidity'.

Such a situation seems to provide a perfect opportunity to approach the question of the factors *defying* the logic of certain social classes supporting given political parties. So, instead of explaining it by patterns and theories which fail to take these factors into account, let us try to *understand* it. This demands an exercise in comprehensive sociology.

In non-local elections the relation is more clear-cut between social strata and political parties. Whichever clan they belong to, a section of the workers vote for the socialist party. But in local elections clan consciousness remains unquestionably stronger than class consciousness. There is no occasion when the workers of different clans are autonomously organised politically. What is fundamental, is that *local* politics represent almost the totality of the daily preoccupations of the people. External, cantonal and national politics only concern them sporadically. For a very large majority of the population, politics means the multiple events and doings of the local life of the clans. Exalting one's clan, denouncing and criticising the rival clan, and reacting to the 'false' accusations of the opponent is what absorbs the essential social and political energies and activities of the population. This is all the more evident since the clans affect all aspects of daily life. As they are not only political groupings but actual complete social groups, a large part of the cultural, social and economic life of the community is, in fact, organised almost autonomously within each clan.

A parallel can be drawn with the conceptual opposition between class consciousness and collective consciousness proposed earlier, in the sense that clan consciousness in the present case is equal to collective consciousness. The characterisation of ideology outlined in the first part permits us a greater understanding of certain elements of this seemingly particular political system.

Since the end of the nineteenth century, clan consciousness, affected by very profound economic changes, has *decreased* somewhat. Originally clan consciousness was based more on myth than on ideology. In the realm of the myth, men believe that myths are inherited whereas we know that ideologies are man-made. The myth selects that which seems to merit lasting significance and in doing so, something absolute is created with what is temporal.[10] Thus, originally, the component facts of class consciousness represented a type of absolute belief, deeply felt by *all* inhabitants (at all levels of the population). There was struggle and incompatibility between those with economic power in the respective traditional clans. Political life focused on the struggle between the privileged families of the two clans. There was absolutely no compromise or understanding between the holders of economic power of the opposed clans. The struggle was permanent and continued even in the municipal executive. The clan with the majority in this executive dominated local politics quite openly (for example dismissing people in executive positions from the rival clan) throughout its period of office (4 years).

Then, with social and economic change, clan consciousness decreased, especially among those holding economic power. On the other hand, this clan consciousness is still quite strong among the population. The bulk of the electorate even go so far as to reprimand its political representatives for being unfaithful to the clan and for collaborating with the 'hereditary enemy' (the rival clan). However, on the local executive level, councillors of the different clans have been getting along fairly well for some years now. Clan consciousness, which has changed progressively from belief to ideology, has become an *instrument of political strategy*. Political candidates (who themselves feel very little clan consciousness) consciously 'use' and invoke clan consciousness among the population (who still believe strongly in it) in order to attain power. Without believing in clan consciousness any longer, they have become aware of its power and *play* on it. They politicise local politics, which indubitably arise from the daily preoccupations of the population, in order to get to or retain power. In spite of the fact that clan consciousness is weakening somewhat (even among the population), they do not hesitate to revive it, in different ways, prior to the municipal elections. In this way class power is maintained by means of clan consciousness.

Instead of laughing off a clan consciousness they no longer believe in, although perhaps they do still feel it subconsciously, those who hold political power are very skilful at using it to a political end. They too have become aware of the power of ideology, and they take the daily preoccupations of the lower classes as a basis for their political programmes. This brings us back to the question of what an ideology is built on and the *purposes* for which it is used. In this region, Left-wing political parties are inclined to reject this clan consciousness categorically instead of making a distinction between its conservative and progressive elements (which do exist, for example, in the intense sociability of each clan) and of basing their political programmes on them.

This example shows that a Left-wing political sector which does not take into consideration the daily preoccupations of the majority of the population, is not only ineffectual but is playing into the hands of conservative parties which seem to revel in ideology. More broadly speaking, this case of local politics shows the autonomy that ideology may acquire and the specific dynamic forces it may release. Although ideology is always determined by given social conditions, it can at times play a determining role.

Xenophobic Movements in Switzerland

For over ten years political movements in Switzerland have been campaigning against migrant workers. These movements, which we call xenophobic, aim drastically to reduce the number of immigrants residing in Switzerland and use the 'popular initiative' as a frequent weapon. Briefly, what this means is that 50,000 signatures of Swiss citizens must be collected to propose an amendment of any part of the federal constitution. After the proposal has been examined by the federal authorities, the Swiss nation is called to accept or reject the project in question and its decision is legally binding.

The Swiss have already had to vote several times on initiatives launched by xenophobic movements — in June 1970 on the all too publicised initiative launched by Mr James Schwarzenbach, and in October 1974 on one by the National Action group.[11] The second was more drastic than the first, requiring the government to expel close to half the immigrants in Switzerland within a short time limit.

These two initiatives met with a great deal of success. Mr Schwarzenbach's initiative was very nearly passed (46 percent voted in favour of it). The other which was not only more drastic but even distinctly 'suicidal' (a term that its opponents used repeatedly) for the Swiss economy, was nonetheless approved by 34 percent of the voters.[12]

Such voting results indicate the gravity of the problem of migrant workers in Switzerland and the widespread passionate feelings it arouses. However, the hostility towards migrant workers is certainly no greater in Switzerland than in any other country harbouring foreign workers. In Switzerland the popular initiative brings this phenomenon right out into the open. It is almost certain that if the initiative procedure existed in other countries it would gain as much support. We do not intend to defend Switzerland at all costs but merely to point out that xenophobia is not a Swiss but a more general problem.

Therefore, the battle cry of these xenophobic movements is the migrant worker. In terms of the well-known scapegoat phenomenon (is it in fact really so well-known?), the migrant worker has been designated by these movements as the cause of all evil. We will try to show that the migrant worker is only the leitmotif and that the xenophobic movements, in point of fact, represent and embody what is a conservative and reactionary *ideology*. It is an out-dated political answer to the present-day Swiss economic and social situation.

From both a socio-political and ideological viewpoint, Switzerland presents certain specific features.[13] Until recently, Switzerland was characterised by a fairly peaceful political climate. Since 1937, following the famous 'Labour Peace' (an agreement between social partners to solve social problems and conflicts by collaboration and negotiation), Swiss politics ceased to develop along the lines of a class struggle. The partners to the agreement deliberately agreed to pass from class struggle to collaboration. This socio-political situation provided an ideal climate for the development of an *ideology of consensus*. Seldom has such wide consensus existed in times of peace. In addition, after the Second World War and until around 1974, the country experienced an enormous economic development and a considerable rise in the standard of living.

On a superstructural level, a whole myth has grown up around Switzerland. The country is given throughout the world as an example for several of its features, among which are stressed: the country's natural beauty, the fraternal and egalitarian coexistence of very different sub-cultures, direct democracy, its neutrality, its humanitarianism, etc. These diverse elements have undoubtedly led to a certain feeling of *superiority* among the Swiss. They have fostered *nationalism* – and the word nationalism necessarily, even as a latent and implicit tendency, implies the devaluation of all that is not Swiss, of all that is foreign, Other. Almost the entire Swiss population (people from all social classes at any rate) is deeply attached to these notions, which are to a greater or lesser degree mythical. They form the basic elements of *collective consciousness*. They form what we shall henceforth call the *Helvetian ideology*.

For several years now, almost all the notions which constitute the 'greatness' of the Helvetian ideology are increasingly in contradiction with reality. Industrialisation and urbanisation have spoiled numerous natural beauties. Other notions idealised by the Swiss are losing ground. There is general uneasiness at all levels. In short, certain elements of Helvetian ideology which are, or at least were, part of reality are becoming more and more chimerical. Helvetian ideology is in crisis. Certain myths are being shown to be no more than myths. Demystification of this kind creates doubt among the Swiss who are disoriented because the notions to which they were most attached and which were deeply ingrained seem to be losing ground. The extent of the confusion is in proportion to the extent of demystification.

This ideological demystification or transformation is obviously related to changes in social and economic conditions. Yet the very sudden change in Helvetian ideology has released specific dynamic forces, a type of ideological autodynamism. Demystification has caused panic and confusion at the level of collective consciousness.

In the face of the disorientation of the collective consciousness, Left-wing movements had no overall or significant alternative to offer. They limited themselves to issuing political directives, half-hearted claims and proposals for small-scale reform which did not however represent a political ideology based on the immediate and new daily needs and problems of the vast majority of the Swiss. Their claims and directives were once again almost entirely limited to objective interests. They hardly took into account collective consciousness or those elements of Helvetian ideology 'in crisis' to which people were still strongly attached. This is yet another example of the lack of understanding on the part of the Left of the primordial role of ideology and its deep nature.

Ideologists who understood the essential role of ideology and the difference between the theorist's class consciousness and collective consciousness, then made their entry into Swiss politics. They used Helvetian ideology to the full as an instrument of political strategy for reactionary purposes. They very rapidly created havoc on the political scene in record time. In this way the xenophobic movements were created.

If we use the term Helvetian ideology today, it is to distinguish it from one which is generally described as the dominant ideology transmitted by the classes in power. Helvetian ideology is related to the progressive birth, growth and extension of Switzerland (let us not forget that the last cantons only became part of Switzerland in 1815). We maintain that Helvetian ideology could also partly be progressively oriented. Let us take just one very general and rather theoretical example: *unity*. When primitive Switzerland was created, this theme was invoked for progressive purposes. Unity was necessary for freedom from foreign domination. With the rise of capitalism, the 'bourgeoisie' played on this feeling of unity first to impose its domination and then to remain in power. Thus, unity became the ideology of consensus. Consensus is an essentially conservative theme. Through consensus unity became an instrument in the hands of the established power. To invoke consensus is to insist on common elements rather than on inequalities and differences, and is an excellent means of defence against confrontation and claims.

These few elements show that in the present example Helvetian ideology is not only a series of reactionary elements, but also that certain themes could be taken up by progressive forces with the advantage that their political programmes would be immediately and directly related to the daily preoccupations of the majority of the population.

Schwarzenbach, the ideologist who best symbolises the xenophobic movements, follows this pattern very closely although obviously for reactionary purposes. Such movements draw from Helvetian ideology only those themes which may be orientated in a conservative way. Furthermore, any progressive aspects contained in these themes would be played down by stressing only those which permit a reactionary orientation.

One of the basic themes of this reactionary ideology, and behind the denunciation of an alleged 'foreign overpopulation', is in fact nationalism. The devaluation of the Other, the foreigner, is directly related to nationalism and the exaltation of this nationalism leads to such devaluation. The insistence on nationalism also provides a possible answer to the Helvetian ideological crisis and to the Swiss collective and individual identity crisis.[14] The supreme subterfuge of these ideologists is that the cause of all evils can be traced to one passionate theme — immigrant workers. Evil and 'contamination' always come from the Other, and this Other has been clearly identified. The theme of foreigners is only a catalyst for these movements and their ideology.

Up till now consensus was regarded as an end in itself. What could be described as consensus on the status quo, was used by the ruling classes to remain in power. The ideologists also made use of this element of Helvetian ideology. They tried to sway the consensus as far to the Right as possible, basing it on the most reactionary elements. Their solution to the crisis was not a new model of society but a *return to the past*, to a Switzerland at once beautiful, pure, harmonious, without conflicts, enclosed within itself and free from external contamination, clean, ordered, superior, ideal, etc. They were trying to revive a mythical past.[15]

In times of crisis there is frequent ideological recourse to a mythical and idealised past and, in this too, the link with collective consciousness is direct and immediate.

In order to overcome possible reservations on the part of the working class, especially among skilled workers and small businessmen, certain *anti-capitalist* themes are added (opposition to the large monopolies, etc.). However, the term anti-capitalist must be carefully examined. To denounce big business or multi-national companies does not necessarily imply a fundamental opposition to capitalist societies. Thus, at the same time, these movements absolutely uphold private property and free enterprise. We all know that at the outset Nazi ideology was rigorously anti-capitalist. Furthermore, it did not hesitate to expound revolutionary themes towards the working classes.

Therefore, at the source of the xenophobic movements there is a definite political ideology which has all the principal characteristics and properties of any other ideology such as the simplification, schematisation, reconstruction, correction and rectification of social reality, together with coherence and impossibility of verification. It is an affirmative and apodictic certainty and closely follows divisions and patterns in terms of Good/Evil and Self/Other.

In our example the simplification and distortion are carried to extremes. The immigrant workers are regarded as the cause of *all* evil. When these ideologists realised that the theme of the migrant worker was even more passionate and more emotional than they had foreseen, they expanded it further. Foreigners who (in the minds of the greater part of the population) were regarded as the cause of certain evils became the cause of all evils, even the most unlikely ones (crime, 'moral decline', pollution, etc.)

In this sense this ideology could truly be described as a pathological one although obviously terms such as 'normal' and 'pathological' are wide open to criticism.[16]

On this point, it is interesting to note the link J. Gabel established between schizophrenia and certain ideologies such as fascism, nazism and stalinism.[17]

The origin of the most pathological forms of distortion must be sought in the inevitable gap between the content of an ideology and the complexity of concrete reality. The intrinsic properties of ideology are precisely what lead to the creation of pathological ones. These ideologies develop according to the logic of identification (Gabel speaks of 'false identification') as in the case of xenophobic ideology with the foreigner identified as the cause of all evils. From the time that this identification is accepted and experienced by the greater part of the population, when it proves effective, it can in certain cases be simplified and lead to an increasing distortion ending in delirium which is no longer individual but collective. There is a delirious awareness of the Other, of the foreigner who is seen as embodying malefic qualities. As in schizophrenia, an hallucinatory collective mental world can be created which leads to a delirious and phantasmic surreality. In this world, suffering, for example, is regarded as the condition or the means to discover or rediscover a wonderful world. Those xenophobic individuals, whilst aware that expelling the foreigners would inevitably lead to further difficulties, nevertheless tell themselves that they are 'ready to suffer in order to rediscover the real Switzerland'. In hallucinatory situations of this nature, ideologists appeal to the most primitive forces (aggresiveness, fantasies of power, etc.). In extreme cases, homicidal tendencies come to the surface (massacres of designated victims, as in the case of nazism).

Our aim is in no way to present an exhaustive analysis of xenophobia but merely to outline, by means of this second example, the autonomy of ideology, the remarkable power it may have, and the fact that, in certain cases, it may become 'the driving force of history' or a basic determining factor of a complete restructuring of social and political relations. Pushing our analysis one step further, could we not conceive of power as the outcome of ideology?

It is as though our knowledge of ideology were only at its beginnings. In the social sciences ideology has only been very partially understood. Some of its essential properties appear to have been hardly analysed in depth and often hardly understood. This lack of knowledge has implications which are scientific and theoretical as well as political.

Furthermore, we have tried to show that an ideology which has a certain influence on the masses is related to their immediate and daily preoccupations. This explains the distinction between the theorists' concept of class consciousness and the class consciousness of the masses or collective consciousness. An ideology which does not take this distinction into account will easily find reasons for its own lack of impact, all the more so when we consider to what extent popular political energy and combativity arise from the direct every-day lives of the people. Furthermore, we believe that Right-wing and extreme Right-wing political parties have a better understanding of the properties, potential and power of ideology and they put their knowledge into practice, but for conservative purposes. The most every-day preoccupations of the people are open to both progressive and conservative solutions.

With regard to the scientific and theoretical aspects of the lack of ideological knowledge, we feel that, broadly speaking, our Western civilisation tends to regard economy and technology as more real than culture and ideology. Ideology is not considered as something particularly real.

Science (the social sciences) is seen, and develops, in opposition to ideology. Science in fact views ideology as a residue, often entirely negative. In such a context and under such conditions, it is hardly surprising that only very minor aspects of ideology are retained, and that its overall reality is overlooked. Indeed, how can one conceive of ideology as at the same time a means of giving science perspective and as an object of science? This viewpoint is fairly evident in the most diverse studies within the social sciences and is consequently opposed to our approach, which attempts to perceive ideology as a formulator of realities, as a specific reality, and as having its own characteristics and its own specific mechanisms.[18]

Our intention in this chapter was merely to outline a problem of ideology and to define some of the possible angles of approach towards a greater understanding of the subject; in particular the puzzling fact that on the one hand power can be the outcome of ideology, and on the other that there should be this profound failure to understand the specificity of ideology.

NOTES

1. Cf. P. Ansart, *Les idéologies politiques* (Paris, 1974), 213. This book was an invaluable source of reference at various levels for this first section.

2. W. Reich, *La Psychologie de masse du fascisme* (Paris, 1972).

3. U. Windisch, *Lutte de clans, lutte de classes* (Lausanne, 1976).

4. A. Gramsci, *Oeuvres choisies* (Paris, 1959).

5. W. Reich, *Qu'est-ce que la conscience de classe* (Nice, 1975), 64 [Editors' translations].

6. Ibid., 91.

7. Ibid., 93.

8. Ibid., 19.

9. U. Windisch, *Lutte de clans, lutte de classes.*

10. F. Dumont, *Les idéologies* (Paris, 1974), 52-57.

11. Members of the second movement broke away from Mr Schwarzenbach's movement because they considered it too 'soft' towards the immigrants.

12. The Swiss people were called to vote on several initiatives of this kind in Spring 1977.

13. For a more detailed analysis of this situation, cf. U. Windisch, 'Travailleurs immigrés, xenophobie et capitalisme, Le cas de la Suisse', *Espaces et Sociétés*, No. 4 (Paris, 1971), 89-105.

14. The ideological use of nationalism in times of crisis, uncertainty and confusion, is a well-known phenomenon.

15. We are at present conducting several practical research programmes on ideology and in particular on the ideology of xenophobic movements. This research is based on numerous very detailed documents and repeated interviews. This is also the subject of a publication we are working on.

16. See P. Ansart, op. cit., 85.

17. J. Gabel, *Sociologie de l'aliénation* (Paris, 1971). Cf. also our criticism of this work: U. Windisch, 'A propos du livre de J. Gabel: La sociologie de l'aliénation', *Revue européenne des sciences sociales*, No. 25, 1971: 209-16.

18. It is to be expected that the results of certain studies on language, for example in the field of socio-linguistics and what may be termed 'discourse analysis', particularly political discourse, will add significantly to a knowledge of ideology. Thus, some of those carrying out research in this field no longer merely inquire into how ideology reveals itself linguistically, but how language itself is ideology. The 'active' and structural aspects of language are receiving greater attention and it is increasingly becoming a matter of a theory of ideology. It would also be appropriate to mention studies on argumentation by B. Grize and G. Vignaux. Furthermore, certain ethnomethodologists (A. V. Cicourel to mention just one) are attempting to reformulate a theory of action and a 'sociology of the implicit' by taking certain linguistic aspects into consideration.

III Individual Action and Collective Choice:
An Evaluation of the New Contractarians

11 Social Contract, Community and Ideology

John N. Gray
University of Oxford, UK

It is widely recognised that the attempted revival by John Rawls and Robert Nozick of the contractarian tradition in political thought occurs at a propitious juncture in the history of ideas. According to a popular view, in their writings political philosophy (recently pronounced dead) emerges from the neglect into which it had fallen as a result of the dominance of the linguistic schools and of positivism. *Anarchy, State and Utopia* and *A Theory of Justice* are viewed, then, as books in which the perennial questions of political philosophy are treated constructively and with all the sophistication achieved in other branches of philosophy. As against this widespread view, I shall claim these are works of salvage and reconstruction, applied to the liberal tradition, whose need of repair is notorious. My argument will be that whatever has value in these writings is obscured if we accept their authors' avowals that they exemplify the fruitfulness of the contractarian method. I shall contend that the contractarian credentials of the theories of Rawls and Nozick are dubious, and that such force as their arguments possess has other sources. In the course of my argument it will become clear why I regard the revival of interest in the contractarian approach as unfortunate. It will also become evident why I do not regard its attempted revitalisation as fortuitous. Rather, it may be seen (though I cannot here show this) as an ideological manoeuvre, inevitably unsuccessful, undertaken in response to the current crisis of liberal society.

I

The avowed aim of Rawls' theory of justice as fairness is to show that there are principles of justice which must command the assent of all rational agents in that they are demonstratively derivable by a species of contractarian argument from premises which are logically unexceptionable and morally non-partisan. My first objection to the Rawlsian programme is that, in so far as the design of the original position incorporates unexamined and controversial moral assumptions, the social contract which supposedly occurs within it cannot justify assent to the principles of justice. Importantly, I am assuming (what is far from self-evident) that rational choice can occur in the circumstances of the original position, that the principles chosen can somehow be shown to be principles of justice, and that they will be Rawls' principles. Equally importantly, my objection to Rawls' theory must be distinguished sharply from another, superficially similar objection, which I believe to be fundamentally misconceived. This latter objection has been made by W. G. Runciman in an exceptionally succinct form: 'The fundamental objection to Rawls' idea of an "original position" in which rational persons ignorant of their interests are supposed to have to decide on principles by which their social institutions will in due course be governed is that it already assumes what it purports to be used to demonstrate.'[1] As it stands, this objection to Rawls' theory is paradoxical; so far as it goes, indeed, such an objection constitutes a testimony to the success of Rawls' theory. For, as Runciman immediately goes on to acknowledge, it is precisely Rawls' claim that the principles of justice are derivable from, or yielded by, the conditions stipulated to hold in the original position. Runciman's objection to Rawls' theory plainly embodies a misconception of the role Rawls himself might reasonably claim to be performed in his theory by the original position. Rawls himself (it will be recalled) supposes the original position to be the most philosophically favoured interpretation of a hypothetical initial situation in which basic agreements would be fair. In answer to the question '. . . how are we to decide what is the most favoured interpretation?', which Rawls puts himself, he responds to the effect that 'the conditions embodied in the description of the original position are ones that we do in fact accept. Or, if we do not, then perhaps we can be persuaded to do so by philosophical reflection'.[2] The question of how we are to establish what is the most favoured interpretation of the initial situation is plainly a question of the first importance, since Rawls later (after having acknowledged that there are many possible interpretations of the initial situation) conjectures that 'for each traditional conception of justice there exists an interpretation of the initial situation in which its principles are the preferred solution'.[3] These remarks make clear that there is a centrally important sense in which the entire burden of the justification of the principles of justice rests on the arguments Rawls adduces in support of the stipulations by appeal to which he characterises the original position. The objection to Rawls' theory is not, then, that 'the stipulated conditions are . . . so framed so to yield the outcome that he requires' (Runciman), but that Rawls' rationale for the stipulations regarding the conditions of the original position is unconvincing. This can, in fact, easily be shown.

It is a truth of capital importance for the understanding of Rawls' theory that intuitive judgements enter into it at two decisive points: in determining what are the appropriate stipulations regarding the conditions of the initial position, and in modifying these stipulations in accordance with our considered moral judgements. At both points it can be shown that Rawls' intuitive judgements fail to correspond with those that many reflective members of his own culture are inclined to make. Let us look first at Rawls' claim that the conditions of the original situation incorporate 'commonly shared presumptions' that principles of justice be chosen under certain conditions – a claim Rawls inflates into the claim that the conditions of the original situation incorporate what he describes as 'the circumstances of justice'. Rawls' motive in advancing this bolder claim is fairly transparent. Manifestly in order to show that the choices his contractors allegedly make under the conditions of the original position are morally relevant, Rawls needs to establish the moral significance of the conditions under which the choices are supposed to be made, and this is what he tries to do by making the claim that the conditions of the original position comprehend typical circumstances of justice or, alternatively, that they represent the formal constraints on having a morality. The implausibility of any such claim must, however, be apparent as soon as it is examined critically. There is an initial doubt whether the expression 'circumstances of justice' has any definite sense; but, granting that it does, it is surely incontrovertible that it does not typically designate a set of conditions in which men are ignorant of their own circumstances and abilities and in which their relationship with one another is one of fair equality. Rawls might, no doubt, want to claim that the conditions of the original position represent formal constraints on the deliberations of the rational contractors – constraints of impartiality, for example – that these constraints are synonymous with the conditions of having a morality. Once again, however, such a claim has only to be clearly stated for its implausibility to be patent. The presumption that the contractors stand in relation to one another on a basis of equality, while it corresponds with the main stream of Judaeo-Christian and Enlightenment morality, cannot sensibly be supposed to express one of the conditions of morality itself. Such a presumption of fundamental human equality would not be made in Aristotelian or Nietzchean moral outlooks — to cite only two fairly obvious examples. If the conditions of the original position do not (as Rawls claims) embody the typical circumstances in which questions of justice arise, or express the formal requirements of having a morality, then a serious problem is posed for his theory. In so far as Rawls' stipulations regarding the original position lack the generality required to make them circumstances of justice or formal constraints on having a morality, then his derivation of the principles of justice from the conditions of the original situation will have little or no moral interest even if it is valid. Rawls' reasoning assumes a character of vicious circularity, then, not at the point when it is noticed that the stipulations regarding the original situation are made in order to secure the derivation of the principles of justice, but at the point when it is established that these stipulations have no independent justification.

The lack in Rawls' work of such a justification for adopting his stipulations regarding the original position is not an incidental defect of his theory, but testifies to one of its most important characteristics. I have alluded to this aspect of Rawls' theory in pointing out that intuitive judgements enter into it at two decisive points — in the construction of the initial position, and in its refinement in accordance with 'commonly shared presumptions' and 'our considered moral judgements'. Rawls' reliance on intuition at these crucial points reveals that, despite its deductivist aspirations, his theory rests ultimately on an intuitionist moral epistemology with strongly subjectivist implications. As his exposition of the notion of reflective-equilibrium makes clear, the validity of an ethical theory for Rawls is partly constituted by its correspondence with our most tenaciously held moral judgements (which it must also account for and systematise): for Rawls, the relation between the validity of a moral theory and our first-order moral judgements is conceptual or criterial rather than a relation between explanation and evidence. The analogy between moral theory and linguistic theory, which crops up frequently in *A Theory of Justice* and which rests on a comparison of ethics as an exploration of human competence, is further evidence in support of the attribution to Rawls of a subjectivist moral epistemology. For, plainly, moral intuitions will be as decisive in ethical theory as linguistic practice is in grammatical theory, only if validity in moral theory is actually constituted by fidelity to the fixed points of moral sentiment and practice. Paradoxically, then, his frequent invocations of the Kantian interpretation of justice as fairness notwithstanding, Rawls' adoption of conformity with moral intuitions as a *criterion* of validity in moral theory warrants us in characterising him as an exponent of a moral sense epistemology with evident Humean affinities.

So far my criticism of Rawls' theory as incorporating unexamined and unjustified moral assumptions — assumptions which I have claimed correspond in Rawls' moral epistemology to basic intuitive judgements or ultimate moral responses — has proceeded at a somewhat abstract level. I want now to illustrate my claim by looking in greater detail at the design of the original position and to show how controversial judgements as to the value of equality and liberty are built into its very fabric. Somewhat platitudinously, it may be worth remarking that the general point of view of Rawls' theory is a strongly emphasised egalitarianism, according to which 'All social values — liberty and opportunity, income and wealth, and the bases of self-respect — are to be distributed equally unless an unequal distribution of any, or all, of these values is to everyone's advantage.'[4] Now, as Kenneth Arrow has noted,[5] the generalised difference principle stated in this quotation is far from tautologous: it entails, for example, a widely accepted but still far from uncontroversial principle of *asset egalitarianism* which affirms that 'all the assets of society, including personal skills, are available as a common pool for whatever distribution justice calls for'.[6] Rawls actually makes explicit this asset egalitarianism when he says in the course of discussion of the main grounds of the two principles of justice: 'The two principles are equivalent ... to an undertaking to regard the distribution of natural abilities as a collective asset so that the more fortunate are to benefit only in ways that help those who have lost out.'[7] It is worth noting parenthetically the grossly counter-intuitive implication of the principle of asset egalitarianism that the able and gifted members of the human race — those endowed with extraordinary artistic talents, for example — are justified in enjoying the primary goods involved in developing and exercising their talents only if in doing so they benefit the rest of society, and, in particular, its least advantaged group.[8] Apart from the fact that Rawls' general point of view has counter-intuitive implications for many of his readers — a fact which casts serious doubt on the claim of adequacy of justice as fairness conceived as a quasi-empirical theory whose data are men's considered moral responses — his commitment to a stringent principle of asset egalitarianism helps to explain his otherwise unaccountable neglect of what Arrow has described as the productivity principle. This is a principle which is widely and unreflectively held, and often thought to be entirely self-evident, according to which an individual is entitled to what he creates.

Once again, it is not accidental that Rawls fails to consider a productivist alternative to his conception of justice: the neglect illustrates some of the most important features of his theory. For, as Robert Nozick has shown, the design of the original position excludes from initial consideration all 'historical' theories of distributive justice (such as Nozick's own quasi-Lockean entitlement theory) and restricts rational deliberation in the original position to critical evaluation of various 'end-state' theories. Nozick distinguishes between end-state and historical theories as follows: 'In contrast to end-result principles of justice, historical principles of justice hold that past circumstances or actions of people can create differential entitlements or differential deserts to things'.[9] Nozick distinguishes also between 'patterned' and 'unpatterned' principles of justice. A patterned principle is one according to which justice of a distribution varies according to some 'natural dimension', such as needs, which would yield an end-state patterned principle, or merit, which would yield a patterned historical principle. According to Nozick's own unpatterned historical theory, the justice of a distribution does not vary according to determinate features of men's actions or characteristics of these sorts. Nozick's argument is not the weak, paradoxical and probably invalid one that Rawls' construction of the original situation is incapable of yielding any conception of justice other than that which it actually yields: rather it is that the veil of ignorance 'ensures that no shadow of entitlement considerations will enter the rational calculations of ignorant, non-moral individuals. . . . Since no glimmer of entitlement principles is built into the structure of the situation of persons in the original position, there is no way these principles could be selected; and Rawls' construction is incapable in principle of yielding them.'[10] The significance of Rawls' neglect of entitlement and, in general, of historical principles of justice is that, since he nowhere justifies their absence from the list of alternative conceptions of justice, he has no independent chain of reasoning which might warrant adopting end-state rather than historical principles. The point, then, is not that Rawls' construction of the original position is designed to yield only end-state principles, nor yet that his list of alternative principles of justice is far from exhaustive (which Rawls readily admits), but that Rawls' reasoning becomes viciously circular insofar as he can give no good reasons for accepting stipulations regarding the original position other than that they allow him to derive the outcome he wants.

I have called attention to an important feature of Rawls' approach to social justice — its *presumptivism* regarding the value of equality. Rawls assents uncritically to the view (endorsed by a long line of liberal thinkers, including Isaiah Berlin (in some of his writings), Bernard Williams and Richard Wollheim)[11] according to which it is supposed that 'though it is absurd to think that justice requires us to treat all men exactly alike, it does require that we give them equal treatment until we have good reason not to, so that "the burden of proof is on the person who wants to treat people differently from one another" '.[12] The most common line of criticism of this approach to equality is that it established only a weak, formal and question-begging principle of equality, so leaving the whole weight of justification of particular discriminatory policies to rest upon the criteria of relevance which are adduced to support them.[13] I want to contend that this criticism, though valid as far as it goes, is misconceived in so far as it endorses the egalitarian presumption which is expressed in Berlin's claim that '. . . if I depart from (a) principle of equal division I am expected to produce a special reason'.[14] For, as Feinberg has pointed out, egalitarian presumptivism is open to the fatal objection that 'Where the "burden proof" actually lies in a given case . . . depends upon what is given (believed or known) about the relevant traits of the individuals involved, and also upon the particular context of justice and its governing norms and maxims. The presumption in favour of equal treatment holds when the individuals involved are believed, assumed or expected to be equal in the relevant respects, whereas the presumption in favour of unequal treatment holds when the individuals involved are expected to be different in the relevant respects.'[15] Rawls' commitment to a narrow, dogmatic and vulnerable form of presumptivism regarding the value of equality is clearly revealed when he asserts that 'this principle (the first principle of justice requiring an equal distribution of all primary social goods), is so obvious that we would expect it to occur to anyone immediately'.[16] Interestingly, Rawls subsequently discloses that he is committed to an analogous form of presumptivism regarding the priority of liberty when he stipulates that the rationality of the contractors in the original position is *partly constituted* by their preference for liberty over other primary goods. Rawls' frequent resort to such presumptivist positions should occasion no surprise to those who accept the characterisation of his moral epistemology as a variant of subjectivist intuitionism: for, after all, if such an epistemology be adopted, it follows that no argument can be adduced in support of basic principles, whose ratification can be conceived only in terms of their endorsement by pre-reflective moral sentiments. It is an implication of my account that Rawls' commitment to an intuitionist moral epistemology reinforces his indisposition to supply independent reasonings for adopting the stipulations regarding the original position in which are embodied the moral assumptions I have in mind. It is a further implication of my account that, if the stipulations expressive of these moral assumptions can be supported independently, then we have found direct moral arguments as to the value of equality and the priority of liberty, and the apparatus of the original position and the social contract is dispensable.

My overriding objection to Rawls' programme — that it endorses a misconceived presumptivism in respect of liberty and equality and that its contractarian argument is superogatory in so far as it is not ultimately incoherent — has large consequences for social philosophy and its ramifying reasonings may accordingly deserve some further elaboration. Rawls' account of rationality gives the reader the impression that he supposes that, from among the extended family of human activities in which reasons may be asked for or given, there might be selected some which, since they are expressive of some of the natural necessities or generic features of human life, may be privileged over the innumerable local, culturally and historically variant practices in which men give an account of themselves and their actions to their fellows, and ponder dilemmas of choice. Indeed, Rawls' theory would plainly fail to achieve the universality to which it aspires if the picture of rationality which Rawls paints in it (especially in Chapter 7) could be shown to be permeated by norms characteristic of his own (but not of all) cultures. In general it is one of the oldest aspirations of philosophers to formulate criteria or legislate norms of deliberative rationality which will be universal and context-independent in that they reflect the natural necessities of man's life, and which (unlike the rules of inference of formal logic) will impose substantive restrictions on the conduct of practical reasoning. This perennial aspiration, notoriously, is open to the objection that the task of distinguishing between what is generic and what is specific in human life, between what is essential and what is accidental, between nature and convention is (logically, or as a matter of fact) impossible to bring off. More plausibly, it is an objection to any such distinction as is involved in Rawls' attempt to isolate generically human and universally binding constitutive principles of practical reasoning, that such principles will either be truly universal in their application but empty of substantive, action-guiding content, or else specific in their practical implications but tainted by culture-dependent norms. I submit that Rawls' attempt to operate with principles of practical reasoning which have the universal validity of the inference rules of formal logic but are yet action-guiding, like that of Kant and H. L. A. Hart, falls between two stools. Specifically, Rawls gives the derivation of the principles of justice from the circumstances of the original position an appearance of plausibility only by building into the deliberate rationality of the contractors normative specifications (such as that embodied in the Aristotelian principle) whose culture-dependency is patent.

The pancultural aspirations of Rawls' theory are, however, most clearly visible in his theory of primary social goods, and it is there that the Rawlsian programme most obviously founders. It is the central claim of Rawls' theory that the concept of a rational life plan, in conjunction with the thin theory of the good that it comprehends, is such as to allow a reasonable choice to be made and for the choice problem posed by the original position to yield a determinate solution, while at the same time being neutral as between rival conceptions of the good life. Are there, in fact, any 'primary goods' that are truly universal? Life and health look unexceptionable items on any list of true primary goods — though such an appearance may be delusive — but it is surely evident that the cultural relativity of the rest of Rawls' candidates restricts the class of primary goods and seriously impoverishes the notion of a rational life plan. Again, one must not follow Rawls in neglecting the possibility that the class of true primary goods is an empty one. After all, it is an implication of some understandings of human life — those of Hegel and the later Marx, perhaps — that human nature is always entirely constituted by a nexus of historically variant, culturally specific and alterable social relations. Admittedly, Hegel might well wish to present an explanation of the indeterminacy of human nature in terms of man's permanent liability to reflexive thought, while neither Marx nor Hegel could sensibly deny that man's biological constitution imposes significant constraints on the range of modes of social life that is open to him. Still, it is an implication of such an understanding of human activity that no distinction can be made between human wants and needs that are local or parochial and those that are generic or universal, such as that the latter can be identified reliably and ranked morally over the former. If the forms of man's life are the creations of his own practice, constrained only by the facts of his constitution and by the circumstances he inherits from his forebears, then it will be seen that no conception of the good life can be privileged over others on the grounds that it is more deeply founded in man's nature.

If there are good reasons for supposing that Rawls' attempt to predetermine the outcome of the contractors' deliberations by supplying them with paradigmatic human wants, from which all traces of motives relating to culturally and historically variable forms of life have been erased, is a project that is doomed to failure, these reasons are only strengthened if we consider the restrictions Rawls wishes to impose on the knowledge available to his covenantors. For, as several writers have perceived, Rawls' hypothesis of the original position is not (strictly speaking) coherent. It will be recalled that Rawls supposes that the contractors might be acquainted with the laws of psychology (including moral psychology), sociology and economics (for example) while being ignorant of any particular facts about themselves or their society. There is the profoundest doubt, however, whether it is at all conceivable that the veil of ignorance could be thick enough to blot out knowledge of particular facts while being thin enough to let in knowledge of such laws. Even if such an objection of incoherence could be shown to be misconceived, it would still be the case that general knowledge let in through the veil of ignorance would be so vague as to be of little assistance in solving the choice dilemma. For, since the contractors are presumed to be ignorant of the stage of development of their own society, the 'laws of economics' and 'laws of sociology' they would be acquainted with would be such as apply to all societies — whatever their stage of development — and, plausibly, they would be laws of such abstract generality as to be almost destitute of predictive or explanatory potency. More generally, I contend that, just as an understanding of the terms and notions used in empirical science such as psychology and economics presupposes logically some knowledge of particular facts, so an understanding of the general conditions of human existence presupposes an experience of living in definite forms of social life. This is only to express assent to the traditional criticism of social contract doctrines, recently powerfully restated,[17] that they attribute to the presocial abstract individuals who make the contract, qualities which are acquired only by living in society. To do this, however, is to say that the original position envisages a logically impossible circumstance, and that the supposition that deliberation and choice can occur within it is incoherent.

If Rawls' hypothesis of the original position is an unintelligible one, we may be inclined to doubt that it has the central place in his theory that Rawls sometimes attributes to it. At first glance Rawls' claim that the theory of justice as fairness represents a revival of the contractarian tradition in political argument raises suspicions in anyone acquainted with the development of that tradition. After all, the traditional social-contract theory addressed itself to different problems from those to which Rawls' theory is intended as a solution. In the writings of Hobbes and Locke, for example, the device of the social contract is used not primarily as a test of the acceptability of candidate principles of social distributive justice, but rather as a metaphorical statement of a consensual theory of the grounds and limits of political obligations (which itself comprehends an account of justice). Even in the more favourable case of Rousseau's political thought, it might plausibly be contended that there are independent moral arguments for the value of equality and the principles of social justice, while the social-contract device retains its traditional role as a solution to the problem of political obligation by appealing to the actual or tacit consent of the representative rational agent. These doubts about the aptness of Rawls' characterisation of his theory as contractarian are amply confirmed if (disregarding the basic question of its coherence) we look at the logic of rational deliberation in the original position. A number of writers have remarked that, in so far as the contractors have access to the same general knowledge and are presumed to undertake the same deliberations, there is no need in Rawls' account of the original position for the supposition of a diversity of choosing selves coming to a unanimous public agreement. I suggest that the claim that Rawls' theory is not a variant of contractarianism can be made more sharply. I suggest that, not only is it the case that Rawls does not need the device of social contract: he cannot afford it. In other words, Rawls characterises the original position in such a way as to exclude even the logical possibility of there being a diversity of choosing selves who come to an agreement. How does Rawls succeed in doing this? In the first place, by laying down stringent conditions regarding publicity of information, identity of motivation and values and of the conduct of practical reasoning, Rawls effectively removes from the original position the possibilities of privacy, diversity of motivation and divergence in reasoning processes which are among the logically necessary conditions of there being a diversity of selves. In noting as part of the logic of selfhood the necessary truth that a diversity of persons is composed of individuals with distinct and differing experiences, values and motives, we see that Rawls cannot have the assurance that the choice problem posed in the original position will have the solution he desires while yet preserving the fiction of a diversity of reasoners and choosers. Another way of making this claim is to say that, in stipulating that 'the parties in the original position are theoretically defined individuals', Rawls deprives the contractors of criteria of identity without which they are interchangeable and undistinguishable.

Against those of Rawls' critics who have argued that the core of his theory is in the conception of the original position as posing a choice problem in which a hypothetical rational individual adopts principles of action under conditions of ignorance and uncertainty, and who contend that this rational-choice core needs to be separated from the redundant expository device of the social contract, I contend that the incoherence of the supposition that there can be deliberation or choice in the original position entails that Rawls' theory is no more a rational choice theory than it is a species of contractarianism. (That the derivation of the principles of justice confessedly fails to be deductive should in any case incline one to be suspicious of the theory's rational-choice credentials.) If Rawls' theory is neither of these things, then what is it? Paradoxical and implausible though such a characterisation of his work appears, the closest affinity exists between Rawls' theory and those theories of the moral sense which flourished during the period of the Scottish Enlightenment. Such an interpretation of Rawls' work is rendered less implausible, perhaps, when one recalls his account of moral theory itself as an elaboration of man's moral capacity, having a method and aim closely analogous to that of the ordinary empirical sciences (though having also important differences which Rawls does not fail to note). The tension between such an account of the final character of Rawls' theory with that which he claims for it himself is not inconsiderable, yet there are evidences in *A Theory of Justice* that (though he might be reluctant to accept many of the arguments I have adduced in support of my characterisation of his theory) he would not find wholly repugnant the description of his work as a subtle, naturalistically based moral sense theory. Given a sufficiently mature appreciation of the richness and complexity of Kant's thought, Rawls' appeal to Kantian interpretation of his theory might be cited as evidence that he would admit some justice in a moral sense interpretation of his theory. For it is a feature of some at least of the classical exponents of moral sense theories that, while they made a primary appeal to the sentiments of sympathy and benevolence as sources of the moral point of view, they recognised also that moral reasoning has constitutive principles and inference rules of its own. Rawls' neo-Kantian critical rationalism is not implausibly construed, accordingly, as a resumption of the Kantian project of displaying the congruence of the intimations of man's fully developed moral sensibilities with the dictates of the principles of practical reasoning.

Once Rawls' programme is so characterised, it becomes apposite to restate and expand the central objection to all arguments having this general character. It is two-pronged. First, as the ineradicable instability of the thin theory of the good reveals most vividly, any research programme in social philosophy which takes as its basic data the deliverances of 'our fully developed moral sensibilities' may expect to achieve determinate results only if it rests on the (erroneous) supposition, clearly endorsed by Hume, that in essential respects 'mankind is much the same in all times and places'. Secondly, a presumptivist fallacy is committed whenever the attempt is made to derive substantive action-guiding maxims from principles of moral reasoning the denial of which would involve self-contradiction or the abandonment of the moral point of view. Since this fallacy is all but ubiquitous in recent writings on questions of distributive justice, it may be worth attending to those features of genuinely formal principles of justice which distinguish them plainly from those principles, at once avowedly presumptive and allegedly action-guiding, which have been acclaimed by a number of recent writers as expressive of some of the constitutive inference rules of 'our moral reasoning'. As Katzner[18] points out, genuinely formal (or 'formalist') principles of justice are endorsed by Aristotle, when in Chapter 5 of the *Nicomachean Ethics* he explicates justice in terms of the notion of proportion, and by Perelman when he characterises formal justice as treating all those who belong in the same essential category in the same way. Such genuinely formal non-presumptivist principles of justice clearly embody a weak ideal of impartiality, in that they require us to treat relevantly similar cases alike, and it is not utterly implausible to regard subscribing to such genuinely formal principles as partly constitutive of the notion of a rational (rule-following) agent; but they make no presumption in favour of (or against) equality, requiring only that beings in the same categories be treated the same and those in other categories differently. Such formalist principles of justice, in other words, differ from such principles as Berlin's or Benn and Peters'. These latter principles require us to treat all beings alike unless good reason can be provided for treating them differently and stipulate that the *onus probandi* lies on those who advocate discriminatory treatment. For, whereas the former are exceptive principles enjoining that we treat all men alike save where there are differences between them, the latter are presumptive principles demanding that we treat all men alike until it has been shown that they are relevantly different. I contend that the former are genuinely formal principles in that they can plausibly be represented as being used in any kind of moral reasoning, whereas the latter are substantive principles embodying a controversial (and in some cases grossly counter-intuitive) egalitarian presumption. Given the easily demonstrated extensional inequivalence of the two sorts of principles, I submit that presumptive principles are fraudulently represented as defining features of the moral point of view. Rather, the egalitarian and libertarian presumptions embodied in such principles as 'treat all men equally until they have been shown to be relevantly different' and 'do not restrict men's liberty until you have been shown a good reason for doing so' endorse a definite form of moral life whose rivals are no less entitled to claim that their practices satisfy genuinely formal rules of moral reasoning. It is to beg the question in favour of the moral standards of a liberal society to characterise the dispute between its supporters and its enemies as a dispute between men who subscribe to common principles regarding liberty and equality but who assent to divergent criteria of relevance for their correct application.

II

What are the implications of my argument so far for the evaluation of Rawls' theory? First, I wish to emphasise that recognition that the contractual aspect of deliberation in the original position is delusive has substantive and important implications for the evaluation of the character and merits of Rawls' theory. Significantly, Rawls himself lays considerable stress on the claim that his theory has a contractualist aspect, alleging that it is this aspect of his theory which distinguishes it most sharply from utilitarianism. He tells us that

> whereas the utilitarian extends to society the principle of choice for one man, justice as fairness, being a contract view, assumes that the principles of social choice, and so the principles of justice, are themselves the object of an original agreement. There is no reason to suppose that the principles which should regulate an association of men are simply an extension of the principle of choice for one man. On the contrary, if we assume that the correct regulative principle for anything depends on the nature of that thing, and that the plurality of distinct persons with separate systems of ends is an essential feature of human societies, we should not expect the principles of social choice to be utilitarian . . . from the standpoint of contract theory one cannot arrive at a principle of social choice merely by extending the principle of rational prudence to the system of rational desires constructed by the impartial spectator. To do this is not to take seriously the plurality and distinctness of individuals, nor to recognise as the basis of justice that to which men would consent.[19]

In view of the arguments I have adduced regarding the logical impossibility of there being a diversity of selves in the original position, it is paradoxical to find Rawls insisting on the supposed contractarian aspect of his theory as a feature which serves to distinguish it from utilitarianism. In blurring one of the contrasts Rawls wants to make between his theory and utilitarian theories of justice, the dissolution of the contractual aspect of justice as fairness may also bring it much closer to a Kantian position than Rawls himself would allow. Rawls tells us: '. . . I have departed from Kant's views in several respects. . . . The person's choice as noumenal self I have assumed to be a collective one. The force of the self's being equal is, that the principles chosen must be acceptable to other selves. . . . This means that, as noumenal selves, everyone is to consent to these principles.'[20] Interestingly, Rawls seems to be aware that the original position might be interpreted in such a way as to omit any reference to a contractual component: for he goes on to say 'Later I shall try to define a clear sense in which the unanimous agreement is best expressive of the nature of even a single self (Section 85).' When he comes to do this, however, Rawls at no point acknowledges that his design of the original position might rule out any possibility that it contains several reasoning, choosing selves.

Secondly, I want to suggest that the considerations which lead me to question the absence of the supposition that there could be rational deliberation in the circumstances of the original position are destructive of state-of-nature arguments, whether or not they contain reference to contractual agreement. Why is this? Clearly, when the contractors consider the merits of rival conceptions of social justice, they are engaged in a species of practical reasoning; they are deliberating a problem of choice, about which they seek to come to a decision. Given the practical character of reasoning in the original situation, it is striking to note the logical oddity of Rawls' references to 'persons' who compose a society, who yet have no knowledge of their own particular abilities or values, or any acquaintance with specific forms of social life. For, according to one widely influential account of the sense of those concepts which apply peculiarly to human involvements — concepts to do with intending, acting, hoping or regretting, to take a few examples — it is said that their meaning is partly constituted by the circumstances in which they are learnt. To understand such a concept, to use it correctly, in this account, is inconceivable without a grasp of the cases in which its typical uses occur. As Pitkin has put it: 'Meaning is compounded out of cases of a word's use, and what characterises these cases is often the speech situation, not the presence of something being referred to. As a consequence, the significance for meaning of situation, of circumstances, of context, is much greater than one might suppose.'[21]

If, then, there is a non-contingent connection between grasping the sense of a concept and knowing the cases in which to use it, then the supposition that one might (as do the contractors of the original position) employ concepts used to characterise human actions (say) without having learnt their uses in the particular circumstances of human life — this supposition breaks down. Specifically, Rawls' account invites the question, 'How can I be sure I would attach such a high value to liberty, when, as Rawls makes clear, liberty is partly constituted by the immunities and security provided by such artefacts as constitutions and bills of rights — if I were ignorant of the character of a liberal civilisation?' This question, in turn, suggests the aptness of Steven Lukes' judgement on Rawls', whose achievement, he says,[22] is 'to have produced *a* theory of justice — a theory of liberal democratic justice'.

Thirdly, it is, of course, a traditional criticism of social contract theories that they attribute to the pre-social abstract individuals who make the contract qualities which are acquired only by living in society.

Alastair Macintyre has said of Hobbes, for example, that he 'makes two incompatible demands of the original contract: he wishes it to be the foundation of all shared and common standards and rules; but he also wishes it to be a contract, and for it to be a contract there must already exist shared and common standards of the kind which he specifies cannot exist prior to the contract. The conception of an *original* contract is therefore ruined by internal self-contradiction and cannot be used even to frame a metaphor of a coherent kind.'[23] Macintyre's argument applies with even greater force to Rawls than it does to Hobbes. The hypothetical rational choosers of the original position are supposed by Rawls to be able to make an intelligent decision regarding the principles by which their conjectural society will be governed though they are denied all knowledge of particular features of any historic society. Like Hobbes' original contract, but perhaps more obviously, Rawls' original position is a metaphor ruined by its internal contradictions. I have claimed that the state of nature arguments adduced by many liberal theorists suffer from this kind of incoherence, regardless of whether they comprehend contractual deliberations. It is important to note parenthetically that the contractarian credentials of Nozick's derivation of the state are as dubious as those of Rawls' principles of justice. Certainly, as a number of recent writers have pointed out, Nozick's invisible-hand account of the emergence of the state goes no distance forward in justifying its existence against the claims of the individualist anarchist. The real force of Nozick's argument must arrive from a theory of inalienable human rights, which is presupposed rather than defended in *Anarchy, State and Utopia*, and whose consistency with the argument for the minimum state is questionable. More specifically, as Murray Rothbard has argued in a recent critique[24] of Nozick's argument for the state, there is a tension between Nozick's endorsement of the classic liberal position on self-ownership and his treatment (under the murky category of 'compensation') of basic human rights as alienable. As Rothbard puts it, according to classical liberal theory, 'the only valid (and therefore binding) contract is one that surrenders what is, in fact, philosophically *alienable*, and . . . only specific titles to property are so alienable. . . . While, on the contrary, *other* attributes of man, specifically, his self-ownership over his own will and body, and the *rights* to person and property which stem from that self-ownership, are "inalienable" and therefore cannot be surrendered in a binding contract.' In general, Nozick's derivation of the state fails because, first, no invisible-hand process could constitute or give rise to a contractual agreement authorising a transfer of rights.[25]; secondly, Nozick's own account of such rights shows them to be inalienable and so insusceptible, even in principle, to transfer by contractual agreements and, thirdly, since no theory of human rights is ever adumbrated in *Anarchy, State and Utopia*, Nozick must perforce invoke an incoherent state of nature in which narrowly conceived rational economic agents are supposed to give rise to the state via their self-interested decisions.

My third and final point about the attempted revival of liberal contractarianism in the writings of Rawls and Nozick follows directly from these criticisms of its internal cogency. It is that their obscurities and inconsistencies become fully intelligible only when they are seen against the background of the current crisis of liberal thought. My aim has been to show that Rawls' theory of justice as fairness and Nozick's derivation of the state are failures in their own terms. I wish to suggest, in conclusion, that they are best understood as responses to the desuetude of liberal institutions under the impact of external challenges and their own internal contradictions. They are to be regarded, accordingly, as contributions to liberal ideology rather than as works in political philosophy as it has been classically conceived. They explore a particular moral and political perspective — that of liberal society — rather than elucidate its presuppositions and they give it no trans-cendental justification. If anything, the revival of liberalism attempted in the works of Rawls and Nozick must be judged to have obstructed rather than assisted the improvement of our understanding of the crisis of liberal society.

NOTES

1. 'Moral intuitions, procedural rules and social justice', a paper delivered by W. G. Runciman to the Scots Philosophical Club Conference, University of Stirling, 10 September 1975. I have found this one of the most instructive of recent writings on questions of distributive justice, and I owe much of my understanding of them to it.

2. J. Rawls, *A Theory of Justice* (Oxford, 1973) 21; see also p. 587.

3. Ibid., 121.

4. Ibid., 62.

5. K. Arrow, 'Some ordinalist-utilitarian notes on Rawls' theory of justice', *Journal of Philosophy*, May 1973.

6. Arrow, loc. cit., 248.

7. *A Theory of Justice*, 179.

8. On this point I have profited from L. Holborow, 'Desert, inequality and injustice', *Philosophy*, 50, 1975.

9. R. Nozick, *Anarchy, State and Utopia* (New York, 1974), 155.

10. Ibid., 204.

11. For Berlin's variant of presumptivism, see his 'Equality as an ideal', in: *Proceedings of the Aristotelian Society*, 56, 1955-56.

12. Joel Feinberg, *Social Philosophy* (New Jersey, 1973), 100.

13. E.g. J. R. Lucas, *Principles of Politics* (Oxford, 1966), Section 56.

14. See Berlin, op. cit., for a development of this claim.

15. Feinberg, op. cit., 101. See also Louis Katzner, 'Presumptivist and non-presumptivist principles of formal justice', *Ethics*, 1971: 253-58. I am indebted to Katzner for much of my understanding of the weaknesses of presumptivism.

16. *A Theory of Justice*, 151.

17. E.g. by Teitelman, 'The limits of individualism', *Journal of Philosophy*, 1972.

18. See Katzner, op. cit.

19. *A Theory of Justice*, 28-29.

20. Ibid., 256-57.

21. Pitkin, *Wittgenstein and Justice* (Berkeley, 1973), 71.

22. S. Lukes, 'No Archimedean Point' (Review of *A Theory of Justice*), reprinted as Chapter 10 of *Essays in Social Theory* by Steven Lukes (London, 1977).

23. A. Macintyre, *A Short History of Ethics* (London, 1968), 137.

24. M. Rothbard, 'Robert Nozick and the immaculate conception of the state', *Journal of Libertarian Studies*, 1 (1), Winter 1977.

25. On this point I am indebted to Hillel Steiner's chapter in this volume: 'Can a Social Contract be Signed by an Invisible Hand?'.

12 Public Goods and the Analytic Theory of State

Hannu Nurmi
University of Turku, Finland

INTRODUCTION

The current interest in the theory of state in Western political science may well be taken as an example of the new fields of inquiry opened by the abolition of behaviouralism and the emergence of what has been called post-behaviouralism. Of course, as a concern of political philosophy and 'theory' in that sense, the state, its nature, function and even essence have occupied scholarly minds for centuries. From that point of view the contemporary interest in the state is no novelty. The reemergence of the theory of state cannot, however, be explained by the mere out-datedness of behaviouralism in political science. Old concepts do not automatically reappear after the tradition which demonstrated their illegitimacy vanishes or loses its supremacy. The reason for their reappearance should rather be sought in the abolished tradition. In the case of theory of state — I would argue — some particular features of behaviouralism made it plausible that the state should appear as a going concern of political scientists of the 'post-behavioural era'. This chapter deals with a few well-known contemporary theories of state from the point of view of explicating their relationship to the underlying tradition of thought. In particular, I shall attempt to evaluate whether any new insights into the problem of the emergence of the state can be and have been gained by employing the conceptual apparatus of analytic theory.

The plan of this chapter is as follows: first I shall briefly summarise some modern state theories. In particular, I shall focus upon their

Author's Note: This chapter has been published as Chapter 6 of the author's essay collection *Rationality and Public Goods: Essays in Analytic Political Theory,* Societas Scientiarum Fennica: Commentationes Scientiarum Socialium, no. 9 (Helsinki, 1977). It appears here by permission of Societas Scientiarum Fennica.

conceptions of the 'original position' from which the formation of the state begins. Secondly, I shall dwell on the theory of public goods as most of the mentioned theories make extensive use of it. Thirdly, I shall attempt to assess whether the analytic theories of state make a contribution to the analytic political theory from which they stem. Throughout the chapter I shall use the concept of analytic political theory as referring to the theories of purposive action taking as their point of departure the notion of the rational individual (formally defined in somewhat varying ways). The employment of the concept 'analytic' seems justified in the sense that the theories deal with formally defined actors engaged in formally characterisable interactions in a well-defined universe of discourse (the latter mostly consisting of acts, decisions and states of affairs). Therefore, the investigation resembles mathematical analysis in its technical sense.

AN OVER-VIEW OF SOME ANALYTIC THEORIES OF STATE

The distinctive features of the modern analytic theories of state become perhaps most readily discernible in the light of their conception of what is called 'the original position', i.e. the state of affairs logically preceding the introduction of state power. This state of affairs is thought of as logically prior to the state in the sense that some of its characteristics provide a rational explanation of the emergence of an institution capable of making binding decisions for the collectivity of individuals considered.

The original position is customarily characterised as the Hobbesian anarchy where 'life is nasty, brutish and short'. In the original position, the only things that count in the descriptions of the situation are the set of individuals, the set of valuable things, the distribution of these valuables among the individuals, and the individual's capabilities of changing the distribution. The starting point of analytic state theories is basically individualistic: the basic and irreducible unit of the collectivity is the individual. Despite widespread agreement about the general characteristics of the original position and the principle of methodological individualism, the views concerning the rationale of the emergence of the state apparatus differ somewhat among the analytic state theorists. In the following I shall briefly sketch some of these views.

The VPI School

Although it may be unjustified in some respects to say that the Virginia Polytechnic Institute economists form a school of thought in 'new political economy', I think for the purposes of state theory such a claim can be made. The distinctive features of this school are methodological individualism and the focus on politico-economic institutions (property rights in particular). In the volume *Explorations in the Theory of Anarchy* two VPI scholars, Winston Bush and Patrick Gunning, present complementary views of the evolution of government. The starting point for both authors is 'the Hobbesian jungle' in which the individual levels of welfare depend on the amount of goods possessed by the individuals and there is no authority to stop people from forcefully taking valuables from each other instead of producing them. In this jungle there are four characteristics of an individual that solely determine his welfare: his share of the initial distribution of income, his ability to produce goods, to protect his property and to take goods from others.

Bush makes a distinction between initial and natural distribution of income. The former refers to what is 'given' in the analysis, the latter to the end result (distribution) of the process whereby people by force or theft take income from each other. Assuming that the marginal utility of income is positive for all individuals and that stealing or the employment of force decreases the utility of the individual engaged in such an activity, it may be the case that the natural distribution is a Pareto-suboptimal state of affairs. In other words, 'strong' individuals might be inclined to be less exploitative with respect to the 'weak' ones if they could find an arrangement by which they would have to apply less coercion or engage in less stealing than in the process whereby the natural distribution is achieved. Basically this is the rationale for the establishment of the state apparatus in Bush's analysis. Strictly speaking the above argument does not entail that an institution called the state will emerge after reasonable men become aware of the subtleties of their situation. As Bush points out, the argument implies the establishment of property rights in the sense that the rules defining these rights and their enforcement will increase the total utility of the individuals involved.

There are several interesting questions to be asked about the analysis of the Hobbesian jungle given by Bush. First, does the number of individuals affect the likelihood of the state emerging out of anarchy? Secondly, provided that the avoidance of coercion makes the evolution of property rights plausible, what about the other functions related to the state in modern societies? Thirdly, to what extent is it reasonable to start with the Hobbesian jungle in the first place? The first of these questions has been the most extensively studied one in the public choice literature. The third one, in turn, has largely been neglected although Nozick (1974) takes as his starting point Locke's state of nature. The second question is, I think, the most interesting one as it deals with the question of the extent to which the public sector can be justified on individual rationality grounds. That particular problem has been discussed by Tullock (1970). We shall not, however, pursue these questions further in this connection (see Nurmi, 1976b).

Gunning's principal argument is that the state emerges not because of the obvious inability of the individuals to move over to the Paretian border of the system of behaviours, but because of the feeling shared by the individuals that the state can enforce contracts made by them. It is its function as a contract enforcer that is the crux of the matter, says Gunning. It is easy to see that Gunning's view is basically in accordance with Bush's, being, however, on a somewhat more general level than the latter's. If the state emerges because of the demand for contract enforcement, then the situation investigated by Bush, falling clearly into the domain of contract enforcement, therefore corroborates Gunning's view. The avoidance of coercive effort in return for a lesser amount of income cannot be accomplished unless a contract can be made and enforced. Otherwise, there would be no reason whatsoever to stop the weak ones from responding to the decrease in the level of coercion placed upon them by retaining in their possession more of the income than the Pareto-optimality with respect to the natural distribution would imply. Therefore, the function of the state as a contract-enforcer is essentially the reduction of uncertainty felt by the parties with respect to the actions (future and present) of their opponents.

It is not difficult to see the interrelations of the analyses of Bush and Gunning and the game known as the Prisoner's Dilemma (hereafter, PD). The connection of this game with analytic state theories is even clearer in some of the theories discussed next. For the moment it is sufficient to notice that both Bush and Gunning see the rationale of the state in terms of natural distribution, not the initial one (see also

Buchanan, 1972). In this respect their view differs from that presented by John Rawls to be discussed next.

Rawls

It could be argued that the discussion of Rawl's theory in the context of analytic state theories is unjustified because of the essential difference between the problem formulations of, for example, the VPI school and Rawls. The latter is known for his theory of *justice* whereas the primary task the former sets for itself is how to make the emergence of the state intelligible in terms of the individualistic calculus of utility. Simplifying the difference, one might say that Rawls' theory — if it is a theory of state at all — is normative, whereas the VPI theorists aim at a descriptive (or positive) theory. But this would be misleading: the original position or two-person models the VPI theorists speak of are hardly descriptive of anything that has ever existed in reality. The models purport to shed light on possible ways of justifying the evolution of the state or — failing that — on possible ways of basing socio-economic institutions on a 'rational' foundation. Seen from this angle the difference between the VPI theorists and Rawls diminishes considerably.

Indeed, after closer scrutiny it vanishes altogether in this respect. What is rational for a person determines — at least in simple cases — what is good for him (or at any rate better than something else). Furthermore, goodness and justice are — as Rawls argues — congruent in the sense that 'this disposition to take up and to be guided by the standpoint of justice accords with the individual's good' (Rawls 1971: 567). Let us now take a look at the original position in the Rawlsian sense in order to see how the need for the state apparatus emerges out of the situation and how the maintenance of the apparatus, once established, can be deemed rational from the point of view of each of the individuals involved.

In contrast to the VPI theorists Rawls is particularly concerned with the principles by which institutions function, not just with their presence or absence. So, the principles of justice are formulated and their rationality assessed in a fictitious situation ('the original position') in which the individuals agree upon the principles of justice to be adopted without knowing the initial distribution of income over the set of individuals, 'behind the veil of ignorance', as Rawls puts it. Indeed, the parties involved in the original position know very little of the particulars of the real society they are going to live in. On the other hand, they do know quite a bit about the general laws and facts pertaining to society and the human psyche. So much really as to water down much of the plausibility of 'the veil of ignorance' (see Barry 1973: 10-18). In particular, they are assumed to know 'the circumstances of justice' and that is for our purposes the most interesting part of Rawls' theory.

Rawls (1971: 126-30) distinguishes two kinds of conditions which give rise to principles that determine the division of advantages and the proper distributive shares: (1) 'the objective circumstances which make human co-operation both possible and necessary', and (2) the subjective aspects of the situation, i.e. aspects of the individuals involved that contribute to the emergence of justice as a virtue of social institutions. In the former class Rawls emphasises the condition of moderate scarcity and in the latter the mutual disinterest of the individuals in the interest of the others. Now, in what way do these conditions 'give rise' to the principles of justice and, hence, to the emergence of the state? In and by themselves these conditions could not 'explain' the emergence, but when connected with the assumption of the rationality of the individuals plus the requirement that the agreement be reached behind the veil of ignorance, the conditions form a part of what Rawls apparently thinks of as a rational reconstruction of the emergence of the principles of justice.

It must be emphasised that Rawls is not particularly interested in the emergence of justice in general, but in the reconstruction of the evolution of the two principles of justice that are by now well known. So, one might say that Rawls in a way *assumes* the solution of what we consider the crucial problem: how men come to think that an enforceable agreement on certain important aspects of human conduct is preferable to no agreement at all. Although Rawls is not explicit on this point, it seems to me that he wants to argue that the principle of individual rationality in the circumstances of justice and behind the veil of ignorance simply dictates that each individual should co-operate in finding an agreement on the principles of justice. My interpretation of Rawls gains support from Robert E. Goodin (1976: 54) who notes that Rawls needs the notion of the veil of ignorance in order 'to introduce sufficient uncertainty to make men agree to the hypothetical contract'. The uncertainty concerning the position which a person occupies in the state to be formed may give some plausibility e.g. to the maximin criterion of justice, but still I cannot see how the uncertainty cum rationality could *explain* the emergence of the state. It can explain how and why men stick to the principles once they have been told that they have to come out of the Hobbesian jungle. But the reason for the need to abandon anarchy is something extraneous to Rawls' theory. So, my conclusion from this brief summary of some aspects of Rawls' theory is that it does not give us a specific theory of the emergence of the state. It may be noticed, however, that Rawls' description of the original position does not essentially differ from that given by Bush and Gunning except in its implicit assumption according to which anarchy is no option.

Nozick

Rawls' main concern in social justice is in the distributive principles. This problem setting has subsequently been challenged by Robert Nozick who claims that a prior problem, that of the nature of social justice, has to be solved before one can meaningfully discuss the principles of justice. In particular, Nozick argues that by speaking of distributive justice, Rawls gives the misleading impression that all there is to social justice is an arrangement by which the resources held by individuals can be redistributed in such a fashion that the end result deserves to be called just in some well-defined sense. In Nozick's (1974: 151) view a proper concept of justice – a theory of entitlements – contains three parts: (1) the principle of a just acquisition of resources or holdings; (2) the principles of a just transfer of holdings; and (3) the principles of the rectification of injustice. The last one is given a specific content: 'no one is entitled to a holding except by repeated application of (1) and (2)'. The three parts taken together, then, determine the algorithm by which a just distribution of holdings is generated from any given initial distribution of income. Of course, the process presupposes that a specific content be given to principles (1) and (2). But the crux of the matter is that in Nozick's view the distribution of holdings is no measure of the justice of the society. To determine what is just, we need to know the process by which the distribution has been achieved.

James Coleman (1976) points out that Nozick (as well as Rawls) omits a question that should logically precede the considerations of just distribution of just entitlements, namely what rights the individuals will agree to give up to the collectivity and what ones they will retain. *This* is a problem that — in Coleman's view — can only be solved by some sort of social contract behind the veil of ignorance. Rawls and Nozick present entirely different solutions to this problem; the former assumes that all individual rights be given to the collectivity; the latter, in turn, starts from the position in which every individual is entitled to the product of his labour and to the income that is voluntarily given to him. It must be emphasised, however, that for Nozick the idea of the veil of ignorance is just a trick that is used as a camouflage by the end-state theorists. According to Nozick in the original position each individual is in possession of a set of natural rights. People already have these rights. So, it is theoretically inconceivable that they be deprived of those rights by such a device as the veil of ignorance. In Nozick's view, then, the whole notion blurs the issue.

Central for Nozick's account of the emergence of the state is the notion of a protective agency, that is an agency which provides protective services for individuals in the state of nature. Out of the interaction of such agencies there arises a dominant one, i.e. one that has a monopoly of protection supply in a given geographical area. This agency does not arise by the design of the individuals in the state of nature, but, on the contrary, by an 'invisible-hand process', as Nozick puts it. The formation of the state results from the individuals' *separately* signing up for personal protection. In considering the process of the interaction between individuals in the state of nature and, in particular, their decisions to join protective associations, Nozick (1974: 124) presents the following pay-off matrix:

		individual II	
		B'	C'
individual I	B	5,5	10,0
	C	0,10	x, x

where B (B', respectively) denotes the strategy 'join a protective association and attempt to prohibit II (I) from joining another protective association' and $C(C')$ stands for 'Don't join a protective association and allow II (I) to join a protective association'. The reader immediately notices that this is a PD if $10 > x > 5$. In contrast to the PD 'explications' of the emergence of the state to be discussed later, it is interesting to notice that in Nozick's analysis 'we assume that it is better to be the client of the powerful dominant protective agency in an area, than not to be; and it is better to be a client of the dominant agency, if the other fellow isn't, . . .' (Nozick 1974: 123). Owing to the interpretation of the strategies and the assumption concerning the profitability of joining protective associations, we now notice that the co-operative outcome (C, C') represents a situation in which the Hobbesian jungle prevails. So, Nozick considers the change from (B, B') outcome to (C, C') outcome as Pareto-optimal.

It is to be emphasised, however, that Nozick's assumption concerning the profitability of joining protective associations actually contains the solution to the problem of the emergence of the state. If the individuals find it more desirable to join the associations, then their emergence follows directly (assuming of course that the individuals are not hindered from what they think is rational). What remains to be considered is why the joining of protective associations is deemed desirable in the first place. I think here Nozick largely agrees with Bush's account. In other words, the costs of the acquisition and holding of goods in the Hobbesian jungle may be so excessive that it is to the benefit of the individuals to reach some enforceable agreement concerning the principles of social justice. As the veil of ignorance is now removed, however, we cannot expect that the benefit accruing to the individuals from undersigning the social contract is the same for all. Nor can we expect that in the society once established the distribution of rewards would follow the maximin principle or would tend to an even distribution of resources among individuals if the original position is that assumed by Nozick.

Another problem is how the state emerges out of the multiplicity of protective associations. Nozick explains the monopoly nature of the state as a consequence of the nature of the good provided by the protective agencies: the good is relative as it depends upon how strong the others are (Nozick, 1974: 17). This nature is especially conducive to the growth of what some public goods theorists call natural monopoly (see, e.g., Musgrave, 1974). We may conclude that for Nozick the rationale of the emergence of the state is the avoidance of the costs of anarchy. In this he comes close to the views of the VPI theorists.

Taylor

In his recently published book *Anarchy and Cooperation* Michael Taylor sets out to challenge the position held by many public goods theorists according to which the provision of public goods is the main rationale for state activity. It is well known that if the provision of public goods can be treated as a PD situation, the non-co-operative strategy dominates the co-operative one for all players by definition of the PD (see, Hardin, 1971; Taylor, 1976: 4-8; Nurmi, 1977). Taylor's rejection of this position consists (1) of an attempt to show that PD is not necessarily a proper model of the situation involving the provision of public goods, and (2) of dropping one of the basic assumptions of the analytic theory of state: that of fixed individual preferences. As we shall investigate the public goods argument more closely in the next section, let us concentrate on the latter point in this connection.

The case Taylor builds against the assumption of fixed individual preferences is based on the observation that states do have an active role in the moulding of the individual consciousness. Hence one can expect that the preferences of the individuals can also be modified by the establishment of the state. Taylor (1976: 132-34) points to the example of nation building in new states. This process often proceeds from state building to nation building; in other words, the state machinery is first established and then is used as an instrument in building a nation, i.e. a community of people having to some extent shared values and interests. In this process the state apparatus plays a crucial role in weakening traditional loyalties and strengthening 'modern' ones. The ensuing new community is larger than the loci of traditional loyalties making it therefore more difficult than previously to invoke voluntary co-operation in the provision of public goods. This fact again enhances the need for state activity in co-ordinating efforts and enforcing agreements. Thus, the process is in the initial phases clearly cumulative resulting in a rapidly expanding state apparatus (or at least an apparatus dealing with the provision of public goods).

Another argument of Taylor (1976: 134) against the fixed individual preference assumption is that the forces conducive to the voluntary co-operation of individuals in the provision of public goods tend to vary inversely with the presence of the state activity. Hence, the self-reinforcing nature of the expansion of the state apparatus.

Taken together these two arguments seem to suggest that there is not much point in trying analytically to reconstruct the emergence of the state in terms of a *given* configuration of individual preferences. Rather, Taylor seems to propose that one should look for the rationale of the state elsewhere, perhaps in notions that are alien to the analytic theory of state. The conclusion of Taylor's account of the emergence of the state is in my view basically negative: the individualistic calculus in terms of fixed preferences is unsatisfactory when applied universally, i.e. without spatio-temporal indexing. On the other hand, Taylor shows in the context of his discussion of the PD how co-operation may be rational from the point of view of an individual if certain assumptions hold.

SOME GENERAL REMARKS

As can be inferred from the above remarks, the provision of public goods is deemed to be the crucial determinant and rationale for the emergence of the state by many authors. In fact, of the authors discussed above only Taylor appears to have doubts about the validity of the public goods argument for the state. Of course, a glance at the writing of these authors shows that there are differences in detailed analyses. Bush points out that property rights are bound to emerge in the Hobbesian jungle, not because it would be individually rational for the parties to agree upon the justice of the original distribution of income, but because in the ensuing natural distribution the parties will find it rational to agree upon the property rights of *that* situation. Anyway, the reduction of uncertainty accomplished by public agreement is the crux of the matter. This reduction is certainly a public good for the parties involved. A very similar account is given by Nozick. As the role of the state as a contract-enforcer becomes very marked in Bush's and Nozick's accounts, it is natural to ask with Gunning whether this role in the last analysis is the only relevant one and not the role of the provider of public goods in general. Be that as it may, it is evident that the theory of public goods is certainly applicable to the effort to pursue further the reason for the existence of the state apparatus.

Now, one observation which has far-reaching consequences for the theory formation on public goods has been that some situations involving the provision of public goods can be considered as PDs. Hence by studying PD we can gain insights into the problematic of public goods. Thus, we have the following inference chain:

$$PD \rightarrow public\ goods \rightarrow theory\ of\ state$$

Both of the inferences are problematic, though: (1) is the public goods provision always and most profitably describable as PD, and (2) is the public goods problematic relevant for the theory of state? The bulk of analytic political theory has answered these questions affirmatively. Furthermore, the inferences in the opposite direction may be even more important from the stand-point of the future of analytic political theory. If this theory cannot provide us with the answer to one of the most fundamental questions of political science – the emergence and functioning of the state – it is very doubtful if it can be of much use in general. At the very least, attempts to pursue foundational matters of politics on this basis seem to be doomed to failure.

In the following I shall concentrate upon the two links of the inferential chain in an attempt to discuss and evaluate the various solutions to problems of PD and public goods provision from the point of view of their bearing upon the analytic theory of state. Thereafter I shall turn the inferential arrow in the opposite direction and ask what sort of effects the theories of state may have upon analytic political theory in general.

PRISONER'S DILEMMA, PUBLIC GOODS AND THE ANALYTIC THEORY OF STATE

I can think of no case that would better explain the failure of naïve falsificationism as a descriptive model of scientific change than analytic political theory. In this theory the basic unit is a political decision-maker considered as rational, usually a utility maximiser of some sort.[1] From this basically individualistic starting point attempts have been made to construct a political theory of a precise nature. Yet the predictive success of the theory has been a major concern of the theorists as it seems that on purely individual rationality grounds, one cannot explain the most pervasive and important phenomena of political life: collective action and voting. The predictive failure can most easily be seen in terms of the PD. Therefore, much of the research effort in the field of analytic political theory has been directed to that particular game. The discussion in this section proceeds as follows: first I shall very briefly comment upon the recent developments in the analytic solutions to the PD. Secondly, I shall introduce more structure to the game situation by introducing the other decision-makers so that anticipation strategies can be considered. Thirdly, I shall discuss an attempt to view collective action as a decision problem of the classic type, i.e. not a problem of strategic calculation under uncertainty in the presence of other calculating players, but a decision problem in a 'passive' environment.

On Analytic Solutions to PD

As is well known, the two-person PD situation is visually described as follows:

	C	D
C	a, a	d, c
D	c, d	b, b

with $c > a > b > d$. C and D denote co-operative and non-co-operative (or competitive) strategies, respectively. The dilemma consists in the fact that the D strategy strongly dominates the C strategy for both players. Thus, regardless of the choice of the other player, both players maximise the payoff accruing to them by choosing D. Hence, individually rational players end up with the outcome yielding the amount b to each. However, if they both choose the C strategy, the outcome yields a ($> b$, by definition) to both. Hence, the change from (D, D) outcome to (C, C) is Pareto-optimal.[2]

For the sake of brevity I shall here omit the generalisations of the PD: the n-person and k-strategy PDs (see Hardin, 1971; Taylor, 1976; Nurmi, 1977). For our purposes it is necessary to point out one more characteristic of the PD, however, i.e. the PD is a strictly non-co-operative game, that is, no enforceable agreements can be made between the players concerning the strategies to be chosen.[3]

Now, the analytic solutions[4] to the PD can be divided into the following groups: (1) solutions obtained by taking into account the time factor, and (2) solutions based on the introduction of conditional strategies. In addition, we might wish to include (3) a group of solutions which actually consist of converting the original PD into some other game with a co-operative solution. (4) Solutions based on asymmetries of the PDs are not as yet available. There are, however, reasons to conjecture that the investigations of the asymmetries may turn out to be rewarding in the long run.

The first group can be further subdivided into (a) sequential PDs in which the future payoffs are discounted, and (b) two-level PDs in which the 'lower' level game is controlled by an 'upper' level one.

The idea of considering the present value of the future payoffs in a sequence of plays of a PD game is due to Shubik (1970). As was mentioned above, Taylor (1976) has made use of the idea taking simultaneously into account the two-level structure that can be discerned in a sequential PD. The approach of Shubik and Taylor should, however, be kept distinct from the study of sequential games that yield PD in the expected values of the payoffs. No 'ordinary' game (i.e. a game from which the sequence is formed) needs to be a PD in the latter case. Experimental evidence suggests that in the expected value PDs in which no ordinary game is a PD, the level of co-operation is significantly higher than in the sequence of ordinary PDs (see Guyer, Fox and Hamburger, 1973). As I have discussed Shubik's 'dynamic' solution at some length elsewhere (Nurmi, 1977), I shall not dwell on it here.

Taylor follows Shubik in introducing a discount parameter a_i in the following fashion: the present value of a payoff A to be made for player i at time t is $A \cdot a_i^t$, where $0 < a_i < 1$. It is assumed that the payoffs to players are given at discrete time intervals $t = 1, 2, \ldots$

Taylor investigates supergames that consist of finite sequences of ordinary PDs. In the supergame the payoff can be defined as the sum of an infinite series of payoffs of the constituent ordinary games. Another common feature in Shubik's and Taylor's analyses is the notion of a conditional strategy committing a player to choose some sequence of actions conditional upon the choice or sequence of choices of the opponent. In Taylor's analysis the sequences of action are the supergame strategies. Now, what Taylor's analysis mainly shows is that co-operation in the ordinary games is, indeed, sometimes rational in a very straightforward sense: there is a set of conditional supergame strategies commanding co-operation in the ordinary games such that a unilateral choice of another supergame strategy by any one player would not result in a larger supergame payoff for him than the choice of the strategy belonging to the set. The supergame strategy set is, then, obviously an equilibrium in the game-theoretic sense. The conditions for the co-operative equilibria need not concern us here. Suffice it to notice that the value of the discount parameter in relation to the values of the entries of the PD payoff matrix is of crucial importance: the value of the parameter should not be too small if the co-operation is to become justifiable on the basis of the supergame considerations.

Taylor's solution belongs both to group (1) and (2) in the above classification. In contradistinction, Howard's (1971) metagame solution belongs to the latter group only, that is no dynamics is involved at all. No wonder, then, that conditions for co-operative equilibrium make no reference to a discount rate. As a matter of fact, not even the values of the entries of the PD payoff matrix matter as long as the defining characteristics of the PD are preserved. Taylor (1976: 65-68) has some doubts about the way in which the metagame approach is claimed to provide a *solution* to PD. In particular, he points to the difficulty of seeing how the metagame considerations can have a bearing upon the *actual* plays of PD. As I have argued, the metagame approach pre-supposes that the players be able to take an over-all picture of the situation and, therefore, at least to some extent to get rid of *strategic* reasoning in favour of a *systemic* one (Nurmi, 1977). I think Taylor is right in maintaining that this comes close to presupposing that the game is not a PD after all but some co-operative game. On the other hand, a 'tu quoque' argument applies to Taylor as he makes the same presupposition quite explicitly in his supergame construction. It is true that Taylor's supergame strategies make allowance for retaliatory behaviour and learning from experience, both of which characterise human behaviour in some game-like situations. But the main virtue of the supergame solution is that it seems more realistic than the metagame one in the sense that it does not assume a sequential conditioning of the strategies in the ordinary game when in reality the only choice for the players is between co-operation and defection. Still, I think the crux of the solution is the same for Hardin, Howard and Taylor: the 'systemic' or global aspects of the situation must take priority over the strategic ones in the players' calculations if the co-operative solution is to be reached.

As for the group (3) solutions — i.e. solutions consisting of converting the PD into some other game — the one with the most direct relevance to the analytic theory of state is perhaps the following. It consists simply of adding positive utilities to the payoffs ensuing from the choice of a co-operative strategy (regardless of what the opponent does) and/or subtracting positive utility from payoffs corresponding to the defective strategy.

	C	D			C	D
C	a, a	d, c	$\rightarrow$	C	$a+x, a+x$	$d+x, c-y$
D	c, d	b, b		D	$c-y, d+x$	$b-y, b-y$

where x and y are utility-increasing magnitudes. The relevance of the above transformation for the analytic theory of state is in its ability to capture the effect of the establishment of the Sovereign with powers over the individual. Now, depending on the specific values of x and y vis-à-vis the entries of the initial payoff matrix, the effect of the reward and punishment system may be that of turning the initial PD into a pure co-operation game in which the co-operative strategies become dominant ones for both players, or into an indeterminate game with neither strategy dominating for the players. By allowing x and y to take on different values in different cells of the resulting payoff matrix, we can obviously obtain quite a few game-situations which could have some state-theoretic plausibility. Instead of dwelling on these modifications we will discuss the effects of asymmetries in the initial PD – the group (4) problem – and their effects on modification of the payoff matrix performed in the above fashion and interpreted as the effects of introducing the state apparatus. The following discussion is very much inspired by Buchanan's (1972) paper.

It is not difficult to imagine that in the original position men are not equal and, therefore, the asymmetry of the PD payoff matrix seems a plausible starting point. As a numerical example, consider the following one borrowed from Buchanan (with some modifications):

	C	D
C	15,8	6,12
D	17,2	10,3

In this example let the (D, D) cell represent the natural distribution in the sense of Bush, i.e. the distribution of goods and bads in the Hobbesian jungle. The (C, C) cell can, then, be interpreted as representing the distribution of income resulting from the agreement concerning the assignment of property rights. It is to be noticed that each of the parties gains 5 units of utility from such an agreement. The gain may be thought of as ensuing from the savings in terms of time and effort in protecting and stealing property. Thus, there is an unequal natural distribution and an equal distribution of gains from the agreement. It is no wonder, then, that the gains from the agreement may be of an entirely different *relative* importance for the parties involved. It is easy to check that the gains from unilateral defection are larger to the column-chooser than to the row-chooser. Now, the conclusion to be drawn from all this is that (1) the agreement concerning property rights may, relatively speaking be more profitable to the party which is less advantaged than to the well-off one, and (2) the gains from unilateral defection may also be greater to the party which was worse off in the original position.

The situation becomes more interesting when we make the model dynamic in the sense that we take into account the possibility of the natural distribution changing in the course of time. This might be due, for instance, to different technological circumstances calling for different talents, etc. If the natural distribution changes in the direction of a more even distribution, the previously less-advantaged party will find it less attractive to commit himself to an agreement on the previous terms. Eventually he may come to prefer the Hobbesian jungle to the agreement.

Now, there are a couple of comments one could make on Buchanan's analysis summarised above. (i) The equal amount of benefit from the agreement that essentially concerns *property rights* needs some justification. The mere fact that both rich and poor have to incur costs in the protecting of and search for property by no means implies that the benefits accruing from the assignment of property rights would be the *same* for both parties. Indeed, it can so happen that the benefits for the poor man ensuing from the agreement may amount to nothing at all so that the PD setting simply does not arise. Property rights benefit, of course, mostly those who possess some property. (ii) Buchanan's analysis is crucially dependent on the level of measurement of utilities; indeed, a cardinal level measurement has to be assumed. Furthermore, there must be a way of performing interpersonal comparisons of utilities. These technical assumptions need some justification especially as it seems plausible to think that the *perceived* utilities determine behaviour and not the interpersonally postulated ones.[5]

Despite these critical comments I think Buchanan's focus on asymmetries in PD like situations is plausible. It does not lead to actual solutions, but is certainly a step toward building a more realistic picture of the role of asymmetries in PD and, consequently, in the analytic theory of state.

Public Goods and Anticipation

As was pointed out above, many writers in the analytic tradition consider the provision of public goods as the main — indeed, the sole —

rationale of the emergence of the state. It is, however, clear that public goods can be provided by others than the state. On the other hand, the state can be engaged in the production of goods of a purely private variety. Yet the equilibrium conditions for private and public goods are so different from each other that the perfect or nearly perfect market mechanism normally fails to result in a Pareto-optimal provision of public goods. Therefore, something other than a purely private alloca-tion of resources is usually called for if an optimal outcome is to be reached.[6] In what follows I shall disregard much of what has been written on the public goods problematic and focus merely on one particular facet of it: the free-rider problem.[7]

If the situation involving the provision of public goods is describable as a PD — which in the n-person case means that the non-co-operative strategy strongly dominates the co-operative one for all players — then, of course, we cannot presume that the good will be provided by voluntary agreement of the group members. It is well known that Olson (1965) — obviously not thinking of all collective actions as amounting to PD-like situations — distinguished between groups of three sizes: large, intermediate and small. For small groups, the existence and potential applicability of selective social and economic incentives turns the situation into a co-ordination game. Hence, rational actors will co-operate on purely individualistic grounds. In intermediate groups Olson leaves the issue open: the public good will or will not be provided depending upon additional facts concerning the group. In large groups the prediction is that no good will be provided. In Olson's analysis the basic concepts are the size of the group, the nature of the good and the preferences of the individuals. One way of accounting for the ir-rationality of the emergence of the state is to argue with Gunning that the essential role of the state is not that of a public good provider in general but that of the contract-enforcer. Hence, the arguments con-cerning the provision of public goods simply do not apply in the case of the emergence of the state, even though the situation is in other respects similar to the large group setting of Olson. Now, if the service of a contract-enforcer is a public good, it certainly need not be consumed in equal amounts by all individuals. Therefore, it is not a pure public good. In particular, valuation of the service of contract-enforcement may be so high among some individuals that it is individually rational for each of them to bear the costs of the service. In this sort of situation we may justifiably speak of a privileged group, as Olson does.[8]

Of course, it may also be the case that the provision of the public good (contract-enforcement or whatever) is not sufficiently highly valued by any one individual for him to cover all the costs, but a group of individuals may have a markedly larger interest in the provision than others. In this situation it may be conjectured that the interested individuals somehow anticipate each other's actions. At the very least we can assume that they become aware of the (conscious or unconscious) 'need' of some of their fellow individuals concerning the good. This awareness may be thought of as resulting in a spontaneous cooperation in the subgroup of interested individuals. This is the 'concerted expectations' solution to the free-rider problem suggested by Frohlich and Oppenheimer (1970). To me it seems that the notion of concerted expectations does not lead us very far in the way of making the emergence of the state rational from an individual rationality point of view. On the contrary, the concerted expectations invoke notions that are completely alien to the individual rationality approach. The mere existence and awareness of common interest does not, strictly speaking, *explain* the emergence of the state. Otherwise we should expect, for instance, every person to play co-operatively in PD once the payoff matrix has been shown to them. But, as is well known, people do not in fact generally play co-operatively (see, e.g., Rapoport, 1974) nor should they do so on the basis of the dominance criterion.

Still, the point raised by Frohlich and Oppenheimer has some intuitive plausibility. They certainly point to a possibility whereby collectively rational action could ensue from individual calculations. In a more extensive presentation with Young, they outline a *mechanism* whereby collective goods provision may in some circumstances be quite rational for everyone (Frohlich, Oppenheimer and Young, 1971: 32-36). Specifically Frohlich et al. consider a situation in which an individual j has to make a decision as to whether or not to contribute to the provision of a collective good X_i. Let $U_j(X_i)$ be j's utility from X_i. It is assumed that j can somehow estimate the probability that X_i will in fact be supplied. This probability is denoted by $P_j(X_i)$. Hence, the gross amount of utility j expects to receive from X_i equals $U_j(X_i)P_j(X_i)$. When deciding upon the contribution j, however, considers the following expression:

$$U_j = U_j(X_i)P_j(X_i) - D_j(X_i),$$

where $D_j(X_i)$ is the utility value of the contribution j is willing to make for the provision of X_i. Now, in the 'ordinary' utility calculus it would never be rational for an individual to contribute as long as $D_j(X_i) > 0$ and the term $P_j(X_i)$ is not affected enough by his decision to contribute or refrain from it.

What Frohlich et al. maintain, however, is that a rational individual will contribute as long as

$$\frac{dU_j}{dD_j(X_i)} > 0.$$

That inequality is, of course, analogous to the cost-revenue calculus of micro-economic theory.

The mechanism referred to above now comes into the picture, namely any of the individuals may notice that by promising to set up an organisation for the provision of the public good and by collecting the resources from the other individuals, he might be able to make a net gain in his over-all level of welfare. Such an individual could be called a political leader or entrepreneur, as Frohlich et al. suggest. Let the political leader be A. Denote by $U_A(L_A)$ the utility he derives from his activities. $U_A(L_A)$ can now be decomposed as follows:

$$U_A(L_A) = U_A(X_A) + \sum_{j=1}^{n} D_j(A) - C(X_A) - C(O_A).$$

The first term on the right-hand side denotes the utility for A of the public good X_A, the second term denotes the sum of the contributions he can raise from the others, $C(X_A)$ is the cost of supplying X_A and $C(O_A)$ denotes the organisation costs of A. Whenever A considers this expression to be positive, there is a presumption that A will organise the supply of the public good.

Now the political leader might be regarded as something like the state in the original position. Therefore, the approach of Frohlich et al. becomes directly relevant to our purposes. Upon closer inspection it seems that the crux of the problem of how to make the emergence of the state individually rational is here solved by pointing to the increased certainty and predictability of phenomena after the introduction of the political leader. It is evident that unless the group is so small that the decision to contribute makes a lot of difference in $P_j(X_i)$ for each j, the situation is a PD. However, by promising to supply the public good, the state modifies the situation so that $P_j(X_i)$ becomes *essentially* different when an individual is contributing than when he is not. Otherwise, it would still not be rational for him to contribute. Now, the state has two ways of making this modification: (i) by collecting the contributions and then supplying the good, or (ii) by making an enforceable agreement between itself and the individuals. By resorting to method (i), the state may attempt to provide selective incentives and thereby turn the original public good into another mixed public or even private good. Method (ii), in turn, amounts to dropping one of the defining properties of the PD. Each of the methods results in a situation that is not a PD.

The solution Frohlich et al. propose is based on the anticipation of the individuals concerning the needs and actions of the others.[9] Recently another solution based on anticipation has been proposed by Brams (1975). Its conclusion is similar to the one discussed above but there are significant differences as well. Brams' starting point, Newcomb's Problem, can be expressed in a generalised form in the following payoff matrix:

Player 2

		predicts a_1	predicts a_2
	a_1	A_2	A_4
Player 1	a_2	A_1	A_3

where A_1, A_2, A_3 and A_4 are the utilities of the respective outcomes for Player 1 so that $A_1 > A_2 > A_3 > A_4$.

Note that the strategies of the column player consist merely of predicting the choices of Player 1. Of course, we may give them whatever additional content we wish as long as a one-to-one correspondence prevails between the additional content and the strategies indicated. Now, approaching the situation from Player 1's point of view and letting p be his subjective probability that Player 2's predictions concerning his (i.e. Player 1's) strategies are correct, the expected utility maximising Player 1 should choose a_1 if[10]

$$pA_2 + (1 - p)A_4 > (1 - p)A_1 + pA_3.$$

On the other hand, if we assign no probability for Player 2's predictions being correct the dominance criterion would clearly dictate the choice of a_2 as this choice leads to a better outcome for Player 1, no matter what Player 2 does.

Now, one could similarly assume that the 'real' chooser is Player 2 and the predictor is Player 1. Thus, a similar matrix could be formulated to obtain the following payoffs for Player 2:

Player 2

		b_1	b_2
Player 1	predicts b_1	B_2	B_1
	predicts b_2	B_4	B_3

If the preference ordering of the payoffs is again $B_1 > B_2 > B_3 > B_4$ we, of course, end up with the same dilemma concerning the individual rationality criteria as previously.

Combining the two previous matrices we get the familiar PD payoff matrix. Brams (1975: 604-6) shows by a simple argument that assuming that one of the players chooses a strategy of conditional cooperation (i.e. chooses the co-operative strategy in each play whenever he thinks that the other party does and otherwise defects) the other player can maximise his expected payoff by co-operating, if the probability of the first player's making correct predictions is sufficiently high. More specifically, if the predictive accuracy of Player 2 is p and he adopts the strategy of conditional co-operation, then it is rational (in the expected utility maximisation sense) for Player 1 to choose the co-operative strategy if

$$\frac{p}{1-p} > \frac{A_1 - A_4}{A_2 - A_3} .$$

I think Brams' discussion very elegantly (and quantitatively) complements the solution of Frohlich et al. (1971). As was pointed out above their solution amounts to making co-operation plausible from the view-point of individual utility calculus when anticipation is allowed for. Brams, on the other hand, gives an estimate of the required *assurance* the individuals must have in order to find co-operation worthwhile in their utility calculus. This assurance must, of course, be given by the state or political leader. Brams does not consider the *n*-person case, but it seems that a somewhat similar reasoning holds there. In the case of the emergence of the state it must be emphasised, however, that for a state apparatus to emerge it is not necessary that *all* individuals co-operate. As the above discussion on asymmetries suggests, the very genesis of the state may benefit different individuals quite differentially in the original position. Therefore, it is to be expected that different levels of predictability are called for by different individuals in order to guarantee co-operative action.

Introducing Others

In their by now classic typology of organisational environments Emery and Trist (1969: 247-48) make a distinction between what they call placid clustered environment and disturbed reactive environment. The former is described as being somewhat organised but essentially 'passive', whereas the latter is a strategic one, i.e. one in which there is more than one organisation of a given type pursuing similar goals. This distinction of environment types also forms the basis of the division between decision and game theories and quite plausibly so, as McWhinney (1968) has pointed out that for each of the environment types in the typology of Emery and Trist there is a corresponding decision modality which fully utilises the information obtainable from the environment. So, for instance, the modality of decision-making in a placid clustered environment is risk, and in a disturbed reactive one uncertainty.

It would seem tempting to consider the types of environments as representing evolutionary stages, so that the passive environment precedes the strategic one in evolutionary sequence. The evolution would, thus, proceed from a simple to a more complex type of organisation. I do not know whether there is any historical justification for such a view but from a theoretical point of view it certainly makes a difference if we think of the original position as consisting of individuals, each making his decisions under risk or under uncertainty. In the preceding sections the problem of the emergence of the state has been approached from the point of view of a strategic decision problem, i.e. as a decision under uncertainty. In the case of the PD this assumption is quite obvious but also in the case of the public goods provision (even when it is not considered as a PD) such strategic features as anticipation enter the analysis. In this section I shall briefly outline an approach in which the emergence of the state may be seen in the light of individual decision-making under risk. This approach has been developed by Ferejohn and Fiorina (1974).

The starting point of Ferejohn's and Fiorina's analysis is not the emergence of the state but the anomalous situation in the theory of voting pointed out by Downs (1957): the act of voting is clearly irrational if the classic expected utility maximisation criterion is applied and two alternative actions (vote versus not vote) are considered. Riker and Ordeshook (1973: 63) express Downs' argument as follows. The voter's utility ensuing from the act of voting can be expressed

$$R = PB - C,$$

where B equals the utility of the voter ensuing from his most preferred candidate being elected minus the utility from his least preferred candidate being elected; P is the probability that the voter by voting can bring about B and C is the cost of voting. R, B and C are expressed in commensurable units (utiles). Clearly, it pays for the voter to vote only if $PB > C$ which situation rarely obtains due to the decline of P as the size of the electorate grows. Hence, the act of voting is normally irrational in terms of utility calculus.

Ferejohn and Fiorina render the act of voting rational by considering the voting situation in the light of Savage's minimax regret rule and introducing the states of nature as is customary in decision theory. Specifically, four states of nature are considered on the assumption that the voter has not yet decided about his voting. Therefore the states of nature express what would happen if the decision maker took no action whatsoever:

X_1: the most preferred candidate (in the voter's opinion) wins by more than one vote,
X_2: the most preferred candidate wins by one vote,
X_3: the most and the least preferred candidate tie,
X_4: the least preferred candidate wins by one vote,
X_5: the least preferred candidate wins by more than one vote.

The acts the voter has at his disposal are assumed to be:

a_1: vote for the most preferred candidate,
a_2: vote for the least preferred candidate,
a_3: abstain.[11]

Ferejohn and Fiorina standardise the utility values so that the utility of the most (least, respectively) preferred candidate being elected is 1 (0). On the assumption that C, the costs of voting in terms of utilities, is less than one-half, we obtain the following table of regrets:

	X_1	X_2	X_3	X_4	X_5
a_1	C	C	0	0	C
a_2	C	$\frac{1}{2}+C$	1	$\frac{1}{2}$	C
a_3	0	0	$\frac{1}{2}-C$	$\frac{1}{2}-C$	0

The minimax regret rule states that an actor should choose a strategy that minimises the maximum expected regret. The maximum regrets for strategies a_1, a_2 and a_3 are C, 1 and $\frac{1}{2} - C$, respectively. Obviously, a_1 dominates a_2 because no matter which state of nature obtains, a_1 leads to lesser or equal regret as a_2. Similarly a_3 dominates a_2. On the other hand, the comparison of a_1 and a_3 is not that straightforward. But for a minimax regretter the optimal choice is obvious all the same: if $C < \frac{1}{2} - C$, choose a_1. In other words, the minimax regret rule states that the voter should vote for his favourite candidate if the cost of voting amount to less than one-quarter of the utility difference between the candidates.

This solution to the paradox of participation has been criticised on many grounds.[1 2] In particular, its total disregard of any probability estimates of the voters has been deemed dubious as the minimax regret rule in fact amounts to giving equal weight to outcomes that, intuitively speaking, occur with widely differing frequencies. It would, indeed, be fantastic if people actually calculated in the minimax regret fashion. But clearly they do not calculate in the Downsian manner, either. However, that is not really the issue here. What we are interested in is whether the procedure delineated by Ferejohn and Fiorina deserves to be called rational and whether it is translatable into the analysis of the emergence of the state.

The answer to the first part of the question is, I think, negative. There is no way of saying that the minimax regret rule would be more rational than, say, the Laplace rule.[1 3] But on the other hand, the expected utility maximisation may also be in doubt as an explication of rationality, especially as it in some cases contradicts the dominance criterion (e.g. in the Newcomb's Problem).

As for the latter part of the question — whether the emergence of the state can be understood or made plausible by introducing the minimax regretting individuals — it must be emphasised at the outset that the solution now under discussion is based on an entirely different logic than the one discussed above. The characteristic feature of a person resorting to the minimax regret rule is pessimism: the decision criterion is based on the scrutiny of the worst possible outcomes that may result from a choice of any given strategy. On the other hand, in the strategic environments previously discussed it is the co-operative-ness-competitiveness dimension that is most crucial for the outcome. One might expect that pessimism or — which in the present context amounts to the same thing — suspicion goes together with competitiveness or non-co-operativeness more often than with co-operativeness. At least it would seem that suspicion generates non-co-operative behaviour. Hence, it is unlikely that minimax regretters would find it appealing to resort to co-operative strategies and, therefore, the emergence of the state cannot be understood at the same time on this basis, and on the basis of co-operation in PD.

It is possible to bring the above conceptual apparatus closer to the problems of state-formation or public goods provision by giving a new interpretation to the strategies a_1 and a_3 as well as to the states of nature.[14] Let a_1 denote the strategy of contributing to the public goods provision. Similarly, a_3 denotes the non-co-operative strategy. Let the states of nature X_1, X_2, X_3, X_4 and X_5 now denote the following states of affairs:

X_1, X_2: enough contributions have been collected for the provision,
X_3:   the amount still needed for the provision to start is less than the individual's contribution,
X_4:   the amount still needed for the provision to start is more than one individual's contribution but less than two individuals'; specifically the amount is less than the contribution of the individual under consideration plus the contribution of a ficti-tious player (chance) contributing with a probability of one-half,
X_5:   more than the amount needed in X_4 is still missing.

With this interpretation we obtain the same regret table (with the middle row deleted) as above if we again assume that the utility of the public good being provided (not provided, respectively) is 1 (0) for the individual whose decision is under consideration. On the other hand, the situation also resembles the setting of an *n*-person PD. But in contradistinction to the ordinary PD, in this non-strategic description the plausibility of the non-co-operative solution disappears. This is due to the fact that in the regret model there is no allowance for probabilistic considerations but we are essentially dealing with a 'no data problem'. Hence, one could claim that the minimax regret solution is based on anti-anticipatory considerations as the introduction of anti-cipatory elements immediately invokes an expected utility calculus.

Now what is the conclusion of all this? First, in a non-strategic setting the emergence of co-operation may be the result of the applica-tion of a decision rule (minimax regret) that conceptually runs counter to the co-operativeness in PD-like situations. Indeed, here might be one possible 'explanation' for the experimentally observed variation in co-operativeness due to format effects, i.e. due to effects presumably resulting from different — although mathematically equivalent — ways of displaying the game situation. Secondly, when there is no informa-tion allowing for anticipation of the state of the environment, the decision rules assumed by suspicious or pessimistic people may be conducive to the emergence of agreements.

INDIVIDUALISM AS A RESEARCH PROGRAMME

In the last twenty years the study of the history of science has been much inspired by Kuhn's *The Structure of Scientific Revolutions*. One of the major theoretical frameworks proposed in the field is Lakatos' (1970) theory of research programmes. In this final section of the chapter I shall look at the developments in the analytic theory of state from the angle provided by the research programme theory, as it seems to me obvious that this theory responds far better to the needs of the social sciences than, for example, the paradigm-guided view of Kuhn or the naïve forms of falsificationism. Anyway, this is not the place for arguing the superiority of any particular view of scientific development. I simply take the view of Lakatos as given and assume that the reader has some familiarity with it. I claim no originality here as a similar analysis has recently been given by Ball (1976) with slightly different foci and conclusions, though.

At the risk of over-simplification one could argue that in essence Lakatos' theory states that the basic units of scientific development are research programmes. These consist of a core of basic assumptions, views, theories, etc. plus a protective belt formed by less fundamental constructs, such as statements derived from the core assumptions with the aid of auxiliary statements and rules. For each research programme there are two systems of instructions or commands called negative and positive heuristics. The former one commands that the protective belt be constructed to save the core from the attacks of tests, observations, etc. The positive heuristics, in turn, deal with the research operations outside the core, i.e. in the potentially changing part of the research programme, the protective belt. The research programme may thus be seen as a sequence of theoretical systems in which each contains the common core defined by negative heuristics. The changes are limited to the protective belt. However, there may be two kinds of changes in the sequence: (1) degenerative and (2) progressive. These result from different types of processing research problems. In the former type a problem is processed into another one (problem-shift) which is solvable but only at the cost of diminishing the predictive value of the whole system. In progressive problem-shifts, on the other hand, the solution increases the predictive value − or information content in the Popperian sense − of the system.

Ball discusses the paradox of the participation problem in the light of Lakatos' theory. The conclusion reached is that the problem-shifts invoking notions like 'doing one's share in maintaining democratic institutions' are clearly degenerative, that is, they decrease the informative value of predictions derivable from the theory. This obviously follows from their ad hoc nature. Besides they seriously challenge the core of the programme as the individual rationality view-point is very difficult to accommodate to such collectivistic notions as 'common interest'.[15] On the other hand, Ball clearly approves the solution of Ferejohn and Fiorina to the participation paradox. In other words, the solution is based on a progressive problem-shift: the minimax criterion suggests novel hypotheses concerning political behaviour. Furthermore, it is clearly an individualistic criterion and, hence, is in accordance with the negative heuristics of the research programme.

If we take a somewhat broader view and consider the significance of the analytic theory of state to the research programme of rational action, we similarly notice progressive and degenerative problem-shifts. As a problem area, the emergence of the state is, of course, a similar although more general challenge to methodological individualism than the paradox of participation. As was pointed out above, Taylor's response to the challenge is an explicit rejection of the individualistic core of the research programme. Hence, it is not meaningful to discuss whether Taylor's problem-shift is a progressive or degenerative one. Both of the VPI theorists, on the other hand, can be located in the mainstream of the rational choice tradition. The solutions proposed by Bush and Gunning are, however, based on the idea that the emergence of the state (or of an agreement concerning property rights) can be rendered individually rational as it represents a Pareto-optimal change. What, however, needs additional specification is whether we are dealing with a PD-type of context or whether some other (e.g. co-ordination) game description would apply. A plausible interpretation — and one that gains support from Buchanan (1975: 64-68) — is that the situation preceding the emergence of the state resembles essentially the co-ordination game, that is, each of the individuals has a dominant strategy, the co-operative one. But once agreement has been reached, it would be in everyone's interest to cheat even though simultaneous cheating by all individuals would end up with a Pareto-suboptimal outcome. In other words, what the VPI authors seem to be claiming is that the PD-situation is bound to arise only *after* the agreement on property rights has been reached. So, states emerge because the original position is not a PD, after all.

There are some comments to be made on this view. First, it certainly makes plausible why it is in the capacity of *enforcing* agreements that the role of the state is important. There is no need for an enforcing agency until the agreement on property rights has been reached. Secondly, in the original position the agreement has to be made by unanimous consent by all individuals. Otherwise, there would be an incentive for some individuals to refrain from entering the agreement and — by maintaining their 'level of armament' while the general disarmament is going on — to increase their possessions at the cost of others who entered the agreement. As the state apparatus is known to have the ability to employ selective incentives to secure the co-operation of the citizens, it is to be expected that the emergence of the state apparatus immediately follows from the agreement because there are reasons — discussed at some length by Buchanan and Tullock (1962) — to expect that reaching unanimous consent will be costly due to negotiation costs. Indeed, those costs would otherwise easily outweigh the benefits gained from an agreement.

As for the progressiveness or degenerativeness of the problem-shift upon which the solution proposed by the VPI theorists rests, it cannot be held progressive as it seems to suggest no further hypotheses except those pertaining to state-formation. On the other hand, due to its restrictiveness in the intended scope of application, it does not decrease the predictive content of the rational choice theory, either.

Rawls sticks also to the individual rationality programme, but whereas it is somewhat difficult to determine whether the problem-shifts of the previous authors are progressive, this can relatively easily be done with respect to Rawls. Indeed, the whole idea of 'veil of ignorance' plus its coupling with a specific explication of rationality — maximin payoff — seems to suggest an array of empirical hypotheses. As was pointed out, the account Nozick gives of the emergence of the state is basically similar to the one given by the VPI theorists. There-fore, the conclusions presented above apply to Nozick as well.

By way of concluding, one could argue that the dominance of the analytic theory of state can be explained by the anomaly that confronts rational choice theorists in the field of collective action. Indeed, so great a problem is the apparent irrationality (from an individualistic view-point) of many common phenomena of human life that the existence of the analytic (individualistic) political theory is a para-mount example of the principle of tenacity of Feyerabend (1970). Eo ipso its existence is obvious evidence against naïve falsificationism: theories do not disappear when they are confronted with evidence that contradicts their predictions. I fully agree with Feyerabend that it is only the principle of tenacity that allows the theories to come to maturity and eventual predictive success. On the other hand, as a sole guideline of scientific development, this principle clearly leads to absurdities. But when connected with the principle of proliferation of theories and research programmes, the principle of tenacity has some descriptive as well as normative plausibility. Applied to the present discussion, these principles taken together would dictate the continued development of analytic political theory and the simultaneous develop-ment of other research programmes possibly of a non-individualistic nature. In view of the extreme artificiality of some of the 'solutions' discussed above, this sounds like a reasonable suggestion.

NOTES

1. I shall not dwell on the hotly debated question of how to define rationality. The reader is referred to Riker and Ordeshook (1973), Leibenstein (1976) and Nurmi (1975).

2. Incidentally (C, C) is also a Pareto-optimal state of affairs.

3. As a matter of fact, introducing rewards and penalties for the keeping and breaking of promises, respectively, would in any case modify the payoff matrix so that if the changes are large enough, the game is no longer a PD.

4. I shall use the term 'analytic solution' to refer to solutions obtained by using formal manipulations only, in contradistinction to 'experimental solutions' in which the experimenter, by manipulating some characteristics of the experimental game situation, may affect the probabilities by which co-operative strategies are chosen by the players (see Nurmi, 1977).

5. I have elsewhere pursued the question alluded to in my second comment in the text, namely the investigation of possible models of subjectively perceived utilities (Nurmi, 1976a).

6. But as Olson (1974) has pointed out, one major problem in determining the optimality of the public goods provision is that the level of their actual supply and/or demand is difficult to observe.

7. For a more general discussion on public goods, see Samuelson (1954) Kohn (n.d.); Nurmi (1976b); Väyrynen (1976).

8. See also Olson and Zeckhauser (1966). In the theory of state I think this situation comes close to the extortion theory referred to by Gunning (1972). As the material he refers to is unpublished, I have no way of knowing exactly how close.

9. In a recent paper Frohlich et al. (1975) have proposed another rationale for collective action based on differently shaped utility functions and various production functions.

10. Here we have to assume that the A_i's (i = 1, 2, 3, 4) stand for cardinal measures.

11. As the reader readily notices we are investigating a two-candidate contest here.

12. See, e.g. Strom (1975); Mayer and Good (1975); Stephens (1975). See also the reply of Ferejohn and Fiorina (1975).

13. This rule simply attaches equal probabilities to each of the states of nature and proceeds to maximise the expected utilities (see Milnor, 1954).

14. We may here omit strategy a_2 as it is dominated by both a_1 and a_3.

15. This has been pointed out first by Barry (1970) in a similar context.

REFERENCES

BALL, Terence, 'From paradigms to research programs', *American Journal of Political Science,* February 1976.
BARRY, Brian, *Sociologists, Economists and Democracy* (London, 1970).
— —, *The Liberal Theory of Justice* (Oxford, 1973).

BRAMS, Steven, 'Newcomb's Problem and prisoner's dilemma', *The Journal of Conflict Resolution*, December 1975.

BUCHANAN, James, 'Before public choice', in: G. TULLOCK (ed.), *Explorations in the Theory of Anarchy* (Blacksburg, 1972).

— —, *The Limits of Liberty* (Chicago, 1975).

— — and Gordon TULLOCK, *Calculus of Consent* (Ann Arbor, 1962).

BUSH, Winston, 'Individual welfare in anarchy', in: G. TULLOCK (ed.), *Explorations in the Theory of Anarchy* (Blacksburg, 1972).

COLEMAN, James, Contribution to the review symposium of Robert Nozick's Anarchy State, and Utopia, *Theory and Society*, Fall 1976.

DOWNS, Anthony, *An Economic Theory of Democracy* (New York, 1957).

EMERY, Fred and Eric TRIST, 'The causal texture of organizational environments', in: F. EMERY (ed.), *Systems Thinking* (Baltimore, 1969).

FEREJOHN, John and Morris FIORINA, 'Closeness counts only in horseshoes and dancing', *The American Political Science Review*, September 1975.

— —, 'The paradox of not voting: a decision theoretic analysis', *The American Political Science Review*, June 1974.

FEYERABEND, Paul, 'Consolations for the specialist', in: I. LAKATOS and A. MUSGRAVE (eds.), *Criticism and the Growth of Knowledge* (Cambridge, 1970).

FROHLICH, Norman and Joe OPPENHEIMER, 'I get by with a little help from my friends', *World Politics*, 1970.

— —, Thomas HUNT, Joe OPPENHEIMER and Harrison WAGNER, 'Individual contributions for collective goods: alternative models', *The Journal of Conflict Resolution*, June 1975.

— —, Joe OPPENHEIMER and Oran YOUNG, *Political Leadership and Collective Goods* (Princeton, 1971).

GOODIN, Robert, *The Politics of Rational Man* (New York, 1976).

GUNNING, Patrick, 'Towards a theory of the evolution of government', in: G. TULLOCK (ed.), *Explorations in the Theory of Anarchy* (Blacksburg, 1972).

GUYER, M., J. FOX and H. HAMBURGER, 'Format effects in the prisoner's dilemma game', *Journal of Conflict Resolution*, 1973.

HARDIN, Russell, 'Collective action as an agreeable *n*-prisoner's dilemma', *Behavioral Science*, 16, 1971.

HOWARD, Nigel, *Paradoxes of Rationality* (Cambridge, Mass., 1971).

KOHN, Leopold, *Probleme der Kolletivgüterallokation* (Zürich, no date).

LAKATOS, Imre, 'Falsification and the methodology of scientific research programs', in: I. LAKATOS and A. MUGRAVE (eds.), *Criticism and the Growth of Knowledge* (Cambridge, 1970).

LEIBENSTEIN, Harvey, *Beyond Economic Man* (Cambridge, Mass., 1976).

MAYER, Lawrence and I. J. GOOD 'Is minimax regret applicable to voting decisions?', *American Political Science Review*, September 1975.

McWHINNEY, William, 'Organizational form, decision modalities and the environment', *Human Relations*, August 1968.

MILNOR, John, 'Games against Nature', in: R. M. THRALL, C. H. COOMBS and R. L. DAVIS (eds.), *Decision Processes* (New York, 1954).

MUSGRAVE, Richard, 'On social goods and social bads', in: R. MARRIS (ed.), *The Corporate Society* (London, 1974).

NOZICK, Robert, *Anarchy, State and Utopia* (Oxford, 1974).

NURMI, Hannu, 'Rationality and analytic political theory', Institute of Political Science, University of Turku, research reports D:2, 1975 (mimeo).

– –, 'Fuzzy sets and game theory' (mimeo 1976a).

– –, 'Political development and theory of collective goods', prepared for delivery at the Xth World Congress of I.P.S.A. in Edinburgh, 16-19 August, (1976b).

– –, 'Ways out of the prisoner's dilemma', *Quality and Quantity* 11 (2), 1977.

OLSON, Mancur, *The Logic of Collective Action* (Cambridge, Mass., 1965).

– –, 'On the priority of public problems', in: R. MARRIS (ed.), *The Corporate Society* (London, 1974).

– –, and Richard ZECKHAUSER, 'An economic theory of alliances', *Review of Economics and Statistics*, 48, 1966.

RAPOPORT, Anatol, 'Prisoner's dilemma – recollections and observations', in: A. RAPOPORT (ed.), *Game Theory as a Theory of Conflict-Resolution* (Dordrecht, 1974).

RAWLS, John, *A Theory of Justice* (Cambridge, Mass., 1971).

RIKER, William and Peter ORDESHOOK, *An Introduction to Positive Political Theory* (Englewood Cliffs, 1973).

SAMUELSON, Paul, 'The pure theory of public expenditure', *Review of Economics and Statistics*, 36, 1954.

SHUBIK, Martin, 'Game theory, behavior, and the paradox of the prisoner's dilemma', *Journal of Conflict Resolution*, 19, 1970.

STEPHENS, Stephen, 'The paradox of not voting: comment', *The American Political Science Review*, September 1975.

STROM, Gerald, 'On the apparent paradox of participation: a new proposal', *The Americal Political Science Review*, September 1975.

TAYLOR, Michael, *Anarchy and Cooperation* (New York, 1976).

TULLOCK, Gordon, *Private Wants, Public Means* (New York, 1970).

VÄYRYNEN, Raimo, 'Theory of collective goods, military alliances and international security', *International Social Science Journal*, No. 2, 1976.

13 Social Contract and Property Rights: A Comparison between John Rawls and James M. Buchanan

Percy N. Lehning
University of Amsterdam, The Netherlands

Recently there has been a revival of social contract theories. Three authors who immediately come to mind when speaking about such a revival are John Rawls, Robert Nozick and James M. Buchanan. At first sight it seems no problem to label these authors as 'the new contractarians'.[1] A closer look will show, however, that apart from the central core of the social contract idea — voluntarily unanimous agreement — all three use the social contract in essentially different ways.[2] In this chapter my aim is to compare John Rawls' *A Theory of Justice* with James M. Buchanan's book *The Limits of Liberty* and his article 'A Hobbesian interpretation of the Rawlsian difference principle'[3] and especially to examine the use they both make of the idea of a social contract.* Therefore only those aspects of Rawls' theory of justice are mentioned that seem relevant to an understanding of his use of the social contract, and it is taken for granted that he has been successful in deriving his specific principles of justice from his theoretical framework. Although Rawls' theory is by now well known we shall, nevertheless, summarise in a few pages those aspects of it that are concerned with his use of the social contract in order to show where this use differs, and where it is similar to Buchanan's contractarian approach.

---

*Citations: (R, . . .) refers to John Rawls, *A Theory of Justice* (Oxford, 1972); (B, . . .) refers to James M. Buchanan, *The Limits of Liberty; Between Anarchy and Leviathan* (Chicago/London, 1975).

I

Rawls and the Social Contract

Rawls conceives society as an arrangement for co-operation between rational individuals. Social co-operation makes possible a better life for all than any would have if each were to live solely by his own efforts. At the same time there is a conflict as to how the greater benefits, produced by collaboration, are to be distributed. Therefore the co-operation has to be regulated by certain principles: the principles of justice;

> they provide a way of assigning rights and duties in the basic institutions of society and they define the appropriate distribution of the benefits and burdens of social co-operation (R, 4).

A central role in Rawls' conception is played by the notion of treating men as ends in themselves and never as means only. In Rawls' theory this means that everyone should be able to fulfil his plan of life. The necessary attributes for each individual to achieve this are primary goods (rights and liberties, powers and opportunities, income and wealth) which are distributed through the basic structure of society. The main question that Rawls wants to answer is: what are the principles that should regulate this distribution? For the derivation of these principles Rawls introduces the idea of a social contract.

> My aim is to present a conception of justice which generalizes and carries to a higher level of abstraction the familiar theory of the social contract as found, say, in Locke, Rousseau, and Kant (R, 11).

In this argument the idea of an original social contract gives the answer to the question how principles of justice and a basic structure of society might be formulated in such a way that it justifies the willing compliance of all members of that society. The original contract is not to be seen as one to enter a specific society; the object of the original agreement are the principles of justice that are to regulate the basic structure of society. This leads to a contractarian theory of justification. Substantive principles of justice are justified by showing that these principles are, in the described initial situation, precisely those that are selected by all rational persons. In Rawls' initial situation there is a hypothetical position of equality. He suggests that this original position of equality corresponds to the state of nature in the traditional theory of social contract. This does not mean, however, that this initial situation is to be seen *as* a state of nature. It is a situation of general egoism in which the basic structure is to be designed from scratch. Essential in this method of justification is, of course, the description of the initial situation. Rawls' by now well-known initial situation – the original position – is characterised by the veil of ignorance:

> . . . no one knows his place in society, his class position or social status; nor does he know his fortune in the distribution of natural assets and abilities, his intelligence and strength, and the like. Nor, again, does anyone know his conception of the good, the particulars of his rational plan of life, or even the special features of his psychology such as his aversion to risk or liability to optimism or pessimism (R, 137).

All characteristics in the situation of the original position that are irrelevant from a moral point of view are omitted. In the original position it is assumed that the parties are roughly similar in physical and mental powers so that no one can dominate the others. The contractors are also assumed to be non-envious, nor are they interested in the welfare of their fellow contractors. At the same time they know that society is characterised by moderate scarcity and that they themselves wish to have at their disposal more rather than less primary goods. The choice of the contractors is an a-moral choice; the principles that are chosen are means for the fulfilment of their self-interest. However, once these principles are chosen as 'the public conception of justice' they have become the yard-stick for right and wrong.

To ensure that the choice of the contractors – being itself an a-moral choice – will get an ethical status it is not only necessary that the initial situation is constructed in such a way that *unanimous* agreement will be possible, but also that the choice of every contractor will be an *impartial* one. The choice of principles, on which a moral judgement is to be based, should itself be based on an impartial judgement of the interests of all persons that have to live with these principles. Now it is, of course, exactly this that is guaranteed by the veil of ignorance. Because 'no one knows his situation in society nor his natural assets, . . . no one is in a position to tailor principles to his advantage' (R, 139). There is no basis for bargaining in the usual sense or the threat of sanctions during the negotiations. In this situation each chooses for everyone. To agree with Rawls that he has succeeded in deriving his principles of justice from a hypothetical social contract it is necessary to distinguish two stages in this method. First we must agree that the veil of ignorance, as Rawls describes it, is an adequate description of an initial situation in which to choose ethical principles. If we do agree, the second question that has to be answered is: does the deduction by rational choice from this specific initial situation lead to the principles specified by Rawls?

Granting that we agree on both points the following familiar principles are chosen:

First principle: each person is to have an equal right to the most extensive basic liberty compatible with a similar liberty for others;

Second principle: social and economic inequalities are to be arranged so that they are both (a) reasonably expected to be to everyone's advantage, and (b) attached to positions and offices open to all.

The principles are to be arranged in a serial order with the first principle prior to the second. Rawls' idea is that these two principles of justice achieve the aim of treating men as ends and not as means. In his theory Rawls makes a distinction between 'liberty' and 'the worth of liberty'; liberty is represented by the complete system of liberties of equal citizenship, while the worth of liberty to persons is proportional to their capacity to advance their ends. The worth of liberty is not the same for all, but this lesser worth is compensated for, in Rawls' conception, by the difference principle. Rawls' theory of justice is a pure procedural theory. The fairness of the circumstances under which agreement is reached transfers this fairness to the principles agreed to. And any outcome that has been arrived at by applying the principles in the correct way are, whatever the outcome may be, just.

II

Buchanan and the Social Contract

At the end of *The Limits of Liberty* Buchanan makes a few remarks on the differences between his book and Rawls' *A Theory of Justice*. His main disagreement with Rawls lies where Rawls wants to – and does – identify precepts of justice. As Buchanan remarks: 'My efforts in *The Limits of Liberty* are simultaneously more and less ambitious than those of Rawls' (B, 1975). He is more ambitious in that he wants to examine the prospects for genuine contractual renegotiations among persons, here and now, who are not placed in some artificial situation of equality. He is less ambitious in that he does not want to identify a set of principles that should define the 'good society'.

The only 'normative foundation' for the analysis is 'that each person counts for one, and for as much as any other' (B, 11). Nevertheless, he is against the idea of postulating a basic equality among men in some initial situation in order to derive the structure of a free society from rational, self-interested behaviour. Society is not a society of equals, but of individuals and individuals

> differ, one from another, in important and meaningful respects. They differ in physical strength, in courage, in imagination, in artistic skills and appreciation, in basic intelligence, in preferences, in attitudes toward others, in personal life-styles, in ability to deal socially with others, in Weltanschauung, in power to control others, and in command over nonhuman resources (B, 11).

Now, Buchanan wants to demonstrate 'that, even among men who are unequal, a structure of legal rights can be predicted to emerge' (B, 54). His aim is to give a conceptual explanation of how social order might have emerged contractually from the rational utility-maximisation of individuals. Social order embodies a definition of assignments of individual rights and the establishment of a political structure that is charged with enforcing rules of personal behaviour with respect to these assigned rights.

For the purpose of this explanation he introduces the idea of a natural equilibrium in a Hobbesian state of nature as an analytical starting point for social order.[4] In this initial conceptual setting individual differences manifest themselves by varying success in the continuous struggle for survival. In this situation there are no laws 'and there is no need for a definition of individuals' rights, either property rights or human rights. There is no society as such' (B, 55). The absence of authority presents the individual with a choice of using his labour to produce goods or to take by force those goods produced by others. The well-being of a person depends on his relative ability to produce, to take from others, and to protect his own. There emerges a natural distribution which can be seen as a conceptual equilibrium 'in which

each person extends his own behavior in securing (defending) shares in
x to the limit where marginal benefits from further effort are equal to
the marginal costs that such effort requires' (B, 24). The idea is that
this natural equilibrium serves as the starting point in which individual
persons are identified and from which contractual agreement becomes
possible, according to Buchanan. This social contracting is concerned to
reach *unanimous* agreement on an assignment of individual rights. Now,
in the natural equilibrium, one will recognise on rational observation,
that a lot of efforts are expended in securing and defending one's stock,
and that these efforts are wasteful. Therefore one should reach contractual   agreement   on   some   disarmament.   This   constitutes   in
Buchanan's analysis the initial leap from the Hobbesian jungle and
represents in itself a Paretian shift. Everyone will be made better off if
this disarmament agreement can be reached,

> [W]hatever might be the characteristics of this distribution, whether rough
> symmetry prevails or whether one participant becomes a consumption giant
> and the other a pygmy, and even if all of *x* is secured by one party (B, 24-25).

In this conception it is even possible that one arrives at a contract of
slavery. Now, the guiding idea is that the natural distribution is the
basis for the emergence of property rights. The distribution of rights
that are laid down in the contract is directly linked to the relative
command over goods and the relative freedom of behaviour that
separate persons in the Hobbesian state of nature had enjoyed. The
considerable differences that exist between persons in the precontract
setting have as a result that 'postcontract inequality in property and in
human rights must be predicted' (B, 25). This is, as remarked over and
over again by Buchanan, the result of the fact that

> [t]here is nothing to suggest that men must enter the initial negotiating
> process as equals. Men enter as they are in some natural state, and this may
> embody significant differences (B, 26).

This means, however, that the measure of differences between persons
will find its way into the unequal distribution of rights that are
contractually secured.

Buchanan makes a distinction between two stages of social contracting: the constitutional stage and the postconstitutional stage. This
makes it possible to distinguish the state in two separate roles. At the
constitutional stage the state emerges as the enforcing agency or institu-

tion, conceptually external to the contracting parties and charged with the single responsibility of enforcing agreed-on rights and claims. This is the legal or protective state; it is not to be seen as a decision-making body but only as a referee and has no legislative function.[5] That function is fulfilled by the productive state, the agency through which individuals provide themselves with 'public goods'.

In the postconstitutional stage (a part of the basic contract) the rules are defined with which the collectivity must operate when making and implementing decisions concerning the provision of 'public goods'.

Although unanimity is required for the constitution itself, this does not imply that decision rules governing the provision of public goods should themselves satisfy the unanimity requirement. For individuals will trade-off the costs of decision-making against the benefits of the veto when negotiating over the allowable departures from unanimity in reaching collective decisions, and these departures will be specified in the constitutional contract. But that does not mean that the collective action under non-unanimity decision-making is unrestrained. The constitutional contract indicates the allowable range over which collective action may take place and specifies the restrictions on the goods to be provided and financed. The purpose of defining individual rights (or, as Buchanan calls them, 'property rights') in constitutional contract is to provide the basis upon which individuals can initiate and implement trades and exchanges. To the extent that collective action would be allowed to break beyond the boundaries imposed by the mutuality of gains from exchange the whole idea of Buchanan's analysis would fall apart; it would mean that the community had made a step backward into the jungle or would not have stepped out of it at all. So the productive state is not allowed to cross the boundaries of the protective state and to intrude or change property rights. The only possibility in this analysis to change these rights is by a new constitutional contract in which *unanimous* agreement has been reached.

III

Discussion

After these two summaries of the social contract idea as used by Rawls and Buchanan the similarities and differences between both can be seen more clearly. Buchanan develops the contractual metaphor to analyse the emergence of property rights in the hope that it offers assistance in finding criteria for social change. The analysis of the emergence of property rights is done in what he calls a 'positive' way. Right from the start Buchanan makes clear that he does not want to give a description of principles that should regulate a 'good' society. That does not mean, however, that he has not an opinion on what is to be labelled 'good': good is that which 'tends to emerge' from the free choices of individuals. 'It is impossible for an external observer to lay down criteria for "goodness" independently of the *process* through which results or outcomes are attained. The evaluation is applied to the means of attaining outcomes, not to outcomes as such' (B, 6).

Now it may be suggested that we have seen the same attitude in Rawls' theory, where it was stated that an outcome could not be analysed independently of the procedure by which it has been reached. The important difference to note, however, is that Rawls' aim is to guarantee that the principles that are chosen are fair principles and these guarantee in their turn that any outcome can be called just as long as the principles are applied in the correct way. Buchanan, also, emphasises the procedure, but in his case the starting point is not agreement on fair principles but the struggle between unequals and he defines as 'good' the agreement on the outcome of that struggle. He places

> ultimate value on process or procedure, and by implication . . . define[s] as 'good' that which emerges from agreement among free men, independently of intrinsic evaluation of the outcome itself (B, 167).

The outcome can only be evaluated through the means by which it has been attained, and in this case that is unanimous agreement. *Any* unanimous agreement is classified as 'good'. The reason for this argumentation lies in the – ethical – choice of Buchanan's starting point for his analysis: the Hobbesian state of nature. (The choice of the Hobbesian state of nature as a starting point and not, for instance, a Rousseauean state of nature, is evidently based on the idea that individuals are self-interested utility-maximizers.) The 'base line' for comparison is the situation where people's lives are 'nasty, brutish, and short'. A society in which one can expect people to act predictably by abiding by rules and, foremost, a situation in which there is no coercion is the best one can strive for, and it is the protective state that guarantees this order in which individual rights are secured.

Now, it will be clear that essential to this analysis is how freedom is defined. Individual liberty has to become, in Buchanan's view, the overriding objective of social policy, due to his idea that every individual counts for one, and for as much as any other. Unfortunately, however, a more specific elaboration of what we have to understand under 'individual liberty' is lacking in Buchanan's analysis; but essentially it means 'freedom of contract'. The role the contract idea plays in his analysis is that it guarantees that people will freely — unanimously — come to agreement, even in a situation in which one of the parties is a 'consumption giant' and the other a 'pygmy'. But what kind of freedom is this? It is certainly not the possibility to be free to fulfil one's plan of life that plays such a central role in Rawls' theory.

In Buchanan's opinion the time has come for a renegotiation of the basic structural arrangement of society, with which he has in mind a change in the legal order and especially a consensual redefinition of individual rights and claims. The existing order (the outcome of some prior contracting process) has recently shown features of instability. A symptom of this instability is, according to Buchanan, that the productive state (for which we can read the welfare state) is making intrusions into the domain of the protective state. The result is that changes are made in the basic arrangement of society *without* the unanimous agreement of all concerned. How should these symptoms of instability be evaluated?

The use of any conception of justice for this evaluative purpose is out of the question. Such a conception cannot give direction to an eventual change of the existing legal structure (and in the distribution of property rights) because Buchanan wants

> to the maximum extent that is possible to derive the logical structure of social interaction from the self-interested utility-maximization of individuals and without resort to external norms (B, 80).

The reason the existing order has lost its stability is that people believe that if they were back in the state of nature right now, there would emerge *another* natural equilibrium and, consequently, another distribution of property rights. Individual holders of a right or a claim defined in the status quo, come to predict that this claim will be eroded or undermined unless the structure is modified . . . Such predictions may be based on imagined shifts in the natural distribution in anarchistic equilibrium which always exists 'underneath' the observed social realities (B, 78-79).

Now, the instability and disruptions in the sixties may have been the signal that there was a shift in the natural distribution; that the existing power structure was no longer a mirror of this natural equilibrium and that there was, therefore, reason to renegotiate the existing legal structure. (As an example of instability Buchanan repeatedly mentions the student rebellion. This unrest, however, is not seen by him as an example of a signal of change in the existing power structure.)

The problem remains to be answered how we are to imagine that one could arrive at a 'consensual redefinition of individual rights and claims', once we know that the holders of rights (rights that are distributed unequally) would agree to make a new social contract in which these property rights will be redistributed in another way (presumably more equally). From Buchanan's point of view such a unanimous redistribution is not as preposterous as it might seem. In this analysis, *not* choosing unanimously for a revised contract may have as a consequence that the existing order may be disrupted completely. Anyone who is in favour of renegotiating, in view of the imagined shift in the natural distribution, can make a threat to no longer co-operate and disrupt the existing order by bringing back the state of nature in which everybody will be worse off. In this analysis, inspired by the shotgun behind the door, the best thing one can do is to choose for a consensual redefinition of individual rights and claims. As Goodin has remarked, the appeal of this kind of analysis is especially strong for the cautious, the paranoid or those that have a lot to lose.[6]

IV

A 'Positive' Derivation of Rawls' Principles?

The main point on which Buchanan disagrees with Rawls is that Rawls derives specific principles of justice. In a recently published article by Buchanan ('A Hobbesian interpretation of the Rawlsian difference principle') he tries to show that it is possible to derive the Rawlsian difference principle from the analysis of Hobbesian anarchy as developed in *The Limits of Liberty* without any resort to a conception of justice. The interpretation given in this article 'places Rawls' construction in a somewhat more positivistic setting'.[7]

We shall make a short digression into the analysis of this article because it makes especially clear where the difference lies between Buchanan's and Rawls' use of the social contract. We have already mentioned that Buchanan shares with Rawls a set of quasi-Kantian contractarian presumptions. The original position provides for both the basis from which the arrangements for the basic structure must be derived. The essential difference, however, lies in the fact that in Rawls' case, once the social contract has been reached, ethical principles are chosen *once and for all.* In Buchanan's case, however, the social contract can be renegotiated at a later point in time. This is due to the fact that the original position, that is the effective alternative in the absence of agreement, is defined as the equilibrium in Hobbesian anarchy and – as we have seen at the end of section III – after the constitutional contract has been reached one or more persons or groups may say: 'let's do it again'. In Buchanan's analysis one can go back to the original position and try to reach a new contract.

For Rawls the social contract is a heuristic device and the readers of *A Theory of Justice* are invited to follow the Rawlsian *Gedankenexperiment* for the choice of ethical principles that should regulate a well-ordered society. The original position is *not* supposed to be a situation to which one can threaten to shift the system back. In the article Buchanan shares Rawls' idea of a 'veil of ignorance':

> In the original position, in Hobbesian anarchy, the persons do not know their respective abilities within the cooperative technology, nor do they know how each will respond to income incentives in participating in joint production. They know only that each of them can, by unilateral action, shift the whole system back into anarchy by the simple expedient of withdrawing cooperation.[8]

Now in this analysis, the difference principle can only be identified as emerging from contractual agreement in the initial position.

> if the participants make the positive prediction that the least-advantaged persons and/or groups will, in fact, withdraw their cooperation in certain situations and that the threats of this withdrawal will be effective.[9]

That is the reason, according to Buchanan, that individuals, acting behind a veil of ignorance, will agree on the difference principle of income distribution because

> they mutually recognize the threat potential possessed by the relatively disadvantaged in any sharing outcome that fails to meet the requirement of Pareto-superiority over the equal sharing solution.[10]

(The equal sharing solution is seen here as a way-station between Hobbesian anarchy and the final position.) In this way the analysis tries to show that (with the presumption of the absence of envy, as in Rawls' analysis) contractual unanimity can be reached on a shift from Hobbesian anarchy to a set of social arrangements that will maximise the income of everyone, *including* that of the least-advantaged.

For Rawls, the difference principle removes the indeterminateness of the Pareto-efficiency concept by singling out a particular point from which the social and economic inequalities are to be assessed: the position of the least-advantaged. As Rawls formulates it:

> the difference principle is compatible with the principle of efficiency. For when the former is fully satisfied, it is indeed impossible to make any one representative man better off without making another worse off, namely, the least advantaged representative man whose expectations we are to maximize. Thus justice is defined so that it is consistent with efficiency, at least when the two principles are perfectly fulfilled (R, 79).

In Buchanan's article the close link that exists between his contract approach and Pareto-efficiency culminates in the derivation from an original position, defined as Hobbesian anarchy, of the difference principle not because of its moral content — which is seen by him as a favourable side-effect — and not because it is equivalent with the Pareto-principle, but because its application is a way to reach Pareto-optimality.[11]

We may summarise this section by saying that in Rawls' case efficiency is a by-product of justice, while in Buchanan's case justice is a by-product of efficiency when using Hobbesian anarchy as the starting-point of analysis.

V

The Problem of Property Rights

We now return to Buchanan's analysis in *The Limits of Liberty.* Since he claims that there should be a renegotiating of individual rights, let us look more closely at his conception of 'property rights'.

The assignment of property rights is a consequence of the way in which capacities are distributed amongst different persons: feud, violence and force are the source of the natural distribution. The logical foundation of property rights lies in the need for boundaries between 'mine' and 'thine'. Being unequal in a variety of aspects, some people will acquire more 'property' than others. Some may get a lot, some hardly anything at all, but in this analysis there is no place to criticise the resulting distribution from a moral point of view.

In Rawls' view the starting point should be exactly the opposite: men should be considered as moral equals. Like Buchanan, he recognises that people differ in their talents and capacities, but for Rawls these initial endowments of natural assets are arbitrary from a moral point of view. There is no moral sense in which talented people deserve their more favourable starting place in society. His two principles are a fair way of meeting the arbitrariness of fortune and can be seen as principles of redress. A distribution of property rights that is the result of force, and the use of one's ability to grab what one can, cannot create an order that will be stable. And what is more: 'To each according to his threat advantage is not a principle of justice at all.' We have already mentioned that Buchanan's normative foundation for his analysis is that everyone counts for one, and for as much as any other. He remarks that this

> must be reconciled with the positive statement that men will necessarily differ among themselves *and in any assignment of rights* (B, 11; emphasis added).

He also states:

> there is really no categorical distinction to be made between that set of rights normally referred to as 'human' and those referred to as 'property' (B, 10).

Now, with this sort of approach it is impossible to derive any set of 'universal' or 'inalienable' rights independently of the analysis of the emergence of property rights in the natural distribution. That means, independently of the distribution of power among individual persons. In Buchanan's view 'there has been relatively too much emphasis on the normative function of property' (B, 9). One may wonder, however, if this 'positive' theory about property rights makes sure that 'everyone counts for one, and for as much as any other'. If persons are defined by the rights they possess and one can get rights only by force, or, after the constitutional contract has been made, by gains from trade, some will count for much less than one!

Buchanan's approach to property rights corresponds with the ideas developed in the literature on 'the economics of property rights'. In a recent book, edited by Furubotn and Pejovich, all relevant articles that paved the way for this approach are reproduced. In it

> property rights are understood as the *sanctioned behavioral relations* among men that arise from the existence of goods and pertain to their use . . . The term 'good' is used here for anything that yields utility or satisfaction to a person. Thus, and this point is important, the concept of property rights in the context of the new approach applies to *all* scarce goods. The concept encompasses both the rights over material things (to sell my typewriter) as well as 'human' rights (the right to vote, to publish, etc.). The prevailing system of property rights in the community is, then, the sum of economic and social relations with respect to scarce resources in which individual members stand to each other.[12]

This properly summarises, we think, how Buchanan sees property rights. In his economic analysis, contractual agreement is vitally important because it represents the means by which bundles of property rights are exchanged. Now, in the real world that Buchanan wants to analyse, the regulations pertaining to property rights are important in delimiting the welfare of the individual members of the system.

This brings us back to Buchanan's notion that everyone should count for one, and for as much as any other. How are we to assess this 'counting' in view of the origin and distribution of property rights? By conceiving rights only as rights in the market-place it is difficult to see how his idea that free men should have free relations among each other can be realised. We think Buchanan's analysis would have gained a lot if he had made a distinction between different kinds of rights. In the first place a distinction should have been made between, on the one hand, rights that are not to be obtained on a quid pro quo base and that recognises the equal worth of every citizen and, on the other hand, property rights. In the second place he should have recognised the complexity of property rights themselves. For instance, the right of ownership may be an exclusive right, but is it also an unrestricted right? Buchanan does not elaborate on such problems as to what one is allowed to do or not to do with one's property rights except, of course, trading them.

It is clear from his whole analysis that his dilemma in the provision of public goods (and therefore of the role played by the productive state) is an efficient provision of these goods while avoiding a build-up of the central government. He is more afraid of Leviathan than of private power based on exclusive property rights. Especially, he is afraid of methods of redistribution that place too much power in the hands of the productive state. That would make expropriation of owners possible *without* their consent, because unanimous agreement is not necessary for the activities the productive state undertakes. Redistribution activities are an example of unallowable coercion and therefore these activities are conceptually not possible, within Buchanan's strict contractarian framework, in the realm of the productive state. To avoid intrusions into property rights by the productive state, bargaining (that should eventually result in unanimous agreement) is the only way by which the affluent can agree to a reduction of their property rights in return for a limit on state redistribution activities.

However, by defining rights only as economic assets, in which Buchanan follows the tradition of the New Political Economy and which is the conventional way to forestall an activist government, he leaves many problems unanswered.[13] What is especially lacking in his analysis is a political theory of property rights. A foundation for rights other than the one given by Buchanan is the view that some 'goods' are especially important to individuals because these enable them to fulfil their own plan of life and to reach self-fulfilment, and should for that reason, be recognised as rights. Rawls' theory can be seen as a good example of this sort of justification of rights. In our opinion his approach leads to a more fruitful starting-point than the one given by Buchanan if one wants to analyse the range of activities a productive state should undertake to give everyone the possibility to fulfil his own plan of life.

NOTES

1. See, for instance, the review of all three authors by Scott Gordon, 'The new contractarians', *The Journal of Political Economy* 84, 1976: 573-90.

2. In this paper we shall not go into Nozick's *Anarchy, State, and Utopia,* New York, 1974. We are not sure that his theory can be classified as a social contract theory at all, due to his hypothetical invisible hand explanation of the origin of the state, as opposed to a contractarian explanation. See also: Percy B. Lehning, 'Een filosoof van de vrijheid protesteert tegen gelijkheid' (A philosopher in favour of liberty protests against equality), *De Gids,* 139, 1976: 73-95.

3. James M. Buchanan, 'A Hobbesian interpretation of the Rawlsian difference principle', *Kyklos,* 29, 1976: 5-25.

4. This analytical starting point for social order was originally developed by Winston C. Bush in his 'Individual welfare in anarchy', in: Gordon Tullock (ed.), *Explorations in the Theory of Anarchy* (Blacksburg, 1972), 5-18.

5. The protective state is similar, according to Buchanan himself, to the minimal state as conceived by Nozick. But: 'My contractarian model does not, however, allow the state to be closed off at these limits. If contractual agreements emerge for the provision of jointly-consumed public goods, there may be a role for a productive as well as for a protective state.' James M. Buchanan,'Utopia, the minimal state, and entitlement'. (A review of Nozick's *Anarchy, State, and Utopia*), *Public Choice,* 23, 1975: 121-26; 125.

6. Robert E. Goodin, 'Possessive individualism again', *Political Studies,* 24, 1976: 488-501; 491.

7. Buchanan, 'Hobbesian interpretation', op. cit., 6.

8. Ibid., 9.

9. Ibid., 23.

10. Ibid., 10.

11. For the difficulties (and differences) that arise from interpreting Rawls' difference principle, see: Percy B. Lehning and R. J. van der Veen, 'De Rechtvaardigheidstheorie van John Rawls', II, *Acta Politica,* XII, 1977: 25-76; esp. 26-49. The relation between Rawls' difference principle and the conventional Paretian approach (like Buchanan's) is analysed in Charles K. Rowley and Alan T. Peacock, *Welfare Economics; A Liberal Restatement* (London, 1975); esp. ch. 7.

12. Erik G. Furubotn and Svetozar Pejovich (eds.), *The Economics of Property Rights* (Cambridge, Mass., 1974), 3.

13. See Goodin, op. cit., 490.

14 Can a Social Contract be Signed by an Invisible Hand?

Hillel Steiner
University of Manchester, UK

In the first part of *Anarchy, State and Utopia*,[1] Robert Nozick advances an argument against the anarchist claim that the state is intrinsically immoral because, in the course of maintaining its monopoly on the use of force and protecting everyone within a territory, it must violate individuals' rights.[2] He purports to show that a state would arise from a state of nature *even though no one intended this or tried to bring it about*, by a process which need not violate anyone's rights. We already possess, in Locke's *Second Treatise*, an account of how a state could come to be established within the parameters of permissibility implied by individuals' natural rights.[3] Hence, what is novel about Nozick's argument is its contention that this development need not be occasioned by a social contract — by a deliberate undertaking, on the part of individuals, jointly to create a state — but rather would occur in any case as the unintended effect of unconcerted choices made by individuals independently pursuing their private purposes. Anarchists' aspirations are held to be, not morally wrong, but unattainable. This attempt to show that the normative effects of a social contract would equally be brought about by an 'invisible-hand process' does raise some interesting issues on the boundary between political philosophy and the philosophy of the social sciences. But in the present chapter I shall not devote much attention to the wider aspects of these issues, and shall concentrate my discussion on Nozick's account of the establishment of the unintended state and on his main (other) example of the operation of invisible-hand processes — the creation of money as a common medium of exchange.

I

Two concepts require some preliminary elucidation. For Nozick, 'the state' is a protective association containing an agency which rightfully possesses a monopoly of the legitimate use of force within a given territory. Legitimate uses of force consist of, and only of, those uses of force that are necessary to uphold individuals' rights which are thus presumed to be capable of independent (non-state) determination. Just how a *single* agency could come to possess such a monopoly is explained by a conjunction of arguments, one of which invokes the notion of invisible-hand processes. To get a grip on what is meant by 'invisible-hand processes' and on why Nozick believes that explanations referring to them have greater explanatory power, we must attend briefly to his introductory remarks on explanatory political theory. He suggests that there are three possible ways of understanding the political realm:

> (1) to fully explain it in terms of nonpolitical; (2) to view it as emerging from the nonpolitical but irreducible to it, a mode of organization of nonpolitical factors understandable only in terms of novel political principles; or (3) to view it as a completely autonomous realm (p. 6).

Only the first of these is held to promise full understanding of the whole political realm and is therefore to be considered the best form of explanation. Only such explanations can be viewed as 'fundamental' inasmuch as they are

> explanations of the realm in other terms; they make no use of any of the notions of the realm. Only via such explanations can we explain and hence understand everything about a realm; the less our explanations use notions constituting what is to be explained, the more (*ceteris paribus*) we understand (p. 19).

Attaching privileged status to this form of explanation seems entirely acceptable and can be seen as an extension of the sound principle that no term which is present in a *definiendum* should enter into its *definiens*. Descriptions of invisible-hand processes, when employed in the understanding of complicated social arrangements or patterns, are one form of such fundamental explanations. Non-fundamental explanations of social patterns explain them in terms of the desires, wants, beliefs, and so on, of individuals, directed toward realizing the pattern. But within such explanations will appear descriptions of the pattern, *at least within quotation marks*, as objects of belief and desire. The explanation itself will say that some individuals desire to bring about something with (some of) the pattern-features . . . (p. 19).

By contrast, the description of an invisible-hand process, as *explanans*, does not contain terms present in the description of the pattern which is its *explanandum*. It explains what looks to be the product of someone's intentional design as not being brought about by anyone's intentions. Nozick names sixteen examples of this kind of explanation, ranging from the subject of evolutionary theory through that of bureaucratic decision-making to trade-cycle analysis and accounts of social group distribution over urban residential neighbourhoods (pp. 20-21). He takes pains to emphasise that the instanced explanations may not be the correct ones, and the same holds with regard to his explanations of the state and money. Rather, they are logically possible explanations of these phenomena.

What I shall try to show in the ensuing argument is that Nozick's explanations of the state and money cannot possibly be correct. The establishment of a monopolistic protective agency and of a common medium of exchange cannot be construed as the effects of the operation of invisible-hand processes. Rather, they must be attributed to the deliberate and concerted efforts of individuals to bring them about. They must be attributed to social contracts. But this demonstration, if valid, should not be taken to cast doubt upon the possibility of invisible-hand processes generally, much less to impugn their explanatory superiority in other areas of investigation.

Like Locke, Nozick starts from the assumption that individuals have certain natural property rights (in their own bodies and other objects) which, in the absence of a state, they are entitled to protect by the personal use of force. It is plausible to imagine that many individuals will find the task of personally protecting their property both inconvenient and, in some cases, impossible. Consequently they will find it worthwhile (less costly) to form or join protective associations and to institute a division of labour whereby some persons are employed to perform protective functions for the members of the association. Protective agencies are thus contractually charged with the duty to employ force (if necessary), both against non-client violators of their clients' rights and in the rectification of inter-client violations. Among the non-client violators of any one agency's clients' rights may be persons who are clients of other protective agencies in the same geographical area. Such violations may give rise to special problems. It is reasonable to assume that each agency would develop a set of adjudicative and enforcement procedures acceptable to those who contract its services. But Nozick claims there is no reason to assume that any one agency's procedures would be the same as those of others. Since clients may have recourse to their agencies' procedures whenever there is occasion for force to be used, either against them or on their behalf against others, difficulties can arise in cases of conflict between persons who are clients of different agencies. If the agencies in question disagree over the merits of the case, they are each thereby obliged forcibly to oppose the other's use of force against their respective clients. Nozick's thesis is that the natural outcome of this state-of-affairs would be the emergence of a dominant protective association in any one geographical area — an association which very much resembles a state. This is said to come about for one of several alternative reasons. Either it is the case that any two opposed agencies do battle and one of them invariably prevails, whereupon the ill-protected clients of the losing agency shift their custom to the winning one. Or it is the case that any two opposed agencies do battle and each tends to win in one geographical area and to lose in another, whereupon those of their respective clients who are ill-protected either move to where their agency wins or shift their custom to the agency which wins where they are. Or it is the case that any two agencies do battle and are evenly matched, whereupon they devise less costly and more successful ways of protecting their clients' rights that amount to establishing a unified (federal) judicial system (pp. 16-17). Thus, purely through the operation of competitive forces in the market for protective services — purely through an invisible-hand process — a state comes into being.[4]

The question we need to address is not the empirical one of whether it is probable that a dominant association would indeed emerge from a state of nature. Rather, what demands consideration is the conceptual question of whether the foregoing account is, in fact, one of an invisible-hand process occurring within the parameters of permissibility. That is, we want to know if Nozick is correct in thus describing the emergence of the complex social pattern represented by the dominant protective association — a pattern in which what were previously maximally dispersed legitimate powers of enforcement have become kaleidoscopically convergent ones — as occurring without anyone's rights being violated and without any individuals entertaining a belief, want or desire that this pattern be brought about.

II

In a passage worth quoting in full, Nozick puts the following query to his readers:

> *How, if at all, does a dominant protective association differ from the state?* Was Locke wrong in imagining a compact necessary to establish civil society? As he was wrong in thinking (sects. 46, 47, 50) that an "agreement", or "mutual consent", was needed to establish the "invention of money". Within a barter system, there is great inconvenience and cost to searching for someone who has what you want and wants what you have, even at a marketplace, which, we should note, needn't become a marketplace by everyone's expressly agreeing to deal there. People will exchange their goods for something they know to be more generally wanted than what they have. For it will be more likely that they can exchange this for what they want. For the same reasons others will be more willing to take in exchange this more generally desired thing. Thus persons will converge in exchanges on the more marketable goods, being willing to exchange their goods for them; the more willing, the more they know others who are also willing to do so, in a mutually reinforcing process. (This process will be reinforced and hastened by middlemen seeking to profit in facilitating exchanges, who themselves will often find it most expedient to offer more marketable goods in exchange.) For obvious reasons, the goods they converge on, via their individual decisions, will have certain properties: initial independent value (else they wouldn't begin as more marketable), physically enduring, non-perishable, divisible, portable, and so forth. No express agreement and no social contract fixing a medium of exchange is necessary (p. 18).

The view that money or a common medium of exchange is an instrument of convenience — a lubricant of the wheels of exchange — is such a well-entrenched belief that it is almost never subjected to analytical scrutiny, even in the most searching theoretical accounts of the foundations of economic activity. For even the writings of those economists — not a few — who find its actual origin in some act of agreement or an authoritative social convention, suggest the plausibility of accounts like the one set out above, whereby the emergence of such a medium *could* equally result from the cumulative effects of individuals' unconcerted rational efforts to expedite interpersonal exchange. Consider the following standard tale from a widely used textbook:

> An individual, for instance, a farmer, who has grown more turnips than he can or desires to eat may find some other farmer who has grown more wheat than he desires to eat and the two may strike a bargain. However, such methods of

trading are useful only when very few such bargains are necessary to channel the produced commodities from the producer to the final purchasers. Otherwise, barter transactions require expenditure of time and effort that could be better spent on production of goods or on leisure. . . . A drastic increase in efficiency may be accomplished when *money* is used as a medium of exchange. Without money, an owner of good A who desired some other good X may have been forced to exchange good A for good B, good B for good C, and so on, whereas with the use of money this chain of transactions may be cut to merely two: the sale of good A for money and the purchase of good X for money.[5]

The problems typically besetting stories such as this one are two-fold. First, their tellers are remarkably incurious about how convenient the above set of barter transactions might have proved for the *buyers* of goods A and B. Secondly, they rarely trouble to inform their readers of what then happens to the cash *seller* of good X, taking it rather for granted that he will presently proceed to purchase good C (or whatever) with his receipts. I do not, of course, wish to query the claim that this is what he will *try* to do. Rather, I should like to draw attention to the nature of the reasons for believing that he will *succeed* in doing so.

In the penultimate quotation above, Nozick misleadingly advances the suggestion, endorsed by many writers on this subject,[6] that the operation of a barter system depends upon what economists have termed the 'double coincidence of wants' — that there must be 'someone who has what you want and wants what you have'. It is the relative infrequency (or non-necessity) of double coincidences of wants among traders that is held to render the use of a common medium of exchange more efficient than barter, inasmuch as it *reduces the number of transactions* required to clear the market, that is, required to achieve the state-of-affairs where everyone has what he wants and can afford of what is available from others. *Is* the use of a common medium of exchange more efficient in this respect? Consider the following state-of-affairs in which eight individuals are each possessed of a different commodity which they wish to exchange for another commodity, and in which there is no double coincidence of wants (Table 1). If there is a medium of exchange, the minimum number of transactions required to clear the market is *eight*. These are as shown in Table 2. If there is no medium of exchange, the minimum number of transactions required to clear the market is *seven*. These are as shown in Table 3.

So, while we must not leap to any hasty conclusions, the claim that the use of money actually reduces the number of transactions necessary

TABLE 1	TABLE 2
1 wants A and has B	1 buys A from 8
2 wants C and has D	2 buys C from 5
3 wants E and has F	3 buys E from 6
4 wants G and has H	4 buys G from 7
5 wants B and has C	5 buys B from 1
6 wants D and has E	6 buys D from 2
7 wants F and has G	7 buys F from 3
8 wants H and has A	8 buys H from 4

TABLE 3

1 exchanges B for A with 8
2 exchanges D for C with 5
3 exchanges F for E with 6
4 exchanges H for G with 7
5 exchanges D for B with 8
6 exchanges F for D with 8
7 exchanges H for F with 8

in the absence of double coincidences of wants is, to say the least, not self-evidently true. Thus, it is sometimes further suggested that one feature of a medium of exchange that renders its use more efficient than barter lies in the fact that it is divisible, whereas some of the commodities offered on markets may not be divisible. Hence, in the absence of any double coincidences of wants, the owners of more valuable indivisible goods would be badly placed, under barter, to obtain the severally less valuable goods they desire from the various persons supplying them, without a larger number of transactions being needed. Again, is this true? Consider the following state-of-affairs (Table 4) in which six individuals are each possessed of varying amounts of different commodities, and in which there is no double coincidence of wants. We shall further suppose that one of these commodities, F, is more valuable than any other and is indivisible. If there is a medium of exchange, the minimum number of transactions required to clear the market is *eleven*. These are as shown in Table 5. If there is no medium of exchange, the minimum number of transactions required to clear the market is *seven*. These are as shown in Table 6.

Again, the fact that the required number of transactions is actually *less* under barter than when money is used, should not immediately lead us to reject long-standing claims for the latter's greater efficiency

TABLE 4

1 has 32A and wants	8B and 4C
2 has 16B and wants	4C and 2D
3 has 8C and wants	2D and 1E
4 has 4D and wants	1F
5 has 2E and wants	16A and 8B
6 has 1F and wants	16A and 1E

TABLE 5

1 buys	8B from	2
1 buys	4C from	3
2 buys	4C from	3
2 buys	2D from	4
3 buys	2D from	4
3 buys	1E from	5
4 buys	1F from	6
5 buys	16A from	1
5 buys	8B from	2
6 buys	16A from	1
6 buys	1E from	5

TABLE 6

6 exchanges	1F for	32A	with	1
5 exchanges	1E for	16A	with	6
5 exchanges	1E for	8B	with	2
4 exchanges	4D for	1F	with	1
3 exchanges	4C for	2D	with	1
1 exchanges	2D for	8B	with	2
2 exchanges	1E for	4C	with	3

in facilitating a set of market-clearing exchanges. Might there not be considerations other than the minimum number of required transactions that would tell in favour of the greater efficiency of money?

In this connection we can, I think, dismiss the fact that money is more portable than (some) goods as a decisive reason for its greater efficiency. For, in the first place, the market is theoretically held to be a place where no transportation costs attach to the performance of transactions (cf. above, Nozick's claim that money is more efficient 'even at a marketplace'). Moreover, there is no reason why a set of barter transactions could not include the exchange of vouchers, each redeemable for one unit of a specified commodity and issued by each commodity's supplier. Such vouchers would not, of course, amount to a common medium of exchange and would thus not necessitate as great a number of transactions as would money. So far as non-market exchanging is concerned, two alternative possibilities exist. If barter is carried on by using vouchers, the amount of goods-transportation (and the number of transactions) required for any given set of exchanges is the same as if money is used. If barter is carried on without vouchers, it is certainly true that a greater amount of goods-transportation is required for any set of exchanges than if money is used. But the use of money, inasmuch as it necessitates a greater number of transactions than barter, thus necessitates a greater amount of trade-transportation in non-market trading. Whether the extra trader-transportation costs of money are outweighed by the extra goods-transportation costs of barter must remain a purely empirical question, leaving money's greater portability as an inconclusive reason for asserting its greater efficiency.

One argument which might be entered in behalf of the greater efficiency of money — and against the conclusiveness of our adverse findings in the foregoing transaction tables — is that, under barter, there is no reason to assume that the set of transactions actually performed by rational traders to clear the market would constitute the *minimum* number required to do so. Whereas this is allegedly not true when money is used. In the barter system and where there are no double coincidences of wants, traders must presume that there will be transactions which some of them undertake that will have to involve them in accepting, in exchange, goods which they will then need to exchange with others for the goods they want. Of course, the same is true — indeed, true without exception — of all exchanges when money is used. But could not those engaged in barter make a 'mistake' in their choice of these intermediate goods? Consider the fifth and sixth transactions in Table 3 above. If 5 had mistakenly exchanged with 7 instead of 8, and if 6 had (then) mistakenly exchanged with 8 rather than 7, the minimum number of transactions then required to clear the market would have been nine and not seven — one more than was required with the use of money.

That occurrences of this kind of mistake are possible seems undeniably true. What needs consideration, however, are the conditions required for such mistakes actually to occur. In the case just mentioned, 5 trades with 7 because he *does not know* that there is someone (namely, 8) who will give him what he wants, B, for what he has, D. Similarly, 6 trades with 8 because he does not know that there is someone (now 7) who will give him his desired D for the F he has. Both had previously traded with 2 and 3 (second and third transactions, Table 3) in the hope, let us suppose, that they were thereby acquiring intermediate goods which they would be able to exchange for the goods they wanted. Their hopes were dashed when, through ignorance, they came to believe that their receipts from these initial transactions would not accomplish this for them.

But, and this is surely the point, the existence of money is no remedy for such ignorance. The fact that there is a common medium of exchange implies only that *if* there is someone wanting to exchange X for something else, he will take money in return for it. But it in no way implies, suggests or otherwise hints that there is such a person. Thus, if I sell my goods in order to obtain X, the fact that this transaction is conducted via a common medium of exchange is no guarantee that I shall succeed in buying X. And if I do not succeed in doing so, the sale of my goods was a mistaken transaction, as I have been left with no goods at all. Had I but known that I would be unable to secure X, I should not have offered my goods for sale and the market would have been cleared without the transaction whereby they were purchased.

Perhaps the case for the greater efficiency of money can be put differently and more persuasively. One might argue that, for any set of wants which traders *already know to be satisfiable* in the market, money more probably minimises the number of transactions performed to clear the market.[7] The grounds for such a claim are held to lie in the fact that under barter, but not under money, traders will need to know more than that the market will be cleared, i.e. more than that their receipts for their goods will secure for them the goods they want. It is this allegedly greater amount of required knowledge that renders barter less likely to be maximally efficient. Again, however, this claim is ill-founded. For even if traders know only that their receipts will secure the goods they want, they will have sufficient reason to accede to any proposal of barter made to them. Hence, all that each need do is approach whomever is in possession of the goods he wants and exchange the goods he has for them. This is precisely the procedure followed when money is used, the only difference being that under money, but not under barter, every trader must engage in at least two transactions.

What follows from all this is *not* that it is irrational to use money rather than to engage in barter. It is that the reasons for using money are not to be found in stories about its expediting the exchange of goods by enabling it to be performed with fewer transactions. These reasons are to be found elsewhere. A necessary, though by no means sufficient, reason for accepting money in exchange for one's goods consists in the belief that the goods one wants are *currently* not supplied by others. A sufficient reason for doing so consists in the belief that, at some time *later* than when one sells one's goods, others will supply one with the goods one wants in exchange for one's current receipts. That this latter sort of belief is not invariably well-founded is a fact to which many can give ample testimony. What then are the possible grounds for this sort of belief?

To answer this question, let us perform a quite modest thought-experiment by trying to conceive of money as itself a good. What kind of good is it? We have seen that it is not a good which increases the trading efficiency with which we can secure the goods we want. Rather, it is (ostensibly) a good which, so to speak, will 'produce' the goods we want when we want them at a later time. In this respect, the appropriate metaphor might consist in depicting money as an ultra-versatile piece of equipment (homogeneous capital?[8]) or, less fancifully and more pertinently, as a stocked storage facility. Indeed, most works on monetary theory list one of its secondary functions as being to act as a 'store of value' (erroneously listing its primary function as being the facilitation of the exchange of goods). But unlike the possession of an effective all-purpose machine or a stocked storage facility, the possession of money does not ensure the availability of the goods one wants at the later time when one wants them. For this later availability necessarily depends upon the choices of persons other than oneself.

Crucially, it depends upon the choices of those who (one hopes) will then be supplying the goods one wants. So one's belief in the later availability of these goods, and in their purchasability with money, must be based upon a belief that others will supply these goods and will prefer to exchange them for money rather than (only) for other goods at that time. That future suppliers will be willing to accept money for their goods is a belief which, in turn, can only be entertained if one believes (i) that they will *then* want — as one *now* wants — to defer purchases of desired goods until a (still) later time, and (ii) that they will then believe that they will be able to secure those desired goods at that (still) later time. The interminably regressive structure of the justification for these beliefs is, perhaps, reasonably apparent. It is certainly true to say that the acceptability of money

> falls within that perplexing but fascinating group of phenomena which is affected by self-justifying beliefs. If the members of a community think that money will be generally acceptable, then it will be; otherwise not.[9]

But the belief that money will be generally acceptable is not itself one which is auto-generated.

For what should be fairly obvious at this point is that we have
ventured on to the familiar terrain of the Prisoner's Dilemma. Consider
the two-person world of individuals I and II, each of whom is possessed
of money and a stock of goods. Four transactional outcomes confront
each of them as alternative possibilities: (a) keeping one's own goods
and acquiring the other's goods; (b) relinquishing one's own goods and
acquiring the other's goods; (c) keeping one's own goods and not
acquiring the other's goods; and (d) relinquishing one's own goods and
not acquiring the other's goods. With respect to the use of money, there
are two alternative strategies which each may pursue: to accept money
in exchange for one's goods, or to refuse money in exchange for one's
goods. A quick glance at the conventional payoff matrix shows that, for
each individual choosing independently, refusal to accept the other's
money is the dominant strategy where $a > b > c > d$.

		individual II	
		accept	refuse
individual I	accept	b, b	d, a
	refuse	a, d	c, c

Hence each, if unable to rely upon the other's acceptance of his money,
will rationally prefer to retain his own goods rather than relinquish
them in exchange for the other's money. And, as in the standard case of
this (c, c) which is worse for each of them than the outcome consequent upon each relying on the other's acceptance of money (b, b).

The wealth of literature on the theoretical ramifications of the
Prisoner's Dilemma makes it unnecessary here either to review its ex-
tendability to n-person games or to rehearse what it implies about the
existence of 'public goods' and the means to secure them.[10] Nor should
the foregoing demonstration, that a common medium of exchange is a
public good, be taken to suggest that its existence presupposes a
state.[11] What it *does* presuppose, as Locke affirms and Nozick denies,
is a general contractual understanding among individuals to accept
money in exchange for goods.[12] Contracts create rights which entail
correlative duties. And in a state of nature, as in civil society, such
duties are legitimately enforceable. In short, the hand which resolves a
Prisoner's Dilemma cannot be an invisible one.[13]

III

Let us now return to consider the emergence of Nozick's dominant protective association. In so doing it is important to bear in mind a constraint on the conditions within which this phenomenon occurs. The dominant protective association's executive agency is said to possess a rightful (near) monopoly on the use of *permissible* force. It can have no title to, and may well lack monopoly control of, the use of impermissible force.[14] An agency which employs force to violate individuals' rights — either by protecting those of its clients who have committed rights-violations, or by inflicting an unwarranted degree of deprivation on those who have violated its clients' rights — is not exercising permissible force and is, in that respect, not a protective agency. So the allegedly unvanquished record of Nozick's dominant protective agency is a chronicle of victories (or, at least, stalemates) in, and only in, upholding rights. It is not a chronicle of either victories or stalemates in resisting the efforts of others, including other agencies, to seek redress for rights-violations committed by its clients. A hardened rights-violator may well wish to engage the services of an agency wielding effective force, but this cannot be a protective agency.

Reverting to Nozick's account of the three alternative ways in which an agency might be expected to emerge as dominant, one is moved to ask what it is that two genuinely protective agencies can have to fight about. Could the outcome of a struggle between them provide any more of an indication, as to which of their respective clients had acted impermissibly, than the outcome of a struggle between a protective agency and a group of avowed gangsters (who might, following a time-honoured practice, call themselves a protection agency)? Nozick's answers to these questions emerge in the course of his discussion about why an *already-dominant* agency is entitled, in effect, to 'mop up' any independents — that is, persons who are interspersed among its clients and who have not contracted the services of any protective agency.[15] His argument on this latter subject is somewhat complex, but can be resolved into essentially three moves: first, he maintains that included among individuals' substantive rights is the right not to have their other substantive rights endangered; secondly, he suggests that the exercise by independents of executive procedures in defence of their own rights, may be seen by dominant agency clients as posing a danger to their rights; finally, he claims that the fact that the dominant agency can exercise a monopoly of the use of force in the area concerned is a sufficient reason to entitle it to do so, i.e. to assume the executive powers of independents (at least in relation to their dealings with its clients), provided it compensates them for any net disadvantage they may thereby incur.

Since the problematic character of the first two of these arguments has been commented upon elsewhere, I shall confine myself to a brief consideration of the third.[16] Apart from the fact that Nozick's reasoning here appears to lean rather heavily on the view that might makes right, he has unwarrantedly leapt from the premiss that an agency is the dominant protective agency in an area to the conclusion that it is also the dominant exerciser of force in that area. That a particular protective agency has managed to distinguish itself as being singularly more adept at upholding its clients' rights than all other such agencies in the same area — and has thus acquired their clienteles — in no way licenses the inference that it dominantly controls the use of force there, not even of permissible force. For it may be that only a very small proportion of the population have ever contracted protective services from any agency. By conferring upon each individual 'the right to oversee others' enforcement of their rights against him' (p. 120), and then making the logically illicit move from an agency's acquiring a monopoly of *contracted* protective powers to its acquiring a dominant share of all protective powers — as well as the further illicit move from this to its acquiring a de facto monopoly of power per se — Nozick opens the way for his claim that the dominant agency's effective capacity to control all use of legitimate force is one to which it is entitled and which arises only by permissible steps.

The fate of independents in Nozick's state of nature, important though it is, is not the central concern of this chapter. Our concern is to examine the reasons why the contracted protective powers of several protective agencies would eventually converge in one such agency. And the story of how independents' executive powers may be conscripted by an already-dominant agency is relevant to this purpose only inasmuch as it throws some light on the alleged relation between individuals' substantive and procedural rights. We return, then, to the question of what it is that two genuinely protective agencies can have to fight about. Evidently one agency cannot oppose the efforts of another to seek redress for its client from a person who has committed a commonly acknowledged rights-violation. Of course, there may be agencies which employ force to resist such efforts and which, if successful, may well attract the patronage of a large number of persons. But, for the sake of clarity, we should do better to call such an agency a protec*tion* agency rather than a protec*tive* agency, since its mode of attracting new clients assumes the customary form of offering them the protection they most need, that is, protection against itself. So if there is to be fighting between genuinely protective agencies, it can only be because the violation alleged by one agency is not acknowledged as such by the other. Hence the difference between the two agencies must be not moral, but epistemic. They disagree about the methods to be used to ascertain guilt.

> The natural-rights tradition offers little guidance on precisely what one's procedural rights are in a state of nature, on how principles specifying how one is to act have knowledge built into their various clauses, and so on (p. 101).

> No one has a right to use a relatively unreliable procedure in order to decide whether to punish another. Using such a system, he is in no position to know that the other deserves punishment; hence he has no right to punish him. But how can we say this? If the other has committed a crime, doesn't *everyone* in a state of nature have a right to punish him? And therefore doesn't someone who doesn't know that this other person has committed the crime? Here, it seems to me, we face a terminological issue about how to merge epistemic considerations with rights. Shall we say that someone doesn't have a right to do certain things unless he knows certain facts, or shall we say that he does have a right but he does wrong in exercising it unless he knows certain facts? . . . In either case, a protective agency may punish a wielder of an unreliable or unfair procedure who (against the client's will) has punished one of its clients, independently of whether or not its client actually is guilty and therefore even if its client is guilty (pp. 106-8).

Nozick is undeniably correct to suggest that natural-rights theory embodies no particular epistemology. But he is mistaken in believing that his proposed essential contestability of procedural rights can be pressed into service as a vehicle for delivering the custom of all clients to a single protective agency.

Since the clients of any protective agency employ it to uphold their rights, not only against its non-clients but also against one another, they will wish to ensure that their agency uses what they consider to be the most reliable judicial procedures available: they will not wish to be penalised for offences they have not committed. And since agencies compete for individuals' patronage, one may assume that each agency's (epistemic) view of what counts as a reliable judicial procedure — that

view being the one which determines the content of its clients' procedural rights — reflects the views of its clients. Moreover, since battles
with other agencies are costly and since those who run protective
agencies wish to make a profit, they each have every incentive to ensure
that the procedures they employ cannot be faulted by other agencies.
Unless it is supposed that different agencies, along with their respective
clienteles, will have different and deep-seated epistemic commitments
and that these differences will lead to opposed views about what counts
as judicial evidence, there can be no reason to imagine that their
respective judicial procedures will depart very far from mutual acceptability, if not outright uniformity.

But Nozick *does* suppose that such differences will exist. In so doing
he fails to appreciate that he is making it more — rather than less —
difficult to account for clients converging on a single agency. The
difficulty he thereby creates for his argument may be expressed thus:
how confident can an aggrieved client of a defeated agency rationally
be about the reliability of the procedures employed by the victorious
agency, in contemplating whether to transfer his custom to it (and
thereby help it along the road to dominance)? The very fact that his
agency has engaged in a violent conflict with the victorious one implies,
on Nozick's account, that his agency's — and his own — view of what
counts as proof of a rights-violation is not shared by the victorious
agency. Consequently, he must have every reason to believe that, were
he to contract its services, conduct which he judged to be a violation of
his substantive rights (and equally, conduct of his own which he judged
to be quite innocent) would not be similarly appraised by that agency.
He would thus suffer violations of his substantive rights at the hands of
the very persons he was employing to protect them. To this Nozick
might reply that such a person, in continuing to patronise a weaker
agency, is in any case liable to incur such suffering. But this is only
partly true. For while the rights of a weaker agency's client are
undoubtedly at risk in his conflicts with clients of stronger agencies,
they are not similarly at risk when his conflicts are with fellow-clients
of the same agency. Where a multiplicity of agencies compete for
clients, it can be assumed that fellow-clients of the same agency share
the epistemic views of their agency and acknowledge the reliability of
the judicial procedures which are informed by those views and which
are applied to their conflicts with one another.

The same cannot be said where the range of available agencies has
been forcibly reduced by one (or more) agencies whose justifications of

such exercises of force invoke epistemic differences. Here the clients of extinguished agencies will find their rights at risk in their conflicts with fellow-clients of the same victorious agency. Here the attraction of a protective service based on epistemic views which are opposed to one's own must necessarily be quite minimal. As far as individual clients are concerned, Nozick's proposed essential contestability of procedural rights is *contagious*: it infects the content of their substantive rights with the same affliction. Thus, if epistemic diversity can generate irreconcileable differences over the content of individuals' procedural rights, universal acceptance of the permissibility of any agency's activities — much less those of any state — is logically impossible. One man's protective agency is another's protec*tion* agency; one man's state is another's robber-band. The very reason Nozick offers as a justification for activity resulting in clients converging on a single agency, is a reason for them to avoid doing so. So if a dominant agency is to emerge by permissible steps from a multiplicity of agencies, it will not be due to military superiority. Inter-agency competition for customers in the protective services market will have to be carried on peacefully. Can agencies do battle peacefully, and is the dominance of one of them the unintended outcome of such a process? If they can and if it is, one may conclude that a dominant protective agency would arise by permissible steps through the operation of an invisible-hand process.

Perhaps one agency's service is more efficient than that of others. That is, the ratio between the fees it charges its clients and the number of successful violation-redresses it secures is more favourable than the corresponding ratios attained by other agencies.[17] Evidently this would constitute a good reason for individuals who patronise less efficient agencies to transfer their custom to it. But it would constitute an equally good reason for those who manage less efficient agencies to improve their services or to lower their fees. Thus customers in the protective services market might be offered a choice between cheaper but less effective services, and more expensive but also more effective ones. There is no a priori reason to believe that a predominant proportion of customers will gravitate in any one direction.[18] Imagine, however, that inefficient agencies cannot lower their fees without becoming unprofitable and thereby ceasing to remain in business. To stay in business they must improve their services. Is there any reason to think that they, or some more enterprising newcomers, will fail to do this? Will not investors and suppliers of protective equipment, seeing the profits which more efficient agencies are able to make, hasten to furnish competitors with whatever they need to turn a similar profit? Is the expectation of making a similar profit necessarily groundless? In short, is there any reason to believe, as Nozick does, that the protective services market must be a naturally monopoliseable one? He offers the following argument:

> Why is this market different from all other markets? Why would a virtual monopoly arise in this market without the government intervention that elsewhere creates and maintains it? The worth of the product purchased, protection against others, is *relative*: it depends upon how strong the others are. Yet unlike other goods that are comparatively evaluated, maximal competing protective services cannot coexist; the nature of the service brings different agencies not only into competition for customers' patronage, but also into violent conflict with each other. Also, since the worth of the less than maximal product declines disproportionately with the number who purchase the maximal product, customers will not stably settle for the lesser good, and competing companies are caught in a declining spiral (p. 17).

I have already indicated why a natural-rights theory of the state cannot employ violent conflict between genuinely protective agencies as the motor for driving all clients into the arms of a single agency. Hence, if it is true that 'maximal competing protective services cannot coexist', this impossibility cannot be attributed to violent inter-agency conflict.

Must a single protective agency be the outcome of any process of non-violent competition between protective agencies? For this to be so, it would indeed have to be the case that 'the worth of the less than maximal product declines disproportionately with the number who purchase the maximal product'. That is, the protective services market would have to be one where it is necessarily the case that a supplier is able to provide more protective service to each of his clients with every additional client he acquires and without raising his fees. Alternatively, he must be able to provide the same level of service to each client at a fee which is reducible with every increase in the number of clients he supplies. Or again, some increasingly favourable trade-off combination of more service and lower fees must be possible with every new customer. Briefly then, the protective services industry must be one in which indefinitely increasing economies of scale prevail.

Two points are worth noting. The first is that it would appear to be a matter for empirical investigation — rather than conceptual analysis — as to whether such economies of scale do in fact prevail in the provision of protective service; there are no grounds for supposing their existence to be *necessary*. A second and related point is that, contrary to

Nozick's suggestion in the passage quoted above, there is no reason to imagine that the protective services market is the only one thus susceptible to natural monopoly — if indeed it is so susceptible — and, consequently, no reason to imagine that it is 'government intervention that elsewhere creates and maintains it'. But these points are not our principal concern here. For what we want to know is whether, in an industry where the worth of any supplier's product is a direct function — and its price an inverse function — of the number of its purchasers, the attainment of a monopoly by a single supplier can be viewed as a development which would occur without any individuals entertaining a belief, want or desire that it be brought about.

Consider the thinking of suppliers. Suppose there is one agency which has somehow secured a larger number of clients than any other agency, and is consequently supplying them with better services and/or charging them lower fees than are supplied/charged by any other agency. Clients of other agencies, irked at the relative advantages enjoyed by those of their neighbours who patronise this agency, complain incessantly to their suppliers urging them to improve their service and/or lower their charges. The harassed suppliers frantically explore every conceivable avenue to meet these demands, but are driven reluctantly to the conclusion that, unless they can increase the size of their clienteles beyond that of the industry leader, they cannot afford to lower their fees (decrease revenues) or improve their service (increase costs) to levels which compare favourably with those of the leading agency. Hence they will seek to engage one another in merger negotiations. Or they will undertake massive advertising campaigns, offering better service and/or lower charges to each client with every additional client they manage to attract. Or they may do both of these things. The leading agency, faced with these negotiations and campaigns by its competitors and concerned that it may lose clients to them, will respond in kind and will resist any temptation modestly to demur from publicising the fact that it already possesses the largest number of clients and is thus potentially better placed to offer still more favourable terms to each of them with every new customer. Thus, each supplier knows that the condition of any agency surviving in this market is that it secures the largest possible number of clients. And each bends his efforts in that direction. Since the 'largest possible number of clients' *means* 'all clients', suppliers may be said to believe, want and desire that a single agency monopoly be brought about.

Consider, now, the thinking of clients. Faced with this competition for their patronage, each knows that it is in his interest to contract with that supplier who contracts with the largest possible number of persons. It is in no one's interest that others patronise agencies other than the one he patronises. If fewer persons contract with one supplier than with another, not only are the clients of the former worse off than those of the latter, but also both sets of clients are worse off than they otherwise might be. Thus clients too will believe, want and desire that a single agency monopoly be brought about. But in a condition where there is a multiplicity of suppliers offering protective services, how is each person to determine with which one he should contract? Clearly, it is in the perceived interest of each person to agree with every other person as to which agency they should all patronise.

The natural monopoliseability of the protective services market – if it is naturally monopoliseable – is a necessary but not a sufficient condition of its being monopolised. The sufficient condition is a social compact. A common protective association – like a common medium of exchange – is the artifact of a concerted plurality of hands, none of which is invisible.[19]

NOTES

1. Robert Nozick, *Anarchy, State and Utopia* (Oxford and New York, 1974).

2. It ought, perhaps, to be noted at the outset that it is doubtful that this is, strictly speaking, the claim which anarchists *do* make. Evidently much depends upon the force of the term 'must'. Nozick appears to treat it as expressing logical necessity – that the very existence of a monopoly of the use of force entails a violation of individuals' rights. But it is difficult to see how anarchists could deny the legitimacy of a title (monopolistic or otherwise) to anything freely transferred to its holder by others who were previously entitled to it; such a denial would invalidate the titles of those doing the transferring. Rather, the anarchist position rests on (i) the not unilluminating tautology that no one can enforce law on its enforcers, and (ii) the claim that justifications of the state, as an alleged antidote to rights-violations in the state of nature, must invoke an empirical postulate – that individuals do not invariably respect one another's rights voluntarily – which itself leaves open the question of whether the state (as a group of individuals) is a suitable remedy for these ills. The fact that this question *is* left open does, however, render the anarchist's 'must' an empirical one.

3. Any action which does not violate rights is a permissible action and thus falls within the 'parameters of permissibility'.

4. Not quite a state, perhaps, for this account does not cover the titles to the use of force to protect the rights of those persons who, interspersed among agency clients, have not contracted protective services with *any* agency. They are still personally entitled to use force for this purpose, and their presence in this area denies the dominant protective association's agency the essential state-like quality of possessing a *monopoly* of legitimate force. Hence the need, on Nozick's part, for arguments in addition to the foregoing account to prove the dominant association's statehood. See below, section III.

5. B. P. Pesek and T. R. Saving, *The Foundations of Money and Banking* (New York and London, 1968), 4.

6. Cf. J. H. Makin, *Theory of Money* (Hinsdale, 1971), 2-3; P. A. Samuelson, *Economics*, 6th edn. (New York, 1964), 51; P. A. S. Taylor, *A New Dictionary of Economics* (London, 1966), 15; R. H. I. Palgrave (ed.), *Dictionary of Political Economy*, Vol. I (London, 1894), 121-22.

7. 'More probably' because, as we have seen, this is far from necessarily true inasmuch as the minimum number of transactions logically required for market clearance is *greater* under money than under barter.

8. But see G. C. Harcourt, *Some Cambridge Controversies in the Theory of Capital* (Cambridge, 1972), passim.

9. W. T. Newlyn, *Theory of Money*, 2nd edn. (Oxford, 1971), 2-3.

10. See, for example, R. D. Luce and H. Raiffa, *Games and Decisions* (New York, 1957); T. C. Schelling, *The Strategy of Conflict* (Cambridge, Mass., 1960); A. Rapoport and A. M. Chammah, *Prisoner's Dilemma* (Ann Arbor, 1965); W. G. Runciman and A. K. Sen, 'Games, justice and the general will', *Mind*, 74, 1965; J. M. Buchanan, *The Demand and Supply of Public Goods* (Chicago, 1968); M. Taylor, *Anarchy and Cooperation* (London, 1976), which contains a useful bibliography on this subject.

11. Menger attributed to Adam Müller the view that it is the development of money that brings the state into being. Cf. Carl Menger, *Principles of Economics* (Glencoe, 1950), 319.

12. In the absence of such a social compact, the rational way to defer acquisition of goods is to obtain — in exchange for one's goods — contractual undertakings from others to supply future goods. Were others to refuse to give such undertakings, would it be rational to take their money instead?

13. It is not my purpose here to discuss the various policies or institutions required to induce the reliance which would render acceptance of money a rational strategy. Nor shall I review the different ad hoc empirical stipulations, found in many works on monetary theory, whereby the dilemma just displayed is, in effect, side-stepped through an ascription of unique substitution properties to money. Rather, the object of this argument has simply been to show (i) that money performs no exchange function independent of its assets — or store of value — function, and (ii) that it performs this latter function only under certain cooperative conditions which are not implicit in the exchange relationships derived from standard individual preference axioms.

14. Indeed, it is quite compatible with the existence of a dominant protective agency that there be, in the same area, a more powerful agency enjoying

monopolistic control of the use of impermissible force, *vide* the south side of Chicago during some periods in the 1920s.

15. See generally, chapters 4-6.

16. Cf. Hillel Steiner, 'Critical notice of *Anarchy, State and Utopia*', *Mind*, 86, 1977: 120-29; 122-23.

17. I leave aside questions about the variability in worth of different kinds of violation-redress. Presumably redress in a case of maiming is, ceteris paribus, more valuable — and more costly to secure — than redress for damage to chattels.

18. For an account of how the number and variety of agencies might well proliferate in the protective services market and, more generally, for a critique of Nozick's anti-anarchist case that ranges over many other of his arguments than are considered here, readers are strongly urged to consult Eric Mack's trenchant paper, 'Nozick's anarchism', in: J. R. Pennock and J. W. Chapman (eds.), *NOMOS XIX: Anarchism* (New York, forthcoming).

19. This paper owes much to the discussion it received from my fellow ECPR Workshop participants, and from my colleagues at the University of Manchester. I am also particularly indebted to the following persons for their extensive and probing comments: Hans Daudt, Patrick Day, John Mackie, Peter Morriss, Ian Steedman and Robert van der Veen.

15 Individual and Collective Interests in Game Theory

Christine Mironesco
University of Geneva, Switzerland

The connection between **individual interest** and collective interest has given rise to a great deal of thought over the years. Particular interpretations of the subject are contained in some important streams of thought — whether we think of Darwinism, economic theories based on laissez-faire or Marxist doctrines. Game theory, which is the modern science of the interdependence of actors' decisions, also tackles that question. The present chapter attempts a critical analysis of the answer which the theory provides.

THE GENERAL ORIENTATION OF GAME THEORY

In many respects game theory claims to make a great contribution to social science. First of all it offers the possibility of alleviating the defects of social and biological determinism. This point of view is clear with some authors for whom the determinist interpretations of society and history are not concerned with the real guiding principles of human behaviour, and thus merely describe what would happen if thinking individuals never used their power of thought.[1] Other authors have aimed at reinstating in its rights human rationality, emphasising the heuristic value of such a concept.[2]

Straight away we would like to make it clear that there is no question of coming back to strictly individualistic views of society where the whole would only be the juxtaposition of the parts. Indeed, the first hypothesis of the theory is that the rational behaviour of an actor consists in maximising his own advantage. But the second hypothesis, no less fundamental than the first, requires that each player should pursue his own interest, taking into account the fact that other participants, who are equally rational, also aim to maximise their advantage. In this context, the concept of 'strategy' takes on a specific meaning: it indicates the social aspect of individual rationality; it lays emphasis on the interdependence of the actors' decisions.[3]

Moreover, as far as method is concerned, game theory derives from mathematical research. Thus, by no means should the term 'game' lead one to take the theory lightly. On the contrary, the question is to calculate probabilities accurately in the same spirit of formalisation as the one applied by Pascal to, among other things, games of chance. But this mathematical tradition extends to include not only the estimate of occurrences of an event, but also the notion of strategy as defined above. The interest of mathematicians in games is perfectly justified; or in other words it seems obvious that the play situation has contributed to the development of mathematics.

What should be observed here is the immediate extension of the 'theory' to other fields of application beyond parlour games. Von Neumann and Morgenstern's book, which is considered the main reference work in this field, was already entitled: *Theory of Games and Economic Behaviour.*[4] It was published immediately after the Second World War, and rapidly inspired research in the field of economics and international relations, to name but those disciplines. The argument put forward by most authors in order to justify this extension seems to us rather simplistic. Nevertheless, it is worth mentioning it, since it is the only one available; there are some common points between game relationships and conflicting interactions in real life: competition, diplomacy, war, etc.[5] The analogy in question is based on the fact that both in games and reality, the theory wants to examine situations where actors' rationality − in its individual and social components − influences their behaviour.

Finally, it should also be stated that side by side with these conceptual and formal concerns, game theory implies the existence of solutions. By virtue of the extension of the theory to other fields of analysis besides games, the very concept of 'solution' covers not only solving equations, but also goes as far as to define the best behaviour an individual should adopt if he is to merit the description 'rational' in a given situation. Thus, in a more or less explicit manner, and despite frequent assertions that the scientific validity of the method is ensured by not taking ethical questions into account, game theory has a distinctly normative aspect.

It is the latter aspect which interests us. The principles of mathematical formalisation that are characteristic of this theory and its application to economics have already been commented upon and criticised.[6] Here the main matter of concern is how, in this light, individual interests are reconciled; how the interaction occurs and is resolved between individuals having in common a rationality which induces them to work towards ends which appear contradictory at first glance. The arguments of game theory will be analysed within the framework of the two typical situations: the fixed-sum games and the variable-sum games which are characterised by the degree of divergence or convergence of the actors' interests.

THE SOLUTION OF THE FIXED-SUM OR ZERO-SUM GAME

We will start with the most simple case: a decision must be taken by two players in interaction, whose interests are opposed to each other, one of whom can only obtain satisfaction at the expense of the other. We know that real situations — games and conflicts — are much more complex than this fictitious case. If it has been possible to evolve the the theory, it is only because a great effort has been made to get over the excessive simplification of the original pattern and take formally into account the multiplicity of possible decisions, their sequence, the quality of information between players, etc. But these subtleties will not detain us, because the 'philosophy' of the proposed solution seems to be completely contained in the discussion of the elementary case.

Players A and B are thus playing for stakes which are either indivisible (if A wins it, B will lose it), or divisible, but with a fixed total value (if A wins a part, the profit of B will be reduced proportionately).[7] Let us suppose that A and B are endowed with rationality: each one wants — and knows that his opponent wants — to maximise his advantage. According to the stakes as defined here, the situation seems of course, from the start, to consist in an 'irreconcilable' conflict of interests.[8] But the outcome of the game, barring a tie, establishes a winner and a loser, that is to say introduces into the association formed by A and B a factor of inequality (in the access to the stakes). This inequality arises from the interaction: no hypothesis allows one to

think that the inequality precedes it, the only theoretical presuppositions being the universal nature of rationality and the recognition by each one of this universal nature. As matters stand, one might
first wonder how, between two persons acting quite rationally, one
alone can assert his interest at the expense of the other. It should be
considered that either rationality is unequally shared out between them
and the more rational wins — which would immediately raise the
problem of empirically measuring rationality; or rationality is equally
shared out, each one does his best to maximise his advantages, but in
this case the victory can only derive from the possession of resources
outside strict rationality — which would immediately call into question
the very usefulness of the game.

What is the 'solution' to this situation of irreconcilable conflict? The
answer to this question throws some light on the meaning which must
be given to the role of rationality. The principal quality of a valid
solution is to be 'stable', that is to say a solution from which no player
can expect to be able to deviate without loss;[9] it is 'the best each player
can expect to achieve facing his opponent's opposition'.[10] Since in this
game the perfect maximisation of individual advantage is very difficult,
not to say impossible, the main thing is to minimise losses as much as
possible, to make 'the best of the worst', to use the time-honoured
expression. Such is the meaning of the 'minimax' resulting from the
player's rational strategy. The end of the game and the solution of the
conflict of interests are determined by the balance of each player's
'minimax'. This balance and the stability of the relationship which
derives from it are presented as an aspect of the common interest. Is it
the essential aspect? Game theory suggests that it is: the solution of
interaction is always valid provided that there is a balance of forces,
independently of whether A's 'best of the worst' is equal, better or
worse than B's 'best of the worst'.

The zero-sum game is, as already seen, a particular case of the
fixed-sum game. In that game the sum of gains of both players is equal
to zero, or what is won by one is lost for the other; and the collective
solution of the conflict of interests corresponds exactly with the
winner's satisfaction alone. What is going on in the fixed-sum games,
generally speaking, those games where the sum of gains is constant but
different from zero? What does the theory suggest as to the rationality
of the distribution of the stakes?

Let us assume, to paraphrase an example dear to theoreticians, that
A and B have to share out a sum of £100. The principle of individual

maximisation of advantages implies that each player prefers to get the total sum for himself, but rationality in its social aspect and the necessity for interdependence of decisions recall that the opponent also tries to maximise his advantage. The main thing once more is to minimise losses due to interaction. If A and B have no other resource for completing the sharing out than an equal will to satisfy their interest and a mutual recognition of this will, the solution must be fifty-fifty. We interpret Rapoport's demonstration in this way, for example: if the structure of this particularly simple game offers several solutions of sharing, the one which minimises the gap between the players has to be preferred. 'A must resist the temptation to choose the mis-leading maximum gain and must adopt B's point of view and reasoning.'[11] The same advice applies to B.

And what if A (or B) does not resist the temptation? If he requires the sharing which privileges him – should we come to the conclusion that he is irrational? Yes, if the opponent considers the requirement unacceptable and if he opposes it. No, if he agrees with it, because in that case the solution would be based on the balance of each one's 'best of the worst', the worst being to win nothing at all. The question is when and why the opponent's efforts to maximise his own advantages are considered unacceptable. Here, in our opinion, the ambiguity of the very concept of rationality, as stated in game theory, becomes obvious. It is as rational to pursue one's interest as to let the opponent define the limit of one's interest.

One might think that the clarification of concepts belongs more to philosophy than to the empirical science of behaviour. Let us recall that game theory studies behaviour or more precisely, individual choices and the balance resulting from them.[12] Nevertheless, the problem we have just raised has not failed to draw the attention of some theoreticians, who tackle it through a debate on the concept of 'symmetry'. Thus, Shubik asserts that the role of symmetry in the outcome of games and conflicts has always caused confusion.[13] Indeed, the least we can say is that there are divided opinions on the subject. The following example is a good demonstration of this.

In his work *The Strategy of Conflict*, Schelling pleads for 'the abandonment of symmetry in game theory'.[14] He upholds the ideas that 'though symmetry is consistent with the rationality of the players, it cannot be demonstrated that asymmetry is inconsistent with their rationality'.[15] The telling arguments stand out in Schelling's criticism of other authors,[16] who wrongly insert symmetry in the very definition of rationality. Harsanyi, for example, to whom Schelling makes explicit reference, asserts that 'two duopolists with the same cost functions, size, capital resources, etc. will reach an agreement giving equal profits to each of them', he also thinks that 'the symmetry axiom is a fundamental postulate' and that 'intuitively the assumption underlying this axiom is that a rational bargainer will not expect a rational opponent to grant him larger concessions than he would make himself under similar conditions'.[17] Such an idea, according to Schelling, has a major weakness: it confuses in a single postulate the rational solution and symmetry in the mathematical meaning of the term; symmetry seems to be derived from the player's rationality.

Let us assume, Schelling adds — and we return to the above-mentioned example — that two players are to be given £100 but only provided that they agree on how to share out the money. They rapidly reach a joint decision, according to which A will be given £80 and B £20. Can B be blamed for making an 'intellectual error'[18] by granting such an advantage to A? No, because he knew that A would claim £80 and that A was aware that he, B, would be satisfied with £20 etc. In short, both knew that the sharing would necessarily be effected in that way. Schelling does not think the question 'How do they know it' worth answering. He merely emphasises the essentials of the game, which is to co-ordinate expectations and in this case the expectations were correct on both sides.

Moreover, he clearly indicates that there are several ways to divide a sum, the symmetrical partition being only one of the possible combinations of a continuum ranging from 1/99, 2/98, . . ., to 99/1. Thus, it should be admitted that the symmetrical distribution enters into competition with many asymmetrical distributions as possible agreement between players. 'The appeal of symmetry is not mathematical' and 'the identification of symmetry with rationality rests on the assumption that there are certain intellectual processes that rational players are incapable of, namely, concerting choices on the basis of anything other than mathematical symmetry'.[19]

Schelling's respect for flexibility of intellectual proceedings is not dictated by some ethical or metaphysical consideration. If he lays so much emphasis on this point, it is on the contrary with a practical reason in mind, since he asserts 'we must be careful not to make symmetry part of the definition of rationality; to do so would destroy the empirical relevance of the theory'.[20] In other words, if the theory is to give an account of real conflicts of interests, it is better not to connect a priori rational behaviour and equality in sharing out gains, as the solution of many real conflicts of interests is very different. Symmetry of the game rules (each player can and must make a decision) should not be confused with symmetry of the game outcome. In a way, Harsanyi and other authors would like to set unnecessary and prejudicial bounds to some particular cases where each bargainer expects neither more nor less from his opponent than what he is willing to grant him, but as far as the problem in question is concerned — namely the connection of individual interests in a collective solution — Schelling's interpretation does not seem to diverge from that of Harsanyi. Incidentally, the latter made a point of stating clearly — in the above-mentioned example quoted by Schelling — that two companies would share profits equally if they had the same costs, functions, size, capital resources, etc.; in other words, if they had the same resources at the start. Schelling's approach implicitly amounts to withdrawing this condition from the overall basic presuppositions in order to apply the theory to any conflictual interaction: it is enough to establish beforehand the possibility of unequal claims by the actors in order to turn the unequal sharing out of stakes into a rational solution. But in conclusion, each of these points of view suggests that the solution of the game is symmetrical or asymmetrical, depending on whether the pre-existing situation is symmetrical or asymmetrical.

As a matter of fact, the 'game' is nothing more than a moment of interaction between individual decision-makers governed by a whole set of formal rules, which clearly indicate the way each one can use resources in order to achieve his own aims.[21] Both in Schelling and in Harsanyi's examples, the whole game is defined by a single rule, which consists for individual decision-makers in explicitly agreeing on a sharing in order to get the sum necessary to complete this sharing. Thus, every factor determining players' decisions arises prior to the game properly speaking. Nevertheless, theoreticians regularly disregard this problem when explaining the solution (this in spite of their own examples): they say that the solution is dictated by the very structure of the game;[22] the game alone determines — through the rationality of individual decision-makers — and legitimises the balance of individual advantages. After having considered the question of the variable-sum game, we will consider the relevance of such an assertion.

THE VARIABLE-SUM OR
MIXED-MOTIVE GAME

The fixed-sum game is only a very small part of the scope of analysis concerned with game theory. Authors like to lay emphasis on this point. On the one hand the most interesting part of the theory is concerned with the study of more complex situations than those where A purely and simply wins what B loses.[23] On the other hand, real conflictual situations, whether it is a question of daily life of international politics, rarely look like fixed-sum games: luckily, some authors state, reality seldom opposes two actors whose interests are completely opposed; the 'irreconcilable' conflict would rather be a point of view permitting some theoretical considerations than a concrete highly probable event.[24] Consequently, situations where each individual's interests are both convergent and divergent should be taken into account.

THE CHARACTERISTICS OF
THE VARIABLE-SUM GAME

Before analysing solutions proposed by the theory regarding these games, the distinction between these games and the fixed-sum games should be clearly stated. It seems that three major characteristics can be drawn from texts, but those characteristics the statement of which was designed to explain the problem raise questions the theory is far from being able to answer.

First of all, as their name indicates, in the games in question the sum of players' gains is not the same for all results of the interaction.[25] Thus, at the end of the game both A and B would get more or less advantages according to the co-ordination of their strategies. The players' rationality no longer applies to the sharing out of a total given reward. On the contrary, everybody knows that the amount of collective reward will differ according to the game result and that, consequently, some results are more favourable for both players. In our opinion the primary question is to know the origin of the overall variation in gain. Why is it that this total reward may vary? The gain surplus does not result from players' interaction, however rational they may be. It is not the players who determine the amount rewarding the co-ordination of their strategies.

The second characteristic of variable-sum games is no longer related to their results but to motivations ruling actors' decisions at the start. These motivations are contradictory ('mixed-motive game'): at the same time friends and enemies,[26] opponents and partners,[27] players are at once competitors — so far as they have opposed interests and each one can take something from the other — and allies — so far as they can increase their gains by uniting their efforts.[28] The rationality of each one amounts in this case to a correct estimation of the proportion of coincidence and the proportion of divergence between his own interest and his partner's interest. What is this estimation based on? Everything leads us to believe that there is no question of a vague intuition, but rather of a calculation in terms of costs and profits. This calculation undoubtedly results from the players' reasoning. But the necessary data are not the fruit of their imagination; they are dictated from 'somewhere else'. The players' decision to co-operate or not does not correspond to a completely free choice, but is linked with this 'somewhere else', a kind of opponent, quite enigmatic so far, and against whom they can unite to defend their common interest.

By putting forward a third characteristic, i.e. the presence of an additional player, some authors have partially disclosed the mystery regarding the total gain variation and the origin of this variation. In some way there would be two levels of interaction: on the one hand between the players who are said to be 'primary', those who draw up their strategy according to the rules of the game while having mutually the above-mentioned contradictory feelings; on the other hand between those same players and the 'secondary' player, whose identity differs according to circumstances: he may be the 'bank' if we think of some games, the 'nature' of some particular persons (for example, the warder facing prisoners) if we think of real situations.[29] Thus, the possible coalition of primary players takes its meaning with respect to this secondary player; we get more or less advantages from him, through co-ordination of strategies. This last detail is meant to satisfy our curiosity and answer the questions raised in connection with the other two characteristics of the variable-sum game.

However, our perplexity grows. Indeed, if the sum of primary players' gains is increasing at the expense of the secondary player (or inversely, if it is decreasing in his favour), we come back to the situation of the fixed-sum game. The additional player loses (or wins) what all the other players together win (or lose). As a matter of fact Von Neumann and Morgenstern themselves mentioned the point,[30] but far from finding it disturbing, they saw it as a way of laying emphasis on the universal scope of the theory.

Why then do they and their successors maintain the distinction between fixed-sum games and variable-sum games? In our opinion the addition of the strange secondary player is a real challenge to logic: either he is a true player subjected to the same rules as the others, and in this case the distinction between fixed-sum and zero-sum is not justified; or he is not a true player, the rules of the game do not apply to him, and in that case the variation of the true players' profits has its origin outside the game as such. Therefore who are the protagonists and what relationships exist between them? This is a question which seems all the more relevant as we give up ordinary games and consider the theory in its application to political conflicts.

THE SOLUTION OF VARIABLE-SUM GAMES:
TWO CASES

Theoreticians rely on various examples to work out their arguments. We will pay particular attention to two of them: the 'game of chicken' and the prisoner's dilemma. Their frequent insertion in texts urges us to consider them as typical examples, deserving a thorough analysis. Furthermore, some authors claim that the problems to be solved during these games have a surprising resemblance to those arising during strikes, rebellions, riots – and even to those presented by collective security in international relations.[31] Here a short description is needed.

The *game of chicken*, also called *game of mutual threats*, seems to be the result of the rich imagination of young Americans. A teen-age gang chooses a straight road; two of them are in cars, standing some distance apart; they start and approach each other at high speed; the gang shouts 'chicken' to the first one who swerves from the middle of the road to avoid crashing, while the driver who does not swerve is treated as an hero.[32] This game is the model theoreticians like to use for nuclear war.[33]

Both A and B can choose between two strategies: to co-operate, that is to say to avoid the crash, thus protecting at best their common interest, which is to survive; or not to co-operate, that is to say to crash straight into each other in pursuit of glory, but running the risk of dying at the same time. The decisions taken by A and B give them different gains, since it is better to survive than to die and to survive with honour rather than without it. The variation of the sum of A's and B's gains depends both on their action and on the evaluation made by observers.

According to the strategy chosen by each player, there are four possible outcomes. The first one results from the double co-operation (*CC*) of A and B, each of them swerving in sufficient time to avoid the crash; they both survive and bear together the burden of their judges' scorn, a burden which is at the same time considerably reduced. The second possibility is the double defection (*DD*), where both drivers keep their course, collide and probably lose their lives. In the third and fourth places we have the situation where one player tries to co-operate whereas the other one refuses, (*CD*) or (*DC*): if A tries to avoid the crash and B goes straight on, A is all the more despised as B is hailed as the only hero; roles are reversed in the case of inverted strategies.

Of course this type of conflict of interests is not described because of its anecdotal character. On the contrary, it contains a whole set of data that game theory with its presuppositions on rationality and its logic of 'minimax' can put together to come out with a rational solution. This solution is unique, clear and mathematical, in Deutsch's opinion for example. Inside a four-fold table, he writes down the figures of each player's joint strategies.[34] We do not insert that table here, as its details are all the less useful for the argument, as numerical values connected with gains (life, glory) are perfectly arbitrary. Let us just keep in mind — and we will have the opportunity to recall it further — that Deutsch gives a distinctly higher value to life rather than to glory (to be fully precise: life is 'worth' 50 and glory 'worth' 5). Afterwards the argument is simple. It is enough to examine the table. It shows to the reader able to make some elementary arithmetical operations that the balance of 'minimax' of each player can only result from their joint co-operation. In everyday language it amounts to saying that for A and B, 'the best of the worst' is to avoid the crash because whatever may be the other player's strategy, one is sure not to risk 'the worst of the worst', which is to die. Deutsch asserts that the verdict of the mathematical structure of the game is obvious: the solution (*CC*) is undoubtedly the most rational.

The necessity of using a matrix of quantitative data to arrive at that conclusion is questionable. By admitting, a priori, that life was preferable to glory, the players necessarily had to be advised to act accordingly. But what should we think about this a priori? Though statistics regarding gangs of American teen-agers and the concrete results of their original game are not available, we can assume that they have not always admitted the verdict of the matrix with the same confidence. The fact that these teen-agers have no degree in mathematics has nothing to do with the present matter. But we have good reason for thinking that they would have neither invented nor repeated this game so often that it has become famous, if they had known in advance that there would never be any winner.

Among the four possible issues of this interaction, there are two in which the gains of A and B are not symmetrical: these are the results of strategies (CD) and (DC), where one player enjoys prestige and the other has lost, although both have saved their lives. If one of those two situations were to arise, should we conclude that the winner has been irrational? This would really be the conclusion for a theory whose central theme is individual rationality. Deutsch's interpretation, however, gives such an impression.

However, other authors have succeeded in eliminating this problem. Kahn, for example, asserts that it is quite possible to want the crash, even if it leads to disaster. In the 'game of chicken' he makes it clear that one can win if one shows determination to crash and if, by doing this, the opponent is frightened and compelled to leave the way clear. Of course if the opponent appears not to understand, it would be irrational to go the whole way.[35] The main thing is to estimate the situation properly before it is too late. But as a matter of fact what does one hope to gain by taking such a risk? It is not prestige for prestige's sake, but for the advantages linked with the winner's position. It is true for teen-agers if we consider that the hero acquires authority within the gang. Kahn emphasises that it is still more true for international relations: 'if a side expresses his refusal to risk war, whereas the other side expresses its willingness to take this risk, the latter will always gain the upper end in further negotiations and will reduce the other side to powerlessness'.[36]

Therefore it can be legitimate for A and B to try to win the game. It is also Schelling's opinion, to whose repugnance for symmetrical solutions we have already had occasion to refer. From this point of view, he looks more particularly at how an opponent can be threatened in order to make him retreat and what the necessary conditions and resources are to make this threat effective.[37] And he comes to the conclusion that, from this point of view, asymmetries between players constitute the whole interest of the interaction and the theory.[38]

But the size and the type of necessary resources are not defined by the rule of the game. This rule merely indicates how these 'resources' can be used. Here, as in the case of the fixed-sum games, the result of the interaction is symmetrical or assymetrical depending on whether the pre-existing situation is symmetrical or asymmetrical. The solution of double co-operation recommended by Deutsch is only rational on the assumption that neither A nor B are able to influence the opponent other than by really risking the worst himself. This is the case if none of them have any other means of coercion, which would favour one player, from the outset, by comparison with his opponent.

In the *prisoner's dilemma*, also called the *game of threats and promises*, the equality of chances seems obvious for both players. Frequently mentioned in texts, this game, according to the authors, has some variations but essentially the story is as follows. Two prisoners are questioned separately by a judge. They are suspected (in fact guilty) of having committed a serious offence, but the judge does not have enough evidence to prosecute them. To do so, he needs formal confessions from them. Then the judge asks the prisoners to think about the following alternatives: if they both confess their offence, they will both be sentenced to heavy penalties, which will however be mitigated because they have confessed; if only one confesses, the other will be sentenced to the maximum penalty (death sentence or life imprisonment, according to the authors) whereas the one who confessed, will not only be freed but in addition will be given a reward; finally if no one confesses, they cannot be indicted and therefore will be released, but of course without any reward. The suspects are not allowed to communicate with each other.[39]

As in the case of the previous game, A and B have two possible strategies: co-operation (*C*) by keeping silent, or defection (*D*) by making a full confession. Hence, there are four solutions: (*DD*), A and B will be imprisoned for some time (*CD*) or (*DC*), A (or B) will be sentenced to the maximum penalty, whereas B (or A) will be released and rewarded, or finally (*CC*), A and B will be released. Which is the 'rational' solution? With the same mathematical method as the one described above theoreticians are amazed to discover that the balance of 'minimax' is produced by the double defection of A and B. We had almost guessed this – but if the figures prove it, there can be no further hesitation: for each prisoner 'the best of the worst' lies in confessing and in betraying his partner, as it is an excellent protection against any risk of maximum penalty. Therefore, being equally rational, A and B decide at the same time to make a full confession.

The theoreticians' amazement turns around a definite point of the verdict given by the matrix of solutions. If A and B had co-operated, if they had kept silent, both would have been released instead of being imprisoned for a certain number of years at a minimum. In fact it would have been a better solution for both of them. As a matter of fact there is nothing akin in the 'game of chicken': in that case it seemed beyond doubt that the collective survival, even without glory, was preferable to collective death, even tempered by posthumous glory.

But in this case, between a higher collective interest (freedom for both players) and a collective interest of inferior quality (a mitigated penalty for both of them), the players, perversely rational, aim at the less desirable goal.

This is embarrassing, because if we cannot rely on individuals' rationality to protect their own interests, what should we rely on? For several authors this issue is an important source of concern. It is sometimes suggested that the situation would be completely different if the prisoners were allowed to communicate with each other and reach an agreement under which both would keep silent.[40] But they are not allowed to do so; the rule of the game is strict in this respect. Other authors recommend that rationality and egoism should not be considered identical: it could be just as logical to base one's argument on social values as on individual ones.

Here a careful comparison between this game and the 'game of chicken' seems to us particularly useful. Let us recall that in order to characterise the variable-sum games, the theory uses the concept of the secondary player, an actor outside the interaction of the players themselves and endowed with the magic power of making the sum of their gains vary. Curiously enough, there is no longer any mention of the existence of a secondary actor when searching for solutions. Solutions seem to spring from the brains of players faced with a set of abstract rules which are there by chance. Now there are links between this secondary actor on one hand and the players, the rules of the game and the solutions on the other hand. These links are implicit in the theory itself.

In the 'game of chicken', the rule is defined by a group of peers, two of whom will come into the action. Only the players are entitled to commit suicide or to kill their opponent. The observers — 'secondary actor' — are only allowed to admire or to despise the players. Both physical and symbolic coercion are thus precisely localised. The former has a heavier weight than the latter: numerical values linked with life, as opposed to numerical values linked with prestige, prove it. Since the power of physical coercion is in the hands of players alone, we can easily understand that, all else being equal, they co-operate with each other and do not betray each other to the advantage of a third person, who moreover would have only admiration to offer to any traitor.

The case is quite different for prisoners. The rules of the game are completely defined by the secondary actor: the judge and, behind him, a fairly well-defined legal system. They are imposed on players who have no part in drawing them up. They are designed to serve the secondary actor's interests: the crime has been committed, the judge has to deal severely with it; he can do so only by using the suspects' confessions as a basis; therefore he offers them a reward for their confession. It is a considerable reward, because this time the power of physical coercion is completely in his hands: he may release the players or sentence them to the maximum penalty. All the prisoners can do is to regret having an informer as a partner. By re-reading the rules of the game attentively, we discover that there was every encouragement for each prisoner to talk. It was possibly a false dilemma for the players.

Thus, when a secondary actor has a power of coercion towards the primary players, he can compel the latter not to co-operate, not to unite against him, to deviate from what constitutes their ideal collective interest. If this re-interpretation of the mathematical verdict of the matrices of games is correct, it would, in our opinion, make an important contribution to the theory.

In conclusion, we would like to question the philosophy of this view. Game theory claims to be a science of rational decision in a conflict situation. On these grounds it aims at defining solutions which are forced on the parties involved, not by virtue of their ethical or metaphysical merits, but because they are based on empirical facts, mathematically provable. It is, however, founded on several ideas which have nothing to do with mathematics.

We have already seen that the dominant concept is that of 'rationality'. It is a universal characteristic of human beings which induces each individual to pursue his interest while knowing that his fellow men do the same. Let us recall that the importance given by the theory to human rationality was aimed at correcting errors of historical, social or biological determinism in the interpretation of struggles and conflicts. It does not seem obvious to us that progress has been made in this respect, inasmuch as the law of the structure of the game to which we must bow, the mathematical verdict given by the matrix of solutions, whose numerical content is most often arbitrary, seems to strike a serious blow to actors' self-determination.

In fact, what remains of their freedom to decide? Curiously, theoreticians answer this question without ever having asked it. To define rationality as trying to maximise one's own interests, while taking into account the aspirations of others, is extremely vague. Authors' disagreement about the necessary symmetry or asymmetry of profits is but one result of it but if we can want, rationally, as much, more or less than our opponent, according to the claims made by the latter, then to make a 'correct' choice amounts to assessing the given situation and to realising that it is desirable to have some interests rather than others. Wanting to change this given situation is a dream which does not fit into the mechanisms described.

What then is left of the very function of the game? We are told that it produces the balance of 'minimax' based on players' complementary choices. But everything in the analysis of concrete examples leads us to think that the game determines nothing; it sanctions choices which were already fixed from the start. It may be considered as a black box, the entrances of which are equal to the exits, the only difference being that the former are said to be 'given', whereas the latter are said to be 'rational' and 'balanced'.

Finally, what is left of the distinction between zero-sum and variable-sum? We are told that the variation of players' gains depends on the co-ordination of their strategies. Everything happens as if they completely determine the quality of their collective interest. We have tried to show that this interpretation hides the influence, sometimes considerable, of a secondary actor on the players' freedom of action.

The logical strictness of game theory does not seem to us obvious. Still less its predictive capacity, considering the arbitrary choice of values from which solutions are extrapolated. But its ideological function seems important: it reconciles the existence of real inequalities with the democratic doctrine of individual self-determination. By advocating the search for 'minimax', we could say — hardly exaggerating — that it recommends to some people that they use effectively their resources (whose origins it is not scientific to question), whereas it recommends to others that they resign themselves to the worst and realise there is nothing better.

NOTES

1. A. Rapoport, *Fights, Games and Debates* (Ann Arbor, 1960).
2. T. Schelling, *The Strategy of Conflict* (New York, 1960), 4.
3. Ibid., 3.
4. J. von Neumann and O. Morgenstern, *Theory of Games and Economic Behavior* (Princeton, 1944).
5. See, for instance, K. Deutsch, *The Analysis of International Relations* (Englewood Cliffs, 1968), 114 or A. Rapoport, op. cit., 77 and 107.
6. See, for instance, a paper by M. Plon and E. Pretéceille, 'La théorie des jeux et le jeu de l'idéologie', *La Pensée*, No. 166, Nov-Déc., 1972: 36-69.
7. A. Rapoport, op. cit., 121.
8. K. Deutsch, op. cit., 114.
9. Ibid., 116.
10. A. Rapoport, op. cit., 96.
11. Ibid., 97.
12. R. D. Luce and H. Raiffa, 'Games and decisions', in: M. Shubik (ed.), *Game Theory and Related Approaches to Social Behavior*, (New York, 1964), 87-91.
13. M. Shubik, 'Game theory and the study of social behavior', in: M. Shubik (ed.), op. cit., 3-79, 51.
14. T. Schelling, op. cit., 267-91 and mainly 278-91.
15. Ibid., 278.
16. Especially J. Nash, 'The bargaining problem', *Econometrica,* 18, April 1950: 155-62; J. Harsanyi, 'Approaches to the bargaining problem before and after the theory of games', *Econometrica*, 24, April 1956: 144-57.
17. Quoted by Schelling, op. cit., 279.
18. Ibid., 281.
19. Ibid., 285.
20. Ibid., 281.
21. M. Shubik, op. cit., 12.
22. See, for instance, K. Deutsch, op. cit., 117 or T. Schelling, op. cit., 282.
23. T. Schelling, op. cit., 5.
24. K. Deutsch, op. cit., 117.
25. A. Rapoport, op. cit., 121.
26. Ibid., 120.
27. T. Schelling, op. cit., 15.

28. K. Deutsch, op. cit., 117.

29. Ibid., 117-18.

30. Quoted by M. Plon and E. Preteceille, op. cit., 49.

31. K. Deutsch, op. cit., 118.

32. Ibid., for instance.

33. See, for instance, H. Kahn, *On Thermonuclear War* (Princeton, 1960), 291.

34. K. Deutsch, op. cit., 119-20.

35. H. Kahn, op. cit., 291.

36. Ibid., 292.

37. T. Schelling, op. cit., ch. 5.

38. Ibid., 131.

39. The description of the dilemma may be found in almost any book on game theory. See, for instance, A. Rapoport, op. cit., 125; or K. Deutsch, op. cit., 120; or A. Rapoport, *Game Theory as a theory of Conflict Resolution* (Dordrecht, 1974), 17.

40. See, for instance, Harsanyi, quoted by Rapoport, ibid., 30; or T. Schelling, op. cit., 213-14.

16 Social Contract and the Limits of Majority Rule

Hans Daudt
University of Amsterdam, The Netherlands

Douglas W. Rae
Yale University, USA

I

The idea of a social contract refers to unanimity or consensus among those who are willing to participate in the contract. In this way a political regime supposedly based on the contract is justified for everybody, even if there is disagreement on specific measures taken by the regime. In this sense the idea of a social contract is a means of giving legitimacy to a regime or denying legitimacy to a regime supposedly not based on a contract.

The idea of a social contract further suggests a political system without coercion. This ideal is never realised and will never be realised, but it emphasises that coercion will only be wholly absent if everybody agrees. In practice, according to democratic theory, a system of majority rule is supposed to come as near to this ideal as is possible in minimising coercion.

But a democratic system with majority rule can only function in a satisfactory way if the conflicts that the system must deal with can be solved by compromises in such a way that everybody's interests are taken into account. Only in that case is it, theoretically at least, possible that there might be *unanimity* about the desirability of majority rule and only in that case will the system not be experienced by anybody as coercive. If a person belongs to a minority that is permanently prejudiced by the system or harmed in what it considers its most fundamental rights, there cannot be any rational argument why he should consider the system as legitimate.

Our thesis is that before the introduction of universal suffrage in Western Europe there was in general agreement (consensus) among the relatively small group of politically relevant members in the system about majority rule within this limited context. Moreover, there was agreement among the group about the limited tasks of the government, which in general ought to refrain from interfering with the economy. After the introduction of universal suffrage and the resulting rise of the welfare state there is increasing doubt about the legitimacy of the system, because (a) there is no consensus about the scope of the government's task, especially in the social and economic fields; (b) there is no consensus about the ensuing problem of lessening inequalities and interfering with personal freedom; and (c) there is no consensus about the question as to who has to bear the costs of increasing government activities. These developments put the system under heavy pressure, worsened by what Brittan calls the generation of excessive expectations and the disruptive effects of the pursuit of group self-interest.[1]

The lack of consensus on such fundamental questions as the scope of the government's tasks means that there is no rational argument to accept majority rule if this leads to decisions in areas which one considers ought to remain free from government interference. Additionally, belief in legitimacy based on religion or tradition is on the wane. This development might explain the revival of contractual political philosophy which, in fact, is a search for fundamentals on which one might (or should) unanimously agree. In what follows we shall analyse how majority rule in various situations can lead to decisions that are opposed by majorities of the people involved. It is based upon the line of thought expounded in 'The Ostrogorski Paradox' by Rae and Daudt,[2] and part of it is a summarised version of a Dutch article about the political future of the welfare state.[3]

II

In the welfare state, more and more demands can be expected to present themselves for consideration in the political sphere. This is in the first place due to interference by the government in an increasing number of fields, but it is also caused by the initiative of a growing number of persons and groups with demands which, until the rise of the welfare state, were little attended to, persons who now enter the political arena with confidence and often with militancy. One could argue that this increase in demands need not present problems if political parties simply attach price-tags to programmes and emphasise in their campaigns the unpleasant things like taxes which will accompany their implementation. In such a case, a public discussion about the political priorities is of course a real possibility, but this would not solve all the problems, as we hope to make clear.

Case I. In a two-party system, party X rallies a majority of voters on the basis of an election campaign which also indicates how many taxes are needed to operate each programme. It is conceivable that all the attractive elements of the programme might benefit one group of people voting for X and the unattractive aspect – financing the programme – might fall to another group, voting for losing party Y. One might say that democracy demands that the will of the majority be decisive, but in the long run this will hardly be convincing to permanent losers. They will, instead, be inclined to talk about the tyranny of a majority that does not take into account the rights of the minority. If such a situation persists long enough, the losers will withdraw their support of a regime which can behave in such a manner.

This is but one of the possible scenarios according to which a democratic regime might be undermined in the welfare state as a result of government activities, the resulting costs and the way in which various groups have to bear these burdens. Again it draws attention to a thesis, of central importance to eighteenth-century political philosophers, that the pursuit of group interests is destructive to a democratic system. It is interesting to notice, however, that in present discussions about democracy, this likelihood does not get much attention. More or less casually remarks are made to the effect that the conditions necessary for the functioning of democratic regimes are self-restraint and tolerance, or belief in democratic norms, or an absence of serious conflict about the nature of the more important issues and the direction society must take to solve these problems.

But what this really implies is that a democracy can function only if there is no basic disagreement about the issues, or if the resolution of fundamental problems of that kind lies outside the jurisdiction of the state. The fundamental problem of the welfare state is disagreement about the *degree* of desirable inequality of incomes, since the welfare of some is at the cost of another. Before the rise of the welfare state, the solution of the problem of inequality was not considered to be the responsibility of the state, but since then the degree of justified (in) equality of incomes has entered the political arena for the first time and, as a result, the government (in our example party X) will have to proceed with great care to keep the regime intact. The supporters of majority party X and of minority party Y run the risk of hostile confrontation. Only if a consensus emerges about a desirable distribution, can measures be taken based on the majority position.

But the democratic process in the welfare state might be undermined in another way, too.

Case II. This case will illustrate the mechanics of a situation wherein not only the supporters of the losing party (minority party Y) but also the supporters of the winning party (majority party X), turn against the government. We can distinguish two variants of this example.

IIa. In the first variant all voters for majority party X agree with a majority of the stands taken by their party and yet a majority of all voters disagree with winning party X on each single issue. This possibility is illustrated in Table 1.

TABLE 1

Voters	Issues			Chosen party	
	1	2	3		
A (20%)	X	X	Y	X	
B (20%)	X	Y	X	X	(60% votes
C (20%)	Y	X	X	X	for party X)
D (40%)	Y	Y	Y	Y	
	60%	60%	60%		
	supports party Y				
	on each issue				

In this illustration we have three issues (1, 2 and 3), two parties (X and Y) and four groups of voters (A, B, C and D). Twenty percent of the voters belongs to group A, which agrees with party X with respect to the first and second issue and with party Y on the third issue. The voters in group A give equal weight to each issue and for that reason they decide to vote for party X, with which they agree on two out of three issues. The voters of group B also agree on two out of three issues with party X, but whereas the voters of group A preferred the point of view of party Y with respect to the third issue, the voters of group B prefer party Y with respect to the second issue. The voters of group C agree with party Y on the first issue and with party X on the second and third issues.

Under these conditions, party X will get 60 percent of the total votes, namely those of the voters from groups A, B and C. But on each separate issue they receive only 40 percent support, or less than a majority of the population. Conversely, although party Y's position is supported by 60 percent of the voters for each of the three issues, party Y receives only 40 percent of the votes. This paradox has been more fully illustrated in 'The Ostrogorski Paradox'. In that article it is argued that with respect to the number of voters who must support the winning party X on each issue, there is a minimum percentage that becomes lower as the number of issues is larger and the victory of the winning party smaller. The limit is at 25 percent. In the example given here with three issues and a victory of 60 percent for party X, the support for party X is 40 percent on each issue, a minimum figure. If, with three issues party X wins with a majority of 51 percent, the minimum support needed on each issue is 34 percent. Only if party X gains a majority of 75 percent, is it impossible that there is a majority against each separate position taken by the winning party. But even if party X gets 100 percent of the votes and if all the voters agree with only two of the three positions taken by the winning party, the support for the party on each issue cannot be higher than $66\frac{2}{3}$.

For the welfare state this phenomenon might be of special significance since the state is involved in so many areas: the result could be that parties in their platforms must take stands on all sorts of issues. Moreover, in such a situation the number of voters who agree with the total programme will decrease. Voters will have to weigh the elements in the programme with which they concur against those with which they disagree. They might decide to support the party with which they agree on a majority of the issues. One might object that it is much more probable that they will select one issue of overriding importance to themselves and vote with the party they think best represents their interest in that situation. This is especially probable when strong group interests are present.

Robert Dahl, in *A Preface to Democratic Theory*[4] describes this situation which since then has been taken to explain the rule of coalitions of minorities. But never is it emphasised, by Dahl or by others, that the phenomenon we have observed in our last example, is aggravated by this situation — even larger majorities can oppose the winning party on each issue. This brings us to the second variant of case II.

IIb. Table 2 illustrates what could happen when with three issues (1, 2 and 3) and two parties (X and Y), the voters decide on the basis of only one issue, which they perceive as of overriding importance.

TABLE 2

Voters	Issues			Chosen party	
	1	2	3		
A (17%)	X	Y	Y	X	
B (17%)	Y	X	Y	X	(51% support
C (17%)	Y	Y	X	X	for party X)
D (49%)	Y	Y	Y	Y	
	83%	83%	83%		
	supports party Y				
	on each issue				

In this example the voters of group A have such an intensive preference for the stand taken by party X on the first issue that they decide to vote for party X, even though they agree with party Y on the other two issues, which they consider less important. In this situation an increasing number of issues might lead to an ever-increasing decline in the percentage of votes that supports the winning party on each issue. With an election victory of 51 percent and ten issues at stake (and what nowadays are ten issues in election programmes?) the support on each of the issues received by the winning party could fall to 5.1 percent. The limit is reached if each one of the voters, who together comprise 51 percent of the electorate, is promised a personal advantage that for him is more important than the advantages promised to others and the cost of which is to a large extent chargeable to the other losing 49 percent of the voters.

Although this extreme situation might be considered very unreal, in less extreme form this phenomenon occurs whenever parties suggest to all kinds of groups that their own group interest is furthered by the party and when members of these groups subsequently allow their own group interest to prevail over all other elements in the programme.

Both variants of this second example illustrate that if not all voters agree with all elements in their party's programme, it is possible that not only are opposition voters against the winning party, but in addition, a large part of the winning party's support. As a result, the implementation of each issue in the programme could lead to the uneasiness, or even complete disillusionment, of a majority of the voters. It is no longer the case, as it was in the first example, that the winning majority can transfer the costs of its programme to the losing minority. The lack of 'budget constraint', which Brittan found characteristic of the voter, is likely to result in numerous votes for programmes which favour small minorities who, on the basis of promised advantage, all voted for the winning party.

Again we have the situation wherein majorities oppose the majority party on individual issues. It might lead to increasing tensions between groups, each of which think that other groups get more benefits and fewer burdens. In this situation the more the welfare state undertakes to do, the greater the chance it will forfeit its credibility, no matter how much support the winning party has before the election.

III

In the preceding pages we gave some simple examples of the way in which the democratic method of decision-making makes it *possible* for the welfare state to suffer from political pressure, namely, the pursuit of group interests which leads to increasing tension between all sorts of groups and, ultimately, to dissatisfaction about a government which tries to do more and more for more and more people. The question is whether this probability becomes a reality in welfare states. One might say that wherever coalitions of minorities pursuing different group interests dominate the political scene, the problems mentioned arise in some degree. In the next section we will analyse some further configurations that might emerge. What can be done to counter these developments dangerous for the welfare state? One starting point might be that political parties must re-evaluate the role which they play and emphasise their unifying function in aggregating the various interests.

They must make clear to the voters that their responsibility is not to satisfy special interest groups but to realise a total vision of society in which group interests can play only a minor role. This implies that group interests will get their due share after their interests are weighed against other criteria. In that way, parties can encourage voters to join politicians in achieving the realisation of a vision of the whole society. Election campaigns therefore ought not in the first place to stimulate competition between interest groups but rather assist the voters in understanding and evaluating the alternatives before the society. Only in that way will voters act not as individuals but as citizens, that is to say, as people with a vision of the public cause. In a sense, the old idea about the need for a consensus re-emerges which, however vague, is always presupposed in discussions about democracy.

But what kind of consensus is required, and according to which criteria should the weighing of alternatives proceed?

We have limited ourselves to the question of how each of the two *parties* might counteract the process of destructive pursuit of group interests. While referring to a vision of society from which the criteria of weighing must be derived, we have arrived at the question of political philosophy and the norms according to which we must strive for social justice. It is evident that the two parties in our examples might disagree about these norms. For socialist parties the question will revolve around the method and the degree in which it is possible to alleviate all kinds of social inequalities. But this is not an objective that might be considered the highest one for the whole electorate in the Western welfare state. More conservative groups will without doubt emphasise the decline of freedom and the greater power of the state which results in this struggle for less inequality. In day-to-day political life this results in one group espousing greater equality as the greatest value and another pleading for individual freedom. We have then returned to the controversy raised by Hayek more than a generation ago.

The implication of all this is that if the pursuit of group interests is de-emphasised, the contrast between the parties will be evident in their differing visions of the social good; or, in other words, consensus about the greatest priority, without which democracy is impossible, is lacking in this situation too.

Instead, we end up with a situation similar to that of case I, where the majority tyrannises the minority because it disagrees with its vision of the greatest good. Will such a confrontation lead to either a Right-wing authoritarian regime or a Left-wing totalitarian regime, or is another solution possible? In theory at least there is another possibility: if indeed the welfare state degenerates into a state severely torn by ideological differences, we might end up with a consensus regarding an acceptable stalemate. It is possible that both parties will prefer this to an ideological show-down where one party loses altogether, accompanied by violence and more threat of violence. The acceptance of such a stalemate must be agreed upon before the critical point is reached, and this presupposes that those who strive for less inequality will turn the burner down before the soup boils over, while the other side agrees to co-operate in eating the final product. Tolerance is essential, of course, and it must emerge as a norm which prevails over other ideologies. The discussion on an ideological or political-philosophical level about the most acceptable norms of social justice will gain in vigour. With John Rawls on one side and Robert Nozick on the other, it appears that the first fighters for this new round are in the ring already. And if we are lucky, a new consensus might emerge.

Another question is whether this idyllic situation could actually succeed in practice. Moreover, the answer will differ from country to country. It depends on the intensity of the various preferences within the electorate, the power relations between the adherents of the various visions of society, thresholds at which people consider the actual situation as unbearable, the measure by which one estimates the risk of a non-democratic regime, and the perceptiveness of the politicians in gauging the right moment to declare a stalemate. These elements will determine whether a national 'balance of terror' or 'peaceful co-existence' is possible. But one thing is certain: if we do not declare a stalemate at some point and fundamental disagreement about norms of social justice persists, democracy as a method for making decisions in the welfare state is doomed to disappear.

IV

In Table 1, illustrating case IIa, we showed an example with *minimum* support for the stand the winning party had on each issue, given the winning percentage of party X. In this situation the voters gave equal weight to each issue and voted for a party if they agreed with the party's point of view on a majority of issues. It turned out that the minimum support, given three issues and an election victory of 51 percent for party X was $\frac{2}{3} \times 51 = 34$ percent. With five issues this minimum support for each of the five issues is $\frac{3}{5} \times 51 = 30.6$ percent.

This minimum value is reached because in the example all voters for losing party Y support their party and oppose winning party X on each issue. The situation is different if the voters for party Y do not form a monolithic bloc. If, for example, every voter, voting for a losing or a winning party, gives equal weight to each of the five issues and if moreover every voter for losing or winning party *only agrees with a majority of the party's issues*, then the *maximum* support for winning party X on each issue is as shown in Table 3. Given these conditions the maximum support for winning party X on each issue is $3 \times 10.2 + 2 \times 9.8 = 50.2$ percent.

TABLE 3

Voters	Issues					Chosen party
	1	2	3	4	5	
10.2%	X	X	X	Y	Y	⎞
10.2%	X	X	Y	X	Y	⎟
10.2%	X	Y	X	Y	X	⎬ 51% for party X
10.2%	Y	X	Y	X	X	⎟
10.2%	Y	Y	X	X	X	⎠
9.8%	Y	Y	Y	X	X	⎞
9.8%	Y	Y	X	Y	X	⎟
9.8%	Y	X	Y	X	Y	⎬ 49% for party Y
9.8%	X	Y	X	Y	Y	⎟
9.8%	X	X	Y	Y	Y	⎠

50.2% supports party X on each issue

In general

$$\frac{n+1}{2n} \cdot X + \frac{n-1}{2n} \cdot (100 - X)$$

in which n is the number of issues and X the winning percentage of party X. In this situation with equal weight on five issues we get the minima and maxima for the various possible winning percentages of party X (see Table 4).

TABLE 4

Minimum and Maximum Support for Each of the Five Issues
with Various Winning Percentages for Party X

Winning % party X	Minimum on each issue (%)	Maximum on each issue (%)
51	30.6	50.2
55	33	51
60	36	52
65	39	53
70	42	54
75	45	55
80	48	56
85	51	57
90	54	58
95	57	59
100	60	60

Up till now we have distinguished two different cases with respect to the support given by the voters to their party's issues. In the first case the voters for party X all disagreed with a minority of their party's issues, whereas the voters for party Y formed a monolithic bloc. We shall abbreviate this case as $\frac{X\,X\,X\,Y\,Y}{Y\,Y\,Y\,Y\,Y}$ (case 1). In the second case the voters for party X *and* the voters for party Y disagreed with a minority of their party's issues $\frac{X\,X\,X\,Y\,Y}{Y\,Y\,Y\,X\,X}$ (case 2).

We now can add a third and a fourth case, namely the situation in which the voters for winning party X form a monolithic bloc whereas the voters for party Y disagree with a minority of their party's issues $\frac{X\,X\,X\,X\,X}{Y\,Y\,Y\,X\,X}$ (case 3), and a fourth in which the voters for both parties form monolithic blocs $\frac{X\,X\,X\,X\,X}{Y\,Y\,Y\,Y\,Y}$ (case 4).

In figure 1 we depict the possible support for each issue of winning party X in these four cases from the various winning percentages of party X.

Before commenting upon this figure, let us give the following definitions:

conflict occurs whenever on any issue some people prefer solution X

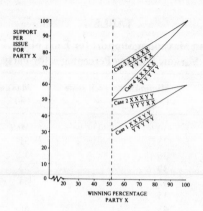

Figure 1

and others solution Y, that is $\frac{X}{Y}$ or $\frac{X\,X}{Y\,Y}$;

party frustration occurs whenever people disagree with some issue on
which their party takes a stand, for example X X Y or Y Y X;

system frustration occurs whenever the system follows a policy on any
issue with which one disagrees.

Let us look at the situation in which party X gets *51 percent of the
vote.*

(1) If the preference pattern of case 1 occurs, then there is *maximum system frustration.* This happens whenever the losing side has a
minority as large as possible; and its voters form a monolithic bloc
which means that they do not have any party frustration; and whereas,
on the contrary, the voters for winning party X have *maximum* party
frustration: $51\frac{X\,X\,X\,Y\,Y}{Y\,Y\,Y\,Y\,Y}$.
          49

(2) With the preference pattern of case 2 there is *maximum party
frustration* in both parties. In this case system frustration is less than in
the first case. With a 51 percent victory of party X the support on each
issue of winning party X is 50.2 percent against 30.6 percent in the first
case (see Table 4). But in both cases, even with a 100 percent victory of
party X, the support on each issue of winning party X cannot be higher
than 60 percent.

(3) If the preference pattern of case 3 occurs, then there is *minimal
system frustration.* This happens whenever the voters for party X form
a monolithic bloc; whereas the voters for losing party Y have maximum
party frustration.

(4) With the preference pattern of case 4 there is *maximum conflict*. This happens whenever the losing side has a minority as large as possible; and voters for both parties form monolithic blocs: maximum conflict: 51 X X X X X.

49 $\overline{\text{Y Y Y Y Y}}$

We see that, with equal weight of five issues, a *51 percent victory* for party X can lead to different support for each issue of the winning party, depending on the prevailing preference pattern. The support for each issue of the winning party can be

(a) 30.6 percent in case 1;

(b) 50.2 percent in case 2;

(c) 51 percent in case 4; and

(d) 70.6 percent in case 3.

Although the support in case 4 starts at nearly the same level as in case 2 and increases more with a higher winning vote for party X, the situation seems more dangerous than in case 2. In case 2 the support for the various issues is derived from winning *and* losing voters. In case 4 the losing voters disagree with the winners on every issue. In case 1 voters from the winning party agree with the losers on some issues.

V

In section IV we analysed various situations that might occur if the voters gave equal weight to each issue and voted for a party if they agreed with the party's point of view on a majority of issues. An example of one of these situations has already been given in Table 1 (section II).

In Table 2 we gave an example in which voters decide to vote for a party because they agree with that party on one issue which is of overriding importance to them. Analogously to section IV, we shall now analyse various possibilities that might occur if all voters for one or for both parties vote in this way.

In the example given in Table 2 all voters for winning party X agreed with only one of the party's issues which was for them of overwhelming importance, whereas the voters for party Y formed a monolithic bloc. In that case the support for each issue of the winning party might fall to $(1/n) \cdot X$ in which n is the number of issues and X the winning percentage of party X. With a 51 percent victory and three issues the support per issue can be 17 percent and with five issues it might fall already to 10.2 percent.

Voters for X have one overriding issue
Voters for Y form monolithic bloc   (case 1).

In the second case *all* voters for *both* parties vote according to their preference for one overriding issue.

Voters for X have one overriding issue
Voters for Y have one overriding issue   (case 2).

Then the situation in Table 5 is possible. In this case the general formula for support for party X on each issue is:

$$\frac{1}{n} \cdot X + \frac{n-1}{n}(100 - X).$$

TABLE 5

Voters	Issues					Chosen party
	1	2	3	4	5	
10.2%	X	Y	Y	Y	Y	
10.2%	Y	X	Y	Y	Y	
10.2%	Y	Y	X	Y	Y	51% for party X
10.2%	Y	Y	Y	X	Y	
10.2%	Y	Y	Y	Y	X	
9.8%	X	X	X	X	Y	
9.8%	X	X	X	Y	X	
9.8%	X	X	Y	X	X	49% for party Y
9.8%	X	Y	X	X	X	
9.8%	Y	X	X	X	X	

support for party X on each issue
10.2 + 4 × 9.8 = 49.4%

In Table 6 the possible support for each of the winning issues is shown for the various possible winning percentages of party X, given one overriding issue for the supporters of the winning party (case 1) or for the supporters of both parties (case 2).

TABLE 6

Possible Support for Each of the Five Issues in Case 1
and Case 2 with Various Winning Percentages of Party X

Winning % party X	Case 1	Case 2
51	10.2	49.4
55	11	47
65	13	41
75	15	35
85	17	29
95	19	23
100	20	20

In the third case the voters for winning party X form a monolithic bloc, whereas the voters for party Y agree with their party on one issue which is of overriding importance to them.

Voters for X form a monolithic bloc
Voters for Y have one overriding issue (case 3).

The fourth case in which voters for both parties form monolithic blocs is identical to the fourth case in section IV, depicted as conflict line in Figure 1.

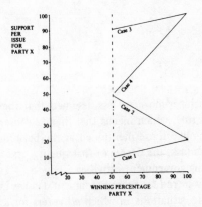

Figure 2

In Figure 2 we show the support that each issue of winning party X might get under these conditions at various winning percentages of party X. There are some remarkable differences compared with Figure

1. If party X again gets a 51 percent victory the possible differences in support for each issue of the winning party are greater than in Figure 1. It might be

    (a) 10.2 percent in case 1 (Figure 1: 30.6);

    (b) 49.4 percent in case 2 (Figure 1: 50.2);

    (c) 51 percent in case 4 (Figure 1: the same);

    (d) 90.2 percent in case 3 (Figure 1: 70.6).

We see that the system frustration can be considerably higher (that is lower support; case 1) or lower (higher support; case 3) than in the situation outlined in Figure 1. It is remarkable that under these conditions, in case 2 the support per issue might decrease if the winning percentage of party X increases. It means that in the situation with maximum party frustration in both parties, system frustration becomes higher if winning party X gets a larger victory!

These various possibilities show that an authoritarian system, which does not feel obliged to follow the rules of majority-vote-elections and feels less obliged than parties to implement its programmes, might be experienced as an 'improvement' in the sense that it can follow a policy that gives more support on issues than the existing system; unless people consider the problem involved in non-democratic regimes (e.g. arbitrariness) as worse than their party or system frustration. This leads to the following problem.

VI

Up till now we have more or less assumed that the voters in general accept majority rule, which means that there is consensus about fundamental questions like those mentioned at the beginning – the scope of the government's task, the degree of (in)equality, and the bearing of the costs of increasing government activities.

We shall now introduce these fundamental issues in our analysis. We limit ourselves to situations in which *all* voters for a party agree with the party if that *party* considers an issue of fundamental importance. If for example issue 1 is considered to be a fundamental issue by party X, then all voters for party X support their party on this issue. Fundamental issues for them will always be more intensely preferred issues, which means that at one extreme they might disagree with their party on all other issues. The other extreme is that they support their party on each issue, forming a monolithic bloc.

For each party we now have the following possibilities.

(1) The party does not consider one issue as fundamental (a).

(2) The party considers one issue as fundamental and all its supporters agree, but they disagree on other issues (b).

(3) The party considers one issue as fundamental and its voters support it as a monolithic bloc on all issues (c).

With two parties involved this gives us the following matrix:

party X

		a	b	c
	a	1	2	3
party Y	b	4	5	6
	c	7	8	9

Case 1 is unimportant because both parties agree that no fundamental issue is at stake. Case 9 can be excluded because it gives the same figures as the conflict line, described in section IV with two opposing monolithic blocs.

In case 2 winning party X (and its voters) consider issue 1 as fundamental but its voters disagree with the party on other issues. Party Y and its voters are not fundamentally opposed to this issue. This might lead to the configuration shown in Table 7. In this case 90.2 percent of the voters support winning party X for what this party considers a fundamental issue and 51 percent agree that the issue is fundamental. Party X's stand on the other issues is supported by 39.2 percent of the voters all belonging to the opposition. For the various possible winning percentages the figures are (see also Figure 3) as shown in Table 8.

TABLE 7

51	1	2	3	4	5
	X	Y	Y	Y	Y
9.8%	Y	X	X	X	X
9.8	X	Y	X	X	X
9.8	X	X	Y	X	X
9.8	X	X	X	Y	X
9.8	X	X	X	X	Y

TABLE 8

Winning % party X	Support for party X on		
	Issue 1 (%)	Issue 1 considered fundamental by (%)	Other issues (%)
51	90.2	51	39.2
55	91	55	36
65	93	65	28
75	95	75	20
85	97	85	12
95	99	95	4
100	100	100	0

In case 3 winning party X considers one issue as fundamental and its voters support it as a monolithic bloc. Party Y and its voters are not fundamentally opposed to this issue (see also Figure 4). Then the figures given in Table 9 are possible.

TABLE 9

51	1 $\boxed{X}$	2 X	3 X	4 X	5 X
9.8%	Y	X	X	X	X
9.8	X	Y	X	X	X
9.8	X	X	Y	X	X
9.8	X	X	X	Y	X
9.8	X	X	X	X	Y

Winning % party X	Support for party X on		
	Issue 1 (%)	Issue 1 considered fundamental by (%)	Other issues (%)
51	90.2	51	90.2
55	91	55	91
65	93	65	93
75	95	75	95
85	97	85	97
95	99	95	99
100	100	100	100

In case 4 winning party X does not consider one issue as fundamental. Party Y does, however, and all its voters agree but they disagree
on other issues with their party (Table 10).

TABLE 10 (see also Figure 5)

	1	2	3	4	5
10.2	*X*	Y	Y	Y	Y
10.2	Y	*X*	Y	Y	Y
10.2	Y	Y	*X*	Y	Y
10.2	Y	Y	Y	*X*	Y
10.2	Y	Y	Y	Y	*X*
49	Y	X	X	X	X

Winning % party X	Support for party X on		Party X's stand on issue 1 fundamentally opposed by
	Issue 1 (%)	Other issues (%)	
51	10.2	59.2	49
55	11	56	45
65	13	48	35
75	15	40	25
85	17	32	15
95	19	24	5
100	20	20	0

In case 4 nearly half of the voters might oppose fundamentally the
stand taken by winning party X on issue 1, that is only supported, *and
not as a fundamental issue*, by 10.2 percent of the voters. With respect
to this issue the situation becomes less worse with a larger victory of
party X, but then the support for X on the other issues might decrease.

In case 5 both parties and their voters consider issue 1 as a fundamental issue on which they have opposing views but voters of both
parties disagree with their parties with respect to the other issues (Table
11).

In case 6 both parties and their voters consider issue 1 as a fundamental issue on which they have opposing views, but, moreover, voters
for party X form a monolithic bloc whereas voters for party Y disagree
with their party with respect to the other issues (Table 12). In this case
the non-fundamental issues cease to be issues because everybody is in
agreement.

TABLE 11 (see also Figure 6)

| 51 | X | Y | Y | Y | Y |
| 49 | Y | X | X | X | X |

Winning % party X	Support for party X on		
	Issue 1 (%)	Issue 1 considered fundamental by (%)	Other issues (%)
51	51	51	49
55	55	55	45
65	65	65	35
75	75	75	25
85	85	85	15
95	95	95	5
100	100	100	0

TABLE 12 (see also Figure 7)

| 51 | X | X | X | X | X |
| 49 | Y | X | X | X | X |

Winning % party X	Support for party X on		
	Issue 1 (%)	Issue 1 considered fundamental by (%)	Other issues (%)
51	51	51	100
55	55	55	100
65	65	65	100
75	75	75	100
85	85	85	100
95	95	95	100
100	100	100	100

In case 7 losing party Y considers one issue as fundamental and its voters support it as a monolithic bloc on all issues whereas winning party X does not consider this issue as fundamental (Table 13).

TABLE 13 (see also Figure 8)

	1	2	3	4	5
10.2%	X	Y	Y	Y	Y
10.2	Y	X	Y	Y	Y
10.2	Y	Y	X	Y	Y
10.2	Y	Y	Y	X	Y
10.2	Y	Y	Y	Y	X
49	[Y]	Y	Y	Y	Y

Winning % party X	Support for party X on		Party X's stand on issue 1 fundamentally opposed by
	Issue 1 (%)	Other issues (%)	
51	10.2	10.2	49
55	11	11	45
65	13	13	35
75	15	15	25
85	17	17	15
95	19	19	5
100	20	20	0

In case 8 both parties and their voters consider issue 1 as a fundamental issue on which they have opposing views, but, moreover, voters for party Y form a monolithic bloc, whereas voters for party X disagree with their party with respect to the other issues (Table 14).

TABLE 14 (see also Figure 9)

	1	2	3	4	5
51	[X]	Y	Y	Y	Y
49	[Y]	Y	Y	Y	Y

In this case, as in the sixth, the non-fundamental issues cease to be issues because everybody agrees. It is difficult to imagine a situation in which a winning party might follow a policy on issues which are opposed by everybody. But a less extreme form might occur if, for example, some supporters of X agree with each of these issues 2, 3, 4 and 5 because they favour interests of small groups.

The most comfortable situation are the cases 1, 2 and 3 in which the voters for losing party Y do not consider any issue as fundamental. In the other six cases the voters for the losing party might experience the system as coercive, because the winning party takes a stand on issue 1 which the losers fundamentally oppose. Most dramatic are the cases 4 and 7 (Figures 5 and 8). In both cases winning party X does not consider any issue as fundamental, but the voters for the losing party do. In case 4 they only fundamentally oppose party X's stand on issue 1, but in case 7 they form a monolithic bloc against party X on each issue. In this last case winning party X might get only 10.2 percent support on each issue, given a 51 percent victory, whereas 49 percent might fundamentally oppose issue 1.

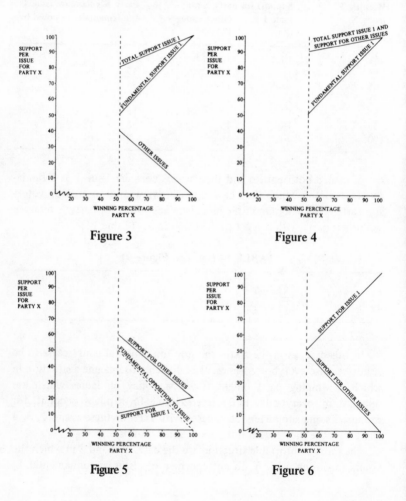

Figure 3

Figure 4

Figure 5

Figure 6

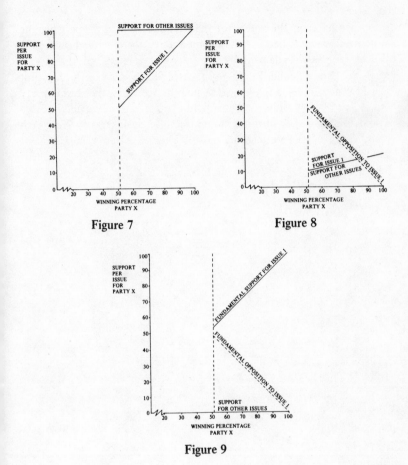

Figure 7

Figure 8

Figure 9

NOTES

1. Samuel Brittan, 'The economic contradictions of democracy', *British Journal of Political Science,* April 1975: 129-59.

2. Douglas W. Rae and Hans Daudt, 'The Ostrogorski paradox: a peculiarity of compound majority decision', *European Journal of Political Research,* 4, 1976: 391-98.

3. H. Daudt, 'The Political Future of the Welfare State', *The Netherlands' Journal of Sociology*, XIII, 2, 1977.

4. Robert A. Dahl, *A Preface to Democratic Theory* (Chicago, 1956), 128.

Notes on Contributors

Elias Berg is a Lecturer in the Department of Political Science at the University of Stockholm. He has published *The Historical Thinking of Charles A. Beard* (1957), and *Democracy and the Majority Principle* (1965).

Pierre Birnbaum is a Professor of Political Science at the University of Paris I. His recent books include *La fin du politique* (Paris: 1975), *Le pouvoir politique* (Paris: 1975), *Les sommets* de l'Etat (Paris: 1977) and, with C. Barucq, A. Bellaiche and A. Marie, *La classe dirigeante française* (Paris: 1978).

Hans Daudt is Professor of Political Science at the University of Amsterdam. His publications in English include *Floating Voters and the Floating Vote: A Critical Analysis of American and English Election Studies* (Leiden, 1961), and with Douglas W. Rae, 'The Ostrogorski Paradox: A Peculiarity of Compound Majority Decision' in the *European Journal of Political Research* (Volume 4, Number 4, December 1976). His paper 'The Political Future of the Welfare State' is to be published in *The Netherlands Journal of Sociology*.

Graeme Duncan is at the University of East Anglia, UK. He has taught politics at Monash and Adelaide Universities in Australia, and Oxford in the UK, and is the author of *Marx and Mill*.

Pierre Favre is Professor of Political Science at the University of Clermont Ferrand. He is the author of *La décision de majorité* (Paris: 1976) and, with Monique Favre, *Les marxistes après Marx* (Paris: 1970).

John N. Gray is Official Fellow and Tutor in Politics at Jesus College, Oxford, and Lecturer in Political Thought at the University of Oxford.

Herman van Gunsteren is Professor of Political Theory at the University of Leiden. He is the author of *The Quest for Control* (New York: 1976).

Percy B. Lehning is Assistant Professor at the Institute for Political Science of the University of Amsterdam. Related to his contribution to this work, he has published, with R. J. van der Veen, a paper 'De rechtvaardigheidstheorie van John Rawls' in *Acta Politica* (Volume 11, Number 4, pp 449-488, and Volume 12, Number 1, pp 25-76).

Jack Lively is Professor of Politics at the University of Warwick, UK. He has been a Research Fellow at St. Antony's College, Oxford, Lecturer at University College of Swansea and the University of Sussex, and Fellow of St. Peter's College, Oxford, where he was also University Lecturer in Politics. His publications include *Social and Political Thought of Alexis de Tocqueville, Joseph de Maistre, The Enlightenment, Democracy,* and *Utilitarian Logic and Politics* (with John Rees).

David Miller has taught at the University of Lancaster and is now Senior Lecturer in Politics at the University of East Anglia, UK. His publications include *Social Justice.*

Kenneth R. Minogue is Reader in Political Science at the London School of Economics, UK. His publications include *The Liberal Mind* (1962), *Nationalism* (1967), *The Concept of a University* (1973), and contributions to many journals.

Christine Mironesco holds an M.A. in Sociology from Columbia University, New York. She is presently a teaching and research assistant in the Department of Political Science at the University of Geneva, where she is preparing a doctoral dissertation on conflict theories.

Hannu Nurmi is Assistant Professor of Methodology of the Social Sciences at the University of Turku, Finland. His publications include *Causality and Complexity* (Ann. Univ. Turkuensis, 1974) and *Rationality and Public Goods* (Societas Scientiarum Fennica, 1977), as well as papers on cybernetics, model-building and game theory.

Geraint Parry has been since 1977 Professor of Government at the University of Manchester. He has previously been Edward Caird Professor of Politics at the University of Glasgow (1974-76), and was earlier both a Lecturer and Senior Lecturer in Government at the University of Manchester (1960-74). He has been a visiting professor at Queen's University, Kingston, Ontario (1972-73). His publications include *Political Elites* and *Participation in Politics.*

Douglas W. Rae is a Fellow in the Center for Advanced Study in the Behavioral Sciences, Yale University. He is the author of *The Political Consequences of Electoral Laws* (1967 and 1971), and *The Analysis of Political Cleavages* (with Michael Taylor, 1970), and is co-editor, with Isaac Kramnick, of *Political Works of Condorcet* (forthcoming). He has also contributed to several other books and to many journals.

Hillel Steiner is Lecturer in Political Philosophy at the University of Manchester. He is the author of 'Individual Liberty' in *The Proceedings of the Aristotelian Society* (1974-75), 'The Concept of Justice' in *Ratio* (1974) and 'The Natural Right to the Means of Production' in *Philosophical Quarterly* (1977).

Uli Windisch is Professor of Sociology at the University of Geneva. His recent books include *Lutte de clans, lutte de classes* (Lausanne: 1976), and, with A. Willener, *Le Jura incompris, Fédéralisme ou totalitarisme?* (Vevey: 1976).